Constitutional Identity

Constitutional Identity

Gary Jeffrey Jacobsohn

Harvard University Press
Cambridge, Massachusetts · London, England
2010

Printed in the United States of America

Library of Congress Cataloging-in-Publication Data

Jacobsohn, Gary J., 1946–
Constitutional identity / Gary Jeffrey Jacobsohn.
p. cm.
Includes bibliographical references and index.
ISBN 978-0-674-04766-2 (alk. paper)
1. Constitutional law—Philosophy. 2. Law—Foreign influences. I. Title.
K3165.J333 2010
342.02—dc22 2010011117

For Steven and to the Memory of Amy Jacobsohn

Contents

Preface ix

1. Introduction: The Disharmonic Constitution 1
2. The Conundrum of the Unconstitutional Constitution 34
3. The Quest for a Compelling Unity 84
4. The Permeability of Constitutional Borders 136
5. The Sounds of Silence: Militant and Acquiescent Constitutionalism 213
6. "The First Page of the Constitution": Family, State, and Identity 271
7. Conclusion 323

Index 357

Preface

THE COMPLETION OF THIS BOOK happened to coincide with what has become one of the more ritualized events in American national politics: the confirmation hearings for a Supreme Court Justice. In her appearance before the Senate Judiciary Committee, President Barack Obama's nominee for the Court, Judge Sonia Sotomayor, followed a familiar script that, since the ill-fated nomination of Judge Robert Bork twenty-two years earlier, more or less guarantees that these proceedings will be as dull as they can possibly be. Candidates for a position on the bench are carefully instructed to reveal precious little about their views on substantive issues; moreover, it is clear that their prospects for confirmation will be enhanced to the degree that they are adept and consistent in uttering platitudes about the role of judges in a constitutional democracy.

If learning very much about the views of judicial nominees to the highest court in the land is not a result realistically to be hoped for, following the hearings may nevertheless yield useful information about the state of mainstream legal thinking as seen from within the political realm. It was instructive, for example, to hear Judge Sotomayor, who had prior to her nomination acknowledged the wisdom of judges remaining open to good ideas from abroad, mainly accede to Republican

Senators' categorical rejection of foreign law and jurisprudence as legitimate sources for decision making on the Supreme Court. While she did not repudiate her earlier openness to learning from foreign law, she emphasized that such law could not be used to influence a decision involving an interpretation of the American Constitution. What is more, the reluctance of Democrats at the hearings seriously to engage their minority colleagues on the question suggested that, whatever the disagreements in legal and academic circles, the safe political position was acquiescence in what could be characterized as a jurisprudence of insularity.

At the same time as these proceedings were unfolding in the American Congress, a court in New Delhi was boldly challenging a long-standing provision of the Indian Penal Code that had criminalized "unnatural" consensual sexual acts between consenting adults in private. Introduced by the British in 1861, the law directed against homosexual conduct was declared unconstitutional by the High Court of Delhi in a ruling that was promptly described by informed observers as a landmark judgment in Indian jurisprudence. As one of these commentators said of the judges in the case, they "fashion[ed] a historic decision heard loud and clear, not only in India, but across the world."[1] Indeed, the judgment "is likely to rival the mango this summer as India's top export!"[2]

Unlike the mango, however, which is indigenous to the Indian subcontinent, the Court's opinion was so heavily influenced by foreign sources that it could with equal justification be described as India's top import of the summer. It fashioned a constitutional right of privacy largely out of materials appropriated from abroad, with copious references to American precedents. Prominent among these references was the majority opinion in Lawrence v. Texas, whose invocation of foreign case law, while tangential to the outcome, did much to fuel the hostility in this country toward constitutional "borrowing" that was much in evidence at the confirmation hearings. To be sure, an ex-Chief Justice of the Indian Supreme Court, whose reaction to the High Court's judgment

1. Vikram Raghavan, Law and Other Things: A Blog about Indian Law, the Courts, and the Constitution, July 7, 2009.

2. Ibid.

was that it should not be interpreted as an endorsement of homosexual conduct nor accorded any constitutive significance, opined that Indians should be more skeptical about incorporating accepted practices in the West into their own jurisprudence.[3] Still, this sentiment was decidedly at odds with the prevailing view in the Court's opinion, which saw the invalidation of the nineteenth-century British-mandated criminalization of homosexual conduct as critical to the furtherance of twenty-first-century Indian "constitutional morality."[4]

The timing of these events—the Sotomayor hearings and the ruling in Naz Foundation v. Union of India—was for me propitious, as they reinforced my sense that the subject of constitutional identity merited sustained consideration. Neither in Washington nor in New Delhi were the underlying identity-related assumptions of the protagonists in the American Congress or the Indian court elaborated. The Indian judges saw themselves as defending "a constitutional morality derived from constitutional values," and they embraced the teaching of B. R. Ambedkar, their nation's Madison, who had said at the Constituent Assembly: "[I]t is perfectly possible to pervert the Constitution, without changing its form by merely changing its form of administration and to make it inconsistent and opposed to the spirit of the Constitution."[5] But these judges failed to explain the relevance of the many pages of their opinion devoted to *other* peoples' constitutions to maintaining the spirit of *their* constitution.

The ironic aspect of this omission was accentuated by the judges' insistence that the contested section of the Indian Penal Code, drafted for the colonial administrators by Lord Macaulay in the nineteenth century, was itself an alien intrusion into the subcontinent. It embodied the "Western concept" that certain sexual practices were "against the order of nature," but the jurists were quick to point out that "in India we didn't have this concept."[6] The clear implication was that in declaring the provision in question unconstitutional the Court was in effect cleansing the

3. J. S. Verma, Law and Other Things: A Blog about Indian Law, the Courts, and the Constitution, July 24, 2009.

4. Naz Foundation v. Government of India, WP(C) No. 7455/2001 (2009), par. 79.

5. Ibid.

6. Ibid., at par. 84.

Indian legal order of foreign ideas that had compromised the integrity of the indigenous culture. Or put differently, the Court manifestly intended its decision to be interpreted as a defense of an Indian constitutional identity that "protects and celebrates diversity."[7] Strangely, however, the ruling failed to include an explanation for why an identity-based defense of this kind required such a heavy reliance on foreign ideas. In moving so dramatically to excise an externally imposed source of constitutional corruption from the Indian Penal Code, what understanding of constitutional identity enabled the Court to achieve its goal by appealing to sources external to the legal order?

As for the Senators and the Supreme Court nominee, the conveniently cobbled together consensus on the dubious standing of any judicial outcome that bore an imprint of extraterritorial sway was noticeably lacking in reflection on just why the most durable constitutional order in the world required assurances that its official interpreters would not be susceptible to foreign influence. "I will not use foreign law to interpret the Constitution," Sotomayor told the Committee, some of whose members rightly suspected that her notion of usage was more narrowly conceived—and thus less categorical—than theirs. For these Senators it would not be sufficient simply to disavow foreign case law as binding or controlling precedent; to be confirmed for the Supreme Court one would have to more broadly renounce comparative usage as a legitimate source of ideas in trying to understand the Constitution.

Given the nature of these proceedings, it should not be surprising that the principals in the highly charged political setting that is a confirmation hearing failed to delve very deeply into the intricacies of the subject. In observing the spectacle, however, I wondered if even in a less fraught environment whether the issue would have received the consideration it deserved. My misgivings had to do with a sense that the problem, which understandably triggers strong opinions about the role of judges in a democratic polity, would be framed in a too limited way for establishing the connection between judicial function—the micro question—and the more macro-level question of constitutional identity. Of additional concern, this projected failure would only replicate the

7. Ibid., at par. 80.

shortcomings of constitutional scholarship, whose inattention to the phenomenon of identity was the difficulty I had sought to rectify in writing this book.

Making the micro-macro connection would mean situating the decision to "use" foreign law within a broader comparative framework that encourages one to assess the contested practice in relation to the particular circumstances of a given constitutional polity. In the same way that one might evaluate jurisprudential commitments—for example, to the original intent of the framers or to the text of the document—in light of the specific constitutional context judges in a given society operate within, the implications of applying legal materials originating outside national borders to cases adjudicated internally are likely to vary accordingly. If judges in India are less inclined than their American counterparts to attach much weight to founding understanding, or if structural principles play a more decisive interpretive role in South Africa than, say, in Australia, it would be foolish reflexively to attribute such differences to the prevalence of a more genuine judicial commitment to the rule of law in one place as opposed to the other. Of course that explanation could turn out to be true, but we should consider the strong possibility that factors associated with the character of the constitutional cultures in question will in the end yield more explanatory value.

As I argue in this book, constitutions may be variously described in terms of the mix of universal and particular attributes that define their identities. The insularity that Judge Sotomayor's questioners seemed implicitly to endorse could have been justified by aspects of American constitutional identity that arguably render such a preference highly desirable and functional. Others, in turn, might have disputed such a justification, perhaps by relying on an alternative account of constitutional identity, or by drawing different inferences from the same rendering. Had there been, for example, an inclination to challenge the prevailing wisdom at the hearings, the argument could have been pressed that the number of constitutional aspirations that the United States shares with other nations is such that following their example in cases raising comparable issues, or at least attempting to learn from them, is surely compatible with American interests. Where these aspirations can be shown to differ, there would still be some benefit, so the argument might have gone, in looking through the prism of the other to deepen the understanding of one's own distinctive constitutional commitments.

Some version of this rationale might also have accompanied the Indian judges' use of foreign law. In anticipating the allegation of inconsistency in their opinion, these jurists could have cogently argued that there is in principle no contradiction between the selective rejection and embrace of legal inputs from abroad. In support of this claim a comparative perspective might suggest that there is no inherent problem in distinguishing among national judiciaries in terms of their propensities to encourage the international transference of law-related ideas and experience. The extensive use of foreign precedents in a transitional regime might not suit the circumstances of a polity where a discernible constitutional identity has been shaped and reinforced over many years; for example, in regard to certain rights questions that manifest a particular historical orientation toward the role of government in enforcing entitlements.

Without necessarily relying upon a carefully elaborated theory of exceptionalism, defenders of a more restrictive policy on extra-national sources could counter the universalistic thrust of the aspirational argument with a more particularist account of identity that underscores the judiciary's obligation to prevent any dilution or erosion of a distinctly American constitutional way of life. This protective posture in turn raises the question—one that I address at length in the pages to follow—of the nature of change in constitutional identity: how it occurs and what it looks like. The debate over interpretive sources—foreign and domestic—is just one instance where the struggle between forces seeking fundamental change in the nature of the Constitution and others intent on preserving its constitutive meaning is often the crux of a controversy incorporated in more mundane matters. Indeed, other events in the summer months of 2009, including constitutionally portentous struggles for power in two countries—Iran and Honduras—were in different ways revealing for the issues they raised about the durability of constitutional identity. These countries were not among those I had studied in this book, but it was easy to recognize in the crises that consumed both places some of the concerns that have been a preoccupation of mine for a number of years.

Indeed, these concerns have been at the center of my work long before I attached the constitutional identity appellation to them. When it was only the American case that was the focus of my research and writing, the questions that interested me most were those that spoke to the larger meaning of the Constitution. I was particularly taken with Lincoln's appropriation of the biblical metaphor of an "apple of gold" framed by a "picture of silver" to understand the role of antecedent principles in constituting a polity that had been compromised at its very inception by practices antithetical to those principles. For Lincoln, American constitutional identity made sense only in aspirational terms, much as it did a century later for Martin Luther King Jr., for whom the propositions of the Declaration of Independence were a "promissory note" creating regime-defining constitutional obligations.

As my scholarly interests took a comparative turn—first to Israel and then to India—the ways in which those aspirations were instrumental in constituting the American polity became clearer to me. The absence in Israel of a formal written constitution that might function as a frame to that country's foundational principles—as they had been inscribed in its Proclamation of Independence—was a testament to the hotly contested nature of those principles. The contrast with the United States was striking and instructive, but not only in highlighting the differences between the two nations and their constitutional circumstances. For while the comparison of Israel and the United States served to accentuate the constitutive prominence in the latter of non-ascriptively based commitments, it also helped me to understand that the process by which a polity's constitutional identity emerges is not necessarily as variable as those differences might lead one to expect. If, for example, the disharmony between the particularistic and universalistic strands in Israeli political culture was critical in driving the formation of constitutional identity, that dynamic existed in the American context as well, albeit in a less obvious way. Viewing constitutional development in the United States through the prism of the Israeli experience enabled me to see with greater clarity that the ascendance of certain foundational principles was not inconsistent with the continuing vitality of opposed principles and thus with an ongoing contest for the American constitutional soul.

As I progressed to my work on India, my sense sharpened that the characteristics that enabled one to draw defining contrasts among constitutions also provided a basis for identifying commonalities among regimes of disparate organizing structure and principles. The Indian Constitution's confrontational deportment vis-à-vis the surrounding social order was distinguishable from the more compliant relationship of its counterpart in the United States; but the difference led me to consider the ways in which the American document, particularly as amended after the Civil War, coexisted in a less harmonious relationship with the institutions of civil society than I had for so long assumed. As important as it is to understand the ways in which constitutions differ—a recognition that reaches back to Aristotle—so too is it vital to the comparative study of constitutionalism to appreciate the continuities in the things we compare. Comparative analysis of course confronts one with the diversity of national experiences in constitutional governance, but it also makes one aware of the ubiquitous quality of the characteristics that, in varying degrees, serve to mark constitutions as distinguishable entities of a certain type. As I hope to demonstrate, the dynamics of constitutional identity are to a significant degree an expression of a developmental process endemic to the phenomenon of constitutionalism. The specific ways in which the process unfolds will vary from one constitutional context to another—and the differences are fascinating to behold—but so too are the elements of constitutional identity that are reflective of the constitutional condition more generally and that will be featured in the pages to follow.

I have been the beneficiary of much good advice and encouragement from people near and far. To my colleagues and friends, Russ Muirhead and Jeff Tulis, I owe a special debt of gratitude for their generous efforts on my behalf. Others to whom I am indebted are Ran Hirschl, Ruth Gavison, Shylashri Shankar, Amnon Reichman, Pnina Lahav, Hahm Chaihark, Sung Ho Kim, Tom Ginsburg, Bill Kissane, Gretchen Ritter, Zach Elkins, and Mark Graber. I am particularly grateful to two of the giants in Israeli constitutional jurisprudence, Justices Aharon Barak and Mishael Cheshin, for allowing me to question them closely about their participation in the controversial case that is the focus of one of my chapters. I wish also to thank Mike Aronson, my editor at Harvard University Press, whose enthusiasm and sage counsel were greatly appreciated during the latter stages of the preparation of this book. Finally, I must acknowledge the two Walters—Berns, my earliest mentor, and Murphy, my more recent mentor—who have played such a large role in helping me to see what is important about constitutions and other significant things. They are like bookends for my scholarly life, very different in style and intellectual orientation, but so much alike in their towering integrity and respect for the life of the mind.

A revised version of some of the material in Chapter 2 appeared in "An Unconstitutional Constitution? A Comparative Perspective," 4 *International Journal of Constitutional Law* 460 (2006). Several sections of Chapter 4 appeared in "The Permeability of Constitutional Borders," 82 *Texas Law Review* 1763 (2004); similarly, revised versions of some of the sections in Chapter 5 appeared in "The Sounds of Silence: Militant and Acquiescent Constitutionalism," in Steven Kautz, et al., *The Supreme Court and the Idea of Constitutionalism* (Philadelphia: University of Pennsylvania Press, 2009). Permission to incorporate this material is gratefully acknowledged.

Constitutional Identity

CHAPTER 1

Introduction: The Disharmonic Constitution

It is our purpose to create completely new laws and thus to tear up the very foundations of the old legal system.

—Mustafa Kemal Atatürk

We need to change the soul of the Turkish Constitution.

—Dengir Firat

The Identity Problem

Four score and three years separate these calls to action by two Turkish political figures. The occasion for the first was a speech in 1925 delivered by Mustafa Kemal Atatürk at a new law school in Ankara, in which the founder and first President of the Republic of Turkey laid out the case for a new civil code that promised to transform the ways in which the people of his nation would henceforth relate to one another. For the second it was an appearance at an old law school in Cambridge, Massachusetts, by the deputy chairman of Turkey's governing party, who was explaining why his Constitution required certain changes that would enable it to reflect the shifting underlying realities of Turkish society. A few months after Atatürk's address, the Turkish Assembly adopted a radical new civil code modeled after the Swiss example; nine weeks after the party leader's appeal for a change in the nation's constitutional soul, the country's highest court invalidated amendments to the Constitution, whose purported anti-secularist ambitions were deemed too radical for maintaining the coherence of the document.[1]

Both of the speakers were arguably indulging in rhetorical excess; for example, it had been a staple of the governing Justice and Development Party's (AK Party) professed ideological commitments to preserve the fundamentals of the secular settlement codified in Kemalist constitutionalism, which, to be sure, the party had conveniently chosen to understand as not having succeeded in completely eviscerating Turkey's preexisting Ottoman legal foundations.[2] From the party's perspective, the constitutional amendments it had sponsored benignly affirmed that an individual's modest assertion of her religious identity—in the form of attire that denoted affiliation with a faith community to which nearly all members of the society belonged—was not incompatible with the secular underpinnings of the regime. But rhetoric aside, these statements call attention to a critical and perplexing issue in comparative constitutional theory and to the subject of this book: What are we doing when we invoke the particular attributes or characteristics of a constitution that enable us to identify it as a unique legal and political phenomenon? Will doing so help to clarify the stakes involved in struggles between the opposing forces of constitutional preservation and change?

The Turkish case, as embodied in the transition from Ottoman rule to secular republicanism, may be an unusually dramatic instance of an attempt to destroy an existing constitutional identity before entrenching a new one that in time can be expected to inspire countervailing initiatives to recalibrate the foundational commitments of the regime. But as we shall see, the issues raised in the course of Turkish constitutional contestation are hardly peculiar to that polity. In one way or another they are implicated in the constitutional sagas of all nations, even if most of these narratives have unfolded more seamlessly than in Turkey. Among these issues are the questions of most obvious and immediate concern to us: just what is a constitutional identity and how does it come into being and change?

1. E. 2008/16, K. 2008/16 (case 2008/16, decision 2008/16) 2008.

2. See, for example, Esra Ozyurek, "Public Memory as Political Battleground: Islamist Subversions of Republican Nostalgia," in Esra Ozyurek, ed., *The Politics of Public Memory in Turkey* (Syracuse, NY: Syracuse University Press, 2007).

In this book I argue that the concept of constitutional identity should be at the center of constitutional theory. Understandably perhaps, many constitutional theorists have been skeptical that identity can be anything more than a tendentiously applied label used to advance a politically and constitutionally desirable result. Laurence Tribe's view is doubtless reflective of a not uncommon attitude: "[T]he very identity of 'the Constitution'—the body of textual and historical materials from which [fundamental constitutional] norms are to be extracted and by which their application is to be guided—is . . . a matter that cannot be objectively deduced or passively discerned in a viewpoint-free way."[3] Much as a term like "identity theft" may have relevance to credit cards and other aspects of our digitally filled lives, the concept's bearing on matters of constitutional salience is at best obscure. Yet, if the philosopher Joseph Raz is correct that constitutional theories "are [only] valid, if at all, against the background of the political and constitutional arrangements of one country or another," and that "[f]ew writings on constitutional interpretation successfully address problems in full generality," then it may behoove us—or at least those of us who do constitutional theory—not to give up too quickly on constitutional identity.[4]

Tribe's skepticism, however, derives from an insight into the American constitutional condition that may resonate even more compellingly in other national contexts where the "unruly plurality of the Constitution's ideas"[5] raises additional questions about the existence of a discernible identity than in the United States. But, even if his belief that the American Constitution "as a whole embraces conflicting, even radically inconsistent, ideas at one and the same time"[6] is an exaggerated claim about a document whose authors held divergent aspirations about fundamental things, the undeniable absence of a unitary constitutive vision places a commonsensical obstacle in the way of declaring this or that identity as definitive.

3. Laurence Tribe, "A Constitution We Are Amending: In Defense of a Restrained Judicial Role," 97 *Harvard Law Review* 433 (1983), 440.

4. Joseph Raz, "On the Authority and Interpretation of Constitutions: Some Preliminaries," in Larry Alexander, ed., *Constitutionalism: Philosophical Foundations* (Cambridge: Cambridge University Press, 1998), 152.

5. Laurence H. Tribe, "The Idea of the Constitution: A Metaphor-morphosis," 37 *Journal of Legal Education* (1987), 173.

6. Ibid.

To some extent I share Tribe's critique of such eminent constitutional theorists as Ronald Dworkin, John Hart Ely, and Richard Epstein for their acceptance of a central, unifying idea that confers unambiguous and lasting meaning to American constitutionalism. Indeed, their work points to a related problem, which is that too often constitutional theory tends to ignore the disharmonies of constitutional dynamics, preferring to conceptualize the Constitution at a level of abstraction that enables apparent tensions to disappear when theorizing is done the right way.

I take the position in the pages to follow that constitutional disharmony is critical to the development of constitutional identity, even as it may make more challenging the task of establishing the specific substance of that identity at any given point in time.[7] I also argue, however, that a vital component of the disharmony of the constitutional condition consists of identifiable continuities of meaning within which dissonance and contradiction play out in the development of constitutional identity. The forging of constitutional identity is thus not a preordained process in which one comes to recognize in the distinctive features that mark a constitution as one thing rather than another the ineluctable extension of some core essence that at its root is unchangeable. The disharmonies of constitutional law and politics ensure that a nation's constitution—a term that incorporates more than the specific document itself—may come to mean quite different things, even as these alternative possibilities retain identifiable characteristics enabling us to perceive fundamental continuities persisting through any given regime transformation.[8]

7. The "Constitution's greatness," as Tribe insists, may lie "in its resistance to neat encapsulation in any one grand tradition" (ibid., 173), yet, as we shall see, following Alasdair MacIntyre, if traditions are viewed correctly as incorporating dissonant perspectives, we will not want to deny their significance in the assessment of constitutional achievement.

8. The political theorist Hanna Pitkin was thus mostly right when she observed, "[T]o understand what a constitution is, one must look not to some crystalline core or essence of unambiguous meaning but precisely *at* the ambiguities, the specific oppositions that this specific concept helps us to hold in tension." Hanna Fenichel Pitkin, "The Idea of a Constitution," 37 *Journal of Legal Education* (1987), 167. To this I would add that such ambiguities and oppositions do not in themselves indicate the nonexistence of a core, but only render less obviously discernible a core that nevertheless endures in the idea of a constitution. As for the distinction between a constitution and a constitutional text, for the most part I follow Walter Murphy, who views the former as incorporating the latter as well as the constitutional order's "dominant

To be sure, the frequency with which constitutional arguments are tendentiously framed in the pursuit of political ends should doubtless temper extravagant claims for the analytical utility of the idea of identity. Skepticism may also follow from the logic and ubiquity of conventional identity politics, which begins with the claims of a part against the whole. Thus identity "is used to underscore the manner in which action—individual or collective—may be governed by *particularistic self-understanding* rather than by *putatively universal self-interest*."[9] Hence one would not expect viewpoint-neutrality to be a part of the political dynamics of representing the felt needs and aspirations of identity-based groups. More likely what is portrayed as a fundamental constitutional norm will be seen as reflecting the strategic requirements of differently situated actors within the larger political process.

Arguably, however, we can specify the features of a constitution so that we can identify that document as a constitution when we see certain attributes incorporated in a particular legal document. These traits enable us at least tentatively to affirm the existence of a constitution before engaging in further analysis of the content of any specific constitutional identity.[10] The certification is similar to our recognition of a table after

---

political theories, the traditions and aspirations that reflect those values, and the principal interpretations of this larger constitution." Walter F. Murphy, *Constitutional Democracy: Creating a Just Political Order* (Baltimore: Johns Hopkins University Press, 2007), 13.

9. Rogers Brubaker, *Ethnicity without Groups* (Cambridge, MA: Harvard University Press, 2004), 33. While there is much in Brubaker's account with which I agree, I do not share his conclusion, in which he insists that "[c]onstruing particularity in identitarian terms . . . constricts the political as well as the analytical imagination" (ibid., 61).

10. As Donald S. Lutz argues, "The distinction between what is held in common by all humans and what is held in common by the people of a given political system reminds us that any constitution must take into account basic human needs." Donald S. Lutz, *Principles of Constitutional Design* (Cambridge: Cambridge University Press, 2006), 203. The distinctions between constitutions generic and specific will become clearer in subsequent chapters. I agree, however, with Stanley N. Katz's criterion for affirming the presence of constitutional government. "[G]eneric constitutionalism consists in a process within a society by which a community commits itself to the rule of law, specifies its basic values, and agrees to abide by a legal/institutional structure which guarantees that formal social institutions will respect the agreed-upon values. . . ." Stanley N. Katz, "Constitutionalism in East Central Europe: Some Negative Lessons from the American Experience," in Vicki C. Jackson and Mark Tushnet, eds., *Comparative Constitutional Law* (New York: Foundation Press, 1999), 285.

seeing something that conforms to the criteria applicable to that particular object. We may then go on further to establish particular identities related to the general type, as when we distinguish a dining room table from, say, a pool table. If we wanted to preserve the identity of the latter we would prevent the removal of its pockets and distinctive felt playing top, just as we would protect the identity of *any* table by guaranteeing that its base and horizontal surface remain in place. We might also consider ways in which we might modify the identity of the specific table to improve its performance, while retaining its essential purpose and character.

That the defining attributes of a constitution will quickly be found more contestable than a table's ought not to discourage further inquiry. Indeed the table analogy is not only apt, but also receives implicit endorsement in the texts of many constitutions. For example, the Guaranty Clause of the American Constitution (Art. IV, sec. 4) in effect says that a republican form of government must prevail throughout the federal system and that failure to secure it would be like cutting the legs out from under the constitutional table. Similarly, a number of constitutions—for example, Turkey's in its commitment to secularism; the French document, in its express prohibition of any change that would destroy the republican form of government—are protective of basic, regime-defining characteristics that provide general definitional content to constitutional identity.[11] In theory, these textual barriers to certain kinds of constitutional change are designed to preserve a preexisting identity by obstructing the removal of those attributes without which the object in question, as in the case of the pool table, would become something very different.[12]

11. In 1992 the French Conseil Constitutionnel ruled that the Maastricht Treaty on European Union did not violate the requirement that the French State adhere to republican principles. Decision 92-308 (1992). At least as interesting as the finding is the fact that the Court did not avoid the question, thus in effect affirming that the question of constitutional identity is a justiciable matter.

12. This is the underlying logic of constitutional entrenchment. When those who frame a constitution act to prevent future actors from changing certain elements of their handiwork, they are in effect establishing an insurance policy in favor of a present identity against an imagined future identity that is deemed unacceptable. As Akeel Bilgrami points out, this logic runs counter to the familiar liberal understanding (exemplified in John Stuart Mill's *On Liberty*) that seeks to accommodate the future by ensuring that all present

Most tables do not require interpretation, even if a specific identification may be obscured by the fact that a table used for dining may function on other occasions as a work surface. With constitutions, however, we are always in the realm of interpretation. Included within this interpretive provenance is one of the most elemental and yet difficult questions of constitutional theory: how does one come to know the identity of a constitution? There is a vast philosophical literature going back to Plato that continues to provide vibrant, and sometimes passionate, debate over the criteria for determining identity, at least on the personal level. Much of this controversy surrounding the status of personhood is not directly transferable to constitutional matters, although constitutional theorists would be wise to give it measured consideration as an aid in structuring the ways in which we might reflect on the subject of identity and constitutions, and why it should matter to those who theorize about constitutions.

I will argue that a constitution acquires an identity through experience, that this identity exists neither as a discrete object of invention nor as a heavily encrusted essence embedded in a society's culture, requiring only to be discovered. Rather, identity emerges *dialogically* and represents a mix of political aspirations and commitments that are expressive of a nation's past, as well as the determination of those within the society who seek in some ways to transcend that past.[13] It is changeable but resistant to its own destruction, and it may manifest itself differently in different settings.

Constitutional theorizing about identity has deep historical roots. In Book III of *The Politics* Aristotle asked, "On what principle ought we to say that a State has retained its identity, or, conversely, that it has lost its

---

arrangements are adhered to in a tentative fashion. See Akeel Bilgrami, "Secularism and Relativism," 31 *Boundary* 173 (2004).

13. I use the word "commitments" in the sense employed by Jed Rubenfeld, who distinguishes it from "intentions," the latter term lacking the temporally extended dimension that creates constitutional obligations. "[D]emocracy does not consist ideally of governance by present democratic will, but also, in fundamental part, of adhering to the nation's fundamental, self-given commitments over time." Jed Rubenfeld, *Revolution by Judiciary: The Structure of American Constitutional Law* (Cambridge, MA: Harvard University Press, 2005), 112.

identity and become a different State?"[14] His answer requires that we distinguish the physical identity of a state from its real identity. Thus, "The identity of a polis is not constituted by its walls."[15] Instead, it is constituted by its constitution, which for Aristotle refers to the particular distribution of the offices in a polis—what the moderns imply by sovereign authority—as well as the specific end toward which the community aspires. When this end changes or when these offices come to be distributed differently, the constitution is no longer the same, and the identity of the state will have been likewise transformed. Much as a chorus is not the same chorus when its members shift from comic to tragic mode, a polis may physically retain all of its recognizable characteristics but project a different identity if its "scheme of composition" is transformed.[16] But, whether comic or tragic, a chorus helps to structure how we, the audience, are to understand what is going on in the drama unfolding before our eyes.

We might call this approach to identity *deeply constitutive,* as it reflects an understanding of the constitution as the foundation for both legal and social relations within a polity. In conflating the identity of the state with the substance of the constitution it suggests "a city could not change its constitution without committing suicide."[17] Such a consequence

14. *The Politics of Aristotle,* trans. and ed. Ernest Barker (New York: Oxford University Press, 1962), 98.

15. Ibid. As has been well documented and chronicled, the judiciary and the military have been the institutions most protective of the militant secularism that is Atatürk's legacy. For an interesting account of the Court and its assumption of a guardianship role in protecting the fundamental collective identity of the polity, see Ran Hirschl, "Constitutional Courts vs. Religious Fundamentalism: Three Middle Eastern Tales," 82 *Texas Law Review* 1819 (2004). Hirschl sees this development as part of the judicialization of politics, in which the judiciary has defended threatened political interests in their efforts to maintain a dominant position in the society.

16. *The Politics of Aristotle,* 99. Rousseau in *The Social Contract* suggests something similar when he says: "[B]efore examining the act by which a people elects a king, it behooves us to examine the act by which a people is a people. For this act necessarily precedes the other and is the true foundation of society." Jean-Jacques Rousseau, *The Social Contract and the First and Second Discourses* (New Haven, CT: Yale University Press, 2002), 162.

17. Richard Robinson, *Aristotle's Politics: Books III and IV* (Oxford: Clarendon Press, 1995), 10.

will appear extreme to those nurtured in the teachings of modern constitutionalism. Who today would say, for example, that the identity of Ireland had changed in the replacement of the Constitution of 1922 with the subsequent 1937 document, or even that a new identity for Poland had emerged from the pages of its post-Communist Constitution?[18] The latter case, to be sure, is a more unambiguous example of radical constitutional change, but would we not still be inclined to say that Polish national identity was continuous through the regime transition?[19] If so, perhaps our hesitancy to affirm otherwise bespeaks a less ambitious view of constitutional determinism, which is to say that what is constitutive of the identity of a polity seems to us to be rooted more in extra-constitutional factors such as religion and culture than in the language of a legal document.

The more encompassing Aristotelian notion of a constitution includes many of the factors typically viewed in the contemporary setting as extra-constitutional. For Aristotle, then, we find a direct correspondence between national and constitutional identities. Even, however, in the less comprehensive and more familiar constitutional model that imagines a clearer separation between these two identities, echoes of this older conception are present in those aforementioned entrenched provisions that, to borrow from Erik Erikson's definition of identity, seem

18. Thus I agree with Frank Michelman, who points out: "To think of a people living under a fundamental-legal regime that they themselves make or adopt is already to confer upon 'the people' an identity that is in some respect continuous across events of constitutional mobilization and change. . . . Agents can change through their acts without loss of identity. . . ." Frank I. Michelman, "Constitutional Authorship," in Larry Alexander, ed., *Constitutionalis: Philosophical Foundations* (Cambridge: Cambridge University Press, 1998), 79.

19. As Baruch Kimmerling argues, "The identity is the core that tends to persist when the government or even the state's regime changes." Baruch Kimmerling, *Clash of Identities: Explorations in Israeli and Palestinian Societies* (New York: Columbia University Press, 2008), 106. Kimmerling rightly points out that new identities will develop out of the dismantling of the Soviet Union and Yugoslavia, as ethnic restructurings and boundary redrawing take place. But, he acutely observes, "[a] transition from an autocratic or totalitarian system to a democratic system is a change in regime but not in identity. The Hungarian identity of post communist Hungary is not different from its identity during the communist era" (ibid., 365).

designed "to maintain inner sameness and continuity."[20] The distinction between national and constitutional identities is also difficult to sustain in situations where the express purpose of the constitution is to separate the future from the past in ways that will have transformative effects on social behavior. Turkey's Kemalist constitutions can, in this sense, be conceptualized as exercises in the conflation of the two identities, with the intended result manifest in the constitutionalization of national identity.

As Erikson also observed, "Identity is safest . . . when it is grounded in activity,"[21] which, in the case of a constitution, points to a correspondence between the words of a document and the behavior of those who fall under its jurisdiction. Some independent empirical demonstration that the text is in fact mainly consistent with constitutional experience will be required. Whether or not one embraces the deeply constitutive meaning of the ancient constitutional understanding, the Aristotelian distinction between a physical identity and a real identity requires that one withhold judgments about identity until after confirming that the codified rules and principles of the document actually resonate in the practices and culture of the body politic. A constitution's language may indicate a commitment on the part of its authors and subsequent interpreters to establish a constitutional identity, but until confirmed in the accumulated practice of a constitutional community, the goal, however noble, will remain unfulfilled. Who would say, for example, that the constitutional identity of the former Soviet Union was discernible within the folds of its governing charter?[22]

But even where constitutional enforcement and protection of rights are taken seriously, where, in Walter Murphy's terms, constitutionalism

20. Erik H. Erikson, *Dimensions of a New Identity* (New York: W. W. Norton, 1974), 204.

21. Ibid., 105.

22. As Andras Sajo notes in a different context, "The text itself has only limited potential for forging identity. A legally binding document is but a first step on the long and winding road from a political design for collective identity to a socially embedded institution that actually fosters such identity." Andras Sajo, "Constitution without the Constitutional Moment: A View from the New Member States," 3 *International Journal of Constitutional Law* 243 (2005).

rather than constitutionism prevails,[23] the question of identity presents challenging intellectual problems. First, as illustrated by Turkey, the relative intractability of a nation's sociocultural experience to legally inspire reshaping means that the relationship between the way identity is inscribed constitutionally and the way of life of the people to whom it is intended to apply—its behavioral identity—will be one of negotiation rather than incorporation. The "document called the Constitution," Michael Perry reminds us, may not be identical with "the norms that constitute the 'supreme Law.'"[24] Many constitutions, of course, do not seek behavioral transformation; what is set out in their provisions is intended to conform to the general configuration of the society, what in Chapter 5 I refer to as acquiescent constitutionalism. Here too, however, one needs to anticipate and consider the changes inevitably occurring in the mores and practices of a social order and their likely impact on the substance of constitutional identity. The case of Ireland, for example, which unlike Turkey embarked on a constitutional journey determined to accommodate the nation's extant cultural reality, illustrates, as we will see, the same adaptive process—albeit in reverse direction—of adjusting constitutional identity to shifting facts on the ground.

But, one might ask if we haven't gotten a bit ahead of ourselves. After all, what the Turkish example also highlights is the contestable nature of constitutional identity and, moreover, doubt as to its very analytical value. In the scholarly debate over the European Constitution, J. H. H. Weiler observes, "Our constitutions are said to encapsulate fundamental values of the polity and this, in turn, is said to be a reflection of our collective identity as a people, as a nation, as a state, as a community, or as a union."[25] Much of the controversy surrounding the proposed

23. "*Constitutionalism* differs from *constitutionism* in demanding adherence not to *any* given constitutional text or order but to principles that center on respect for human dignity and the obligations that flow from those principles." Walter F. Murphy, *Constitutional Democracy: Creating and Maintaining a Just Political Order* (Baltimore: Johns Hopkins University Press, 2007), 16.

24. Michael J. Perry, "What Is 'the Constitution'? (and Other Fundamental Questions)," in Alexander, *Constitutionalism: Philosophical Foundations,* 99.

25. J. H. H. Weiler, "On the Power of the Word: Europe's Constitutional Iconography," *International Journal of Constitutional Law* 184 (2005).

Constitution focused on the problematic application of the concept of identity to an entity comprised of states with their own separate identities. Thus, the "collective identity" of a union of states, as the American experience at its founding would also seem to exemplify, appears oxymoronic when contrasted with the other entities mentioned by Weiler. For those who see the American experience as showing the opposite—that a constitution can frame and establish the identity that fills the union's deficit of traditional integrative resources—there is in this instance a history that clearly makes the weighing of costs and benefits a worthwhile undertaking.

But this also raises the question of whether the union's identity problem is arguably only an extreme case of the dilemma confronting all forms of collective political identity, which is, as Mark Tushnet notes, that " 'who we are' is often—perhaps always—contestable and actively contested."[26] The dilemma is particularly acute for the "expressivist," who views constitutions as instruments through which "a nation goes about defining itself."[27] Tushnet rightly points out that for the expressivist, preambles to constitutions are exceptionally informative in conveying the underlying meaning of the collective enterprise that is the constitution. For example, the first words of the Turkish Preamble read: "In line with the concept of nationalism and the reforms and principles introduced by the founder of the Republic of Turkey, Atatürk. . . ." By contrast, the corresponding opening in the Irish document invokes "the Most Holy Trinity, from whom is all authority and to whom, as our final end, all actions both of men and States must be referred. . . ."

To the extent that expressivism finds in these emphatic proclamations the essence of Turkish and Irish identity, it asks that language bear more weight than it should or can. It also invests the words with a declarative meaning, asserting that this is what these identities are—Turkey is defined

26. Mark Tushnet, "Some Reflections on Method in Comparative Constitutional Law," in Sujit Choudhry, ed., *The Migration of Constitutional Ideas* (Cambridge: Cambridge University Press, 2006), 82. Or as Sanford Levinson observes, "[T]he Constitution can be said to be a model instance of what the philosopher W. B. Gallie has labeled an 'essentially contested concept.'" Sanford Levinson, *Constitutional Faith* (Princeton, NJ: Princeton University Press, 1988), 124.

27. Tushnet, "Some Reflections on Method," 79.

according to the (extreme secular) principles of its founder, and Ireland in accordance with the precepts of Christian theology. This in turn tends to yield a static view of constitutional identity, fixing its content in the codified affirmations of a specific time and place, whereas a more modest understanding of the constitution's expressive function is compatible with the position taken in this book. To this end, I argue for a more fluid concept of identity, in which constitutional assertions of self-definition are part of an ongoing process entailing adaptation and adjustment as circumstances dictate. It is not fluidity without boundaries, however, and textual commitments such as are embodied in preambles often set the topography upon which the mapping of constitutional identity occurs.

In this I am in partial agreement with the philosopher Michael Kenny, who says of "[t]he presumption that a cultural community possesses a core or bedrock identity," that it "encourages the idea that group identities can be grasped in isolation from wider social and cultural processes."[28] As applied more specifically to constitutional communities, I am less skeptical than Kenny (or Tribe) of the supposition concerning the existence of a core, believing with Aristotle that the specific end toward which the community aspires is critical to the concept of identity; but, I embrace the idea that a dialogical engagement between the core commitment(s) and its external environment is crucial to the formation and evolution of a constitutive identity. In this sense the identity of any constitution presumes that, as noted by Robert C. Post, "[C]onstitutional law and culture are locked in a dialectical relationship, so that constitutional law both arises from and in turn regulates culture."[29]

This relationship is an essential element in understanding the ways in which constitutional disharmony drives the process of identity

28. Michael Kenny, *The Politics of Identity: Liberal Political Theory and the Dilemmas of Difference* (Cambridge: Polity, 2004), 101.

29. Robert C. Post, "The Supreme Court, 2002 Term—Forward: Fashioning the Legal Constitution: Culture, Courts, and Law," 117 *Harvard Law Review* (2003), 8. Beau Breslin expresses a similar sentiment. "The act of writing a Constitution . . . commences a dialogue between text and citizen (and future generations) about the pursuit of political perfection." Beau Breslin, *From Worlds to Words: Exploring Constitutional Functionality* (Baltimore: Johns Hopkins University Press, 2008), 49.

development and clarification. "Those who constitute themselves in writing," Anne Norton acutely observes, "too often remain willfully unconscious of the unending dialectic of constitution. They prefer to see the writing of the Constitution as the perfect expression of an ideal identity."[30] In the Turkish case, for example, the "soul" of the constitution reflected the secular republican vision of its founder, but the actual constitutional identity of the polity had not been irrevocably fixed in the inscribed details of the document's provisions. "The written text, which exists beyond the moment of its composition, speaks to the people and their posterity of their identity and aspirations. It claims to speak to them not as artifacts of the past, but as present Law. No text, however transcendent, is unmarked by its time. No text, however abstract, speaks to all circumstances. For all these reasons there will be disjunctions between what is said to be and what is, between a people and its Constitution."[31] To the extent, then, that the commitment to secularism was constitutive of the Turkish regime, its specific content would vary over time, tethered to the text, but only loosely, so as to accommodate the dialogical interactions between codified foundational aspirations and the evolving mores of the Turkish people. "[C]onstitutional law will be as dynamic as the cultural values and beliefs that inevitably form part of the substance of constitutional law."[32]

Of course, the balance of political forces at any given time is always a key variable in how this all plays out, with the judiciary, as Ran Hirschl points out, often serving as the vehicle through which questions of "foundational collective identity" are addressed.[33] Whether in Turkey, where secular and non-secular (or at least less secular) parties compete for recognition as the authentic voice of traditional values; in Israel, where a persistent and fragile political equilibrium is traceable to the dual commitments of the nation's founding; in India, where a dominant, inclusive nationalist outlook has regularly been challenged by an alternative view

30. Anne Norton, "Transubstantiation: The Dialectic of Constitutional Authority," 55 *University of Chicago Law Review* (1988), 467.

31. Ibid., 469.

32. Post, "Supreme Court, 2002 Term—Forward," 10.

33. Ran Hirschl, *Towards Juristocracy: The Origins and Consequences of the New Constitutionalism* (Cambridge, MA: Harvard University Press, 2004), chap. 6.

with strong ethnic aspirations; the course of constitutional identity is impelled by the discord of ordinary politics within limits established by commitments from the past.

Identity and Disharmony: A Chapter Preview

The "Disharmonic Constitution" does not refer to the incoherence of constitutions—though that may indeed be the condition of some—but to the dissonance within and around the constitution that is key to understanding its identity. Thus, far from being fatal to the inquiry, the contestability of constitutional identity is a crucial element in our attempt to comprehend it. "Identities are held together by values as well as interests. Rarely, however, do they cohere. Rather, the tensions among them are played out in different sites, both temporal and geographical."[34] In subsequent chapters I explore several aspects of the disharmonic constitutional condition that illuminate the question of identity in topical contexts that have attracted the interest of American constitutional theorists but that have suffered from a deficit of comparative analysis and reflection.

Consider, for example, constitutional change. In the United States the difficulties in adapting the document to changing circumstances is a staple of Government 101. That predicament, however, has inspired some very creative efforts to construct alternative understandings to overcome the formal obstacles to constitutional transformation. These constructions focus on different political actors—mainly on the interpretive ingenuity of judges—but also on the activities of an aroused citizenry, which, in the most prominent intellectual venture of this kind to date, have been at the center of an unfolding project in constitutional theory.[35] Bruce Ackerman has developed a non–text-based understanding of constitutional change, which in the American context means forgoing an exclusive reliance on Article V's amendment procedures. He finds "revolutionary

34. Seyla Benhabib, Ian Shapiro, and Danilo Petranovic, "Editors' Introduction," in Seyla Benhabib, Ian Shapiro, and Danilo Petranovic, *Identities, Affiliations, and Allegiances* (Leiden: Cambridge University Press, 2007), 1.

35. Bruce Ackerman, *We the People: Foundations* (Cambridge, MA: Harvard University Press, 1991); Bruce Ackerman, *We the People: Transformations* (Cambridge, MA: Harvard University Press, 1998).

reform of the old regime" emanating from efforts that "did not respect established norms for revision."[36] In two volumes he has examined several "constitutional moments," transformative exertions of popular sovereignty—including post–Civil War developments that culminated in the formal incorporation of Martin Luther King Jr.'s promissory note—that he believes to have fundamentally redefined constitutional meaning in the United States. Indeed, as noted by John Finn, for Ackerman, "American constitutional history is best understood as an ongoing struggle over our collective constitutional identity."[37]

But in distinguishing between normal and transformative change, has Ackerman provided an adequate understanding of constitutional identity? Finn argues forcefully that he has not, that the account fails to identify "who 'We the People' are, and how we are constituted."[38] This alleged failure results from a miscalculation of the significance to be attached to entrenched constitutional principles. Thus, Ackerman's commitment to "dualist democracy" (requiring deference to all legitimate expressions of the popular sovereign will) as opposed to foundationalism (requiring resistance to any deeply constitutive changes) leaves him, in Finn's view, incapable of "address[ing] fundamental questions of constitutional identity."[39]

Finn's own account may attribute too much importance to entrenchment, thereby making evolution in the substance of constitutional identity hard to apprehend. Does the framing of a constitution effectively establish a fixed identity, such that prospects for change must focus on what Lincoln referred to in his First Inaugural as the revolutionary option? When this option is exercised there is no doubt that the goal sought is a substitution of one constitutional identity for another (assuming the post-revolutionary regime is a constitutional one); less certain is whether the constitutional process can be legitimately used to effect such a change, and whether there are implicit substantive limits to change

36. Bruce Ackerman, *We the People: Transformations,* 12.

37. John E. Finn, "Transformation or Transmogrification? Ackerman, Hobbes (as in Calvin and Hobbes), and the Puzzle of Changing Constitutional Identity," 10 *Constitutional Political Economy* (1999), 355.

38. Ibid., 355.

39. Ibid., 363.

achieved through procedures enumerated in the document.[40] As Walter Murphy argues, "The word *amend,* which comes from the Latin *emendere,* means to correct or improve; amend does not mean 'to deconstitute and reconstitute,' to replace one system with another or abandon its primary principles. Therefore, changes that would make a polity into another kind of political system would not be amendments at all, but revisions or transformations."[41]

Murphy's view has not penetrated very deeply into the American legal or scholarly imagination. More consonant with conventional opinion is Ackerman's sovereignty-based theory of constitutional change, which, in addition to allowing for sweeping transformation outside of the procedures outlined in Article V, requires accepting the legitimacy of any amendment—even one that would make Christianity the state religion—as an expression of the authentic voice of the demos. In Chapter 2 I examine the puzzle of the unconstitutional constitutional amendment in varying constitutional contexts—India, Ireland, and Sri Lanka—to introduce us to the challenge of constitutional identity. The Irish and Sri Lankan cases point to the dilemma adverted to by Murphy, that a constitutional order is fully capable of furnishing those committed to its subversion with the lawful means to secure their objective. In contrast, in Indian jurisprudence we find a sustained effort to engage the deepest issues of identity implicated in the genus of constitutional change that may culminate in a reconstituted order. But this effort, while impressive in the magnitude of its ambitions, is limited in its theoretical reach; thus it provides a rationale for identity-motivated judicial activism on behalf of the constitution that *is,* without offering guidance for those committed

40. Jeffrey Tulis criticizes Ackerman for not "distinguish[ing] amendment from revolution." "Amendment presupposes a constitution whose identity persists over time. Revolution presupposes the disjunction of identities, the possibility of marking a change in fundamental political attributes that make a new polity truly new." Jeffrey K. Tulis, "Review of Bruce Ackerman, 'We the People: Foundations,'" in 55 *The Review of Politics* 540 (1993), 542.

41. Walter F. Murphy, "Merlin's Memory: The Past and Future Imperfect of the Once and Future Polity," in Sanford Levinson, ed., *Responding to Imperfection: The Theory and Practice of Constitutional Amendment* (Princeton, NJ: Princeton University Press, 1995), 177. Murphy has elaborated in other writings, most expansively in *Constitutional Democracy* (2007).

to a better constitution that *could be.* In other words, the jurisprudential record is slim in theorizing the changes in constitutional identity that extant circumstances may require, even if, ironically, Indian constitutional identity is in its essentials, predominantly about the urgency of change.

In Chapter 3 I try to address this insufficiency, which prevails in the precincts of contemporary constitutional theory as well as in the decisions of faraway courts. "[C]onstitutional identity," Michel Rosenfeld suggests, "can take many different forms, and evolve over time, because it is often immersed in an ongoing process marked by substantial changes."[42] But what is the nature and dynamics of this process? Within what constraints does it proceed?

The most important constraint is generic. While I direct most of my attention in this book to the factors that provide polities with their specific and distinctive constitutional identities, I assume, in the spirit of Lon Fuller's famous account of the "morality of law," that there are certain criteria that enable us to determine the existence of constitutional governance.[43] Fundamentally, these have to do with the presence or absence of a pervasive arbitrariness in the conduct of public affairs. It is no coincidence that the doctrine of the unconstitutional amendment originated in German jurisprudence, which had in the immediate post-War period come to accept the idea that there are implied and enforceable limits to constitutional change, particularly as these changes go to the very essence of what it means to be governed constitutionally. Indeed, the German interest in the subject of constitutional identity is historically obvious, as would the interest in the individual identity of anyone who had been close to another whose personality appeared at some point to have drastically changed for the worse.

Elsewhere the concern for identity may be more politically motivated. In the Indian case that is celebrated for having pursued the conceptual logic of German legal thinking, one of the justices concluded, "The

42. Michel Rosenfeld, "Modern Constitutionalism as Interplay between Identity and Diversity," in Michel Rosenfeld, ed., *Constitutionalism, Identity, Difference, and Legitimacy* (Durham, NC: Duke University Press, 2004), 10.

43. Lon Fuller, *The Morality of Law* (New Haven, CT: Yale University Press, 1964).

personality of the Constitution must remain unchanged."[44] From here it is not very far to opposing constitutional change when it is viewed as a threat to the specific commitments one associates with the constitution's particular identity, as eventually transpired in India in connection with the intense struggle over the meaning of secularism. Such threats may be tactically described as subversive of the generic constitution, as happened in response to the amendments in Turkey easing the restrictions against religious expression in the public domain, but the reality is that what is opposed is not the end of constitutionalism but rather a contested way of practicing it.

My argument in Chapter 3 is that the shaping and evolution of constitutional identity is a function of such contestation. I draw upon Alasdair MacIntyre's analysis of tradition to consider constitutional identity as an artifact of the dissonance in a nation's divided inheritance. Tradition for MacIntyre is more than a source of societal stability, or as Edmund Burke emphasized, an "idea of continuity"; rightly conceived it embodies an adversarial component—"continuities of conflict"—that connects it to the historical narrative within which it unfolds while preventing it from becoming moribund. As T. S. Eliot put it in a famous essay, "[I]f the only form of tradition, of handing down, consisted in following the ways of the immediate generation before us in a blind or timid adherence to its successes, 'tradition' should positively be discouraged."[45]

But, as constitutional experience demonstrates, tradition rarely presents itself neatly as the harmonious gift from the past, rather it comes to us encumbered with the discordant strands of a complicated history. Burke's "prescriptive constitution" need not connote, as is often seen, sameness and predictable continuity in the course of constitutional development. As I contend in this chapter, a satisfactory account of constitutional identity cannot ignore the various disharmonies that are embedded in a nation's constitutional history. If we think again of Turkey, we would not be remiss in seeing the course of twentieth-century constitutional development as the progressive entrenchment of a secular identity. Ultimately,

44. Kesavananda Bharati v. State of Kerala, A SC 1461 (1973), 1624.

45. T. S. Eliot, "Tradition and the Individual Talent," in *The Sacred Word and Major Essays* (Mineola, NY: Dover Publications, 1997), 28.

however, we must recognize the contingent quality of that identity, which is not to suggest that in the foreseeable future it is likely to experience a radical transformation in its core assumptions and aspirations. Nevertheless, the determinative power of those assumptions and aspirations may become attenuated through a dialogical process of engagement with newly energized forces having roots in the nation's constitutional history and inspiration from events occurring in contemporary civil society.

Constitutional change comes in many forms, and in Chapter 4, I consider it in the guise of emulation, specifically the use of foreign sources and precedents of one national court by justices from another. This practice has become an intensely debated issue in scholarly circles, on the American Supreme Court, and in the halls of Congress. Among the various criticisms of the practice is that it has the potential for obscuring and perhaps undermining the distinctively unique character of American constitutionalism. Its most outspoken critic is Justice Antonin Scalia, who argues, "[I]rrelevant are the practices of the 'world community,' whose notions of justice are (thankfully) not always those of our people. We must never forget that it is a Constitution for the United States of America that we are expounding. . . ."[46] Or, as a scholar much more sympathetic than Scalia to constitutional borrowing writes, "If law and individual legal systems can be understood as having distinct local identities with identifiable authentic experiences, what happens when such experiences are continually exposed to external influences?"[47]

As with the amendment process, assessing the costs and benefits of foreign legal experience is entwined in the details of constitutional identity. In 2004, following the Supreme Court's controversial gay rights decision in Lawrence v. Texas, in which the majority had cited foreign law to augment its argument in support of the case's homosexual petitioner, the U.S. Congress debated the Constitution Restoration Act (CRA).

46. Atkins v. Virginia, 536 US 304 (2002), at 347.

47. Sarah Harding, "Comparative Reasoning and Judicial Review," 28 *Yale Journal of International Law* 410 (2003), 462. One answer to this query is that attention to other possibilities abroad might actually underline the distinctive features of the local identity. As J. H. H. Weiler writes, "My continued existence as a distinct identity depends, ontologically, on [the national] boundary and, psychologically and sociologically, on preserving the feeling of otherness."

Included in the proposed legislation was the following provision: "In interpreting and applying the Constitution of the United States, a court of the United States may not rely upon any constitution, law, administrative rule, Executive order, directive, policy, judicial decision, or any other action of any foreign state or international organization or agency, other than the constitutional law and English common law."[48] The main purpose of the bill to which this provision was attached was to prevent courts from adjudicating cases involving the public "acknowledgment of God as the sovereign source of law, liberty, or government."[49] Abundantly clear from the arguments advanced by the bill's supporters was an understanding of the American Constitution as having incorporated a Christian identity within the folds of its spare provisions. Restoring the Constitution to its status as a God-friendly charter meant, to a large degree, excluding foreign influences—mainly European—from undermining that distinctive identity.

That the CRA was never enacted into law is at least partly attributable to the failure of its proponents correctly to characterize the constitutional identity they intended to defend. It was not the result of the opponents' cogent defense of the migration of constitutional ideas. As Sujit Choudhry rightly remarks, the increasing judicial reliance on foreign sources "has outgrown the conceptual apparatus that legal actors use to make sense of it."[50] In this chapter I seek to clarify some of the conceptual issues involved in this debate by shifting the geographical focus away from the United States, thereby insulating the analysis from the polemical noise that has too often drowned out thoughtful consideration of the problem. My departure from the predominantly U.S.-centric discussion of the issue allows us to factor out the heavy dose of American exceptionalism that has led some commentators to establish categorical objections to any outside penetration of constitutional borders.

Of course, the very idea of constitutional identity carries with it some connotation of exceptionalism. But a more comparative perspective does

48. Constitution Restoration Act of 2004, Section 201.

49. Ibid., Section 101.

50. Sujit Choudhry, ed., *The Migration of Constitutional Ideas* (Cambridge: Cambridge University Press, 2006), 10.

two things: (1) It highlights the extent to which all constitutional polities represent a blend of characteristics revealing what is particular to the constitutional culture as well as what are widely viewed as common attributes of a universal culture of constitutionalism. The tensions—and sometimes outright contradictions—in this mix provide an incentive structure within which judicial actors may attempt to reconcile and accommodate the disharmonic elements of their constitutional circumstance. One way of doing it is to engage with the external legal environment for interpretive insight; and (2) It demonstrates across a range of cases that the manner in which foreign materials are integrated into the local constitutional setting matters much more than the categorical acceptance or rejection of such infusions. As we shall see, critical to the success or failure of the enterprise is the impact that the insinuation of foreign examples into the domestic arena exerts on the balance of disharmonic constitutional elements in a given society. Much here will depend on the aspirational content of the prevailing constitutional ethos; thus, a more confrontational document, one devoted to an agenda of societal transformation, may, in view of its less deferential take on the status quo, benefit from a greater openness to the possibilities of foreign influence.

Of all of the bases for distinguishing among constitutional identities, one of the most revealing concerns the ways in which polities have imagined the relationship between a constitution and its surrounding social order. In Chapter 5 I discuss two models of constitutionalism that exhibit divergent orientations with respect to the expected impact of a constitutional presence in the life of the larger community. Thus, we might think of a constitution in a quite unconventional way, as an expression of defiance directed against an existing social structure whose transformation had been deemed desirable by the document's framers. Prototypical of this constitutional model is the Turkish Constitution, which, it is safe to say, was not given to complacency in the mission assigned to it for the governance of society. Kemalist aspirations required that it assume a profoundly subversive role in re-constituting the personal and institutional priorities that had come to define public attitudes and behavior.

I characterize constitutions of this type as *militant,* which indicates that critically important for understanding their identity is the large space that separates founding ideals and entrenched reality. While law and society are always in some tension with one another, the level of disharmony that prevails between the two in places where militancy is the dominant constitutional ethos sets it apart from the comfortable fit that distinguishes the more familiar constitutional situation. This latter model may be characterized as *acquiescent,* which does not mean that it leaves the institutions of civil society immune from revision; indeed, the two types of constitutions contrasted in this chapter should not be viewed as dichotomous, but as distinctive points on a broad spectrum. Acquiescence signifies that the constitution itself is not the proximate source of societal transformation. Fundamental to the identity of these constitutions is a preservative predisposition, a commitment to maintain the essential continuity of such structures of societal stability as the church and private property.

The focus in this chapter is on the family, an institution whose importance as a bastion of civil society is evident in the ubiquitous specification for its protection among the constitutions of the world. In Ireland, for example, the 1937 Constitution's privileging of the "inalienable and imprescriptible" rights of the family in Article 41 embodied commitments central to the aspirations of Irish constitutionalism. To attempt a description of Irish constitutional identity without featuring this centrality would be strange indeed. In Ireland the textual acknowledgment of the non-textually based standing of the family—its presumed natural law pedigree—renders the institution a rather obvious candidate for inclusion in what is constitutive of identity in that polity. But the centrality of the family to all societies and to the individual lives of their members means that the institution has the potential for illuminating the question of constitutional identity in many polities, including those which, unlike Ireland, are more muted in their recognition of its societal significance.

In India the family is embedded in a social structure whose reconstruction had been vital to the project of Indian constitutionalism. The transformative nature of Indian constitutional identity is implicit in the reach of the powers granted public authority as well as the rights that are withheld from the ambit of constitutional protection; thus, one of the world's longest constitutions does not contain language mandating state guarantees for the family. To the framers of the document, who were well versed in the constitutional arrangements of other places and also very receptive to borrowing ideas that seemed promising for their own venture, the absence of such language was arguably not accidental. So, for example, the Irish Constitution, which had been an important source of ideas for the Indian framers, was not emulated with respect to its explicit protection for the family. The dominant religions in both countries—Catholicism in Ireland and Hinduism in India—emphasized the sanctity of the family, but this emphasis has had different implications for the constitutional identities of the two respective polities: in the first it culminated in the preservative provisions of Article 41, and in the second it led to the political vulnerabilities attendant to textual indifference. As Donald S. Lutz, following Aristotle, notes, "[W]hen it comes to matching a government to a people for purposes of constitutional design, the relative absence of barriers to intermarriage across a population may be a very important consideration."[51] In this regard, the Indian Constitution's explicit targeting of caste is also a way of taking aim at the constitutionally exposed family; indeed, India is an example of constitutional silence facilitating societal reconstruction, and hence reinforcing the particulars of constitutional identity.

Silence, however, may also facilitate the goal of societal preservation; in the American Supreme Court's jurisprudence of the family, constitutional acquiescence in the traditional family is, as we will see, a reflection of a more pervasive acquiescence in the configuration of the larger social order. In contrasting the Indian and American constitutional approaches to the family, I build upon Alexis de Tocqueville's famous comparative insight concerning the democratic condition and the origins of regimes, specifically the important political implications that derive from being "born equal [or not], instead of becoming so." Among these implications is the shaping of constitutional identity, which to a significant degree reflects the nature of prevailing social conditions at the inception of new polities. Constitutional aspirations are not framed in a vacuum; they are rooted in the past and adapted to the circumstances of the moment. As these circumstances change over time the mutability of identity becomes

51. Donald S. Lutz, *Principles of Constitutional Design,* 201.

a reality that cannot be ignored. This may manifest itself, as I explain in connection with recent Irish experience, in a questioning of acquiescent constitutional assumptions that no longer comport with modifications in social behavior. While the constraints of the prescriptive constitution work to prevent a radical swing from acquiescence to militancy, the pull of secularization produces a discernible shift in the family's constitutive meaning in Ireland, one consistent with my consideration of the dynamics of identity in Chapter 3.

In Israel, too, the family has become an important site for reflection on constitutional identity. As in India, there is a regime of personal laws in place that survived the transition from empire to national independence. It is a more entrenched arrangement than exists in India, leading to a less interventionist state vis-à-vis the autonomy of religious communities and their determination of family policy.[52] But in the cauldron of conflict that is the setting for debate over Israeli constitutional identity, issues occasionally arise that transcend the particulars of family policy, implicating the most fundamental and divisive fault line in the nation's politics. One such issue arose in connection with the passage in 2003 of the Nationality and Entry into Israel Law (Temporary Order),[53] which prevents the spouse of an Israeli citizen—in effect a Palestinian Arab—who lives in the Gaza Strip or the West Bank from joining his or her family in Israel. In 2006 the Israel Supreme Court ruled on the constitutionality of the law, narrowly upholding it and thereby creating a firestorm

52. To be more precise, as Marc Galanter and Jayanth Krishnan note, the state in Israel, in the rulings of the Supreme Court, has become increasingly interventionist with regard to personal status issues of the majority Jewish community. It has, on the other hand, scrupulously avoided such issues as they apply to the minority communities, including the Muslim population. The key difference between the regimes of personal law in Israel and India is this: "In Israel, personal laws are administered by qualified religious specialists in courts that are part of, or attached to, religious institutions. By contrast, in India, personal law is applied by common-law-trained judges in the regular state courts." Mark Galanter and Jayanth Krishnan, "Personal Law Systems and Religious Conflict: A Comparison of India and Israel," in Gerald James Larson, ed., *Religion and Personal Law in Secular India: A Call to Judgment* (Bloomington: Indiana University Press, 2001), 284.

53. Khok Ha-Ezrakhut V'Ha-Knisa L'Yisra-el (Hora-at Sha-a), 2003, S.H. 544.

over the question of family unification and the very essence of the Israeli political community.[54]

In Chapter 6 I examine the family unification decision as a case study in the disharmonics of constitutional identity. Indeed, the contest over family rights was, perhaps most importantly, a struggle over the meaning of Israeli constitutional identity. Thus, it may be true, as the dissenting justice in the case pointed out, that democracies do not act in the way that the Israeli government did in this instance. Yet, the conflicting strands of Israel's national identity suggest that the constitutional meaning of the family, like so much else in that country, cannot be finally resolved without addressing questions of more fundamental import that would clarify the actual relationship of democracy to Israeli constitutional identity.

The debate within the Israeli Supreme Court was about immigration policy but was conducted largely through the discourse of constitutional jurisprudence. Focusing on the alternative interpretive strategies employed in the opposing opinions, I call attention to an issue that transcends the particulars of the Israeli case: as courts increasingly are asked to resolve what Hirschl has referred to as the "meta-narrative" questions of constitutional disputation, we need to develop thick, ethnographically detailed accounts of the local constitutional scene (including specific judicial decisions) that provide entry into the theoretical constructs we have devised to illuminate the object of our general interest (i.e., constitutional identity). In the landmark family unification case that is the subject of the inquiry in Chapter 6, the Basic Law on Human Dignity and Liberty, the most recent addition to Israel's evolving constitution, served as the vehicle through which the justices addressed the interdependent issues of identity and judicial role; in the end, how they differently assessed the disharmonies in the nation's historical narrative dictated their contrasting conclusions about constitutional identity. Their differences transcend the parameters of the immediate case and contain lessons that carry well beyond Israeli borders.

In the concluding chapter I review the lessons learned from this episode as well as from others detailed in earlier chapters. A nation's constitutional

54. Adalah, et al. v. The Minister of Interior, et al., H.C. 7052/03.

document is not coterminous with its constitutional identity; thus, in a sense the Israeli example, in which no comprehensive formal document exists, offers at once a notably idiosyncratic display of constitutionalism and a portal into the developmental dynamics attendant the formation of constitutional identity in more conventional settings. The consciously cumulative nature of constitutional rights and structures in Israel openly reveals the "unending dialectic of becoming and overcoming"[55] that prevails in all constitutional polities, but which is often obscured by the appearance of finality misleadingly projected by the all-embracing legal codification that is the common experience of constitutions around the world. Thus, the blatant incompleteness of the Israeli constitutional project produces a serial reenactment of foundational contestations whenever the polity confronts a further constitutionalization of governing practices. Additionally, there is on these occasions no escaping consideration of whether the proposed constitutional accretion should seek a ratification of what exists in the patterns of prevailing societal conduct or attempt to transform it.

Indeed, this determination—ratification or transformation—is the challenge that all constitutional regimes confront. My concluding reflections include return visits to issues that received earlier consideration—the unconstitutional amendment conundrum and the constitutional status of the family—but in venues that were not featured in the initial analyses. These examples from Turkey and South Korea leave us with the thought that the dynamics of constitutional identity may be common to the constitutionalist condition, that, for example, the mutability of identity is both attributable to constitutional disharmony and constrained by its prescriptive content.

The Three "I's"

In this book I cite various examples from around the world to illustrate and develop my arguments, but with the United States, my focus is on three nations: India, Israel, and Ireland. For the reader who perhaps is

55. Anne Norton, "Transubstantiation: The Dialectic of Constitutional Authority," 463.

wondering if the common first letter in the names of these countries dictated my case selection, I want to conclude this introductory chapter with some observations about these polities that should make clear that the choices were not randomly determined.

The British Empire is, of course, the shared backdrop to the constitutional histories of these places. Indeed, for Edmund Burke, whose thoughts on the prescriptive constitution carry considerable weight in the chapters to follow, the burdens of England's colonial ties to the Americans, the Indians, and the Irish were the constant preoccupation of his extended political career. Moreover, it requires only some imaginative energy to hear echoes of Burke's censure of eighteenth-century British imperial policies in pointed denunciations of his country's administration of Palestine two centuries later.

Thus a prominent particular in Burke's condemnation of British practices is applicable to pre-independence Israel as well, namely, the baneful effects of the colonial presence on relations among major population groups in the local setting. Niall Ferguson's magisterial history of violent conflict in the twentieth century captures this sad fact very well: "The decline and fall of the British Empire was attended by bitter intercommunal violence between Hindus and Muslims in India; between Israelis and Arabs in Palestine; between Sunnis and Shi'ites in Iraq [another "I" country!]; between Protestants and Catholics in Ireland."[56] The similarity in this regard between India and Israel is especially striking, with both countries "emerg[ing] as a nation state in the first wave of de-colonization through a partition process that reduced the presence of its largest minority and increased the preponderance of its largest religious group."[57] In Ireland, too, a war of independence from British rule was followed by a continuation and exacerbation of deep religious divisions that placed church/state matters at the center of the constitutional identity question. And in time the courts of all three common-law countries played a critical role in addressing these issues of identity.

56. Niall Ferguson, *The War of the World: Twentieth-Century Conflict and the Descent of the West* (London: Penguin Books, 2006), 610.

57. Mark Galanter and Jayanth Krishnan, "Personal Law and Human Rights in India and Israel," 34 *Israel Law Review* (2000), 101, 102.

More importantly, these similarities allow us better to appreciate the significance of the differences, beginning with the question of fit.[58] In contrast with India and Israel, Irish constitutional identity developed in more harmonious conjunction with the sociocultural-economic environment within which it came into being. The observation by an Irish commentator that his constitution gave expression to "characteristics of the polity that already exist[ed],"[59] may seem a commonplace of general applicability. What is more, the predominant characteristic of his nation parallels that of the other two countries, namely, the religion of the vast majority of the population.[60] And like Hinduism in India and Judaism in Israel, the constitutional salience of Catholicism in Ireland is as much

58. For an interesting discussion of similarities and differences in relation to case selection, see Ran Hirschl, "On the Blurred Methodological Matrix of Comparative Constitutional Law," in Sujit Choudhry, ed., *The Migration of Constitutional Ideas.* Hirschl cites his own research on Egypt, Israel, and Turkey to illustrate what he calls the "most different cases" approach. This involves "compar[ing] cases that are different on all variables that are not central to the study but match in terms that are, thereby emphasizing the significance of consistency on the key independent variable in explaining the similar readings on the dependent variable" (ibid., 51). While my trio of cases does not quite match the variability in the countries' interpretive approaches to questions of religion and state that his embodies, their selection parallels his in important respects, particularly as relates to the "emergence of constitutional courts as important guardians of secular interests in these countries" (ibid., 53).

59. Garrett Barden, "Discovering a Constitution," 7.

60. The constitutional significance of this is manifest in the Preamble's invocation of "the Most Holy Trinity, from whom is all authority and to whom, as our final end, all actions both of men and States must be referred." Section 2 of Article 44 in the original Constitution (deleted in 1972) also recognized "the special position of the Holy Catholic Apostolic and Roman Church as the guardian of the Faith professed by the great majority of the citizens." Section 3 (deleted at the same time) went on to recognize other denominations, including, uniquely, "the Jewish congregations." It should be noted that the Section 2 language was not as emphatic as some of the Catholic advisors to Eamon de Valera had preferred. For example, de Valera rejected the Jesuit priest, Edward Cahill's, recommendation that the Constitution proclaim: "The Holy Roman Catholic Church . . . occupies in the social life and organization of the Irish nation a unique and preponderant position, which is recognized as a fact by the Constitution and shall be duly recognized by the state." Quoted in Sean Faughnan, "The Jesuits and the Drafting of the Irish Constitution of 1937," 26 *Irish Historical Studies* (1988), 94. For a thoughtful treatment of de Valera's balancing of religious and political factors in the framing of the Irish Constitution, see Bill Kissane, "Eamon de Valera and the Survival of Democracy in Inter-War Ireland," 42 *Journal of Contemporary History* (2007).

political as theological. But there is a difference. In considering the process of constitutional design, the imprint of the dominant religions in India and Israel on the formation of identity is a more complicated story than in the Irish Republic, where the Christian spirit of the document was incorporated as a relatively noncontroversial feature of the document. In India, constitutional identity evolved in creative tension with the religious identity of the majority; its imprint, therefore, was substantial but decidedly confrontational in character. In the Israeli case, the failure to adopt a formal comprehensive written constitution after the establishment of the state was partly attributable to a fundamental disagreement over the role that the religion of the majority should play in constituting the polity. A half-century later the controversy over the judicially inspired "constitutional revolution" essentially reenacted the early debates over the shape and substance of constitutional identity, the contestants still arguing over the appropriate balance between democracy and Judaism.[61]

None of these countries has an established religion, and yet religion is at the center of the most vexing questions concerning their constitutional identities. The Trinitarian cast to the Irish Constitution does not mean that the nation's highest law is deeply constitutive in the theocratic sense that applies, say, to the Iranian Constitution.[62] The adoption of a document in 1937 that made no effort to conceal the sectarian sources of its deepest commitments did not appreciably alter the identity of a polity that had previously been governed by a constitution notably lacking in any explicit religious identification. "If the constitution differed from its predecessors in introducing religious values into constitutional law for the first time, it was also a return to the democratic ethos of the 1922 document, which had been inspired by very radical ideas."[63] More than a new departure in constitutional engineering, the document was, in es-

61. I have examined this controversy in Gary Jeffrey Jacobsohn, "After the Revolution," 34 *Israel Law Review* 139 (2000).

62. Nevertheless, in the first few decades under the 1937 Constitution the state proved itself unwilling or unable to make policy opposed to the Catholic Church's wishes. As Basil Chubb suggests, this record could qualify as "theocratic" by some definitions. Basil Chubb, *The Politics of the Irish Constitution* (Dublin: Institute of Public Administration, 1991), 48.

63. Kissane, "Eamon de Valera," 218.

sence, a confirmation of the prescriptive constitution.[64] As Basil Chubb points out, the Catholic Church was not made an established church under the Irish Constitution because it did not need to be.[65] All that was necessary (or at least desirable) was for the document to validate an identity that had long been instantiated in centuries of religious tradition and political struggle. The behavioral reality of the Irish people was expressed in what was approvingly referred to as "the wonderful Christian spirit, which animates the whole constitution."[66] An expressive component is present in all constitutional identities; where, as in the Irish instance, the principal marks of identity are largely a projection of the extant social or cultural condition rather than mainly or even partly a reproach to it, expressiveness might be viewed as a synonym for the concept of identity and not merely a component of it.

Israel's constitutional experience is also a reflection of its social condition. As Alexis de Tocqueville pointed out, "Social condition . . . may justly be considered as itself the source of almost all the laws, the usages, and the ideas which regulate the conduct of nations. . . . If we could become acquainted with the legislation and the manners of a nation . . . we must begin by the study of its social condition."[67] In Tocqueville's usage the term included the beliefs and ideas that shape the political consciousness and identity of a nation. As in Ireland, those ideas and the chronicle associated with them are tethered to a particular faith community; when, however, this similarity is viewed against other background conditions, it is clear why the course of constitutional development in the two countries has been widely divergent. The principal difference of

64. In saying this I do not mean to overlook the obvious break with British colonial ties signified by the 1937 charter. For Ireland this was indeed a new departure, and so a complete account of constitutional identity must include the triumph of republicanism. For a different view of Irish constitutional identity that views the Constitution as a text similar to the contradictory texts of literary modernism (for example, James Joyce's *Finnegans Wake*), see Patrick Hanafin, *Constituting Identity: Political Identity Formation and the Constitution in Post-Independence Ireland* (Aldershot, England: Ashgate, 2001).

65. Ibid., 36.

66. The comment of a Catholic theologian at the time of the adoption of the Constitution, as quoted in Faughnan, "The Jesuits," 97.

67. Alexis de Tocqueville, *Democracy in America,* ed. Phillips Bradley (New York: Vintage, 1945), 48.

course involves the presence in Israel of a large ethnic population whose marginal status in the polity creates an omnipresent challenge to the realization of liberal democratic aspirations.[68] But the other point of distinction is no less significant in generating constitutional disharmony. The orthodox Jewish establishment is responsible for setting rules to govern the conduct of Israeli Jews in matters of personal status—for example, marriage and divorce—but its authority to do so, unlike the Catholic hierarchy in Ireland (which formally does not have such powers), has always been contested within the Jewish community in Israel and in the diaspora. Taken together, these rifts in the body politic create the perception that the achievement of constitutional identity is persistently beyond the reach of the present.

Although in India, too, struggles over the status of a substantial minority population—most of whom, as in Israel, are Muslim—leave the substance of constitutional identity exposed to perennial disputation, it is, ironically, the abiding fissures in the nation's social terrain that provide a unifying thrust and stability to that identity. As Bruce Ackerman rightly suggests, "[B]y the standard criteria of political science [India] should never have been able to sustain constitutional democracy."[69] That it *has* is attributable in part to the "increasing prominence of the Constitution, and its judicial institutions, as the guardians of the nation's fundamental constitutional commitments."[70] Exactly how much a part is so attributable is a much-debated subject. The constitutional commitments to which Ackerman refers would have to include a transformational aspiration intended to transcend the sectarian fragmentation

68. There is a huge literature on this subject. Among the most prolific (and outspoken) commentators has been Baruch Kimmerling, whose work persistently pursued the question of identity. "As powerful and strong as it is, the state cannot be detached from the identities and mythic self-perceptions of the population composing the society, referring in this case to the population that considers itself to belong to the somewhat abstract term of Israel, which cuts across state, family, and civil institutions. We are also dealing with a notion of a nation-state—the term 'nation' indicates a generalized kind of identity with some structural implications—wherein the identity of the Israeli state is primarily and ultimately a Jewish nation-state." Kimmerling, *Clash of Identities,* 105.

69. Bruce Ackerman, "The Rise of World Constitutionalism," 83 *Virginia Law Review* 713 (1997), 781.

70. Ibid., 782.

that produced so much communal violence in the inception of the state. These horizontal divisions in the polity—played out in different ways—are part of the historical narratives of Ireland and Israel as well; but it is the vertical fragmentation in the dominant religious group in India that is unique and that stamps the Indian constitutional experiment with its distinctive identity. As we will see in the next chapter, the Supreme Court's commitment to that identity is such that it has forged a role for itself that has led some to see it as the most powerful court in the world. But if we are to make sense of that role—in India and in other judiciaries as well—we will need to clarify and elaborate the concept of constitutional identity. It is in pursuit of that end that this book is written.

CHAPTER 2

The Conundrum of the Unconstitutional Constitution

> To enable us to correct the constitution, the whole constitution must be viewed together; and it must be compared with the actual state of the people, and the circumstances of the time.
>
> —Edmund Burke

> The notion of a *constitutional* identity of a people, and particularly its relation to the *constituent* power possessed by the people, is perplexing.
>
> —Martin Loughlin and Neil Walker

Introduction: Constitutional Change and the Legitimacy Question

Can a constitution be unconstitutional? In most countries this is not a question that is generally given serious consideration. We might also think of the query as slightly bizarre, sort of like asking whether the Bible can be unbiblical. But it is in fact a profoundly important question—for students of constitutionalism *and* for citizens and prospective citizens of a constitutional regime. The latter category includes the great mathematician, Kurt Gödel, who, as a well-known anecdote has it, entertained last minute doubts about acquiring American citizenship after discovering that under Article V it would be possible to change the Constitution into something with which he, a refugee from Nazi tyranny, would not wish to be associated. He ultimately set aside his reservations with the help of another refugee, Albert Einstein.[1]

Constitutionalism is about limits and aspirations; whether there are implicit substantive constraints on formal constitutional change is a question that implicates our most basic intuitions—but also our most troubling uncertainties—about constitutions. Perhaps the critical moment in the design of constitutional arrangements occurs when drafters confront the vexed issue of how much freedom to extend to subsequent amenders of their handiwork. Should the later agents of change enjoy an equivalent status to that of the architects of original design, such that the creations of both would be similarly immune from assaults upon their legitimacy? Surely there are things that should not be done through the invocation of constitutional language; yet if these things are so horrible to contemplate, much less to integrate with our sense of what it means to live constitutionally, then a known solution exists: prohibit them from happening by explicitly making them illegal through the power of amendment. In the United States, for example, one might, like Gödel, think there are things worse than altering representation in the Senate, but inasmuch as these things were not textually designated untouchable by the founders, it is easy to sympathize with those—and they include most commentators on the subject—who find the idea of an implicitly unconstitutional constitutional amendment deeply problematic, to say nothing of hopelessly circular.[2] In this chapter I argue that we should view that idea sympathetically. I also argue that it is an idea from which important implications pertaining to constitutional identity flow. But the importance of the issue to constitutional theory—and sometimes its practice—requires that we retain a healthy skepticism toward arguments that might be advanced on its behalf.

Globally there has been great variability in the extent of judicial consideration of the issue.[3] If in some places—for example, Turkey—the

1. The most recent telling of this story may be found in *The New Yorker,* February 28, 2005, 84.

2. See, for example, Raymond Ku, "Consensus of the Governed: The Legitimacy of Constitutional Change," 64 *Fordham Law Review* 535 (1995–1996), 540.

3. For a useful survey of this variability see Kemal Gozler, *Judicial Review of Constitutional Amendments: A Comparative Study* (Istanbul: Ekin Press, 2008).

question has assumed jurisprudential center stage, the American Supreme Court has largely ignored it. Cases involving the Eighteenth and Nineteenth Amendments provided the justices opportunities to consider whether substantive limits on constitutional amendments warranted the imprimatur of the Court, but that tribunal avoided any serious engagement with the issue even while evincing a lack of sympathy for it.[4] In the nineteenth century, the original Thirteenth Amendment, better known as the Corwin Amendment, likely would have presented a less avoidable target had it not been for the untimely intervention of the Civil War. So we will never know whether an amendment removing congressional abolition of slavery from the parameters of Article V would itself have been held to be an abuse of the amendment provision.[5] We can only speculate whether the implications of such an entrenchment were sufficiently revolutionary to have given pause to even the most committed defender of amendatory prerogative, someone perhaps equally attached to an aspirational understanding of American constitutional identity at odds with the contradictory implications of a slavery-accommodating amendment.

But my principal purpose in this chapter is to draw upon a rich vein of jurisprudential thinking from judiciaries outside of the United States to address the conundrum of the unconstitutional constitutional amendment and its importance for the subject of constitutional identity. While American jurisprudence has been spare in its consideration of the question, other national courts have given it detailed attention and reflection. Indeed more judicial commentary on the subject may be found in Africa

4. The cases are *National Prohibition Cases,* 253 U.S. 350 (1920) and Leser et al. v. Garnett et al., 258 U.S. 130 (1922).

5. The text of the Corwin Amendment: "No amendment shall be made to the Constitution which will authorize or give to Congress the power to abolish or interfere, within any State, with the domestic institutions thereof, including that of persons held to labor or service by the laws of said State." Cong. Globe, 36th Cong., 2d sess. 1263 (1861). The Amendment was ratified in two states—Ohio and Maryland—but the proposed amendment was essentially forgotten after the inauguration of Abraham Lincoln, who had expressed openness to it in his Inaugural. For further discussion of the amendment, see Mark Brandon, *Free in the World: American Slavery and Constitutional Failure* (Princeton, NJ: Princeton University Press, 1998); and A. Christopher Bryant, "Stopping Time: The Pro-Slavery and 'Irrevocable' Thirteenth Amendment," 26 *Harvard Journal of Law & Public Policy* 501 (2003).

and Latin America than from the bench of the U.S. Supreme Court.[6] For example, a recent examination appears in an extensive treatment of the issue by the Supreme Court in Peru that, while upholding the constitutional amendment in question, embraced the concept that it had the authority to do otherwise.[7] According to the Court, all institutions must be faithful to the Constitution, including the Congress. The idea that the reform of the Constitution is a political act that cannot be revised by the judiciary was rejected; thus the Peruvian Court must guarantee the Constitution's principles *(principios jurídicos)* and basic democratic values *(valores democráticos básicos)*.[8] But it is in India where the debate has been pursued at greatest length and where one finds some of the most daring and innovative decisions on the reach of constitutional power. To be sure, opinions in India go to great lengths about all manner of things; still, the patient reader will be amply rewarded by a discussion of constitutional maintenance and change whose comprehensiveness is unrivaled in world jurisprudence.

This will not, however, be a discourse on the activism of the Indian Supreme Court; in fact before arriving on the subcontinent I want to make a stop in Ireland, where the categorical rejection of implied limits on constitutional amendments is perhaps as surprising as is the openness to the idea in India. Ultimately, though, my concern is less with the experiences of these countries than it is with the ways in which we theorize about constitutions and their identities.

For those polities that are constitutional democracies in more than name only, the classic tension between popular governance and restraints on power has been addressed through sovereignty-based arguments that suppose that in the limitations imposed on the expression of the popular

6. See the Uganda case, Ssemogerere et al. v. Attorney General, Constitutional Appeal No. 1 of 2002 (2004). Another decision from Africa, the famous South African Certification case, while not technically an amendment case, is critical in revealing the reasoning that can lead judges to declare constitutional amendments unconstitutional. *Certification of the Constitution of the Republic of South Africa, 1996,* CCT 23/96.

7. The occasion was a group of cases known as the "Reform of the Pensionary System of Law" cases (No. 0050-2004-AI/TC, No. 004-2005-PI/TC, No. 007-2005-PI/TC, No. 009-2005-PI/TC), decided in 2005.

8. Ibid., Section VI, A.

will there exists a more profound manifestation of democratic legitimacy, the constituent power. This is the power that represents the people in a regime's foundational enactment and that, according to some, is activated on those occasions when the trigger of formal constitutional transformation is pulled, and to others can only be approximated in these subsequent amendations. The conflation of parliamentary and popular sovereignty that allowed the British to function without a written constitution was a fiction that Americans, in establishing a new nation, were required to reject.[9] Their new fiction allowed them to establish a basis for the belief that other institutions—principally the Court—could, through the invocation of a written constitution, embody the original popular will and in this way legitimately check democratic transgressions. On balance it has proved to be a useful fiction.

I want to suggest that we reduce our dependency on theorizing predominantly in these terms, because it has sometimes obstructed clear thinking about constitutionalism, and specifically constitutional change. Those who have argued for implicit limits on the power of amendment have often invoked the theory of popular sovereignty, and those who have opposed them have just as often found the theory sufficiently supple to provide justification for their counterarguments.[10] So on one side we have arguments that use popular sovereignty to establish the immutability of certain constitutional rights; as, for example, in Jeffrey Rosen's claim that "By refusing to enforce the Flag Burning Amendment, a Court would defer to, rather than thwart, the sovereign will of

9. The best account of the transition from British to American notions of sovereignty will be found in Edmund S. Morgan, *Inventing the People: The Rise of Popular Sovereignty in England and America* (New York: W. W. Norton, 1988).

10. For a discussion of how arguments about unconstitutional amendments relate to popular sovereignty claims, see Richard Albert, "Nonconstitutional Amendments," 22 *Canadian Journal of Law and Jurisprudence* 5 (2009). Albert's argument that regimes that countenance judicial invalidation of constitutional amendments on substantive grounds are premised on "judicial sovereignty" possesses, at a minimum, a certain plausibility (ibid., 34–35). But see Dietrich Conrad, "Constituent Power, Amendment and Basic Structure of the Constitution," *Delhi Law Review* 1 (1977–1978) for a different view, specifically "that judicial review of amendments need not be, undemocratic, quite on the contrary" (ibid., 18).

the people."[11] And on the other side one finds claims like that of Walter Dellinger, that "An unamendable constitution, adopted by a generation long since dead, could hardly be viewed as a manifestation of the consent of the governed."[12]

Here we hear the echoes of James Madison, who insisted "The people were in fact, the fountain of all power, and by resorting to them, all difficulties were got over. They could alter constitutions as they pleased."[13] Madison, of course, also famously cautioned against "frequent reference of constitutional questions to the decision of the whole society," concerned as he was not to "deprive the government of that veneration which time bestows on every thing."[14] And there is, in addition, a further difficulty to disturb one's philosophically derived equanimity: what if the people exercise their presumed constituent authority to destroy the Constitution in the name of change and progress?[15] While the Indian

11. Jeffrey Rosen, "Was the Flag Burning Amendment Unconstitutional?" 100 *Yale Law Journal* 1073, 1092.

12. Walter Dellinger, "The Legitimacy of Constitutional Change: Rethinking the Amendment Process," 97 *Harvard Law Review* 386, 387 (1983).

13. James Madison, *Notes of Debates in the Federal Convention of 1787* (New York: W. W. Norton, 1987), 564. Akhil Reed Amar is perhaps the most prominent exponent of the theory of popular sovereignty as a continuing source for the legal authority to "alter or abolish," in his account even independently of the Article V process. Among others, principally James Wilson, Amar enlists Madison in support of his (and controversially the American Framers) position that popular sovereignty provides a license to change the Constitution in accordance with majoritarian sentiment. Akhil Reed Amar, "The Consent of the Governed: Constitutional Amendment outside Article V," 94 *Columbia Law Review* 457 (1994), 470–471.

14. *Federalist 49* in Clinton Rossiter, ed., *The Federalist Papers* (New York: Mentor, 1961), 314–315. See in this regard Sanford Levinson, "'Veneration' and Constitutional Change: James Madison Confronts the Possibility of Constitutional Amendment," 21 *Texas Tech Law Review* 2425 (1990).

15. Lest anyone worry about the scope of my ambitions, I hasten to add that challenging "government of the people, by the people, and for the people" is not my purpose here, although it may be of more than passing interest that the author of that immortal prose once saw fit to refer to popular sovereignty as "a pernicious abstraction." The abstract character of the discourse on sovereignty is of course present throughout its history. As Gordon Wood has noted, the doctrine of sovereignty "was the single most important abstraction of politics in the entire Revolutionary era." Gordon S. Wood, *The Creation of the American Republic, 1776–1787* (Chapel Hill: University of North Carolina Press, 1969), 345.

Court has been innovative in creating jurisprudential barriers to such a path to destruction, in Sri Lanka, a place that has occasionally experienced the direct intervention into its constitutional affairs by its powerful larger neighbor, the judiciary has resisted the placement of impediments in the way of popular sovereign prerogative. As we will see, their efforts, while seriously flawed, have served to highlight the under-theorized nature of the Indian Court's commitment to preserving its constitution's identity, while pointing the way to a more satisfactory understanding of that much vexed concept.

To help solve—or at least illuminate—the amendment puzzle I turn first to Edmund Burke, whose sympathy for popular sovereignty is not among the sentiments for which he is known. It is not, however, this thinker's coolness to the consent of the governed that I embrace. Burke spent a career being mainly correct about India, Ireland, and the United States. His opposition to the tyrannies of George III in America and Warren Hastings in India were directed at both of these rulers' abstract appeals to sovereign rights. Ultimately, though, Burke's attractiveness here transcends his notable political track record and inheres in the clarifying lens he offers into critical issues of constitutional change and identity. I refer specifically to his depiction of the nation as an "idea of continuity," his commitment to a politics of identity uncompromised by the destructive lure of "geographical morality," and his elevation of reform as a strategy to conserve the fundamentals of constitutional structure.

Yet even as Burke illuminates the object of our concern, his emphasis on conservation—albeit with the appropriate attention to reform—is limited in capturing the more dynamic aspects of constitutional change. In the last section I suggest reasons why it will be necessary to build upon his discussion of constitutional development in order to do justice to the concept of identity. But first I want to explore the dilemma of the unconstitutional amendment in three nations where it has given rise to some fascinating and instructive jurisprudence.

Ireland: Process and Substance

In 1934 at Arbour Hill Military Detention Barracks in Ireland a special tribunal was meting out summary justice under the terms of an amendment adopted three years earlier to the Irish Free Constitution of 1922. Perhaps the only thing uncontroversial about that amendment was that it was inconsistent with the provisions of the Constitution as originally enacted. By authorizing the exercise of judicial power by persons who were not judges appointed in the manner provided by the Constitution, it permitted actions in clear violation of at least two articles clearly set out in the document. Passed as a Public Safety Act, the amendment should not be mistaken for an emergency measure, as it conferred upon the executive permanent authority to exercise its special powers whenever in its uncontrolled discretion it deemed it expedient to do so. Thus the terms of the amendment could be brought into effect during conditions of absolute peace, and under these terms the tribunals could do just about anything, including sentencing people to death without a semblance of due process. As the one dissenting judge in State (Ryan) v. Lennon pointed out, "The more one dwells [on its provisions] the more one is staggered by the contemplation of the range of its operations and the scope of the matters authorized by [them]."[16] The provisions were, according to this judge, "the antithesis of the rule of law," bringing Ireland alarmingly close to "the rule of anarchy."[17]

The objection to this constitutional monstrosity was that it was too radical to be fairly considered anything other than a de facto repeal of the Constitution. As an assault on the basic scheme and principles of the document, it could only be upheld under the principle of *lex posterior*, according to which the recency of a law establishes its priority over an earlier law of the same type. This also describes the essential process of parliamentary supremacy, which is, of course, a *very* British way of doing things. And so one might have imagined that its rejection could have been a source of satisfaction for Irish judges seeking to affirm their nationalist bona fides. But only a single justice, Hugh Kennedy, who was in

16. State (Ryan) v. Lennon, IR 170 (1935), at 197.

17. Ibid., at 198.

fact a nationalist lawyer and one of the drafters of the Constitution, was so inclined, "a lone voice," as he was later to be called, "crying in a positivistic wilderness."[18]

The majority justices were unmoved by Justice Kennedy's argument that any purported amendment repugnant to natural law would necessarily be unconstitutional and hence null and void. While not denying that the provision in question would be impossible to justify as an act sanctioned by God, they firmly asserted a judicial incapacity to determine what constitutional features were fundamental and what were not, which left the legislature, within the constraints of correct procedure, with total freedom to amend in any manner it saw fit. In response to the claim that a constitutional authority to amend provisions had to be distinguished from an unauthorized power to repeal them, Justice Fitzgibbon cited the Twenty-first Amendment to the U.S. Constitution as evidence for the fact that amendments need not only add or clarify. Of course, the repeal of prohibition left the essential character of the American Constitution unchanged, thus making it a curious example to help legitimate the repeal of due process in the Irish Constitution. But the reference underscores the central point in the majority's ruling: distinguishing essential constitutional features from nonessential ones is ultimately an exercise in imponderables.[19] "As a provision is not incorporated into a Constitu-

18. Quoted in Rory O'Connell, "Guardians of the Constitution: Unconstitutional Constitutional Norms," 48 *Journal of Civil Liberties* 48 (1999), 60.

19. The repeal of prohibition and its connection to the unconstitutional amendment issue and constitutional essentials came up in an interesting way in a 2005 case involving "dormant power" Commerce Clause jurisprudence. The state of Michigan (and in a companion case, New York) had enacted a law preventing out-of-state wineries from shipping products directly to consumers in the state. Some local residents, joined by wineries outside the state, sued Michigan officials, claiming that the state's laws discriminated against them and were blatantly in violation of the Commerce Clause. The obvious goal of the law was to provide in-state wineries with a competitive advantage, which should have made this an easy case under the broadly held consensus view of the main purpose behind the adoption of the Commerce Clause—protecting the "foundations of the Union" from economic conflicts among the states. In Granholm v. Heald the law was struck down over the strenuous objections of a minority, who did not disagree with the justices in the majority about the discriminatory impact of the law and its constitutional problems under the dormant power orthodoxy. The twist in the case, however, was evident in the Court's framing of the question before it: "Does a State's regulatory scheme that permits in-state wineries

tion unless it is regarded as of fundamental importance, the distinction between Articles of primary and secondary importance is difficult to maintain."[20] Moreover, there was no purpose in invoking a "spirit embodied in [the] original Constitution" to prevent the enactment of provisions antagonistic to it. And so, given this view of the Constitution, the Court easily reached the one conclusion that was logically required by its reasoning: "In cases where the Legislature professes to amend the Constitution itself, the only function of the Court is to see that the proposed Amendment is within the scope of the power granted by the Constitution, and that the requisite forms insisted upon by the Constitution shall have been duly observed."[21]

---

directly to ship alcohol to consumers but restricts the ability of out-of-state wineries to do so violate the dormant Commerce Clause in light of section 2 of the Twenty-first Amendment?" The complexity of the case, then, turned on whether the law could be saved by language in a constitutional amendment that, in addition to repealing prohibition, conferred upon the state's regulatory authority over the "transportation and importation . . . of intoxicating liquors." Justice Kennedy, in his opinion for the Court, insisted that the amendment had not, and could not, authorize the states to do something forbidden to them under another part of the Constitution. His claim raises the question of whether an amendment to the Constitution must comport with a part of the existing document that is not being amended. The dissenters, on the other hand, argued, in Justice Stevens's words, that with the Twenty-first Amendment "our Constitution has placed commerce in alcoholic beverages in a special category." "Today's decision," he went on, "may represent sound economic policy and may be consistent with the policy choices of the contemporaries of Adam Smith who drafted our Constitution; it is not, however consistent with the policy choices made by those who amended our Constitution in 1919 and 1933." A similar point was made in Justice Thomas's dissent: "[T]he ratification of the twenty-first Amendment . . . freed the States from negative Commerce Clause restraints on discriminatory legislation." *Granholm* thus holds importance for both aficionados of wine and constitutional theory. For the former, it will facilitate access to bottles that might otherwise have not come to their attention, and for the latter it should stimulate reflection about interpreting a constitutional document. For example, if the dormant Commerce Clause theory is as critical to American constitutional identity as the views of the justices would seem to suggest, should the Court exercise its interpretive function consciously to ensure that its rulings maintain a consistency between their outcomes and the underlying premises of the crucial theory? But since a constitutional amendment is not ordinary law, embodying as it does a more profound exercise of popular sovereignty, must the Court not defer to such expressions even at the cost of regime-defining consistency?

20. *Ryan,* at 180.

21. State (Ryan) v. Lennon, at 242.

Among the constitutional theorists writing at this time, the one who would have been least surprised by this result was not an Irishman but a German—Carl Schmitt. While doubtless preoccupied by his own country's rendezvous with constitutional disintegration, he might well have viewed what was happening across the Channel as confirmation of his controversial ideas about the inadequacies of the liberal state. That the amendment process in Ireland culminated in a result he would have applauded—the transfer of all power to the executive—should not obscure the fact that in doing so it provided a compelling demonstration of what Schmitt saw as the fundamental flaw at the heart of constitutional liberalism. An amendment process functioning in total indifference to itself and its own system of legality was a testament to the blind subordination of substance to form that was the basis of modern constitutionalism, of which, of course, the Weimar Republic was exhibit A. In such a system, Schmitt wrote, "A purely formal concept of law, independent of all content, is conceivable and tolerable."[22]

Schmitt might have recognized in the opinions of the prevailing justices in *Ryan* echoes of his positivist adversaries in the 1920s. He would have seen the same conflation of parliamentary and popular sovereignty that could sustain the imagination in visualizing the constituent power whenever constitutional change emerged from the legislature.[23] His own conception of the sovereign will of the people identified it with certain principles of substantive law that could, on the one hand, justify

22. Carl Schmitt, *Legality and Legitimacy* (Durham, NC: Duke University Press, 2004), 20.

23. This chapter addresses only the kind of formal constitutional change that occurs through the amendment process. There is a vast literature that is concerned with constitutional transformation occurring outside of the officially designated procedures set out in constitutional provisions. In this regard, the work of Bruce Ackerman has been critically important. His ongoing *We the People* project is devoted to the understanding that the people are the source of all legitimate constitutional change, both formal and informal. Sanford Levinson has drawn attention to the affinities between Ackerman's popular sovereignty-based theory of constitutional change and the views of Carl Schmitt. For Levinson, the "sovereignty-oriented positivism" of both of these theorists would lead them (contra Jeffrey Rosen and others) to accept as legitimate, the repeal of the First Amendment, as long as this decision emanated from the authentic voice of the demos. Sanford Levinson, "Transitions," 108 *Yale Law Journal* 2215 (1999), 2224.

the infamous Enabling Act *(Ermächtigungsgesetz)* of 1933, by which the Nazis commenced their descent into pseudo-legal hell, and on the other, resist the dominant interpretation of Article 76, by which the constitution could be amended in an infinite variety of ways.[24] It was a conception whose reach extended to India, when in the tumultuous decade of the 1970s Schmitt again provided theoretical support for both sides in a struggle between dictatorial power and the judicial forces arrayed against it.

But before departing Ireland, it is important to see how a different Court under a different Constitution arrived at a very similar result with regard to the amendment issue. This Constitution for the Republic of Ireland was inaugurated with Eamon de Valera's proclamation that "If there is one thing more than any other that is clear and shining through this whole Constitution, it is the fact that the people are the masters."[25] It included an amendment provision that required a popular referendum as the final step in any alteration of the document. The requirement was satisfied when in 1995 the Fourteenth Amendment was adopted, providing for a right to receive and impart information relating to abortion services lawfully available outside the state. A bill passed under its authority was submitted to the Court for constitutional review, and as part of the challenge to its legality the claim was made that the amendment itself was unconstitutional. It was said to be in direct conflict with the Eighth Amendment, which acknowledges the right to life of the unborn. Imagine for a moment the passage in the United States of the Flag Burning Amendment, and the sure objection that it violated the guarantee of free speech under the First Amendment, and you have the case that confronted the Irish Court.

24. As the German scholar, Dietrich Conrad, pointed out, the Enabling Act was considered at the time to be a legitimate use of the amending power, and thus its revolutionary implications in creating unsupervised dictatorial power should not be seen as an example of emergency power. Dietrich Conrad, "Limitation of Amendment Procedures and the Constituent Power," 15–16, *The Indian Year Book of International Affairs* 1970, 387. It thus bears a resemblance to what happened in Ireland.

25. Quoted in John A. Murphy, "The 1937 Constitution—Some Historical Reflections," in Tim Murphy and Patrick Twomey, eds., *Ireland's Evolving Constitution, 1937–97: Collected Essays* (Oxford: Hart, 1998), 13.

Imagine, too, a further claim, that in addition to the allegation concerning conflict between two provisions, the newer amendment should not be allowed to stand because it repudiates principles of natural justice embodied in the Constitution. This, recall, was the core of Jeffrey Rosen's effort to put into play the idea that if the Flag Burning Amendment were to be adopted, it deserved to be nullified by the Court. A similar effort was undertaken in Ireland, with greater ease actually, since the natural law commitments of its Constitution were, in contrast with the United States, much more explicitly set out in the language of the document. The counsel for the unborn, as they were called, maintained that the Court could not enforce any provision of a law or amendment that was contrary to natural law. And so the question was sharply posed: "[Is it] permissible for the People to exercise the power of amendment of the Constitution by way of variation, addition or repeal as permitted by Article 46 . . . unless such amendment is compatible with the natural law and existing provisions of the Constitution, and if they purport to do so, [does] such amendment [have] no effect[?]"[26]

The lead opinion by Justice Hamilton was emphatic in its response: "The Court does not accept this argument."[27] Without denying either that there was a conflict between two amendments or that the Abortion Information Amendment ran afoul of constitutionally significant natural law precepts, the Court confidently upheld the Fourteenth Amendment as the legitimate expression of the will of the people. In affirming the supremacy of popular sovereignty, it effectively left unimpeded the people's right to amend the Constitution. As in the earlier *Ryan* case, it was the sovereign prerogative that was decisive; the change from one constitution to another, however significant as a historical transformation to real independence, was of no consequence with respect to intra-constitutional transformation through the amendment process. It mattered not at all that the first transformation was marked by the replacement of parliamentary by popular sovereignty; ultimately the same reasoning dictated the same positivist result.

26. Article 26 and the Regulation of Information (Services outside the State for the Termination of Pregnancies) Bill 1995 IESC 9 (1995), 38.

27. Ibid.

To make clear that this result was not an anomaly somehow driven by the special status of the abortion issue in Irish politics, a trilogy of cases decided in the late 1990s, in which the Court waxed worshipfully at the altar of people power, suggests a deeper cause. If one had to differentiate the voices in the various judicial opinions delivered in these cases, the only distinguishing mark would be the decibel level at which the several justices proclaimed their complete devotion to the demos. Said one: "There can be no question of a constitutional amendment properly placed before the people and approved by them being itself unconstitutional."[28] More emphatically still: "No organ of the State, including this Court, is competent to review or nullify a decision of the people."[29] And finally, there is this justice's quasi-religious intonation: "The will of the people as expressed in a referendum providing for the amendment of the Constitution is sacrosanct and if freely given, cannot be interfered with. The decision is theirs and theirs alone."[30]

Clear and unambiguous as this is, one should be mindful that the Irish Constitution begins "In the name of the Most Holy Trinity, from Whom is all authority and to Whom, as our final end, all actions both of men and States must be referred. . . ." That these words, and their relationship to commitments in the subsequent constitutional text, weigh heavily in any assessment of Irish constitutional identity can scarcely be denied, pointing as they do to a tension between Ireland's Catholic and democratic commitments. While there are limits to how seriously to take that language, or indeed the language of any Constitution's preamble, how are we to reconcile the democratic positivism of the Court's decisions with some of the provisions in the body of the Constitution, provisions that were clearly inspired by the same divine authority? For example, Article 41 recognizes the family as "a moral institution possessing inalienable and imprescriptible rights, antecedent and superior to all positive law."[31] In

28. Riordan v. An Taoiseach, IESC 1 (1999), www.bailii.org/ie/cases/IESC/1999, 4.

29. Hanafin v. Minister of the Environment, ILRM 61, 183 (1996).

30. Ibid. As we shall see shortly, another excellent application of this principle may be found in Sri Lanka.

31. For more discussion of the tension between Article 41 and popular sovereignty see Gerard Hogan and Gerry Whyte, *J. M. Kelly: The Irish Constitution,* 4th ed. (Dublin: Butterworths, 2003), 1258.

Ireland being a good constitutional positivist means showing a proper respect for natural law.

This is not to say that the outcome in the abortion case was wrong, only that the reasoning in it was instructively deficient. It failed to confront the fundamental dilemma concerning constituent power and constitutional identity. "[O]nce it is conceded that a 'constitutionalized' collective political identity is necessarily malleable and fluid, so too the constitutional form cannot be regarded as unassailable; if the *influence* of constitutional form lies in its ability to refine the meaning and import of collective political identity, its *authority* must nevertheless in some measure depend upon its continuing capacity faithfully to reflect that collective political identity."[32] The referendum requirement in the 1937 Constitution's amendment provisions enabled the Court to invoke the constituent authority of the people as cover for its inability or unwillingness to engage the threshold question of what precisely an amendment *is,* or indeed the antecedent question of what a constitution is. The idea that any duly enacted amendment to the Constitution carried with it the legitimating aura of sovereign authority embodied the brilliant obfuscation of a noble fiction. The flaws in this reasoning would have been recognized by Edmund Burke, who, in his "Tract on Popery," opposed an earlier Irish policy by saying, "No arguments of policy, reason of state, or preservation of the constitution, can be pleaded in favour of [the position . . . that laws can derive any authority from their institution merely and independent of the quality of the subject matter.]"[33] With the Court's categorical rejections of implied limits, the moral-laden commitments of Article 41 only serve to remind us that Irish constitutional development had not offered much to blunt the challenge posed by Carl Schmitt, to wit: how can one "put marriage, religion, and private property solemnly under the protection of the consti-

32. Martin Loughlin and Neil Walker, "Introduction," in Martin Loughlin and Neil Walker, eds., *The Paradox of Constitutionalism: Constituent Power and Constitutional Form* (Oxford: Oxford University Press, 2007), 2.

33. Edmund Burke, "Tracts Relating to Popery," in R. B. McDowell, ed., *The Writings and Speeches of Edmund Burke, Vol. IX, I: The Revolutionary War, II: Ireland* (Oxford: Oxford University Press, 1991), 1765.

tution and in the same constitution offer the legal means for their elimination[?]"[34]

If the Irish decisions provided a weak response to Schmitt's critique of proceduralism, *insisting* that the validity of a formal constitutional change was conditional on its strict adherence to natural law, as was argued in the dissent in *Ryan,* or in the right-to-life brief in the abortion information case, or in the claims made by Rosen in objecting to the proposed Flag Burning Amendment, also fails. It does not explain why a right, even one thought to have a natural endowment, cannot be modified by "addition or variation." Modifications, after all, are basic to our enjoyment of rights in civil society. As to the question of "repeal," there may very well be grounds for principled resistance to excision of a constitutionally prescribed guarantee, but the claim on behalf of resistance would still have to be made upon a demonstration that the result of this more radical change is at least constitutionally incoherent. By this I mean it would have to show not just that something important has changed, but that the change has, in some deep sense, disturbed the fundamentals of constitutional identity. To see how this argument unfolds, we need to go to India.

India: "A Precious Heritage"

It is here, in India, where the words of Lincoln's First Inaugural take on a special significance. They are words that invite us to be very particular in what we comprehend by the power to amend, such that the kind of change that inspired Gödel's hesitation could only properly come about through extra-constitutional deliverance. "This country . . . ," Lincoln said, "belongs to the people who inhabit it. Whenever they should grow weary of the existing government, they can exercise their CONSTITUTIONAL right of amending it, or their REVOLUTIONARY right to dismember or overthrow it."[35] Lincoln did not explore this

34. Carl Schmitt, *Legality and Legitimacy,* 46.

35. Abraham Lincoln, "First Inaugural Address," in Donald P. Kommers, John E. Finn, and Gary J. Jacobsohn, eds., *American Constitutional Law: Essays, Cases, and Comparative Notes* (Lanham, MD: Rowman & Littlefield, 2004), 1050. The German constitutional theorist, Ulrich K. Preuss, has made a similar point: "[N]o constitution can contain rules which

distinction between two types of constitutive restructuring—amendment and dismemberment—to elaborate its meaning is to describe the signal achievement of Indian jurisprudence.

It is an imperfect achievement made possible only by the dictatorial ambitions of a politician bearing the two most revered names in modern Indian history. Moreover, it is an achievement that, like the success of Indian democracy itself, seems somehow counterintuitive. The Indian Constitution, after all, was designed in significant measure to accomplish the goal of radical social reconstruction. To this end, as one of the early justices of the Supreme Court pointed out, "The Constitution-makers visualized that Parliament would be competent to make amendments . . . so as to meet the challenge of the problems which may arise in the course of socio-economic progress and development of the country."[36] The provision for amending the document was shaped expressly to conform with the Jeffersonian idea that each generation should be free to adapt the Constitution to the conditions of its time. Borrowing also from the Irish experience, the framers included a section in the Constitution devoted entirely to Directive Principles of State Policy, a section that came to assume a place of prominence in subsequent constitutional development that it never attained in its place of origin. Indeed, the Irish have been a frequent source of inspiration for many Indians, as is amusingly evident in an Indian judge's slightly amended reference to Justice Fitzgibbon's opinion in the *Ryan* case. "This . . . Eden demi-paradise, this precious stone, set in the silver sea, this blessed plot, this earth, this realm, this India. If it is not that today, let us strive to make it so by using law as a flexible instrument of social order."[37]

---

allow its abolishment altogether; this would permit revolution, whereas it is the very meaning of constitutions to avoid revolutions; and to make them dispensable. Political revolutions change political institutions in ways that those institutions prohibit; whereas constitutional amendments change political institutions in ways which the constitution authorizes." Ulrich K. Preuss, "Constitutional Powermaking for the New Polity: Some Deliberations on the Relations between Constituent Power and the New Constitution," in Michel Rosenfeld, ed., *Constitution, Identity, Difference, and Legitimacy* (Durham, NC: Duke University Press, 204), 157.

36. Justice Gajendragadkar as quoted in Kesavananda Bharati v. State of Kerala, 1973 SC 1461, 1492 (1973).

37. Ibid., at 2027.

Add to this effusive embrace of change the rootedness of a legal culture in the British legal tradition, and it is natural to suppose a hostile Indian reception to the notion of implied constitutional limits. Thus it is not surprising for a judge to declare, "The power of amendment is in point of quality an adjunct of sovereignty. If so, it does not admit of any limitations."[38] So what, then, might explain the unexpected receptivity to the idea?

Perhaps the answer lies, at least in part, in judicial practice developed in constitutional domains at the core of Indian self-understanding, most prominently the question of secular identity. Thus in formulating an appropriate constitutional response to a religious presence that is pervasive and deep, Indian judges have proceeded along a path that their American counterparts have always studiously avoided. They have applied an "essentials of religion" test to isolate what is integral to religion from what is not, so that the constitutional goal of social reform will not be impeded by religious practices—for example, polygamy—erroneously claiming sanctified theological significance.[39] It may be that this defining feature of Indian church/state jurisprudence allows for greater openness to a similar test for amendments, the sort of test that was so categorically rejected by the Irish Court. At least it helps to understand why a judge might conclude that the Constitution cannot legally be used to destroy itself.[40] Or believe: "[Our Constitution] is based on a social philosophy and every social philosophy like every religion has two main features, namely, basic and circumstantial. The former remains but the latter is subject to change."[41]

But how to determine what remains and what is subject to change? In its wrestling with the amendment issue, the Indian Supreme Court has

38. Ibid., at 1495.

39. I have discussed this development in detail in Gary Jeffrey Jacobsohn, *The Wheel of Law: India's Secularism in Comparative Constitutional Context* (Princeton, NJ: Princeton University Press, 2003). Because religion in India is so deeply embedded in the existing social structure, indifference to the substance of religious belief is a much costlier indulgence than it is in places where the spiritual and temporal are not so tightly entwined.

40. As was said in Minerva Mills Ltd. v. Union of India, AIR 1980 SC 1789, "The power to destroy is not a power to amend." *Minerva Mills,* at 1798.

41. *Kesavananda Bharati,* at 1624.

struggled mightily with this perplexity. On the one hand, its task here has been less difficult than in confronting the challenge of religion, where the Court's authority to make this distinction was always more dubiously asserted; on the other hand, its effort has been complicated by the fact that the key cases testing the limits of the amendment power have directly implicated the justices' own institutional self-interest. A very brief outline of the progression of these cases should be sufficient to pursue the logic of the Court's rather weakly theorized, if boldly formulated, rationale for its chosen path.

Unlike the episodic character of the Irish experience, the Indian history with the amendment problem presents a compelling narrative. Indeed there are at least two stories one can tell, the first concerning a decades-long political give-and-take over the place of private property in India, and the second featuring a protracted struggle by the Supreme Court to establish its credibility and independence in the face of repeated attempts to diminish its standing as a significant force in Indian politics. These stories are tightly entwined and are distinguishable only by the theme one chooses to emphasize. In both accounts they are dominated by the looming presence of Indira Gandhi.

The use of the amendment process to insulate certain issues from the oversight of judicial review began in the early days of the Republic, long before Indira Gandhi's ascendance to power. In a 1951 decision (and again in 1965), the Supreme Court upheld the plenary power of Parliament to amend the Constitution over the claim that the process had been used to deprive landowners of fundamental property rights guaranteed under the document.[42] These rulings stood up rather well until 1967 and the landmark decision of Golak Nath v. State of Punjab[43] in which a divided Court announced that duly enacted amendments could not be permitted to render a constitutional right unenforceable. It was, as one commentator has described it, a case that "began the great war . . . over parliamentary

42. Shankari Prasad Deo v. Union of India, 1952 (3) SCR 106; Sajjan Singh v. State of Rajasthan, 1965 (1) SCR 933. The use of the amendment process to preclude judicial review of particular issues (mainly property) began under Indira Gandhi's father, Prime Minister Nehru, although his efforts never aroused the same concerns as did his daughter's in subsequent years.

43. Golak Nath v. State of Punjab, AIR SC 1643 (1967).

versus judicial supremacy."[44] Technically the decision did not invalidate the amendments in question, as the Court issued a prospective judgment essentially putting Parliament on notice that the days of its amendatory interference with fundamental rights were over. But the intense political reaction to the Court's move left little doubt that something very important had occurred.

The opinions in the case were noteworthy more for having established a foundation for debating the meaning of constitutional change than for the quality of the judges' own initial contributions that were, for the most part, underdeveloped. The main opinion by the chief justice introduced the critical question of what the word "amend" actually means; his preference for a limited understanding must be seen in connection with his main point, which was that "fundamental rights are given a transcendental position under our Constitution and are kept beyond the reach of Parliament."[45] Not surprisingly, his natural rights claim—he called them "primordial rights"—provoked some Holmesian grumblings among his dissenting colleagues, one of them quoting the American justice to the effect that "The Constitution is an experiment as all life is an experiment."[46] No reference was made to Justice Hugo Black's memorable denunciation of natural rights as an "incongruous excrescence upon the Constitution,"[47] although when viewed comparatively, it is clear that however suspect may be its descriptive value in the United States, this unappealing appellation has more resonance in India.

This became evident in the 1973 case, Kesavananda Bharati v. State of Kerala, arguably India's most important constitutional decision.[48] *Golak Nath* had provided Indira Gandhi with a splendid issue for a populist

44. Granville Austin, *Working a Democratic Constitution: The Indian Experiment* (New Delhi: Oxford University Press, 1999), 198

45. Ibid., at 1656.

46. Ibid., at 1736.

47. Adamson v. California, 332 US 46 (1947), 75.

48. Choosing a nation's most important decision is not easy. But I hold it to be a mark of a decision's ultimate importance that it both fits within the aspirational DNA of a constitution and that it elevates the Court as a potentially vital institutional actor in the realization of the document's constitutive goals. These criteria are decisively met in the *Kesavananda* ruling.

campaign that ended in electoral triumph in 1971.[49] Her substantial victory quickly translated into passage of no less than four constitutional amendments, one of which—the Twenty-fourth—explicitly overturned the earlier decision on fundamental rights, extending to Parliament authority to adopt amendments that were immune from judicial review. War with Pakistan precipitated a declaration of presidential emergency and subsequent nationalization, which in turn led to the litigation that ended in the landmark judgment in *Kesavananda.* Its massive content (approximately 800 pages) and numerous crosscutting opinions are not conducive to easy recapitulation. In essence the Court—seven of the thirteen participating judges—affirmed the authority of Parliament to amend constitutional provisions involving fundamental rights, while rejecting its authority to place statutes enacted to implement the Constitution's Directive Principles beyond the power of judicial review. It thus reversed *Golak Nath,* but narrowly asserted its own authority to invalidate a constitutional amendment that was in defiance of the "basic structure" of the Indian Constitution. While relenting on its authority to designate specific provisions as immune from constitutional change, the majority invested the Court with a broader supervisory jurisdiction over the fundamental meaning of the document.[50] In the fashion of Marbury v. Madison, the Court avoided a direct confrontation with the government, yet appreciably strengthened its powers in anticipation of battles ahead.

At the core of *Kesavananda* is the "basic structure" doctrine, according to which specific features of the Constitution are deemed sufficiently

49. As noted by Granville Austin, the Court's decision "was a masterpiece of unintentional timing, for it gave Indira Gandhi a cause and an enemy in her quest for renewed power." Granville Austin, *Working a Democratic Constitution,* 198.

50. The essence of the Court's ruling is in line with William Harris's theoretical reflections on constitutional change. "Even for important existing features it would seem that rather than ranging over the constitutional scheme to pick out elements that might arguably be more fundamental in the hierarchy of values, it would be more advisable to develop essential principles that would guide a choice as to whether a particular Constitutional change were substantively invalid. That is, a Constitutional provision would be fundamental only in terms of some articulated political theory that makes sense of the whole Constitution." William Harris, *The Interpretable Constitution* (Baltimore: Johns Hopkins University Press, 1993), 188.

fundamental to the integrity of the constitutional project to warrant immunity from drastic alteration. Under the theory that *constitutional* change must not destroy what it modifies, the Court affirmed its institutional authority to invalidate any constitutional amendment whose adoption would, in its judgment, result in radical transformation of regime essentials. The political and jurisprudential implications of this unenumerated power were extraordinary, easily making the countermajoritarian difficulties of conventional judicial review pale in comparison. Armed with its new doctrine, the contents of which would be determined over time, the Court in effect designated itself enforcer of constitutional entrenchment at its deepest level, able now to nullify the results of legislative rule making even when such action expressed itself in the exalted form of the constituent power.[51]

But the era of natural rights in India was short-lived. Should any legitimacy attach to the idea of implied limits to the amendment power, it would not be found in natural rights arguments. While there were differences in the Court over epistemological questions concerning such rights, a broad consensus emerged that "Fundamental rights . . . are given by the Constitution, and, therefore, they can be abridged or taken away by the . . . amending process of the Constitution itself."[52] The judges were mindful of how arguments from natural rights had been employed elsewhere—notably in the United States—to impede efforts to achieve greater social and economic equality, and they seemed determined to avoid the potential damage to constitutional values associated with the ambiguity surrounding these rights. A characteristically Indian objection expressed what is, for better or worse, a reality of our time: "Natural

51. Of course, an achievement of such noteworthiness—particularly one enhancing the political power of the judiciary—will engender mixed reviews. While the doctrine is now a staple of Indian constitutional law, it remains highly controversial in Indian legal circles. For example, a not atypical negative assessment worries about the effect of the judgment on the very fabric of constitutional government. "Prior to *Kesavananda Bharati,* the Constitution, with all its checks and balances, was considered supreme. The Supreme Court has emerged as the strongest wing of the state with unlimited and illimitable power." P. P. Rao, "The Constitution, Parliament and the Judiciary," in Pran Chopra, ed., *The Supreme Court Versus the Constitution: A Challenge to Federalism* (New Delhi: Sage Publications, 2006), 73.

52. *Kesavananda Bharati,* at 1691.

law has been a sort of religion with many political and constitutional thinkers. But it has never believed in a single Godhead. It has a perpetually growing pantheon . . . The pantheon is not a heaven of peace. Its gods are locked in internecine conflict."[53]

Notice that this rejection of a rights-based bar to first-order constitutional change did not culminate in acceptance of the government's extraordinary argument to the Court that Parliament could do anything it wanted through the amendment power, no matter how revolutionary or destructive. To be sure, the ghost of Holmes returned—and with a vengeance—but only to a small minority of the justices, among whom Justice Chandrachud was most expansive: "If the people acting through the Parliament want to put the Crown of a King on a head they like, or if you please, on a head they dislike . . . let them have that liberty. . . . [As Justice Holmes said], '[W]hen the people . . . want to do something I can't find anything in the Constitution expressly forbidding them to do it, I say, whether I like it or not: God-dammit it, let 'em do it.' "[54] But these sentiments ultimately lost out to the proponents of "basic structure," a doctrine that might not have made it very far beyond the ruling in this case had it not been for the overreaching of the Indian prime minister.

On June 12, 1975, a high court judge in Indira Gandhi's electoral constituency upheld criminal charges against her for the crime of electoral fraud. Two weeks later, faced with the possibility of removal from office, she introduced India's first domestically driven emergency regime, which quickly evolved into a harsh and unremitting dictatorship. Among its first acts were a series of constitutional amendments that were, shall we say, unusual. One of them, the Thirty-ninth Amendment, prevented any judicial inquiry into the election of the prime minister. As one noted Indian legal scholar remarked, "Nowhere in the history of mankind has the power to amend a Constitution thus been used."[55] Another, the

53. Ibid., at 2006.

54. Ibid., at 2044. A similar sentiment appears in the opinion of Justice Sikri: "[S]hort of repeal of the Constitution, any form of Government with no freedom for the citizens can be set up by Parliament by exercising its powers under Article 368" (ibid., at 1490).

55. Upendra Baxi, *Courage Craft and Contention: The Indian Supreme Court in the Eighties* (Bombay: N. M. Tripathi Private Limited, 1985), 70.

Thirty-eighth, shielded from judicial review any laws adopted during the emergency that might conceivably impinge upon fundamental rights. Gandhi's claim was Schmittian in the extreme: in essence the constituent power, as an expression of the sovereign will of the people was all-embracing and at once judicial, executive, and legislative. It was such an extravagant claim that it accomplished what all previous debate over property-related amendments had not succeeded in doing—establish the legitimacy of the unconstitutional constitutional amendment.

It was even too much for the aforementioned Holmesian justice, who would appear to have experienced an epiphany in concluding in the face of these events that the Constitution could indeed be subverted by revolutionary methods, and that constitutional provisions should not, after all, be the vehicle for such change. While Indira Gandhi's election was prudently upheld, the Court decisively repudiated the Thirty-eighth and Thirty-ninth Amendments. "The common man's sense of justice sustains democracies,"[56] wrote another of the prime minister's expected judicial supporters, and the outrage provoked by these travesties must, he felt, be given due regard in determining the attributes of basic structure. In particular, these provisions were a blatant negation of the right of equality and were in sharp contravention of the most basic postulate of the Constitution. Hence, following *Kesavananda,* they could not stand.

Of course one could question just how meaningful these developments were in light of the unusual circumstances that brought them about. That is why the last of the cases in this brief summary—involving a government takeover of a failing business—is so important. In 1980 the Court decided Minerva Mills, Ltd. v. Union of India,[57] better known as the "sick textiles" case, in which parts of yet another amendment, the Forty-second, were invalidated in a ringing affirmation of the basic structure doctrine. The amendment represented Indira Gandhi's last strike at the Court, including the provocative declaration that "No amendment . . . shall be called into question in any court on any ground."[58] Again it was left

56. Indira Gandhi v. Raj Narain, AIR SC 2299 (1975), at 2469.

57. *Minerva Mills,* AIR SC 1789 (1980)

58. Text of the Forty-second Amendment.

to Justice Chandrachud to articulate what he called "the theme song of *Kesavananda*," for which he was now fully prepared to become a part of the chorus. "Amend as you may even the solemn document which the founding fathers have committed to your care, for you know best the needs of your generation. But, the Constitution is a precious heritage; therefore you cannot destroy its identity."[59]

Sri Lanka: Another Thirteenth Amendment

The legal scholar, Frederick Schauer, asks, "What makes a constitution constitutional?" "Nothing," he answered, "nor does or can anything make a constitution unconstitutional."[60] The Indian cases provide another answer, even if much of the jurisprudence that emerged from it was forged in the extreme circumstances of emergency power, and much of what was innovative about it flowed from the Court's own institutional needs. One lesson to draw from them might be to follow the Brazilian example and preclude the enactment of constitutional amendments during periods of emergency.[61] But surely more can be learned from the account; moreover, the rather extreme conditions that provided the context for what judicially transpired are in fact useful in clarifying the stakes in the debate over implied limits.

Hence we should not be surprised to learn that it was the German experience that offered the Indian judges guidance in their extended parrying of Indira Gandhi.[62] She, of course, had a lot to learn from it as well, if alas, from an earlier decade. But both the judges and the prime

59. *Minerva Mills*, at 1798.

60. Frederick Schauer, "Amending the Presuppositions of a Constitution," in Sanford Levinson, ed., *Responding to Imperfection: The Theory and Practice of Constitutional Amendment* (Princeton, NJ: Princeton University Press, 1995), 145.

61. The Constitution of Brazil may not be amended during a state or federal intervention, defense, or siege. Art. 60, section 1. It is popularly viewed as a mechanism of self-preservation in a country with a history of authoritarian interventions in the constitutional text.

62. Instrumental in the education of Indian judges to the German experience was the work of Dietrich Conrad, a German scholar of Indian politics and law. See, for example, Conrad, "Limitation of Amendment Procedures," 15–16. Conrad's work was cited by Indian justices in several of the decisions discussed in this article.

minister could find in the person of Carl Schmitt a source of ideas for their conflicting agendas, for that controversial theorist is at once the guru of emergency power and the proponent of the notion that there are fundamental principles that limit the amendment power. Indeed, his argument that the amendment power was not an expression or reincarnation of the original constituent power, and therefore limited by its original mandate, was incorporated into the jurisprudence of the Basic Law of the Federal Republic. While never actually invalidating a constitutional amendment, the post-War German Court had declared such an act conceptually possible, and had expressly invoked the nation's recent past to affirm that never again would formal legal means be used to legalize a totalitarian regime.[63]

If proximity to the abyss has a way of concentrating the mind on the essentials of constitutionalism, judicial enforcement of implied limits to the amendment power should not rest solely on reasons fashioned for the dire circumstances of the worst case. For Schmitt, it was the doctrine of popular sovereignty traceable to the French Revolution that animated his views on the subject, just as it did his defense of executive dictatorship.[64] Perhaps it was the tragically induced awareness of the multiple

63. *Southwest Case,* 1 BverfGE 14 (1951): "That a constitutional provision itself may be null and void, is not conceptually impossible just because it is a part of the constitution. There are constitutional provisions that are so fundamental and to such an extent an expression of a law that precedes even the constitution that they also bind the framer of the constitution, and other constitutional provisions that do not rank so high may be null and void, because they contravene those principles. . . ." *Privacy of Communications Case (Klass Case,* 30), BverfGE 1 (1970): "The purpose of Article 79, paragraph 3, as a check on the legislator's amending the Constitution is to prevent the abolition of the substance or basis of the existing constitutional order, by formal legal means of amendment . . . and abuse of the Constitution to legalize a totalitarian regime." Fundamental constitutional alteration is not prohibited as long as it meets the criterion of coherence. "Restrictions on the legislator's amending the Constitution . . . must not, however, prevent the legislator from modifying by constitutional amendment even basic constitutional principles in a system-immanent manner."

64. Schmitt's thoughts on popular sovereignty and constitutional change are well treated in Peter C. Caldwell, *Popular Sovereignty and the Crisis of German Constitutional Law: The Theory and Practice of Weimar Constitutionalism* (Durham, NC: Duke University Press, 1997). The popular sovereignty claims of the French Revolution find their modern echo in the figure of Charles de Gaulle. "The power of a Constitution consists in the fact that it originates from the people and it responds to the conditions in which the

ends to which the doctrine could serve that led the German Court to emphasize as a basis for the conceptual possibility it had countenanced, the further idea of preserving the "inner unity" of the Constitution. Thus a constitutional amendment could be subject to nullification to the extent that it was responsible for transforming the document to which it was added into something fundamentally incoherent.

Of the raft of reasons adduced by the Indian Court in the reams of paper it devoted to the analysis of the unconstitutional amendment, the one that stands out is a version of the requirement of coherence—the need to preserve the Constitution's identity. If anything, however, it is a more demanding criterion than the German test. Thus the incongruities and inconsistencies that could lead to a finding of constitutional incoherence might mean only that the document's identity has been obscured in a manner that casts doubt on its fundamental character and commitments. Also, the exigencies of constitution making often leads to an original constitution's incoherence, in the sense that necessary compromise produces contradictions affecting its "inner unity" even before any subsequent amending hand is laid upon it. That is arguably the American story, which holds that in its finest moment Article V served the nation well by enabling its fundamental law to begin the process of working itself pure.

There is, of course, a different narrative that sees in the post-Civil War amendments more than the insertion of a critical course correction; rather it discerns a fundamentally new constitutional departure incorporating a radical transformation in identity.[65] Whether the American polity

---

State must live." Quoted in Lucien Jaume, "Constituent Power in France: The Revolution and its Consequences," in Martin Loughlin and Neil Walker, "Introduction," in Martin Loughlin and Neil Walker, eds., *The Paradox of Constitutionalism: Constituent Power and Constitutional Form,* 80. For additional insight into Schmitt's thinking on these questions, see his *Constitutional Theory,* Jeffrey Seitzer, ed. and trans. (Durham: Duke University Press, 2008).

65. See, for example, Brandon, *Free in the World*, 200–203. For the view that the new additions to the Constitution did not establish a rupture in constitutional continuity see Walter Murphy, "Slaughter-House, Civil Rights, and Limits on Constitutional Change," 32 *American Journal of Jurisprudence* (1980). An insightful discussion of the relevant issues in this fascinating debate appears in Wayne D. Moore, "(Re)construction of Constitutional Authority and Meaning: The Fourteenth Amendment and Slaughter-House Cases," in

was in effect re-constituted by the addition of these amendments need not be debated here. But the question calls attention to an obvious point that can too easily be overlooked after reflecting on the Indian experience: amending a constitution need not threaten the existence of constitutional government. When it does not, when, in other words, it is intended to bring about change that expands rather than truncates the rights of large numbers of people, it may inspire a more skeptical attitude about a preservative role for the Court in defending a nation's constitutional identity. Imagine, for example, a Court sympathetic to the objection that the Thirteenth and Fourteenth Amendments so radically transformed the relationship between the states and the federal government (to the disadvantage of the former) that they threatened the existence of a "basic structure" of constitutional design. Would judicial intervention in defense of constitutional identity—the "precious heritage" under assault from forces within the polity—be justified?

Some light may be shed on this question in the constitutional jurisprudence of a small neighbor of India, whose policies—including ones involving law-related matters—are often influenced by what happens in the subcontinent's dominant nation. Thus in 1987 the Supreme Court of Sri Lanka directly confronted an amendment's challenge to constitutional identity in a case described by its chief justice as "the most critical, the most important and the most far-reaching [case] that had ever arisen in the history of our courts."[66] It concerned the constitutionality of the Thirteenth Amendment, which like its American counterpart number, was challenged for its alleged radical restructuring of constitutional arrangements pertaining to the balance between central and local authority. But unlike what transpired in the United States, the proposed change in Sri Lanka involved a devolution of power to the local level, albeit for a purpose comparable to what lay behind the American amendment—the enhancement in the power and prospects of a much-abused minority.

Ronald Kahn and Ken I. Kersch, eds., *The Supreme Court and American Political Development* (Lawrence: University Press of Kansas, 2006).

66. In re The Thirteenth Amendment to the Constitution and the Provincial Councils Bill, 2 Sri L. R. 312 (1987), 333.

The Thirteenth Amendment arose from the decentralization agreement negotiated under Indian auspices in the Indo–Sri Lanka accord of 1987. The agreement came after years of bloody conflict between a guerilla group, the Liberation Tigers of Tamil Eelam (LTTE), and the Sri Lankan government. The accord's devolution of power to provincial councils necessitated changes in Article 2 of the Constitution, which had entrenched the unitary nature of the state. The shift toward federalism (and India's role in this development), and the perception that the reforms effectively eroded the sovereignty of the country, aroused violent protests from sections of Sinhalese society, in particular an armed insurgency led by the Janatha Vimukthi Peramuna (JVP). The President, J. R. Jayawardene, needed the Supreme Court's approval for the constitutional amendment after Buddhist organizations challenged it in court. It was then narrowly affirmed by a 5–4 margin.

The devolution of political power at the center of the controversy had been advanced as a solution to Sri Lanka's destructive and debilitating ethnic conflict. Yet its strangeness in the political culture of the island nation can scarcely be overstated. As one Sri Lankan scholar commented, "The idea of devolution was so alien to Sinhalese political vocabulary at the time, we who were engaged in political debates had to coin a new Sinhalese word, 'belaya bedaherima,' to convey the meaning of devolution."[67] Politics in Sri Lanka is inextricably linked to the ethnic struggle between the majority Sinhalese (who are predominantly Buddhist) and minority Tamils for power and recognition.[68] While the first constitution in 1948

67. Jayadeva Uyangoda, "Search for the Indian Model," *Economic and Political Weekly*, November 3, 2007. For the views of another Sri Lankan analyst who views the devolutionary structure as critical to political accommodation, see Neil DeVotta, "Control Democracy, Institutional Decay, and the Quest for Eelam: The Case of Post-Independence Sri Lanka," 46 *Pacific Affairs* (2000).

68. Approximately 70 percent of the 19.4 million Sri Lankans are Buddhist, 15 percent Hindu, 8 percent Christian (mainly Roman Catholics), and 7 percent Muslim (mainly Sunnis). Christians live mainly in the west, with much of the east Muslim and north almost exclusively Hindu. The customary law of each religious group adjudicates family law with final appeal to a secular authority, the Supreme Court. Separate ministries in the government address religious affairs, namely the Ministry of Buddha Sasana, the Department of Muslim Religious and Cultural Affairs, the Ministry of Hindu Religious Affairs, and the Ministry of Christian Affairs.

did not address the position of Buddhism, and in fact incorporated specific safeguards for minorities, later constitutions omitted these protections and gave primacy to Buddhism. Since independence, the Sri Lankan state has grappled with maintaining the hegemony of Sinhalese Buddhist national identity without explicitly undermining other ethnic and religious identities. Buddhism was harnessed and politicized to respond to ethnic and linguistic differences, prompting commentators to liken it to Hindu nationalism in India. Sinhala nationalism has emphasized the unitary nature of the state controlled by the Sinhala majority;[69] Article 9 of the Constitution, introduced in 1972 and carried over in 1978, assigned pride of place to Buddhism.

The contested amendment, which was roughly patterned on the Indian model of federalism, was designed to address two demands of the Tamil minority—equal language rights and greater autonomy. Article 18 was amended to include Tamil as an official language and English as a link language. A Provincial Councils Bill decentralized power to the provinces, thus seemingly undercutting the unitary basis of governance.[70] As a result it was constitutionally challenged as a breach of Article 2's guarantee of a unitary state, as well as Article 3's affirmation of the sovereignty of the people, and Article 9's provision for the preeminent position of Buddhism. The issue before the Court was whether the amendment was in fact a contravention of these entrenched articles; the consensus view of the case's importance reflected some of the most profound concerns that can be raised about a constitution, chiefly whether changes to it that transform its identity into something very different from what it was ought to be recognized as legitimate.

In answering this question both the majority and minority were importantly influenced by Indian constitutional design and interpretation.

69. See Jayadeva Uyangoda, "The State and the Process of Devolution in Sri Lanka" in Sunil Bastian, ed., *Devolution and Development in Sri Lanka* (ICES, Colombo, 1994); N. Tiruchelvam, "Federalism and Diversity in Sri Lanka" in Yash Ghai, ed., *Autonomy and Ethnicity* (CUP, 2000), 198–200.

70. The amendment, however, can be seen as merely providing a veneer of devolution while retaining vast powers with the center. Not only did the Provincial Councils have incomplete control over any subject, they could be abolished or their power curtailed by unilateral actions of the central Parliament.

On the key point—did the Thirteenth Amendment so decisively alter the Constitution's basic structure as to render it illegitimate?—the majority found the Indian experience inapposite and the minority held it essential to reaching the correct outcome in the case, namely the invalidation of the constitutional changes. Transcending their disagreements was a fundamental agreement that the amendment could not affect the preeminent position of Buddhism or the unitary nature of the state, which were thought to be the main elements of Sri Lankan constitutional identity. As we see in Chapter 4, this constitutional identity's differences with its Indian counterpart make constitutional borrowing a problematic and risky enterprise, but one that holds potential strategic advantages for sustaining the home country's basic commitments.[71]

While the majority interpreted devolution within a unitary framework, the minority rejected the changes, insisting that their radical features required submission for popular approval through a referendum.[72] Justice Sharvananda's opinion for the Court concluded, "[T]here is no foundation for the contention that the basic features of the Constitution have been altered or destroyed by the proposed amendments. The *Constitution will survive without any loss of identity* despite the amendment. The basic structure or framework of the Constitution will continue intact in its integrity."[73] He argued that Sri Lanka's unitary state would be

71. Here, again, consider the observation of Uyanganda. "The Indian political class, with some occasional exceptions, has by and large trusted the ethnic and religious minorities and it continues to do so. It has designed constitutional and administrative structures to empower minorities, because they are not afraid of the minorities. But in Sri Lanka, the Sinhalese political class . . . does not trust the minorities. They are mortally scared to empower the minorities. There lies the anomaly with the Indian model." Uyangoda, "Search for the Indian Model."

72. Four justices agreed that there was no need for a referendum since the nature of the pertinent changes was consistent with the Constitution. One judge agreed with that general assessment but said that the Thirteenth Amendment's adoption nevertheless required the referendum. Four judges dissented, arguing that both bills required a referendum.

73. *In re The Thirteenth Amendment to the Constitution and the Provincial Councils Bill*, at 329 (emphasis added). In this sense the opinion may be compared to Justice Samuel F. Miller's famous opinion for the U.S. Supreme Court in *The Slaughter-House Cases*. He did not see in the post-war amendments "any purpose to destroy the main features of the general system." There was in the Fourteenth Amendment no "great . . . departure from the structure and spirit of our institutions" (ibid., at 82). As Wayne D. Moore notes, "For

unaffected by devolution, that the changes would not convert it into a federal or quasi-federal state. Sharvananda characterized the unitary state as one possessing the supremacy of the central parliament and the absence of subsidiary sovereign bodies; in contrast, a federal state has coordinate authorities independent of each other. "The concept of devolution is used to mean the delegation of central government powers without the relinquishment of supremacy. Devolution may be legislative or administrative or both. It should be distinguished from 'decentralisation,' which is a method whereby some central government powers of decision-making are exercised by officials of the central government located in various regions."[74]

In addition to finding that the entrenched provisions of the Constitution had not been violated, the justice rejected the reliance by some

---

Justice Miller . . . the Fourteenth Amendment had not brought about fundamental change. Its provisions could be construed as consistent with the main features of the antebellum Constitution." Wayne D. Moore, "(Re)construction of Constitutional Authority and Meaning: The Fourteenth Amendment and Slaughter-House Cases," 250. On the other hand, Justice Noah H. Swayne viewed the amendment much as the chief justice in the Sri Lankan case viewed that country's Thirteenth Amendment. Thus Swayne described it as "a new departure" that "mark[ed] an important epoch in the constitutional history of the country" (ibid., at 78). Of course for the South Asian justice the radically transformative nature of the constitutional change was for that reason grounds for the Court to invalidate it as an unwarranted assault on the Constitution's identity.

74. *In re The Thirteenth Amendment,* at 327. Interestingly, the judgment regarding the undiminished authority of the central government anticipates the Indian Supreme Court's ruling in that country's leading case on secularism, S. R. Bommai v. Union of India, 3 SC 1, (1994). There the Court upheld the president's authority, in the aftermath of the destruction of the Babri Masjid mosque in Ayodyha, to dismiss three elected state governments for failing to comply with the (secular) provisions of the Constitution. Because nothing in the Thirteenth Amendment reduces the power of "the President to hold that a situation has arisen in which the administration of the Province cannot be carried out in accordance with the provisions of the Constitution and take over the functions and powers of the Provincial Council, there can be no gainsaying the fact that the President remains supreme or sovereign in the executive field and the Provincial Council is only a body subordinate to him" *In re The Thirteenth Amendment,* at 327. In India the president's power was exercised to affirm the Constitution's basic structure as a protection for a threatened religious minority, whereas the Court in Sri Lanka was in effect reassuring the Sinhalese majority that, appearances to the contrary notwithstanding, devolution would not interfere with the central government's ability to defend the state's Buddhist identity, which is to say, "the Constitution will survive without any loss of identity."

(including the minority) on the Indian cases affirming the Court's authority to declare amendments unconstitutional when they violated basic structure. Thus even if one disagreed with the majority and believed with the minority that the Thirteenth Amendment ran afoul of entrenched article requirements, there would still be no judicial warrant for nullifying a procedurally correct amendment to the Constitution.

> [B]oth our Constitutions of 1972 and 1978 specifically provide for the amendment or repeal of any provision of the Constitution or to the repeal of the entire Constitution. . . . We are of the view that it would not be proper to be guided by concepts of "Amendment" found in the Indian judgments. . . . Fundamental principles or basic features of the Constitution have to be found in . . . some provision or provisions of the Constitution and if the Constitution contemplates the repeal of any provision or provisions of the entire Constitution, there is no basis for the contention that some provisions which reflects fundamental principles or "incorporate basic features" are immune from amendment. Accordingly, we do not agree with the contention that some provisions of the Constitution are unamendable.[75]

In other countries—again consider Ireland—the amendability of all provisions of the Constitution is defended in accordance with a theory of popular sovereignty: the people must always retain the power to alter any part of their governing document. Hence the Constitution, as was pointed out earlier, is treated more like ordinary law than as a sacred document. Yet it is in Chief Justice Wanasundera's dissenting opinion that we find a popular sovereignty argument, invoked, however, to legitimate the nullification of the Thirteenth Amendment. "[O]ur Constitution, like the US Constitution and unlike the Indian or UK Constitutions, vests Sovereignty in the People and the organs of Government hold a mandate and are agents of the People."[76] But if Sri Lankan constitutionalism is to be distinguished from India's on democratic grounds, it does

75. *In re The Thirteenth Amendment,* at 327.

76. Ibid., at 335.

not gainsay the fact that the Indian precedents on striking down constitutional amendments should be scrupulously followed in the present instance. Thus the constitutional changes cannot be regarded as "entrenching the basic features of the Constitution."[77] "[T]he 13th Amendment seeks to create an arrangement which is structurally in conflict with the structure of the Constitution and with its provisions both express and implied."[78]

For the majority, Indian cases such as *Kesavananda* and *Minerva Mills* were unnecessary as touchstones for constitutional guidance, while for the minority they were essential to achieving the identity-preserving result important to all the Court's judges. To be sure, the nature of the threat to the Constitution's identity could be formulated in abstract structural terms as a radical transformation of a duly mandated unitary system into a federal system whose decentralization of power represented a blatant transgression of constitutional design. But it was hard to conceal—not that the effort was made—the elemental essence of the alleged constitutional infirmity: the assault on the Buddhist and Sinhalese identity of the polity.

The majority had insisted "the Provincial Councils can place no impediment in the way of the State giving Buddhism the foremost place and protecting and fostering the Buddha Sasana in terms of Article 9 of the Constitution."[79] To which the chief justice responded, "[T]he official recognition of the traditional homelands of the Tamils will toll the death knell of the Sinhala people in those Provinces."[80] The reliance of this justice on Indian jurisprudence was also an effort to avoid an unwanted Indian fate, namely the adoption of a "two-nation theory," which, while it arguably serves the interests of the Tamils, would surely undermine the "ideal of a Sri Lankan [translate: Sinhalese Buddhist] nationality." Reduced to its essentials, it is an argument that mirrors the rhetoric of Hindu nationalism in India, where, according to its proponents, the content of Indian nationality should reflect the culture of the

77. Ibid., at 336.
78. Ibid., at 383.
79. Ibid., at 332.
80. Ibid., at 337.

Hindu majority. In Sri Lanka, however, ethno/religious nationalism is sanctified by constitutional language that is nowhere to be found in its Indian counterpart.[81]

The primacy of Buddhism in Sri Lankan identity is explicitly expressed in the Constitution, and implicitly in the structural attributes of constitutional design—mainly in the intentions behind the unitary state. "The Indian proposals acceded to by us clearly indicate a shift in views, no doubt under pressure tilting the scales in favour of the Tamil demands for autonomy."[82] That the minority assessed the implications stemming from the externally induced constitutional changes with more alarm than did their colleagues on the other side is less interesting than is the unity of purpose upon which they both predicated their jurisprudential choices: maintenance of the ethno/republican character of Sri Lankan constitutionalism. All of the arguments made in both opinions—about federalism, popular sovereignty, the relevance to Sri Lanka of India's basic structure doctrine—were embraced and deployed with that predominant end in mind.

What might the Indian proponents of the basic structure doctrine have learned from the uses of their jurisprudence by the Supreme Court of their offshore neighbor?[83] Since most of them were (and are) fervent supporters of Nehruvian secularism, the embrace of which leads one to recoil from any move in the direction of an ethnically or religiously defined state, they might conclude that not all heritages are so "precious" as to justify an aggressive and unyielding defense of constitutional identity. Setting aside such speculation, it should nevertheless be clear that resistance to major transformations in a nation's constitutional identity

81. The Sinhalese chosen people narrative in Sri Lanka parallels the Hindu version in India, but the latter is not a narrative inscribed in the Constitution. Nor in India is religion implicated in the federal division of constitutional power; as has often been told, that is a story whose theme is linguistic diversity.

82. *In re The Thirteenth Amendment,* at 353.

83. Sri Lanka is not the only neighbor to have relied on India's basic structure jurisprudence. Thus the Bangladesh Supreme Court has invalidated a constitutional amendment that would have removed the authority of the Court to transfer and retransfer judges at its discretion. The ruling was justified as a defense of an independent judiciary, a critical basic feature of the Constitution. The case was in this sense similar to the key Indian precedents that employed the doctrine to preserve the institutional prerogatives of the judiciary.

ought not to be an occasion for reflexive celebration. As we see in Chapter 6 when we examine the Israeli case, one can have a serious argument about the merits of "ethnorepublicanism"; that, however, the immutability of an identity in tension with the precepts of liberal constitutionalism should be held sacrosanct by a judicial tribunal is by no means self-evident. Similar concerns about preserving an identity at the possible cost of a diminution in the prominence of principles of constitutional governance have, as I highlight in Chapter 7, been raised in Turkey in relation to the unconstitutional amendment question. The Indian basic structure doctrine was forged against the backdrop of a determined threat to constitutionalism in its generic form, leaving open the question of its applicability to constitutional change that preserves the essentials of a constitution but is transformative with respect to its specific identity.

"An Idea of Continuity"

We might think of an amendment as a new chapter in an ongoing constitutional story. How well it fits the existing narrative will be a factor in assessing its quality; it may, like the Fourteenth Amendment in Ireland or the proposed Flag Burning Amendment in the United States, raise concerns about coherence, or what Ronald Dworkin refers to as "integrity."[84] But if the lack of fit is so extreme as to either call into question whether the addition has subverted the genre itself—for example, is it still a novel?—or to lead one to conclude that a key element of the plotline has been disregarded, then the legitimacy of the undertaking might well be placed in doubt.[85] Constitutionally these two possibilities translate into first- and second-order amendment defects. Both are serious, even if the culturally contingent elements of the latter significantly reduce the

84. Ronald Dworkin, *Law's Empire* (Cambridge, MA: Harvard University Press, 1986), chap. 6–7. My example of a constitutional narrative follows Dworkin's chain novel illustration (ibid., 228–238).

85. As William Harris points out, "[T]he kinds of alteration an example of a genre can bear are limited and . . . going beyond these limits will not only change the characteristics of the example but also will change the genre that it represents." Harris, *Interpretable Constitution*, 171.

urgency of the need to impose implied limits. Thus an amendment that assaulted the very foundations of constitutionalism would be direr than one that challenged some constitutional practice or tradition of particular importance to a given regime. It is not the introduction of significant and far-reaching change, however, that is per se objectionable; rather it is the content of this change insofar as it implicates the question of constitutional identity. Indeed, Edmund Burke, whose resistance to change has often been exaggerated, once wryly pointed out that when a man says he only means "a moderate and temperate reform," what he really means to do is "as little good as possible."[86]

A constitutional amendment may thus be considered problematic in one of two ways: (1) The change it portends could subvert the essentials of constitutional government, at the core of which is the rule of law and the administration of impartial justice; and (2) The change it portends could substantially transform or negate a fundamental political commitment of the constitutional order that had been central to the nation's self-understanding. The second possibility may be considered as a variant of the first, but it may also stand separately. Thus both the American and Sri Lankan Thirteenth Amendments cannot reasonably be interpreted as threats to constitutional government; although in each instance a plausible case can be made that the constitutional changes embodied in the amendments represented a critical departure from the ways and aspirations of the past. In Ireland, the Seventeenth Amendment was a perilous challenge to constitutional governance in the Free State, while the later Fourteenth Amendment to the 1937 document reflected the societal change in that country that had come to express itself—radically for those of strong traditional Catholic commitment—in the Constitution. In India, the constitutional amendments that were an extension of Indira Gandhi's dictatorial ambitions were deeply disturbing as examples of type (1), but how, for example, should an amendatory challenge to secularism be viewed? Surely it would fundamentally transform Indian constitutional identity; would its violation of the spirit of liberal constitutionalism

86. Edmund Burke, "Speech On a Motion Made in the House of Commons, the 7th of May 1782, for a Committee to Inquire into the State of the Representation of the Commons in Parliament," in David Bromwich, ed., *On Empire, Liberty, and Reform,* 278.

justify concerns of the sort aroused by the innovations associated with the first type?

Reforming a constitution is, as Walter F. Murphy points out, different from re-forming a constitution.[87] The latter, one might say, extends beyond incoherence and implicates identity. According to the Oxford English Dictionary, to speak of identity is to refer to that condition or fact that makes something unique, *especially as a continuous unchanging property throughout its existence.*[88] This follows the account of the eighteenth-century Scottish philosopher Thomas Reid's observation that "Continued uninterrupted existence is . . . necessarily implied in identity."[89] As it has evolved in Indian jurisprudence, the meaning of a constitutional amendment has essentially conformed to these definitions of identity. Thus in *Kesavananda,* Justice Khanna, the author of the decision's most important opinion, wrote, "The word 'amendment' postulates that the old constitution survives without loss of its identity despite the change and continues even though it has been subjected to alterations."[90] In *Minerva Mills,* Justice Bhagwati, one of the last holdouts against the idea of implied limits, argued, "If by constitutional amendment, Parliament were granted unlimited power of amendment, it would cease to be an authority under the Constitution, but would become supreme over it, because it would have power to alter the entire Constitution including its basic structure and even to put an end to it by totally changing its identity."[91]

The question of constitutional identity is, as we have seen, much more easily asserted than enforced. Given the exceedingly high probability

87. Murphy, "Slaughter-House," 17. For Murphy, the addition of the Thirteenth and Fourteenth Amendments provided the Constitution with the intellectual coherence it had previously lacked, and in doing so enhanced, rather than undermined, the integrity of its core principles.

88. *The New Shorter Oxford English Dictionary*, Vol. 1, Lesley Brown, ed. (Oxford: Clarendon Press, 1993), 1304.

89. Quoted in Udo Thiel, "Individuation," in Daniel Garber and Michael Ayers, eds., *The Cambridge History of Seventeenth Century Philosophy—Volume 1* (Cambridge: Cambridge University Press, 1998), 253.

90. *Kesavananda Bharati,* at 1860.

91. *Minerva Mills,* at 1824. Some constitutions, we should note, expressly provide for the possibility of their total revision through constitutional amendment. See, for example, the constitutions of Spain, Austria, and Switzerland.

that any such assertion will be vigorously contested, judges are understandably reluctant to enforce it. This is because, as Christopher Eisgruber notes, "Isolating the mechanism that makes invocations of identity . . . persuasive would take us into deep philosophical waters."[92] While such an exercise could prove quite beneficial, the safer judicial route is to avoid these waters entirely. Thus in the American case, Coleman v. Miller, Justice Black said of the Article V process that it "is 'political' in its entirety, from submission until an amendment becomes part of the Constitution, and is not subject to judicial guidance, control or interference at any point."[93] The judicial practice of invoking this "political question" doctrine to avoid difficult constitutional questions began in Luther v. Borden,[94] which was in essence a case of constitutional identity in which the Supreme Court refused to say what it was that the republican guaranty clause (Article IV, section 4) guaranteed. The same jurisprudential choice to avoid the question of identity underlies the unwillingness to find implied limits to formal constitutional change.[95] When, several years later, the abolitionist senator from Massachusetts, Charles Sumner, suggested that republican identity was incompatible with slavery, and hence the federal government should do what the Constitution commanded and remove those governments that supported it, his arguments were defeated by John C. Calhoun and the logic of *Luther*.

92. Christopher Eisgruber, "Is the Supreme Court an Educative Institution?" 67 *New York University Law Review* 961, 971 (1992).

93. Coleman v. Miller, 307 U.S. 433 (1939), at 459.

94. Luther v. Borden, 48 U.S. 1 (1849).

95. At the state level there has occasionally been less reluctance to engage such issues. In Downs v. City of Birmingham, 198 Southern Reporter 231, the Supreme Court of Alabama held that an amendment to the State Constitution must be consistent with a republican form of government as required by the federal Constitution. Some states (California, Delaware) distinguish in their constitutions between "amendment" and "revision," the latter intended to apply to pervasive changes in constitutional arrangements. The Spanish Constitution of 1978 has a similar two-tier amending system. For a comparative analysis of the various approaches to constitutional amendment see Elai Katz, "On Amending Constitutions: The Legality and Legitimacy of Constitutional Entrenchment," 29 *Columbia Journal of Law and Social Problems* 251 (1996). Katz argues that while everything in a constitution should be amendable, certain clauses should be harder to amend than others.

Very different was the result in India when in 1994 the Supreme Court upheld the authority of the central government in dismissing the elected governments in three states for their complicity in undermining the polity's commitment to secularism.[96] The provision under which this was done had been modeled after the American Guaranty Clause. As a prominent delegate at the Constituent Assembly said, "In putting in that Article [for dismissing state governments], we are merely following the example of the classical or model federation of America."[97] The Court's main concern was Indian constitutional identity, and so, following *Kesavananda,* secularism was declared essential to the unchangeable "basic structure" of the Constitution. But here, as in the earlier case, the Court's boldness in defending against the assault on constitutional foundations was not matched by its effort in articulating a theory by which the properties of a protected domain of identity might be known. Moreover, as we have noted earlier, the determination to preserve this domain begs the question of why, as an axiom of constitutional policy, this "precious heritage" must be shielded from destruction.[98] "[T]o say your Constitution is what it has been, is no sufficient defense for those, who say it is a bad Constitution."[99]

These last words belong to Burke, whose disparaging reflections on the dramatic changes in one country have unfortunately obscured his decades of engagement in the transformation of others. In South Asia, where some said he stubbornly—others prefer tenaciously—championed the rights of Indians against the numerous depredations of the British Empire, he is given more regard as a visionary thinker, albeit one whose

96. *S. R. Bommai,* 3 SC 1 (1994). The case is discussed at length in Jacobsohn, *Indian Secularism,* 125–160.

97. *Constituent Assembly Debates,* Official Reports, vol. 7 (Delhi: Lok Sabha Secretariat), 150. The delegate, Alladi Krishnaswami, was a future Supreme Court justice.

98. Thus the judge in *Kesavananda* who raised the following question did not get a satisfactory answer: "And what is the sacredness about the basic structure of the Constitution? Take the republican form of government, the supposed cornerstone of the whole structure. Has mankind, after wandering through history, made a final and unalterable verdict that it is in the best form of government? Does not history show that mankind has changed its opinion from generation to generation?" *Kesavananda Bharati,* at 1948.

99. Burke, "Speech On a Motion," 275.

gaze was never fully diverted from the past.[100] There are approving references in the *Kesavananda* ruling to Burke's famous injunction about the need to accommodate change in order to conserve what is truly important.[101] But in the development of their ideas on constitutional identity and basic structure, the Indian justices got less mileage than they could have from one whose unique Irish perspective led him to condemn the injustices done to their ancestors.[102]

Indeed, Burke's immersion in the struggles of Ireland and India had much to do with what I would describe as his dual track understanding of constitutional identity, one that parallels the two aforementioned amendment threats. At the most basic level there are for Burke certain attributes of the rule of law that are the necessary condition for generic constitutional governance. What the American legal philosopher, Lon Fuller, called the "inner morality of law"[103] is a fair representation of Burke's unequivocal denial of constitutional identity to a dominion that failed to meet its minimum requirements. These are the requirements of due process in the Magna Carta sense, not the more contemporary version of substantive guarantees. In fact, in arguing for Fox's East India Bill, Burke said it was "intended to inform the Magna Carta of Hindostan."[104] To this end his impeachment prosecution of Warren Hastings for the latter's maladministration of India was premised on the idea that

100. In fact, not only in South Asia has he been so viewed. Thus Harold Laski pointed out that "[on] Ireland, America, and India, he [Burke] was at every point upon the side of the future. . . ." Quoted in Uday Singh Mehta, *Liberalism and Empire: A Study in Nineteenth-Century British Political Thought* (Chicago: University of Chicago Press, 1999), 155.

101. For example, Justice Khanna, author of the ruling's most important opinion, quoting Burke: "A state without the means of some change is without the means of its own conservation. Without such means it might even risk the laws of that part of the Constitution which it wished the most religiously to preserve." *Kesavananda Bharati*, at 1847.

102. The best study of how Burke's Irish roots shaped his political ideas is Conor Cruise O'Brien, *The Great Melody: A Thematic Biography of Edmund Burke* (Chicago: University of Chicago Press, 1992).

103. Lon Fuller, *The Morality of Law* (New Haven, CT: Yale University Press, 1964), 42.

104. Edmund Burke, "Speech On Fox's East India Bill," in David Bromwich, ed., *On Empire, Liberty, and Reform: Speeches and Letters of Edmund Burke*, 292.

"The laws of morality are the same everywhere."[105] Whatever one might think of the identity of an authority that does not provide Magna Carta-like liberties, it is not an identity that is properly constitutional. For Burke this did not mandate a particular form of government, as it did for the theoreticians of natural rights whom he often scolded, but it did mean that to be properly identified for what it was, a constitution would have to be able, in Fuller's words, to "save us from the abyss."[106] It is unlikely that Indira Gandhi's amendments or, for that matter, the Seventeenth Amendment to the Irish Free Constitution, would have satisfied this Burkean requirement.

But the most vexing questions about identity concern constitutions, not constitutionalism. One of the justices in the Indira Gandhi case, in speaking of the principles of the rule of law, pointed out that they "must vary from country to country depending on the provisions of [the] constitution."[107] Burke's second track concerns this variability, which is about the identity of a particular constitution. In his Speech on Reform of Representation, delivered just one year before his better-known speech on the East India Bill, Burke explained why he favored the concept of the prescriptive constitution: "Because," he said, "a nation is not an idea of local extent, but is an idea of continuity, which extends in time as well as in numbers, and in space. And this is a choice not of one day, or one set of people, not a tumultuary and giddy choice; it is a deliberate election of ages and generations; it is a Constitution . . . made by the peculiar circumstances, occasions, tempers, dispositions, and moral, civil, and social habitudes of the people, which disclose themselves only in a long space of time. It is a vestment, which accommodates itself to the body."[108]

Tempting as it is to think of Burke as a precursor of modern moral relativism, that interpretation is ultimately unpersuasive, even if excerpts like this offer insight into why some have held that view. His emphasis on particularities and prescription, and on the constitution as

105. Quoted in Frederick G. Whelan, *Edmund Burke in India: Political Morality and Empire* (Pittsburgh, PA: University of Pittsburgh Press, 1996), 281.

106. Fuller, *Morality of Law,* 44.

107. *Indira Gandhi,* at 2470.

108. Burke, "Speech On a Motion," 274.

something that evolves to conform to the circumstances and habits of a people, is surely suggestive of a moral sensibility strongly deferential to entrenched cultural norms. But the deference was not unqualified, as illustrated in Burke's rejection of Hastings's main argument for his morally questionable actions in India. Hastings had framed a defense of "geographical morality," which held that whatever happened in India was compatible with local customs and therefore could not be judged by external standards. Burke was categorical in rejecting this moral perspective, arguing in response that the governance of Indians had to respect the same universal laws of right conduct that applied to Englishmen. Necessary, for Burke, was a prudential balancing of the universal and the particular. "The foundations of government [are . . . in the constitution] laid . . . in political convenience and in human nature; either as that nature is universal, or as it is modified by local habits."[109]

While there were preconditions for *a* constitution to exist, the nation as an "idea of continuity" meant that *constitutions* had to be viewed as embodiments of unique histories and circumstances. "I never was wild enough to conceive that one method would serve for the whole; that the natives of Hindostan and those of Virginia could be ordered in the same manner. . . ."[110] One would never mistake the constitutional

109. Quoted in Francis Canavan, "Prescription of Government," in Daniel Ritchie, *Edmund Burke: Appraisals & Applications* (New Brunswick, NJ: Transaction Publishers, 1990), 259. One of the most thoughtful accounts of Burke's views on India is contained in Mehta's *Liberalism and Empire,* in which Burke is distinguished from such theorists as John Stuart Mill on the basis of his—Burke's—preference for the local over the universal, such that it led him to see, in a way that was not evident to these other thinkers, the abuses of empire. Mehta's argument is very persuasive, although he overstates Burke's renunciation of universal principles. Thus it is incomplete to say, "For Burke . . . obligations and the norms of justice spring from the local and the conventional" (ibid., 176). A similar account, highlighting Burke's aesthetic theory, may be found in Luke Gibbons, *Edmund Burke and Ireland: Aesthetics, Politics, and the Colonial Sublime* (Cambridge: Cambridge University Press, 2003), 166–180. "Geographical morality" is present in some of the sentiments expressed in *Kesavananda.* For example, "Law varies according to the requirements of time and place. Justice thus becomes a relative concept varying from society to society according to the social milieu and economic conditions prevailing therein." *Kesavananda Bharati,* at 1735.

110. Edmund Burke, "Letter to the Sheriffs of Bristol," in *The Works of Edmund Burke—Vol. II* (Boston: C. C. Little & J. Brown, 1839), 119.

identities of these wildly divergent peoples, just as one would not confuse the aesthetic identities of an ornate eighteenth-century French writing table and its minimalist twentieth-century Finnish counterpart. Much as the presence of a horizontal surface on a base assures the viewer that the latter contrast pertains to the category of tables, the constitutional observer will have to be satisfied that analogous generic criteria establish a common basis for comparing the two bodies politic. The accommodation of the vestment to the body implied a tolerance for diverse practices; abstract theory could not dictate constitutional form or identity. One can debate whether Burke was too permissive in the span of constitutional variability he imagined as compatible with legitimate rule. The point is that the Burkean understanding of constitutions as artifacts of time and experience supplies the necessary background assumption for Justice Khanna's criterion for the legitimacy of an amendment: that the old constitution survive without loss of its identity.

In the philosophical literature the relationship between survival and identity is a much contested subject;[111] according to one account, "[W]hat matters in survival is mental continuity and connectedness. . . . What matters in survival is identity."[112] Accordingly, "Change should be gradual rather than sudden, and (at least in some respects) there should not be too much change overall."[113] Although meant to apply to personal identity, a similar idea may be said to give meaning to identity at the constitutional level. In Indian jurisprudence this can lead, as in Justice Khanna's opinion, to basic structure, and in Burke to the constitutional principle of inheritance, more familiarly known as *prescription*. Burke, as Francis P. Canavan noted, "supposes that [the

111. See, for example, David Lewis, "Survival and Identity," in Amelie Oksenberg Rorty, ed., *The Identities of Persons* (Berkeley: University of California Press, 1976); and Derek Parfit, "Personal Identity," 80 *Philosophical Review* 3 (1971).

112. Lewis, "Survival and Identity," 17–18. Similarly, Thomas Reid wrote, "[Identity] admits of a great change of the subject, providing the change be gradual; sometimes even of a total change. And the changes made . . . consistent with identity differ from those that are thought to destroy it. . . ." From *Essays on the Intellectual Powers of Man* (1785), excerpted in Raymond Martin and John Barresi, eds., *Personal Identity* (Oxford: Blackwell, 2003), 51.

113. Lewis, "Survival and Identity," 18.

Constitution] is a contingent part of the moral order and for that very reason imposes an obligation that overrides the alleged right of each successive generation to scrap the existing constitution and frame a new one for itself."[114]

The constitutional text is usually a critical component of constitutional identity but not coterminous with it.[115] India, for example, has embraced secularism as an essential component of its constitutional identity, an embrace denoted only partially by its formal constitutional codification. More significant is the historical backdrop to that codification, which establishes the prescriptive force of the commitments included in the document. Thus the principle of secularism may be understood as an element of the basic structure of the Constitution, and accordingly may not be subject to amendment, but a specific provision intended to configure secular relations in a particular way may be changed within the constraints of the broader principle. The variability of changing conditions may necessitate modifications in the structure and design of particular institutions, as well as in the manner in which these institutions interact with one another and with other agents, but the transient character of formal arrangements will generally reflect the larger purposes and principles that are the continuous thread of constitutional identity.[116]

Burke, then, provides a sound argument for constitutional maintenance, for protecting the basic core of constitutional identity against radical changes that would disrespect fundamental law as an "idea of continuity." But for those who say of their constitution that "it is a bad constitution," is the only available recourse that they go outside of the Constitution to make it good? Our sympathy for Indian judges whose

114. Francis P. Canavan, *The Political Reason of Edmund Burke* (Durham, NC: Duke University Press, 1960), 134.

115. Those of the view that going beyond the text for an answer to the identity question is illegitimate are likely to find the doctrine of implied limits to constitutional change similarly problematic. See, for example, Kemal Gozler, *Judicial Review of Constitutional Amendments,* 67.

116. This is a point well made by the astute scholar of Burke, Gerald Chapman, who points out that the House of Commons, for example, need not as a matter of prescriptive requirement assume any particular form, but that the basis for the existence of the House "authorizes its permanence as a principle in the constitution" (ibid., 166).

high regard for the Constitution's secular aspirations has reinforced their determination to redefine the meaning of judicial supremacy is understandable given the nobility of those aspirations. But is continuity the virtue to be exalted when the nobility of defining aspirations is less obvious—in the case of Sri Lanka, for example, where ethnic domination is the feature of constitutional identity most likely to inspire the judicial invalidation of a constitutional amendment?

Conclusion

Consider the strange course of events that occurred in Honduras during the summer of 2009. The elected president of that country was arrested by the armed forces and summarily dispatched to Costa Rica, prompting nearly universal condemnation in official circles. The consensus view in the international community was that a military *coup* had occurred, and that the perpetrators of this appalling disruption of constitutional processes should be required to reinstall the deposed president and be held accountable for their illegal actions. In response, the defenders of the president's removal insisted that, far from constituting a *coup,* what transpired was not only consistent with constitutional procedure, it was, in effect, preservative of Honduran constitutional identity—or at least what they hoped had been an emerging constitutional identity.

The identity issue was directly implicated in the actions that precipitated the presidential ouster. The deposed leader, President Manuel Zelaya, had initiated a process designed to amend the Constitution to enable him to serve another term in office. Article 239 of that document was clear, however, in establishing that the provision limiting a president to a four-year term was unamendable, and, moreover, that any effort by the president to eliminate the limitation would constitute a basis for removal from office.[117] The order to arrest Zelaya came from the Supreme Court, a directive overwhelmingly supported by the Honduran Congress,

117. "No citizen who has already served as head of the Executive Branch can be President or Vice-President. Whoever violates this law or proposes its reform, as well as those that support such violation directly or indirectly, will immediately cease in their functions and will be unable to hold any public office for a period of 10 years."

which shared the Court's belief that the succession rules were critical to the essence of Honduran constitutionalism. Other considerations were doubtless also in play, but the principle—taken for granted in many places—that presidents should not be continuously reelected, has been difficult to institutionalize in Latin America, a fact that gives added weight to the strong textual commitment entrenched in the document. Indeed, Article 4 of the Constitution provides that any infraction of these rules constitutes no less than an act of treason.

The motives and politics in this constitutional crisis were, to say the least, complicated; understandably, then, reactions to the events were largely colored by ideological and strategic considerations. Arguably there were other courses of actions that might have been undertaken to address the crisis, yet, viewed from the specific perspective of this chapter, one's assessment of the Honduran Supreme Court's central role will likely reflect how one chooses to evaluate the standing of an unconstitutional constitutional amendment. If the change (or in this case, proposed change) is truly of constitutive importance, does its toleration threaten the essence of the constitutional project? The judicial behavior in Honduras was consistent with the actions of other courts—most notably in India—that have held it to be a legitimate function of the nation's highest court to affirm the immutability of certain commitments. To be sure, the Honduran Court's exertion was an unusual variation on the exercise of this power, but as in the more conventional instance of a simple declaration of an amendment's unconstitutionality, it may be viewed as a daring—perhaps even imprudent—effort to defend foundational norms that are deemed vital to the stability of a nation's constitutional identity. Whatever the ultimate resolution of the Honduran crisis, that identity will have undergone significant alteration.[118]

The challenge faced in subsequent chapters is to accommodate major changes in constitutional identity while respecting the critical role that Burke's prescriptive constitution plays in shaping that identity. In the next chapter I begin this effort by introducing the idea of disharmony as the key to constitutional identity as a developmental concept. Thus as

118. As of this writing, there is much uncertainty regarding the settlement of the succession issue.

vital as was the Indian Supreme Court's role in the amendments crisis, its larger role as a shaper of constitutional identity cannot be adequately described without recognizing the institutional, dialogical context within which it operated. As Sarbani Sen points out, "[T]he separation of powers allowed rivals in different branches to square off against one another and present to the people, as forcefully as they could, alternative perspectives to the question of constitutional identity at the center of the political agenda."[119] The same might be said of Honduras.

"At bottom," wrote one of the dissenting Indian judges in *Kesavananda,* "the controversy . . . is . . . whether the meaning of the Constitution consists in its being or in its becoming."[120] He then called attention to the country's national symbol, the *chakra,* which is the wheel that appears on the Indian flag. It signifies, he said, that the Constitution is "a becoming, a moving equilibrium."[121] Hence he concluded that "true democracy and true republicanism" are incompatible with judicial review of constitutional amendments. His only error was in creating a false dichotomy between being and becoming. As Burke reminded us, "[B]y preserving the method of nature in the conduct of the state, in what we improve, we are never wholly new; in what we retain, we are never wholly obsolete."[122] What a constitution becomes can never be considered separately from what it has been; it is, in Burke's words, "a deliberate election of ages and generations." But that is not all, as was implicitly understood by the Indian justice.

The dissenter was appropriately concerned that an expansion of the Court's review function to incorporate the legality of constitutional amendments might "blunt the people's vigilance, articulateness and

119. Sarbani Sen, *The Constitution of India: Popular Sovereignty and Democracy* (New Delhi: Oxford University Press, 2007), 190. Sen, a student of Bruce Ackerman, presents a different account from my own, viewing the struggle over the controversial amendments as an example of her mentor's thesis concerning popular expressions of sovereignty and transformative constitutional moments. For a critique of this view see Rajeev Dhavan, "Sarbani Sen, Popular Sovereignty and Democratic Transformations," 2 *Indian Journal of Constitutional Law* (2008).

120. *Kesavananda Bharati,* at 1986.

121. Ibid., at 2010.

122. Edmund Burke, *Reflections on the Revolution in France* (Indianapolis, IN: Bobbs-Merrill, 1955), 38.

effectiveness."[123] That concern should not be taken lightly; indeed, it is as valid as when it was expressed years ago in the American Judge Learned Hand's oft-quoted and eloquent thought about self-government and the judiciary: "This much I think I do know—that a society so riven that the spirit of moderation is gone, no court *can* save; that a society where that spirit flourishes, no court *need* save; that in a society which evades its responsibility by thrusting upon the courts the nurture of that spirit, that spirit in the end will perish."[124] The lesson in the unconstitutional constitution conundrum is not that the courts can be counted on always to save a people from the immoderate excesses of the amendment process. Once one recognizes that there are applications of that process that may exceed acceptable limits, perhaps the wisest course is to then rely on the body politic to see that these actions are not adopted. But such reliance first requires knowing why there *are* limits and why this matters.

Thus, understanding that constitutional change may produce an unconstitutional result does not in itself prescribe a particular remedy. Indeed, endowing courts with a judicial review responsibility over constitutional amendments might, when prudently considered, be thought of in relation to the relative ease or difficulty of altering the document. Profound as is Hand's teaching, the provision in some polities for straightforward and simple amending increases the likelihood that in these places deeply problematic change could occur while the spirit of moderation remained generally prevalent. Elsewhere the amendment process itself encourages, if not guarantees, moderation. What Lawrence Sager has aptly called "the obduracy of the [American] Constitution to amendment"[125] may, as he points out, be structurally conducive to achieving change agreeable "to generations unborn in circumstances unknown."[126] This is a point with which Edmund Burke would no doubt agree. Where, as in the American case, amending the Constitution is such a formidable undertaking, there should perhaps be a much stronger

123. *Kesavananda Bharati,* at 2009.

124. Learned Hand, *The Spirit of Liberty* (New York: Alfred A. Knopf, 1953), 164.

125. Lawrence Sager, *Justice in Plain Clothes: A Theory of Constitutional Practice* (New Haven, CT: Yale University Press, 2005), 82.

126. Ibid., 164.

presumption against the exercise of judicial review than, say, in India, where the adoption of amendments is only slightly more challenging than the enactment of ordinary law. In principle, however, it might be desirable to keep the option open, if for no other reason than that this could serve to remind politicians and citizens that, as Kurt Gödel understood, constitutional change is inherently bounded. Of course if ever confronted with the felt need to exercise this option, sober heads might well wonder whether it was any longer worth doing.

CHAPTER 3

The Quest for a Compelling Unity

> When we speak of a body of law, we use a metaphor so apt that it is hardly a metaphor. We picture to ourselves a being that lives and grows, that preserves its identity while every atom of which it is composed is subject to a ceaseless process of change, decay, and renewal.
>
> —F. W. Maitland

> We serve our constitutional mandate by expounding the meaning of constitutional provisions with one eye towards our Nation's history and the other fixed on its democratic aspirations.
>
> —Justice John Paul Stevens

Introduction

The possession of philosophic insight is not listed in most people's job description for Supreme Court justices, but there are times when one wishes it were. Such an occasion presented itself when the Court decided the case of a mentally retarded man who had been designated for execution by the state of Missouri. A sharply divided Court ruled in favor of the man, but the case has come to be known as much for its division over the appropriateness of American judges citing foreign law in their opinions. Defending the practice, Justice Anthony Kennedy offered the following explanation:

> Over time, from one generation to the next, the Constitution has come to earn the high respect and even, as Madison dared to hope,

> the veneration of the people. The document sets forth, and rests upon, innovative principles original to the American experience, such as federalism; a proven balance in political mechanisms through separation of powers; specific guarantees for the accused in criminal cases; and broad provisions to secure individual freedom and preserve human dignity. These doctrines and guarantees are central to the American experience and remain essential to our present-day self-definition and national identity. Not the least of the reasons we honor the Constitution, then, is because we know it to be our own. It does not lessen our fidelity to the Constitution or our pride in its origins to acknowledge that the express affirmation of certain fundamental rights by other nations and peoples simply underscores the centrality of those same rights within our own heritage of freedom.[1]

Justice Scalia, whose views on the subject are aired more fully in Chapter 4, gave short shrift to Kennedy's argument, saying in dissent, "Either America's principles are our own, or they follow the world; one cannot have it both ways."[2]

Had there been an opportunity to respond, Justice Kennedy might very well have said, "Oh yes you can." But to support such a claim—or its denial—would require delving more deeply into the questions of identity that are hinted at in the sentiments preceding the reference to the experience of other nations and peoples. Among these groups of questions are (1) In what sense are constitutional doctrines central to self-definition and national identity? Is the suggestion that they are important in this regard tantamount to affirming a correspondence between constitutional and national identities? (2) Is there a connection between a contemporary political self-definition and a constitution whose veneration is in large part attributable to its existence over time? If so, what is its nature? How helpful is the idea of the "self" for conceptualizing constitutional identity? and (3) Do the innovative principles that are original to the nation's experience serve an aspirational role in

1. Roper v. Simmons, 543 U.S. 551 (2005), 578.

2. Ibid., at 627.

constitutional development, or are they the indicia of a fixed constitutional identity? To what extent is the originality that bespeaks a particularity uniquely expressive of a nation's history and tradition also convergent with certain universals of constitutionalism? Is constitutional identity in essence the adaptation of these universals to fit the circumstances of a given polity?

Pursuing answers to these questions would lead to others with a less U.S.-centric focus. For example, we might agree that constitutional ideas are constitutive of national identity but view this as a predominantly American phenomenon of limited applicability elsewhere. Similarly, the American constitutional experience, including the role of its Supreme Court, differs in significant respects from that of other countries in ways that surely impinge on the question of identity. Will one account of identity be able to speak to the comparative variability in which constitutional change occurs in different places? Is constitutional identity a viable notion within a radically transformative constitutional environment such as South Africa?[3] Will it illuminate the situation of a constitution, for example, India, designed to challenge a way of life that is inscribed in a nation's traditions and politics? And the question that is perhaps least likely to be addressed by a Supreme Court justice, but which is vital to the concerns of those who study constitutional politics: how does constitutional identity take shape and develop?

This chapter presents a theory of constitutional identity that offers some tentative answers to these queries, followed in subsequent chapters by treatments of different aspects of the problem in specific constitutional contexts. The first section briefly elaborates some of the philosophical dimensions of the problem, and the second ties these reflections to the more political concerns that must animate the work of comparative constitutional analysis. I argue for a dialogical understanding of identity that incorporates an easily overlooked feature of the universal constitutional condition, which is that in one way or another all constitutions confront

3. As Justice Albie Sachs wrote in the South African gay marriage case, "[O]ur Constitution represents a radical rupture with a past based on intolerance and exclusion, and the movement forward to the acceptance of the need to develop a society based on equality and respect by all for all." *Minister of Home Affairs v. Fourie,* CCT 60/04 (2005), 10.

or embody the problem of *disharmony.*[4] Sometimes this condition exists in the form of contradictions and imbalances internal to the constitution itself, and sometimes in the lack of agreement evident in the sharp discontinuities that frame the constitution's relationship to the surrounding society.[5] The question of identity is prominently implicated in the various permutations of the disharmonic constitution, embodied principally in the determination to eliminate or maintain the discordant aspects of the constitutional predicament.[6] Disharmony is a precondition for change,

4. As far as I know the idea of disharmony as applied to political things originated with the distinguished scholar of Indian society, André Bétaille, who was prominently followed in his usage of the term by Samuel Huntington in his 1981 study, *American Politics: The Promise of Disharmony* (Cambridge, MA: Harvard University Press, 1981). For Huntington, disharmony refers to the gap between promise and performance, and the attempt to close this gap is the main explanation for social change in the United States. In his account, the United States is the most disharmonic of all polities, since the existential and normative orders are necessarily inconsistent with one another, given the presence of a high degree of ideological consensus and the inevitable failure of the society to measure up to its principled commitments. As explained below, my use of the term as applied to constitutional orders is a more expansive understanding that imagines different forms of disharmony, of which Huntington's version is only one.

5. The latter form of disharmony is what André Bétaille had in mind in distinguishing between harmonic and disharmonic societies. "A disharmonic society . . . shows a lack of consistency between the existential and the normative orders: the norm of equality is contradicted by the pervasive existence of inequality." André Bétaille, *The Idea of Natural Equality and Other Essays* (Delhi: Oxford University Press, 1987), 54. For Bétaille, a scholar of caste in India, the 1950 Indian Constitution, with its promise of a casteless and classless society, exemplifies the disharmonic circumstance. I use the term more broadly to accommodate other kinds of contradictions as well, including those preventing a constitution, for example Israel's, from being harmoniously composed.

6. This constitutional predicament includes, according to William F. Harris II, a further disharmonic antinomy, which he characterizes as the positive and negative constitutions. "Any distinct constitution will have specific traits of failure matched of itself, as negative *attributes,* which, when assembled, set up a comprehensively negative Constitution." William F. Harris II, "Constitution of Failure: The Architectonics of a Well-Founded Constitutional Order," in Stephen Macedo and Jeffrey Tulis, eds., *The Limits of Constitutional Democracy* (Princeton, NJ: Princeton University Press, forthcoming 2010). Harris traces this opposition to Aristotle, who "matched good and bad constitutions as an essential part of 'constitution' itself" (ibid.). These two constitutions—in the United States, a Constitution of Order and a Constitution of Disorder—illuminate each other as they function in tandem over time. For our purposes, this persistent interplay is one manifestation of the dialogical unfolding of constitutional identity.

and efforts to reduce or defend it reveal that constitutional identity is therefore not a static or fixed thing. To apprehend constitutional identity is to see its dynamic quality, which results from the interplay of forces seeking either to introduce greater harmony into the constitutional equation or, contrariwise, to create further disharmony. One could imagine the latter development culminating in a rupture of constitutional continuity, thereby setting in motion a process whose goal might be the reconstituting of the polity. But even in cases of radical transformation, the shaping of a new constitutional identity is never simply a matter of "reflection and choice."[7]

In the previous chapter we saw in the emergency-inspired amendment initiatives of Prime Minister Indira Gandhi a much larger assault on the institutions of constitutional government and with it the real danger that a still fledgling democracy, instituted within an inauspicious supportive socioeconomic environment, might descend into the netherworld of harsh authoritarian rule. The identity that was the object of so much judicial concern in these cases was mainly generic, implicating the cluster of attributes or characteristics that makes *a* constitution (rather than *this* constitution) a distinctive governing code. It was less a question of distinguishing the personality of Jerry from Fred, but of investigating allegations concerning the very personhood of Jerry or Fred. Invalidating an assault on personhood itself is one thing; to do the same to preserve *a* personality from changing into another is not as easily defended. Edmund Burke said of Warren Hastings's crimes that they were "not against forms, but against those eternal laws of justice, which are our rule and our birthright."[8] In this chapter I delve more deeply into issues related to the development of specific constitutional identities that, rather than expressing immutable principles

7. *Federalist 1*, Clinton Rossiter, ed., *The Federalist Papers*, 33.

8. Edmund Burke, "Speech in Opening the Impeachment of Warren Hastings, Esq.," in David Bromwich, ed., *On Empire, Liberty, and Reform* (New Haven, CT: Yale University Press, 2000), 388. Burke wished to emphasize that approval of this argument would, in effect, challenge that aspect of British constitutional identity that expressed a universal commitment to constitutionalism. "I impeach him in the name, and by virtue, of those eternal laws of justice, which he has violated" (ibid., 400).

of constitutionalism, are formed in the arena of real-world political, social, and legal contestation.

The Constitutional Self

In his nineteenth-century classic, *The English Constitution,* Walter Bagehot often used the American Constitution as a comparative foil. Addressing one notable contrast, Bagehot wrote, "The United States could not have been monarchical, even if the constituent convention had decreed it—even if the component states had ratified it. The mystic reverence, the religious allegiance, which are essential to a true monarchy, are imaginative sentiments that no legislature can manufacture in any people. These semi-filial feelings in government are inherited just as the true filial feelings in common life."[9]

There are, one supposes, additional and arguably more convincing explanations for the absence of a monarchical presence among the institutions of American constitutionalism, but one of the benefits of Bagehot's reasoning is that it invites us to pursue the heuristic possibilities in a "common life" analogy to the constitutional regime. It asks us to consider how the lives of individuals—their heritage, their intimate social relations—can perhaps illuminate what happens at the governmental level. Bagehot's suggestion that certain paths of constitutional development are effectively foreclosed by the traditions and collective mindset of a people, has its parallel in the progress of the individual, who also finds available options for growth shaped and limited by the circumstances that have identified that individual as someone more or less inclined to pursue one developmental course rather than another. "We live our lives, both individually and in our relationships with others in the light

9. Walter Bagehot, *The English Constitution* (Cambridge: Cambridge University Press, 2001), 4. Another classic work on the English Constitution, A. V. Dicey's *Introduction to the Study of the Law of the Constitution,* uses a different species to make a similar point about constitutional development. Building sound and lasting institutions is achieved "much as bees construct a honeycomb, without undergoing the degradation of understanding the principles on which they raise a fabric more subtly wrought than any work of conscious art." A. V. Dicey, *Introduction to the Study of the Law of the Constitution* (London: Macmillan & Company, 1961), 3.

of certain conceptions of a possible shared future, a future in which certain possibilities beckon us forward and others repel us, some seem already foreclosed and others perhaps inevitable."[10]

That students of British constitutionalism might proceed in this manner is not surprising given that nation's unique reliance for the stability and moderation of its institutions on a people long habituated to a culture of restraint. But the relevance of personal identity to a broader range of constitutional experience should not be dismissed. "What is better or worse for X depends upon the character of that intelligible narrative which provides X's life with its unity."[11] The same logic in this observation by Alasdair MacIntyre applies to constitutions, including those whose success is less dependent than the British on the existence of a mature and uninterrupted political culture. Poland's most recent constitutional arrangements, for example, draw significantly on a long-term constitutional heritage that preceded the country's extended participation in various experiments in despotic rule.[12] In the broad sweep of Polish history, one punctuated by critical moments such as the adoption in 1791 of a strikingly progressive constitution, and lesser but still important instances involving numerous interventions by the Catholic Church in the affairs of state, one can perceive the outlines of a discernible constitutional identity without which contemporary constitutional developments would be difficult to explain. Much like the "concept of a self whose unity resides in the unity of a narrative which links birth to life to death as narrative beginning to middle to end,"[13] there are national narratives within which the struggle to achieve unity provides coherence and integrity to the constitutional project. In Poland's case this narrative helps supply the inner resources to sustain the commitment to constitutional democracy; elsewhere, as in the case of South Africa's indigenous rights tradition, it provides a constructive, if surprising, backdrop for

10. Alasdair MacIntyre, *After Virtue: A Study in Moral Theory* (Notre Dame: University of Notre Dame Press, 1981), 200.

11. Ibid., 209.

12. For a good discussion see Mark Brzezinski, *The Struggle for Constitutionalism in Poland* (New York: St. Antony's, 2000), 206.

13. MacIntyre, *After Virtue,* 194.

launching an innovative and ambitious design for rights enforcement.[14] "Viewed in context, textually and historically," wrote Justice Kriegler in an early and important case for the new South African Supreme Court, "the fundamental rights and freedoms have a poignancy and depth of meaning not echoed in any other national constitution I have seen. . . . [O]ur Constitution is unique in its origins, concepts and aspirations."[15]

In other words, the South African Constitution has an identity of its own. How is it known? By its beginning ("origins"), its middle ("concepts"), and its end ("aspirations"), understood within the unity of a narrative ("viewed in context . . . historically"). A constitution may thus be likened to a human life, which of course requires that we settle on an approach to understanding the latter that can illuminate the former. For this I rely on MacIntyre's theory of the unity of a human life, as famously explicated in his *After Virtue*. One need not share the controversial critique of modernity that animates much of that work to develop insights applicable to important constitutional questions relating to identity. But first I need to situate the argument within some very old issues concerning the nature of the individual.

The philosopher Kwame Anthony Appiah has described two approaches to individuality with suggestive possibilities for the task at hand. The first, deriving from romanticism, emphasizes the idea of authenticity and argues that identity is fundamentally concerned with discovery, that the "meaning of one's life is already there, waiting to be found."[16] In contrast, what Appiah refers to as the existentialist account stresses invention and the view that "existence precedes essence," that

14. There is an interesting discussion of how the first claim for a justiciable bill of rights emerged out of the "bantustan" system in Heinz Klug, *Constituting Democracy: Law, Globalism and South Africa's Political Reconstruction* (Cambridge: Cambridge University Press, 2000), 75. As in the case of Poland and other nations transitioning from authoritarian to democratic rule, these analyses that rely on an earlier tradition and experience to account for a regime of newly constituted rights should be supplemented by more strategically oriented explanations that situate the adoption of mechanisms for rights enforcement in the calculations of threatened political and economic elites. See especially Ran Hirschl, *Towards Juristocracy* (Cambridge, MA: Harvard University Press, 2004).

15. DuPlessis v. DeKlerk, 3 SA 850 (1996).

16. Kwame Anthony Appiah, *The Ethics of Identity* (Princeton, NJ: Princeton University Press, 2005), 17.

individuality is basically volitional, a function of deciding for oneself how one wishes to live one's life.[17] Or as MacIntyre had earlier put it, "From the standpoint of individualism I am what I myself choose to be."[18]

Appiah argues that both of these understandings are not quite right. The authenticity approach, in holding that our individualities are essentially determined by our natures, goes too far in excluding creativity from the making of a self. On the other hand, the existential approach overstates the role of creativity, resulting in a decontextualization of individuality, which is to say, a fundamentally flawed understanding of identity construction as a process involving no "response to facts outside oneself, [to] things that are beyond one's own choices."[19] Not surprisingly, Appiah prefers a middle position, which he finds best articulated in the writings of John Stuart Mill, and to a lesser extent in Charles Taylor. In Mill's view, man "has, to a certain extent, a power to alter his character." Thus, "His character is formed by his circumstances (including among these his particular organization); but his desire to mould it in a particular way, is one of those circumstances, and by no means one of the least influential."[20] Taylor echoes this view with a somewhat greater emphasis on external circumstance: "I can define my identity only against the background of things that matter. But to bracket out history, nature, society, the demands of solidarity, everything but what I find in myself, would be to eliminate all candidates for what matters."[21]

Appiah's conclusion is very much in the spirit of MacIntyre: "To create a life is to create a life out of the materials that history has given

17. Ibid.

18. MacIntyre, *After Virtue,* 205.

19. Appiah, *The Ethics of Identity,* 18. It is worth considering this balanced view against that of Norbert Wiley, who appears to accept both internally developed and externally imposed identities without the need to reach accommodation between them. See Norbert Wiley, "The Politics of Identity in American History," in Craig Calhoun, ed., *Social Theory and the Politics of Identity* (Oxford: Blackwell, 1994), 130.

20. Quoted in Appiah, *The Ethics of Identity,* 17.

21. Quoted in Ibid., 18. H. Patrick Glenn makes a similar point in his consideration of tradition and identity: "Concern with identity arises from external contact; identity is then constructed by explicit or implicit opposition. The other becomes essential in the process of self-understanding. H. Patrick Glenn, *Legal Traditions of the World* (Oxford: Oxford University Press, 2000), 31.

you."[22] For MacIntyre, "We enter upon a stage which we did not design and we find ourselves part of an action that was not of our making."[23] It is an illusion to think that personal identity can be abstracted from the larger historical narrative of which it is a part, and so too with constitutions. MacIntyre was critical of the classical empiricist accounts of identity in John Locke and David Hume that were overly dependent on psychological states or events.[24] Much of the debate in the seventeenth century had centered on the role of consciousness in personal identity, which in Locke was, controversially, all that mattered. It was this that accounted for "the unity of one continued life"; stated otherwise, a person's accumulated memories *constitute* an individual as a person. For Hume and Thomas Reid, we get different understandings of the significance of consciousness or memory in establishing identity (the latter was particularly critical of Locke's views), but the larger point of agreement was the requirement, in Reid's words, of "an uninterrupted continuance of existence." "Identity in general I take to be a relation between a thing which is known to exist at one time, and a thing which is known to have existed at another time."[25]

All well and good, we might say, but as critical as the consciousness of the individual is, to be intelligible as a mark of identity it needs to be situated within a larger historical setting. In the above formulation an identity is inscribed in a personal history of what we know of someone at different points in time. But for MacIntyre the story of a life has a broader sweep than what is included within the span of a lifetime. "I am born with a past; and to try to cut myself off from that past, in the individualist mode, is to deform my present relationships. The possession of an historical identity and the possession of a social identity coincide."[26] But

22. Appiah, *The Ethics of Identity,* 19. As Appiah, following Taylor, observes, "[B]eginning in infancy [I am] in dialogue with other people's understandings of who I am that I develop a conception of my own identity" (ibid., 20). On this point, at least, there seems little reason to think that moving from the personal to the constitutional would not entail a similar consequence with regard to the phenomenon of identity.

23. MacIntyre, *After Virtue,* 199.

24. Ibid., 202.

25. *Works of Thomas Reid—Vol. II* (Charlestown, MA: Samuel Etheridge, 1814), 339.

26. MacIntyre, *After Virtue,* 205.

does the past render identity so beholden to the historical narrative to which it is tethered as to leave it without agency, without the means of altering or transcending the story line within which it is a character?

This of course is a question with considerable implications for constitutional identity, where the balance between organic and agency-driven development looms large in critical constitutional calculations of design and growth, perhaps nowhere more pointedly than in episodes of dramatic regime transformation. The Japanese Constitution, for example, has often been perceived as an alien transplant, but a more accurate account emerges from a considered assessment of that nation's complex history. "The struggle between . . . competing visions of the State and the individual arose at the founding of the modern Japanese State, the so-called Meiji Revolution, and the revolution remains unfinished. Far from being brought by the American occupying forces, notions of democracy and human rights had been percolating inside Japan for generations, growing out of both Confucian and Western sources."[27] General Douglas MacArthur's belief that American governing principles and institutions were "fit for all peoples everywhere" drove the process of constitutional imposition in Japan, but how much of the subsequent success of that venture resulted from the rightness of his vision or the fact that, as one study of Japanese political reconstruction contends, the "commitment to democratic constitutionalism . . . rested on deep cultural foundations"?[28]

27. Sylvia Brown Hamano, "Incomplete Revolutions and Not so Alien Transplants: The Japanese Constitution and Human Rights," 1 *University of Pennsylvania Journal of Constitutional Law* 415 (1999), 419. www.law.upenn.edu/conlaw/issues/vol1/num3/hammo .htm, 2. Hamano argues "the period from the founding of the State in 1868 until 1945 was far from harmonious" (ibid., 421). Or in the framework of this study, constitutional identity emerged from the cauldron of this disharmony.

28. Ray A. Moore and Donald L. Robinson, *Partners for Democracy: Crafting the New Japanese State under MacArthur* (Oxford: Oxford University Press, 2002), 14, 34. In relation to this exercise, Walter Murphy writes, "[T]o maximize the constitutional enterprise's chances, founders must take their past into account. They cannot, at will, erase myths and memories. . . . To minimize trauma, the language of the new or revised institutions and aspirations must demonstrate respect for much of what the society has historically cherished. Walter Murphy, *Constitutional Democracy* (Baltimore: Johns Hopkins University Press, 2007), 201.

The same question may be asked of societies whose foundations are more discordant, for example, India, where the imposition of Anglo-Saxon law over an extended period of time by a British administration resolutely committed to the moral superiority and transferability of its governing ideas confronted an indigenous cultural and legal tradition of markedly dissimilar convictions. How are we to understand the remarkable achievement of Indian constitutional democracy: as the welcome, if surprising, outgrowth of a conflicted inheritance; as the proof that what is inherited, no matter its significance for personal identity, is not an inevitable constraint in shaping a constitutional identity; or, as Lloyd and Susanne Rudolph suggest, as evidence that when the conflicting strands of a divided inheritance engage one another dialectically rather than dichotomously, good things can happen?[29]

To make the leap from the personal to the political, consider again Edmund Burke, the most eloquent and persistent critic of British imperialism in India.[30] Like MacIntyre, who, as we will see, found Burke wanting in important respects, the eighteenth-century statesman and philosopher saw constitutions as embodiments of unique histories and circumstances. As someone totally consumed by the political debates of his time, Burke did not participate in the philosophical debates over personal identity that raged among his contemporaries, notably David Hume and Thomas Reid, both of whom were struggling with the legacy of empiricism bequeathed to them by Locke from the previous century. Yet in Burke's account of the prescriptive constitution one sees how his

29. Lloyd I. Rudolph and Susanne Hoeber Rudolph, *The Modernity of Tradition* (Chicago: University of Chicago Press, 1967), 10. An interesting variation on the problem of constitutional identity and external imposition is playing out in the politics of European integration. As Bruce Ackerman points out, "The basic legal order of the European Union . . . has neither originated in a decision made by its citizens, nor is attributed to them. . . . This is not an act of self-determination but of external determination." Quoted in J. H. H. Weiler, "On the Power of the Word: Europe's Constitutional Iconography," 3 *International Journal of Constitutional Law* 173 (2005), 207.

30. See especially Uday Singh Mehta, *Liberalism and Empire: A Study in Nineteenth-Century British Liberal Thought* (Chicago: University of Chicago Press, 1999). "None of the well-known liberals or socialists of the nineteenth century expresses anything like Burke's indignation and searching critique of the empire" (ibid., 155).

concerns fit well within the terms of those debates, and also how his ideas, even when problematic, help to clarify the question of identity.

In Burke's thought, the nation was a "moral essence" and, in the apt phrase of one of his interpreters, "a cultural personality in time."[31] "Against the images of an age that saw the constitution as a formal and explicit founding contract, Burke sets the image of a constitution as that imperfectly known order—an order that none directly intends—that is set up between people as they live together."[32] At the core of his theory of the constitution was, as we saw in the previous chapter, the principle of inheritance, more familiarly known as *prescription*.[33] Again, "[A] nation is not an idea of local extent, but is an idea of continuity, which extends in time as well as in numbers, and in space. . . . [It] is a deliberate election of ages and generations; it is a Constitution . . . made by the peculiar circumstances, occasions, tempers, dispositions, and moral, civil, and social habitudes of the people that disclose themselves only in a long space of time."[34] Or as framed by the legal philosopher Michael J. Perry in regard to the American Constitution, "Both as a description of our practice and as a prescription for the continuance of the practice, the Constitution also consists of premises that, whether or not any genera-

31. Gerald W. Chapman, *Edmund Burke and the Practical Imagination* (Cambridge, MA: Harvard University Press, 1967), 90.

32. Garrett Barden, "Discovering a Constitution," in Tim Murphy and Patrick Twomey, eds., *Ireland's Evolving Constitution 1937–1997* (London: Hart, 1998), 3.

33. The prescriptive constitution has been the subject of insightful scholarly treatment. See in particular, Francis P. Canavan, *The Political Reason of Edmund Burke* (Durham, NC: Duke University Press, 1960); Chapman, *Edmund Burke*; and Michael Freedman, *Edmund Burke and the Critique of Political Radicalism* (Chicago: University of Chicago Press, 1980).

34. Edmund Burke, "Speech On a Motion Made in the House of Commons, the 7th of May 1782, for a Committee to Inquire into the State of the Representation of the Commons in Parliament," in David Bromwich, ed., *On Empire, Liberty, and Reform* (New Haven, CT: Yale University Press, 2000), 274. Or as Laurence Tribe, whatever his skepticism concerning the concept of constitutional identity, eloquently points out: "To be free is not simply to follow our ever-changing wants wherever they might lead. . . . [T]o make . . . choices without losing the thread of continuity that integrates us over time and imports a sense of our wholeness in history, we must be able to . . . choose in terms of commitments we have made." Laurence Tribe, "Ways Not to Think about Plastic Trees: New Foundations for Environmental Law," 83 *Yale Law Journal* 1315, 1326–1327 (1974).

tion of "We the People" meant to establish them in the Constitution . . . have become such fixed and widely affirmed and relied upon (by us the people of the United States now living) features of the life of our political community that they are, for us, constitutional bedrock—premises that have, in that sense, achieved a virtual constitutional status, that has become a part of our fundamental law, the law constitutive of ourselves as a political community of a certain sort."[35]

These sentiments are echoed in the argument cited by Justice Kennedy from *Federalist 49,* in which Madison wrote of the new American regime's need to achieve a "requisite stability" against a too-frequent appeal to the people for constitutional change. Like Burke, he calculated the benefits of consistency in terms of winning over the "prejudices of the community," so as not to "deprive the government of that veneration which time bestows on every thing."[36] It was, after all, only in "a nation of philosophers" that "[a] reverence for the laws would be sufficiently inculcated by the voice of an enlightened reason." Implicit in Madison's calculation is the idea that a constitution, however reasonable and clear in its articulation of rules and principles, can only succeed in translating word into deed (and thereby establish a discernible identity) if fundamental continuity in basic law and actual constitutional practice are seen as two sides of the same coin.[37]

As the key to constitutional identity, prescription represents continuity, what endures through the changes occurring within the natural progression of any society. Burke's critique of the British in India is premised

35. Michael J. Perry, "What Is 'the Constitution'? (and Other Fundamental Questions)," in Larry Alexander, ed., *Constitutionalism: Philosophical Foundations* (Cambridge: Cambridge University Press, 1998), 107.

36. *Federalist 49* (Madison) in Clinton Rossiter, ed., *The Federalist Papers* (New York: Mentor, 1961), 314.

37. Continuity, then, is a necessary, but not sufficient condition for establishing a viable basis for a genuine identity. That the guardians of the Soviet constitution were in a position to maintain its continuity, and to keep the document essentially the same over the many decades of its existence, did not mean that it represented anything more than a cruel, if transparent, hoax in the lives of the Soviet people. The constitution was a decidedly insignificant presence in the actions of citizens and state and the relations between the two. The durability of the regime—or in the language of personal identity, its survival—did not hinge on the polity's reaching a particular level of constitutional legitimacy.

on the same assumptions that formed his better-known reflections on the excesses of the French Revolution. In Uday Mehta's apt comparison, "[F]or Burke, the British Empire, especially in India, was nothing less than a revolution, with all the psychological naïveté and theoretical arrogance that he associated with the revolution in France."[38] The collective memories that persist as part of the cultural personality of a nation form the core of that identity, which, rather than issuing from acts of abstract reason, is developed over time, evolving in tandem with the habits and experiences of the body politic. This places severe limits on change, particularly so for the essentials of constitutional identity. Burke often distinguished between reform (healthy) and innovation (problematic), the latter having more to do with change that is disconnected from principles engrained in the prescriptive constitution.

But suppose it is innovation that is in fact required. A theory of constitutional identity that cannot account for the more radical departures from constitutional continuity is, as suggested in Chapter 2, an incomplete theory.[39] Again, MacIntyre is instructive. Indeed, just at the point in his argument when he appears most Burkean—invoking the historical narrative, the importance of tradition, and the constraints of inheritance—he turns on Burke with surprising vehemence, saying, "[W]hen a tradition becomes Burkean, it is always dying or dead."[40] How much distance there really is between the two is contestable, but MacIntyre's reasons for distinguishing his views on tradition from Burke's infuse the concept of identity with a dynamic quality that broadens its applicability to the constitutional experience.

These reasons center on tradition itself, or with reference to Burke, the unfortunate contrast between conflict and stability. "[T]radition," as

38. Mehta, *Liberalism and Empire,* 159.

39. What the Israeli sociologist Baruch Kimmerling wrote about the identities that make up a nation's social order can be said of its constitutional identity as well: "Collective identities constitute the most basic components of any social order and are products of culture, but they are not fixed social and political variables. They are flexible, oscillating, and changeable, sometimes dramatically and visibly, other times subtly and gradually. They include a wide range of different identities that individuals and collectivities hold simultaneously." Baruch Kimmerling, *Clash of Identities: Explorations in Israeli and Palestinian Societies* (New York: Columbia University Press, 2008), 271.

40. MacIntyre, *After Virtue,* 206.

Justice John Marshall Harlan II wrote, "is a living thing."[41] The same point is echoed by MacIntyre, "[W]hen a tradition is in good order it is always partially constituted by an argument about the goods the pursuit of which gives to that tradition its particular point and purpose."[42] Vital traditions are those that "embody continuities of conflict."[43] As opposed to Burke's dying traditions, "A living tradition is . . . an historically extended, socially embodied argument, and an argument precisely in part about the goods which constitute that tradition. . . . [A]n adequate sense of tradition manifests itself in a grasp of those future possibilities which the past has made available to the present."[44] Traditions are part of the historical narrative that is the necessary antecedent to the unity of a human life, but it is an incomplete story that must be advanced by carriers of these traditions, whose disagreements about their import leaves the future as indeterminate as the meaning of the past is debatable.[45]

What is the significance of this correction for the prescriptive constitution? For Burke, prescription is "a presumption in favour of any settled scheme of Government against any untried project. . . ."[46] Within the framework of Appiah's alternative visions of identity, one expects to find

41. Poe v. Ullman, 367 U.S. 497 (1961), 542.

42. MacIntyre, *After Virtue,* 206. For a thoughtful application of MacIntyre's thinking to the American constitutional tradition see H. Jefferson Powell, *The Moral Tradition of American Constitutionalism* (Durham, NC: Duke University Press, 1993). "A tradition is . . . historical not merely in the sense of being temporally extended but more fundamentally in that it is constituted by an ongoing argument in which its fundamental agreements are expressed, defined, and revised" (ibid., 24).

43. MacIntyre, *After Virtue,* 206. For a provocative and erudite discussion of tradition as a non-static form of social order, see Glenn, *Legal Traditions,* 21–25.

44. MacIntyre, *After Virtue,* 207. Elsewhere MacIntyre elaborated on his critique of Burke: "Burke was . . . an agent of positive harm. For Burke ascribed to traditions in good order, the order he supposed of following nature, 'wisdom without reflection.'" Alasdair MacIntyre, *Whose Justice? Which Rationality?* (Notre Dame, IN: University of Notre Dame Press, 1988), 353.

45. Peter James Stanlis presents Burke quite differently on this question. Contrary to MacIntyre, Stanlis argues that Burke "favored that harmony of discordant powers that tested ideas through an incessant and vigorous opposition . . . [thus he] was by temperament a man who would not regard the ultimate test of a philosophy that it be a totally unified system." Peter James Stanlis, *Edmund Burke: The Enlightenment and Revolution* (New Brunswick, NJ: Transaction Publishers, 1991), 97.

46. Burke, "Speech On a Motion," 274.

Burke among the partisans of discovery, and not surprisingly he has been so interpreted.[47] "Constitutions are to be discovered, that is, the constitution that people have given themselves in their interaction with one another is to be discovered. . . . One may think of [the constitution] not as the attempt to found and establish the polity but as the attempt to discover and express the characteristics of the polity that already exists."[48] The flip side of this, of course, is suspicion (or hostility, as in Burke's scathing condemnation of French political creativity) of efforts to invent the essentials of constitutional identity out of the building blocks of theoretical materials.

A "presumption" in favor of settled practice is just that—a presumption. To the extent that prescription is critical for establishing the core of constitutional identity, it should allow for the possibility that what is settled is also mutable. Burke, however, provides an insubstantial foundation for challenging such presumptions, for resisting settled practice when the need exists to accommodate course corrections in the path of constitutional identity. In MacIntyre's critique, Burke's conception of tradition is lacking in adversarial vitality; the weight of habit and routine represents continuity without conflict; constitutional identity comes to be identified with, and rigidified in, the dominant will in the community. As Christopher Eisgruber asks, "Why should it matter whether a claimed constitutional right has solid foundations in tradition? Traditional practices may, after all, be exquisitely unjust."[49] Slavery in the

47. "By viewing place and history as constitutive of human identity, Burke takes identity as something partially, though importantly, given and hence not wholly an artifice of individual choice." Mehta, *Liberalism and Empire,* 161. To be sure, this view does not rest wholly on the side of discovery.

48. Barden, "Discovering a Constitution," 6–7. Surprisingly, Tom Paine, the un-Burke, expressed similar sentiments: "A constitution is a thing *antecedent* to a government." Quoted in Charles McIlwain, *Constitutionalism: Ancient and Modern* (Ithaca, NY: Cornell University Press, 1966), 2. What Anthony D. Smith has written in regard to national identity applies as well to constitutional identity: "[T]he role of 'invention' and 'construction' in the formation of national identity varies considerably depending in part on the pre-existing local ethnic configuration." Anthony D. Smith, *National Identity* (Reno: University of Nevada Press, 1991), 101.

49. Christopher L. Eisgruber, *Constitutional Self-Government* (Cambridge, MA: Harvard University Press, 2001).

United States, for example, may have produced a body of settled law, but its incompatibility with other parts of the American historical narrative—formal and informal—rendered its status as a constitutionally sanctioned inheritance fatally suspect. The argument over its presumptive validity was a way of addressing the question of whether the peculiar institution had any purchase in a fair account of American constitutional identity. But that argument required a reasoned critique rooted in the tradition that could transcend "through criticism and invention the limitations of what had hitherto been reasoned in that tradition."[50] Or as MacIntyre has put it, "A tradition becomes mature just insofar as its adherents confront and find a rational way through or around those encounters with radically different and incompatible positions. . . ."[51]

One's inheritance provides a "moral starting point" that gives a life "its own moral particularity."[52] But the self does not have to accept the moral limitations of the particularity that it has acquired through its historical connections. "Without those moral particularities to begin from there would never be anywhere to begin; but it is in moving forward from such particularity that the search for the good, for the universal, consists."[53] Yet particularity can never be simply left behind. As Julie Mostov has observed, "Individuals have fluid, multiple, and overlapping identities, which are not always in harmony, but that do not necessarily inhibit them from holding consistent views, pursuing coherent interests, making and keeping commitments, and having long-lasting affiliations or allegiances."[54] At the constitutional level, identity is often shaped

50. MacIntyre, *After Virtue,* 206. H. Patrick Glenn's extended study of world traditions has led him to a similar conclusion. Internal traditions "are forms of internal dialogue or argument, known so long that they have become identifiable by name—shorthand references to whole bundles of argument . . . which achieve some form of incorporation into the larger tradition. Even when they contradict the larger tradition they have become in most cases indispensable parts of it, providing correction judged necessary or variation judged unavoidable." Glenn, *Legal Traditions,* 319.

51. MacIntyre, *Whose Justice?* 327

52. MacIntyre, *After Virtue,* 205.

53. Ibid., 205.

54. Julie Mostov, "Soft Borders and Transnational Citizens," in Seyla Benhabib, Ian Shapiro, and Danilo Petranovic, *Identities, Affiliations, and Allegiances* (Leiden: Cambridge University Press, 2007), 139.

through the creative interaction between divergent strands within an extant tradition; whatever ultimate convergence to universal norms of constitutionalism emerges will continue to bear the imprint in practice of distinctive primary sources.[55] The disharmonic constitutional self embodies the specific components of an identity that evolves as these elements play off against each other within the circumscribed parameters of the national historical narrative. As the outlines of a "generic constitutional law—a skeletal body of constitutional theory, practice, and doctrine that belongs uniquely to no particular jurisdiction"[56]—becomes increasingly visible in a rapidly globalizing world order, new adaptations in constitutional identity will result from the disharmonic interplay of national and international experience.[57]

Subsequent chapters offer specific illustrations of these somewhat abstract points. For example, a satisfactory account of Israeli constitutional identity must address how the competing strands in the political tradition of that society contest against the backdrop of intersecting historical narratives involving two peoples and an international community very much implicated in the country's domestic tribulations. Upholding "the

55. On this point see as well, Michael Kenny, *The Politics of Identity* (Cambridge: Polity, 2004). "Neither identities nor cultures are coherent wholes that can be passed unaltered across time and space. . . . [B]oth are better seen as internally differentiated products of many different individual interactions and intentions" (ibid., 101).

56. David S. Law, "Generic Constitutional Law," 89 *Minnesota Law Review* (2005), 659. Consider, too, Paul Kahn's observation: "It would be too much to say of comparative constitutionalists that their ambition is to find the hidden science of constitutionalism that should unite all liberal constitutions as varieties on a common theme—but it would not be exaggerating all that much." Paul W. Kahn, "Comparative Constitutionalism in a New Key," *Michigan Law Review* (2003), 2684.

57. Jeffrey Goldsworthy has sketched the attributes of a "common model of liberal democratic constitutionalism." Jeffrey Goldsworthy, "Questioning the Migration of Constitutional Ideas: Rights, Constitutionalism, and the Limits of Convergence," in Sujit Choudhry, ed., *The Migration of Constitutional Ideas* (Cambridge: Cambridge University Press, 2006), 116. These include democratic elections, guarantees of individual rights, an independent judiciary with review authority, and special procedures for amending the constitution. "[T]hese elements are . . . unspecific, and capable of being implemented in so many different ways . . ." (ibid., 119). Or, we might say, convergence (or not) with the common model will vary in accordance with the particular constitutional culture of a given polity, and the subsequent evolution of that nation's constitutional identity will reflect in part the dynamics of local—universal interaction.

values of Israel as a Jewish and democratic state," as is required under the Basic Laws, entails multiple dialogic interactions, with the Supreme Court serving as the main (but not exclusive) recipient "of core collective identity questions."[58] What these values mean will reflect the particularities of the Israeli experience, but they will also incorporate universalist aspirations that, while addressing the needs of specific interests and elites within the society, will also become a part of the polity's evolving constitutional identity. The uniqueness of the Israeli situation may mean that the various disharmonies that make up the constitutional reality of the state play out in exceptional ways, but polities constituted very differently will experience versions involving comparable developmental patterns. Whether it is Canadian judges seeking to clarify their Constitution's Section 1 standard of a "free and democratic society" by engaging with what other societies have concluded in reference to these terms; or Irish judges (and legislators) pursuing strategies for navigating the turbulent waters of the secular/sectarian divide over the constitutionally sacrosanct protections for the family, all the while anticipating the inevitable encounters with European family and privacy law jurisprudence; the quest for a compelling unity will be the common preoccupation of all who are concerned with the problem of constitutional identity.

The Fundaments of Identity

To bring together the key elements in these reflections on constitutional identity, consider three interrelated thematic focal points: aspirational content, dialogical articulation, and generic/local balancing. Framing them are the two ubiquitous ideas that drive the dynamic of constitutional identity: prescription and disharmony. The first has a verb form that can mean either *to recommend* or *to impose.* One way to interpret the MacIntyre critique of Burke is to see it as an effort to soften the determinative power of prescription by moving it away from imposition toward recommendation, stopping somewhat short of the latter. Thus the past cannot be excised from the developmental path of constitutional identity, but it need

58. Ran Hirschl, "Constitutional Courts vs. Religious Fundamentalism: Three Middle Eastern Tales," 82 *Texas Law Review* 1819, 1858 (2004).

not establish its precise direction. It is the second idea—disharmony—that infuses an element of uncertainty into the future course of constitutional identity and gives it its dynamic quality.

Aspirational Content

The seventeenth- and eighteenth-century philosophers maintained that continuity in consciousness is the key to establishing the identity of a person. One of the difficulties, however, in moving from the personal to the political is that nations, more so than individuals, have multiple and conflicting self-understandings. How are we to talk about a nation's constitutional identity if, within "its constitution and constitutional traditions, 'who we are' is often—perhaps always—contestable and actively contested."[59] This question will of course resonate in many places, although one need go no further than the United States where, as Mark Graber reminds us, "Slavery was embedded in a way of life that most Southerners and some Northerners thought intrinsically valuable and expressive of the highest constitutional aspirations."[60]

That they so believed may call into question the significance of aspiration as a constitutionally viable concept. Graber, for instance, finds that the presence of competing aspirational commitments provides dubious interpretive standing for the idea. "Racist and other ascriptive ideologies are as rooted in the American political tradition as liberal, democratic, and republican ideals."[61] To anoint one ideal over another—as one would by assigning it special meaning in distinguishing constitutional identity—is an arbitrary intrusion into a constitutional process which, properly conceived, should not be identified with a specific aspirational agenda. "Constitutionalism . . . mediates the controversies that arise among citizens who hold clashing political aspirations."[62]

59. Mark Tushnet, "Some Reflections on Method in Comparative Constitutional Law," in Choudhry, *Migration of Constitutional Ideas,* 82.

60. Mark A. Graber, *Dred Scott and the Problem of Constitutional Evil* (Cambridge: Cambridge University Press, 2006), 83.

61. Ibid., 78.

62. Ibid., 2.

The problem with this view is that it makes an erroneous inference from the presence of a disharmonic constitutional tradition. It assumes that a conflicted constitutional tradition enables all sides to the conflict to make a plausible claim to speak *for* the constitution. But in his critique of the *Dred Scott* decision, Abraham Lincoln disagreed, articulating a theory of aspiration in which eighteenth-century principles of natural right were at the core of constitutional meaning and therewith a standard for evaluating the work of the Court.[63] Chief Justice Roger Taney had, in Lincoln's estimation, denuded the Declaration of any constitutive significance by transforming it into a positivist document of no moral consequence. But for its signers, "They meant simply to declare the *right* [to human equality], so that the *enforcement* of it might follow as fast as circumstances should permit."[64] The failure to achieve unity of purpose was less an indication that the aspiration to human equality was of no constitutive meaning than it was evidence for the inability of many of the framers immediately to solidify its content within the folds of the constitutional identity they were shaping. In declaring that people of African descent should not expect enforcement of a right to which they were ascriptively excluded, Taney had failed to understand how the aspirations of the Constitution defined Americans as a people, and thus his ruling obligated other actors—principally Congress—to mount a political challenge to it.[65] As I argue later, a constitution of aspiration is

63. I pursue this Lincolnian theory in *The Supreme Court and the Decline of Constitutional Aspiration* (Totowa, NJ: Rowman & Littlefield, 1986). Rogers Smith, whose work in important ways complements Graber's argument, nevertheless gets it right when he says, "[F]ew can seriously contend that the nation would have been better off if Lincoln had agreed that slavery was a vital expression of an authoritative vision of America as a white man's nation instead of insisting that it was hostile to American commitments to liberty." Rogers Smith, *Civic Ideals* (New Haven, CT: Yale University Press, 1994), 502.

64. Abraham Lincoln, *The Collected Works of Abraham Lincoln,* ed. Roy Basler (New Brunswick, NJ: Rutgers University Press, 1953), Vol. 2, 406.

65. Taney's failure was also a failure of textualism. As Garrett Barden has said in discussing the Burkean constitution, "[A] written constitution, being a linguistic instrument, cannot but presuppose an entire language and operative background of political aspirations, ideas and agreements that cannot be made totally clear." Garrett Barden, "Discovering a Constitution," 4. Taney's confidence that the passages he cited in the Constitution accommodating slavery cinched his case gave inadequate attention to the context within which

incompatible with the idea that the Supreme Court exercises an interpretive monopoly over the document.

The American Constitution's Preamble affirms that the document is about several things, among them establishing justice for ourselves and our posterity. One way to understand this commitment is to see it in aspirational terms; thus constitutional fulfillment can be measured and assessed in accordance with the progressive achievement of goals identified by constitutional actors. For some, these goals are the ones inscribed in the Declaration of Independence, which Martin Luther King Jr., following Lincoln, described as "a promissory note to which every American was to fall heir."[66] In this account, which recalls similar sentiments by Frederick Douglass a century earlier, *We the People* was unable (and in many cases unwilling) contemporaneously to extend the justice of the Constitution to all those who fell under its sway, but the posterity of the excluded would in due course see their promised constitutional entitlement fulfilled with or without the help of the Court. The Constitution is both a legal code and a codification of certain ideals that, according to this view, are historically tethered to moments of constitutional framing and subsequent revision.[67]

Constitutions provide structures to mediate among conflicting political aspirations, but that they must or can be neutral with respect to them does not necessarily follow. As Walter Murphy notes, "When . . . a nation has no history of harmonious civil life under free government and groups are set against groups, it is essential that the constitutional charter remind, or even instruct, the people and their officials why they have come together to try to form a national community."[68] There are constraints, however, on the options available to framers. "Every society has

---

a written constitution develops and becomes intelligible. Even the infamous 3/5 clause may be interpreted consistent with Lincoln's aspirational perspective.

66. Martin Luther King Jr., "I Have a Dream," speech delivered in Washington DC, August 28, 1963.

67. "[A] written constitution requires some awareness of its heritage and tradition; the polity's evolving aspirations will be deemed legitimate only if they account for the promises that were made at earlier moments in time." Beau Breslin, *From Worlds to Words* (Baltimore: Johns Hopkins University Press, 2009), 49.

68. Murphy, *Constitutional Democracy,* 198.

its own values, traditions, and customs. Leaders who try to transform a people operate under conditions of restricted choice. The text's values and aspirations must build on some of the existing culture's norms and will likely have to repudiate others."[69]

All of this building and repudiating, incorporating and negating, is consistent with the primacy of particular aspirations within an ongoing dynamic of disharmonic contestation. This contestation can result in the further legitimation and entrenchment of the aspirations—for example, the adoption of the post–Civil War amendments—or it can lead to their delegitimation and erosion in the name of alternative aspirations that are intelligible in light of the broader historical narrative that sustains both. Radical constitutional transformation may be conceptualized as the replacement of one aspirational agenda for another, an ascendance—for example, the adoption of the post-War German Basic Law, the adoption of the new South African Constitution—that invariably retains much from constitutional antecedents in a given nation's prescriptive constitution.

Dialogical Articulation

Charles Taylor, much like MacIntyre, has proposed that we understand identity as an interactive process in which a person develops a self in

69. Ibid., 199. For Murphy, these aspirations serve to reconstitute a people and provide them with a common creed. Constitutional theorists must consider the degree to which these aspirations rely on the past as opposed to a rejection of that past. Bruce Ackerman, *The Future of Liberal Revolution* (New Haven, CT: Yale University Press, 1992). Frederick Schauer, emphasizing the close relationship between constitutions and national identity, views the making of a constitution as a critical step in the establishment of independence. While this means relying on indigenous constitutional sources, to what degree they should also be independent from past practices is not entirely clear. Frederick Schauer, "On the Migration of Constitutional Ideas," 37 *Connecticut Law Review* 907 (2005). Michel Rosenfeld argues that "Constitution making involves an act of negation, a break with a preconstitutional past." Michel Rosenfeld, "The European Treaty-Constitution and Constitutional Identity: A View from America, 3 *International Journal of Constitutional Law* 316 (2005), 318. Rosenfeld contends that the construction of a constitutional identity usually entails a conscious act of negation coupled with unconscious acts of incorporation from the past. "[B]oth negation and reincorporation are essential for a constitution to materialize in form and substance" (ibid., 320).

response to an environment consisting of religion, state, family and so on.[70] "My own identity crucially depends on my dialogical relation with others."[71] The dialogical view also functions in the constitutional arena, although a contingent aspect, not present in the personal domain, is distinctive to the identity of a constitution.[72] In practice the dialogical enterprise comprises interpretive and political activity occurring in courts, legislatures, and other public and private domains.[73] Such activity will be most evident where the responsibility for constitutional development is not clearly identified with the judiciary; where, that is, the notion of a court as principal shaper and articulator of constitutional identity is not

70. Taylor has expressed his disagreements with MacIntyre, but on the question of most concern here—the latter's dialogical understanding of tradition—he has come to his defense: "[MacIntyre's] concept of a tradition is actually close to the reality, and not the caricature that is bandied about in rationalist thought. Traditions, including those of practices with their internal goods, are the site of ongoing debates, internal revisions, critical turns, and so on." Charles Taylor, "Justice after Virtue," in John Horton and Susan Mendus, eds., *After Virtue: Critical Perspectives on the Work of Alasdair MacIntyre* (Notre Dame, IN: University of Notre Dame Press, 1994), 34.

71. Charles Taylor, *The Ethics of Authenticity* (Cambridge, MA: Harvard University Press, 1991), 48.

72. As Frederick Schauer points out, "[A] nation that is not perceived—by itself and others—as having made its own constitution is likely perceived as being for that reason just so much less independent and less mature a country." Schauer, "Migration of Constitutional Ideas," 912. In philosophic terms, a person may be said to have an identity even in the absence of widespread agreement on what exactly it is. One might not be true to that identity in how one chooses to present oneself to others, but the resulting misperceptions are only relevant if their cause is a direct extension of who that person is. Within the philosophical literature this is a subject of some controversy. In their historical overview of Western theorizing about personal identity, Raymond Martin and John Barresi distinguish between an *intrinsic* relations view and an *extrinsic* relations view. In the first, or Lockean, perspective, "what determines whether a person at one time and one at another are the same person is how the two are physically and/or psychologically related to *each other*." In the more recent account, "what determines whether a person at one time and one at another are the same person is not just how the two are physically and/or psychologically related to *each other*, but how they are related to everything else—especially *everybody* else." Raymond Martin and John Barresi, eds., *Personal Identity* (Oxford: Blackwell, 2003), 1.

73. As William Harris argues, "A constitutional order both creates the larger public identity that is to be recognized and constructs the conditions by which those who have their political life through it come to realize its preexistence as something they are established as identifiable entities to have made." William Harris, *The Interpretable Constitution* (Baltimore: Johns Hopkins University Press, 1993), 177.

reflexively assumed. It will, for example, be more prominently revealed in many European countries where, as Alec Stone-Sweet has shown, practices such as abstract review facilitate greater legislative engagement in the determination of substantive constitutional meanings.[74] Or, as I have demonstrated elsewhere, it will be more obvious in polities—for example, Israel before its "constitutional revolution" established judicial review of legislation as an acceptable practice—where the elaboration by courts of regime aspirations possesses a politically tentative or intermediate status in the decision-making process.[75] Yet when the aspirations of the nation's founding agenda are at an unusually high level of disharmonic equilibrium, achieving a greater unity of constitutional purpose might not follow from institutionally based dialogic engagement. Alternatively, as we see with the Israeli case in Chapter 6, it is not clear that failure to so engage will enhance these prospects.

Pursuing identity along a dialogical path may require reconsideration of the juri-centric model that has long dominated contemporary constitutional theorizing, exemplified in the work of Ronald Dworkin, whose considerable achievements have not, it must be said, flowed from their attention to comparative issues. In this model the judge, idealized in Dworkin's Herculean philosopher-jurist, is guardian and expositor of the moral principles that structure and guide the nation's constitutional development.[76] The Indian legal theorist, Upendra Baxi, has called attention to the limited reach of Dworkin's theory, particularly when applied to the experience of postcolonial constitutionalism.[77] One need

74. Alec Stone-Sweet, *Governing with Judges* (Oxford: Oxford University Press, 2000). Much of the recent literature concerning the Constitution outside of the courts also emphasizes this point. See for example, Mark Tushnet, *Taking the Constitution Away from the Court* (Princeton, NJ: Princeton University Press, 1999); and Larry Kramer, *The People Themselves: Popular Constitutionalism and Judicial Review* (New York: Oxford University Press, 2004).

75. Gary Jeffrey Jacobsohn, *Apple of Gold: Constitutionalism in Israel and the United States* (Princeton, NJ: Princeton University Press, 1993).

76. Ronald Dworkin, *Taking Rights Seriously* (Cambridge: Harvard University Press, 1977), 105–130.

77. Upendra Baxi, "'A Known but an Indifferent Judge': Situating Ronald Dworkin in Contemporary Indian Jurisprudence," 4 *International Journal of Constitutional Law* 557 (2003).

not embrace Baxi's account of constitutional texts as "multidimensional spaces of inscription" to share his concern that "the Dworkin of the Fit and the Dworkin of the One Right Answer" has not convincingly incorporated the untidy realities of disharmonic constitutional traditions into his theory.[78] To be sure, the quest for unity, central to the idea of constitutional identity, is fully compatible with Dworkin's abiding commitment to law as integrity, but realizing that commitment through the exercise of judicial unilateralism is problematic, and perhaps more so in places where a nation's historical narrative remains deeply contested. Think again of *Dred Scott.*

The "republican revival" of the 1980s may offer a more promising approach. To advance a republican conception of politics, its leading theorist, Frank Michelman, defended the "dialogic constitution" as more attuned to the plurality of views he wanted to include in "the debate of the commonwealth."[79] "A constitution cannot retain its claim to republican validity without changing in response to historical change in the people's composition and values, its identity and 'fate as a people.' "[80] Michelman envisions a process of self-revision under "social-dialogic" stimulation, involving "a self whose identity and freedom consist, in part, in its capacity for reflexively critical reconsideration of the ends and commitments that it already has and that makes it who it is."[81]

There is much that is appealing in this account, in particular its accommodation of change. This too is its weakness, as its stance toward tradition effortlessly renders everything negotiable, premised on "the contested re-collection . . . of a fund of public normative references conceived as narratives, analogies, and other professions of commitment."[82] It promises dialogic constitutional activity without a prescriptive constitution. It thereby strips away the preservative function of constitutional identity, leaving its substance vulnerable to the vagaries of imagined

78. Ibid., 579, 574.

79. Frank Michelman, "Law's Republic," 97 *Yale Law Journal* 1493 (1988), reprinted in David Kennedy and William W. Fisher III, eds., *The Canon of American Legal Thought* (Princeton, NJ: Princeton University Press, 2006), 798.

80. Ibid., 808.

81. Ibid., 817.

82. Ibid., 805.

histories. Traditions, in MacIntyre's depiction, embody "continuities of conflict"; the historical narrative of which they are a part contains room for contestation and disagreement, but not for revisionary assaults on the narrative itself. The very idea of conflict that is continuous suggests stability as a predicate for the changes that might flow from dialogic interaction.

In India, for example, there are two powerful claims on constitutional identity, both firmly rooted in centuries of conflict and contestation. Since independence one of these claims—for a secular composite culture nation—has been in ascendance, but the other—for a Hindu nation—has influenced the aspirational content of constitutional identity, and at times posed a distinct threat to the hegemony of the predominant view. The identity that has emerged from this extended discordant chronicle reflects the entrenched realities of both visions; the constitutional text embodies them (by no means equally given one side's effective control of the framing process), as does the history of constitutional construction and interpretation. Along the way there have been efforts to reinvent the past, most notably by Hindu nationalists determined to create a history expunged of the truths that complicate their ethno/religious story.[83] The prescriptive constitution, however, places limits on these inventions, and the process of dialogic interaction ultimately determines the substance of identity.[84] The process will be open to various possibilities, but reconsideration of ends and commitments cannot be boundless and open-ended; the development of a constitutional self must be constrained in its grasp of future possibilities by what "the past has made available to the present."

83. See Romila Thapar, "Secularism, History, and Contemporary Politics in India," in Anuradha Dingwaney Needham and Rajeswari Sunder Rajan, eds., *The Crisis of Secularism in India* (Durham, NC: Duke University Press, 2007).

84. As Thapar, one of India's most distinguished historians, writes, "History retrieves multiple pasts that underlie the pluralities of societies and cultures. This plurality is essential to exploring and advancing knowledge about the Indian past and in understanding the Indian present" (ibid., 207). See also James Johnson, "Inventing Constitutional Traditions: The Poverty of Fatalism," in John Ferejohn, Jack N. Rakove, and Jonathan Riley, eds., *Constitutional Culture and Democratic Rule* (Cambridge: Cambridge University Press, 2001). Johnson discusses the threat embodied in the resurgence of ethnic nationalism in Eastern Europe to societies lacking preexisting traditions needed to sustain liberal democratic politics (ibid., 75).

So too the Israeli case. As Ruth Gavison observes, "[T]he conflicts within Israeli society . . . translate to deep debates about the identity and the legitimacy of the state itself."[85] These conflicts refer to the nation's dual aspirational commitments to develop the polity as both Jewish and democratic. The discordant notes in the Israeli constitutional tradition have provided the backdrop for a judicial commitment to complete what may be conceptualized as an unfinished or complex revolution.[86] The success of Israel's "constitutional revolution" is, to be sure, an oft-debated story; how one evaluates it depends on one's judgment about the Supreme Court's management of the constitutional disharmony bequeathed to it by the nation's divided historical legacy.[87] But as Gavison, echoing MacIntyre, rightly points out, "Ultimately, it is the interplay of deep cultures that make legal traditions robust and solid, because they are then based on deep sources of meaning and continuity."[88]

Generic/Local Balancing

Much of the aspirational content of a nation's specific constitutional identity consists of goals and principles that are shared by other nations and that are indeed part of a common stock of aspirations we have come to associate more generally with the enterprise of constitutionalism. These aspirations may be described collectively as "the inner morality

85. Ruth Gavison, "Law, Adjudication, Human Rights, and Society," 40 *Israel Law Review* 13 (2007), 30.

86. I have discussed these developments at length in Gary Jeffrey Jacobsohn, "After the Revolution," 34 *Israel Law Review* 139 (2000).

87. Gavison has been an outspoken critic of the "revolution," in part because she views the Court's intervention as an inappropriate short-circuiting of the democratic process's efforts to address the issues of disharmony in the polity. Farther to the left the "revolution" has been attacked as a sham designed to sustain the advantages of the dominant group (and vision) within the polity. For example: "[I]n the guise of progressive liberalism, [it] perpetuates basic discrimination on the basis of ideology." Kimmerling, *Clash of Identities,* 197. As for the Court's management of the divided legacy, as an "integral part of settler-immigrant society," it is "a central tool in reproducing a hegemonic regime, particularly regarding the inter-ethnic conflict being waged in the land and region . . ." (ibid., 187).

88. Gavison, "Law, Adjudication," 37.

of law"[89] or the requirements of "generic constitutionalism"[90] implicit in a nation's discourse of justice. Such norms need to be reconciled with the particularistic commitments of local traditions and practices; the contours of constitutional identity will to a large extent reflect how these disharmonies get resolved. As Heinz Klug notes in his study of South African constitutional framing, "[T]he challenge is to understand the specifics of [a globalizing constitutionalism's] incorporation into particular national legal systems as well as to understand the potentially multiple roles that constitutionalism is playing in the reconstruction of different polities."[91]

The South African case's "interaction of local participation, context and history with international influences and conditionalities"[92] provides a textbook example of dialogic constitution making. The reasons for the international engagement can be characterized in various ways, including, of course, explanations that emphasize the economic advantages to elites within South Africa inhering in the reintegration of the state into the world community. Nothing in this explanation is inconsistent with alternative accounts that stress the gain in legitimacy to be anticipated from the clear break from the past that would be symbolized in an auspicious debut on the world stage. But as the deliberative process that culminated in a new constitution made abundantly clear, separating from the past is not so easily accomplished, whatever the benefits associated with it. Incorporating international standards—for example, equal treatment of individuals under law—within the set of newly mandated constitutional aspirations would still require reconciliation with a quite different aspirational legacy that was as intractable as the historical narrative from whence it derived.[93]

89. Lon Fuller, *The Morality of Law* (New Haven, CT: Yale University Press, 1964).

90. Kahn, "Comparative Constitutionalism," 2702.

91. Klug, *Constituting Democracy*, 3.

92. Ibid., 117.

93. The South African Constitution, like its Indian counterpart, can be characterized as a "militant" constitution in the sense that it was intended by its framers to confront and challenge critical aspects of the existing social and economic structure. But this ambition was quickly tempered by a set of realities carried over from the old regime. I examine the Indian model of militant constitutionalism in Chapter 5.

A very different angle on the challenge to constitutional design posed by the tension between universalistic and particularistic demands appears in the effort to adopt a constitution for Europe. The issue here is also focused on the question of identity, not so much how extra-national precepts and principles are to be integrated into the jurisprudence of nations possessing unique histories and ways of doing things, but how—or whether—the distinctive political and legal cultures of a diverse group of nations can be incorporated within an over-arching framework of international governance such as to create a constitutional identity for the new entity as a whole. So far the effort has been more encouraging for constitutional theorists than for politicians.[94]

Emphasizing the integrative function of constitutions, Dieter Grimm, the prominent German jurist, has questioned whether the European Union can realize the necessary preconditions for sustaining a constitutional democracy, most importantly a collective identity. "[Th]ese prerequisites cannot simply be created."[95] This is not, Grimm hastened to point out, an incapacity of ethnic significance, but one principally of political import. "What obstructs democracy . . . is not the lack of cohesion of Union citizens as a people, but their weakly developed collective identity and low capacity for transnational discourse."[96] While giving much weight to linguistic considerations, Grimm's concerns seem to go deeper, connecting with the fundaments of the prescriptive constitution; or as Burke put it, "a constitution . . . made by the peculiar circumstances, occasions, tempers, dispositions, and moral, civil, and social habitudes of the people that disclose themselves only in a long space of time." A constitution, Grimm maintains, "is a document in which

94. See, for example, the entries in the special issue on the proposed European Constitution published in the *International Journal of Constitutional Law* in May 2005.

95. Dieter Grimm, "Does Europe Need a Constitution?" 1 *European Law Journal* 282, 297 (1995).

96. Ibid., 297. Or as J. H. H. Weiler suggests, "A constitution will have an integrative effect only if it embodies a society's fundamental value system and aspirations, and if the society perceives that its constitution reflects precisely those values with which it identifies and which are the sources of its specific character." J. H. H. Weiler, "On the Power of the Word: Europe's Constitutional Iconography," 3 *International Journal of Constitutional Law* 173, 199 (2005).

society finds its basic convictions and aspirations expressed."[97] A European Constitution can surely express the universal aspirations that are the generic articulation of liberal constitutionalism, but what would be the prospects for its viability without, in MacIntyre's useful formulation, the particular "unity of a narrative quest"?

The absence of a European people has not dissuaded Grimm's countryman, the philosopher Jürgen Habermas, from his belief that the constitution is achievable in both the short and long term. "What unites a nation of citizens as opposed to a *Volksnation* is not some primordial substrate but rather an intersubjectively shared context of possible understanding."[98] Rejecting "notions of identity" premised on "an historical-cultural *a priori*," Habermas argues that "an abstract, legally mediated solidarity among strangers" will support European constitutional institutions.[99] All that is required is a public sphere transcending the boundaries of the nation-state, within which democratic discourse can productively occur. If a people may be imagined in this broader communicative sense, then Grimm is mistaken in his opinion that "One could not credibly begin the European Constitution with those famous words introducing the US Constitution, 'We the People'. . . ."[100] Indeed, one could imagine the sentence continuing, "of Europe, in order to form a more perfect Union, whose identity is affirmed in our commitment to the procedures of constitutional governance, do ordain and establish. . . ."[101]

The failure to this point of Europeans to ratify a constitution does not tell us which of these positions has the stronger argument. Obviously Grimm's comports more with the theory of constitutional identity I have

97. Dieter Grimm, "Integration by Constitution," 3 *International Journal of Constitutional Law* 191, 195 (2005).

98. Jürgen Habermas, Remarks on Grimm's "Does Europe Need a Constitution?" 303, 305.

99. Ibid., 305, 307.

100. Grimm, "Integration by Constitution," 208.

101. See, however, Jed Rubenfeld's distinction between American and European constitutionalism, highlighting the U.S. Constitution as "self-given" law, as opposed to the constitutional law of the European Union, which in emphasizing human rights that transcend national politics, would surely be skeptical of any assertion claiming the people as the authors of the law to which they commit themselves in the future. Jed Rubenfeld, "Unilateralism and Constitutionalism," 79 *New York University Law Review* 1971, 2000 (2004).

been elaborating; on the other hand, Habermas's captures quite well the pre-constitutional situation prevailing in the constitutional practice of the European Union. As Jed Rubenfeld notes, "[W]hat makes the new European constitutionalism cohere—what gives European constitutional courts their claim to legitimacy—is the ideology of universal or 'international human rights,' which owe their validity to no particular nation's constitution, and which possess therefore a supranational and almost supraconstitutional character, making them close to unamendable and rendering them peculiarly fit for interpretation by international juridical experts."[102] There is, then, an abstract solidarity inhering in a human rights regime that may accomplish what its proponents seek without worrying about the question of constitutional identity.

But the problem of balancing the generic and the local will not go away. One need look no further than the evolution of Irish law on abortion (discussed in Chapter 5) to appreciate how, from the perspective of the constituent members of the Union, the disharmonies between international human rights law and domestic jurisprudence impact the face of constitutional identity.[103] Balancing the universal and the particular is also central to the debate over constitutional borrowing (or if one prefers, migration), the subject of Chapter 4. "If law and individual legal systems can be understood as having distinct local identities with identifiable authentic experiences, what happens when such experiences are continually exposed to external influences? Put another way, if law has a dynamic relationship with local culture, then do we risk a 'feeling of lost authenticity . . . ruining some essence or source' in the

102. Ibid., 1997.

103. Ireland's rejection in 2008 of the Lisbon Treaty, a thoroughly and meticulously negotiated design for governing the European Union, reflected widespread popular uncertainty about the treaty's possible impact on the particularities of Irish identity. The campaign against the treaty "played to Irish voters' deepest visceral fears about the European Union." *New York Times,* June 14, 2008, A1. As reported in the press at the time, "Opponents of the treaty . . . were able to capitalize on voters' . . . feelings of alienation from the political entity of Europe . . ." (ibid., A9). Another way of putting this is that the referendum on the treaty gave voice to pervasive long-standing worries that Irish identity—constitutional and otherwise—was being threatened by an integration into Europe that, for all its economic benefits, had a distinct downside attached to it.

process of globalizing legal analysis?"[104] Finally, balancing lies at the core of many of the transitions from colonial to postcolonial constitutional governance, as the formal withdrawal of external power from their countries left resident constitution makers and interpreters with a puzzling and challenging dilemma: how to calibrate the universalist residuals of colonialism—for example, British law in Palestine and India—against the traditional jurisprudential requirements and expectations of indigenous law.[105]

Preliminary Applications

Subsequent chapters provide extended and more textured accounts of these issues in varying jurisprudential and political contexts. To conclude this chapter I want briefly to make some applications of the conceptual framework for understanding constitutional identity to two polities—South Africa and India—whose constitutions symbolize a clear break with the past, in which the document seeks consciously to distance it from this past without entirely escaping it. Both countries made ample use of the experience of other nations in the framing of their constitutions—for instance, the South African framers relied extensively on the Indian example—and their Supreme Courts have not been reluctant to use foreign judgments to advance their constitutions' aspirational agenda.[106]

South Africa

The South African Constitution has often been referred to as "the birth certificate of a nation." One of the participants in its creation describes it

104. Sarah K. Harding, "Comparative Reasoning and Judicial Review," 28 *Yale Journal of International Law* 409 (2003), 462.

105. On the British and Palestine, see Assaf Likhovski, *Law and Identity in Mandate Palestine;* for India see Lloyd I. Rudolph and Susanne Hoeber Rudolph, *Modernity of Tradition.* Both books highlight the tensions between the British attempts to impose a universalist rule of law regime in the colonial country and the latter's resistance to Anglicization through its more communally based legal practices.

106. For India, see Adam M. Smith, "Making Itself at Home: Understanding Foreign Law in Domestic Jurisprudence: The Indian Case," 24 *Berkeley Journal of International Law* 218 (2006).

as "the growing soul of a nation."[107] In this account it represents the "discovery of nationhood."[108] While such references reflect an understandable sense of pride in a remarkable achievement, they also serve to call attention to the question of how a constitution comes to acquire a specific identity. Such terms as "birth," "soul," and "discovery" are reminders of the philosophical debates concerning personal identity; does the story of one of the most important constitutional developments of our time expand the significance of their application to polity-level questions of identity?

In 1996 the Constitutional Court of South Africa delivered a judgment in a case that it properly referred to as unprecedented. Pursuant to a provision of the Interim South African Constitution of 1993, the Court's ruling concerned certification of the newly adopted permanent Constitution. Was the new document in compliance with criteria set out in language from the earlier constitution's preamble, which had stipulated that "in order to secure the achievement of this new goal, elected representatives of all the people of South Africa should be mandated to adopt a new Constitution in accordance with a solemn pact recorded as Constitutional Principles"?[109] To reach its decision the Court was required to assess the provisions of the new document in light of the 34 Constitutional Principles enumerated in the 1993 iteration. It found that eight provisions of the draft text were inconsistent with these principles and sent the document back to the Constituent Assembly. It was unlikely that any of the judges could have minimized the significance of this undertaking, for they all knew, in accordance with the express language of the constitutional directive from whence their ruling derived, that a decision to certify would be final and could never again be raised in any court of law, including their own.

The power exercised by the Court was as extraordinary as it was unprecedented: to legitimate (or not) a governing code by which a people commit to the structuring of a constitutional way of life. Indeed, this

107. Hassen Ebrahim, *The Soul of a Nation: Constitution-Making in South Africa* (Cape Town: Oxford University Press, 1998), 256.

108. Ibid., 4.

109. Certification of the Constitution of the Republic of South Africa, 1996, CCT 23/96, par. 15.

was the first and only occasion when a court had been given the responsibility of certifying a constitutional text.[110] Of the constitutional principles (CPs) that were the touchstone for the certification exercise, the Court said:

> The CPs must be applied purposively and teleologically to give expression to the commitment "to create a new order" based on a "sovereign and democratic constitutional state" in which "all citizens" are "able to enjoy and exercise their fundamental rights and freedoms". . . . The CPs must not be interpreted with technical rigidity. They are broad constitutional strokes on the canvas of constitution making in the future. All CPs must be read holistically with an integrated approach. No CP must be read in isolation from the other CPs, which give it meaning and context.[111]

The judges and the Constitution's drafters were thus constrained in their creative efforts by guidelines adopted several years earlier, but within the broad parameters of these directives they had considerable leeway in designing and shaping constitutional policy.[112]

Another way of appreciating the novelty of the Court's assignment is to note the resemblance between the task at hand and the Indian Supreme

110. Namibia in 1989 also incorporated a set of constitutional principles, but unlike in South Africa, these were to serve only as guidelines for the final document.

111. Certification of the Constitution of the Republic of South Africa, 1996, 34, 36, 37.

112. The certification process was well within the spirit of the negotiating process among various groups and interests that guided the entire constitution-making arrangements. For an analysis of the process that discusses certification in light of competing models—consociationalism and justice—see Siri Gloppen, *South Africa: The Battle over the Constitution* (Aldershot, UK: Dartmouth, 1997). Firoz Cachalia also looks at the contrasting models and makes a passionate argument for adopting a Rawlsian interpretation of South Africa's Constitution, which he finds "especially valuable in societies that are 'deeply divided' by competing identities." Firoz Cachlia, "Constitutionalism and Belonging," in Penelope Andrews and Stephen Ellmann, eds., *The Post-Apartheid Constitutions: Perspectives on South Africa's Basic Law* (Johannesburg: Witwatersrand University Press, 2001), 367. Cachalia advocates forging "a distinction between constitutional identity and cultural identity," although it is difficult to perceive the constitutional process in South Africa as having culminated in a solution in which the former has been made separate from the latter.

Court's position on amendments to the Constitution that violate its "basic structure." "For constitutional lawyers the role of the [South African] Constitutional Court introduced an 'Alice in Wonderland' element to the process. It meant that it was possible to adopt an unconstitutional constitution."[113] But during the extended hearing on the Certification Case the question of whether constitutionally entrenched rights should be immune to amendment was left unresolved. Justice Albie Sachs at one point asked one of his colleagues, "Are you saying that there are certain fundamental features that cannot be changed even with special majorities, since that would not be amending the Constitution?"[114] The response invoked the *Kesavananda* ruling upholding the Indian judiciary's authority to defend such features against hostile amendments, yet the Court's failure to take a clear stand on the question left one of the attorneys arguing the case concerned: "Our worry is that the CA [Constituent Assembly, but also presumably the Court as well] does not accept the [Indian Court's] *Kesavananda* decision."[115] In effect, this worry expressed the concern that the judges deciding a case explicitly about South Africa's constitutional identity might be reluctant to affirm the legitimacy of a power deemed essential by the Indian Court for preserving that identity.[116]

In what sense, if at all, may the culmination of this judicial exercise be understood as having shaped a constitutional identity? Did the mandate to pursue a purposive and holistic application of enumerated principles suggest the presence of a unified vision of constitutional

113. Christina Murray, "Negotiating beyond Deadlock: From the Constituent Assembly to the Court," in Andrews, *Post-Apartheid Constitutions,* 105.

114. Quoted in Carmel Rickard, "The Certification of the Constitution of South Africa," in ibid., 253.

115. Ibid., 253.

116. In its decision, however, the Court insisted on a more stringent amendment procedure to safeguard entrenched rights against easy abridgement. It did say that the CP's do "not require that the Bill of Rights should be immune from amendment or practically unamendable" (at 1311F–H). It also said, echoing the basic structure jurisprudence of the Indian Court, that provisions "which are foundational to the new constitutional state" should be less vulnerable to amendment than ordinary legislation (at 1310B). This led one commentator to conclude that the issue of the unconstitutional amendment was still on the table. Rickard, "Certification of the Constitution," 272.

practice that represents the core of this identity? Would compliance with the commitments of the drafters of the interim document of 1993 be evidence for the successful construction of a constitutional identity in 1996? Answers to such questions presume a stance on the prior, more abstract question of the status of creativity in the process of identity formation.

As discussed earlier, this is a much vexed issue, but both an existential account emphasizing invention, and a more romantic alternative holding identity to be some preexisting essence waiting to be discovered, seemed problematic in light of their difficulties in balancing organic and agency-driven considerations within a dialogical framework of development. Thus the "birth certificate" of a nation would constitute a misleading marker if it conveyed the idea that a document could bring into the world some constitutional article whose identity was discernible in the details of its very existence. Who would say, for example, that the constitutional identity of the former Soviet Union was discernible within the folds of its governing charter? Nor would the idea that a constitutional "soul" existing independently of the larger environment surrounding the entity within which it was contained capture the interactive reality of the identity-forming process.

Applying these thoughts to the South Africa queries leads then tentatively to the conclusion that the declaratory act of enumerating principles that are subsequently incorporated in a final governing legal code cannot in itself establish or confirm the existence of something we might call a constitutional identity. Were the opposite true, then one of two explanations would apply: (1) The constitutional architects of 1993 and 1996 invented an identity by the choices they made in embracing a particular constitutional way of life and mandating its formal recognition; or, (2) The constitutional architects of 1993 and 1996 authenticated an identity by inscribing in law a particular constitutional way of life expressive of a preexisting essence unique to the South African experience. Without additional information about the political context within which the CPs were adopted, both explanations fail the dialogic test because they suggest that a constitutional identity may be understood as a purely wrought product of the theoretical imagination or the inevitable outgrowth of a fixed and essentially unalterable nature.

Of course, the actual course of South African constitutional design did not occur in a vacuum; indeed, an extensive public record reveals a very complex and nuanced political process culminating in a final constitutional product.[117] Ample evidence exists that the CPs enunciated in the 1993 document were neither discovered nor invented in the fashion outlined in Appiah's two models of personal identity formation. Rather, in the dying days of the old apartheid regime these principles became the focus of a deliberate effort to incorporate contradictory visions—in other words, disharmony—within the project of constitutional design. The Constitutional Court was then given the assignment of mediating these conflicting aspirations so as to leave space for all major parties to accept the legitimacy of the new arrangements while engaging the political process in developing a coherent vision of a constitutional future for the country.

For example, the constitutional framers (and subsequent judges on the Constitutional Court) openly engaged in a systematic and comprehensive effort to incorporate the experience of other nations in the provisions of, and interpretive approaches to, their newly constituted arrangements.[118] Sujit Choudhry has shown how the South African Court quickly developed a distinctive "dialogical" interpretive approach to structure the judicial appropriation of foreign materials into its constitutional jurisprudence.[119] In some cases this led to an emulation and transplantation of the foreign experience in others to a conscious rejection. Critical, however, to both has been the use of "comparative jurisprudence [as] . . . an important stimulus to legal self-reflection."[120] Thus the engagement with other constitutional cultures and practices has, Choudhry argues, sharpened the understandings of South Africans about their own

117. See, for example, Ebrahim, *Soul of a Nation,* which chronicles the framing process and includes many of the most important documents related to the events associated with it.

118. Section 39 of the South African Constitution reads: When interpreting the Bill of Rights, a court, tribunal, or forum . . . b) must consider international law; and c) may consider foreign law.

119. Sujit Choudhry, "Globalization in Search of Justification: Toward a Theory of Comparative Constitutional Interpretation," 74 *Indiana Law Journal* 819 (1999).

120. Ibid., 836.

legal culture, while making clear that this culture is not developmentally tethered to an indigenous core requiring only discovery and nurturing. As Appiah, following Charles Taylor, observes, "[B]eginning in infancy [I am] in dialogue with other people's understandings of who I am that I develop a conception of my own identity."[121] On this point, at least, there seems little reason to think that moving from the personal to the constitutional would not entail similar consequences for the phenomenon of identity.

In like manner, the principles adopted to structure the constitution-making process, while deeply expressive of aspirations for universal justice, were also directly responsive to the realities of a complex pluralism and the extraordinary history out of which it had emerged.[122] How else to comprehend the requirement that "The institution, status and role of traditional leadership, according to indigenous law, shall be recognized and protected in the Constitution"? (#13) Or that "Equality before the law includes laws, programmes or activities that have as their objective the amelioration of the conditions of the disadvantaged, including those disadvantaged on grounds of race, colour or gender"? (#5) The certification process can be viewed as a forward-looking program that launches a novel constitutional experiment, or as a prudent necessity, a way "to facilitate the transition to democratic rule by assuring the white minority that democratic rule would not simply be an invitation to majoritarian retribution."[123] Or more critically, the principles can be understood as establishing "the essential link between the past and the present; through them the old order would ensure its survival."[124] However depicted, the constitutional project must be seen, in other words, as a political effort to address the multiple and often

121. Appiah, *Ethics of Identity*, 20.

122. The first ten principles, concerning commitments to nondiscrimination and other basic human rights, express the universalist aspirations of the document. This is succeeded by a number of principles, including protections for collective rights and indigenous law, expressive of particular societal realities.

123. Samuel Issacharoff, "Constitutionalizing Democracy in Fractured Societies," 82 *Texas Law Review* 1876 (2004).

124. Makau wa Mutua, "Hope and Despair for a New South Africa: The Limits of Rights Discourse," 10 *Harvard Human Rights Journal* 63 (1997), 81.

countervailing demands and pressures that define the South African historical experience.[125] The solution represents an exercise in creative political architecture, but surely not a purely existentialist one of "*only* creativity, [where] there is nothing . . . to respond to, nothing out of which to do the construction."[126]

So it is sensible to say, given the known facts surrounding the language set down by the framers, that the two-stage constitution-making process in South Africa, whether evaluated as a case study in self-discovery or self-authorship, conforms to minimal dialogical criteria for ascertaining the presence of a constitutional identity.[127] Nevertheless, it would be premature to speak at this point of having found this elusive entity, even if the framers of the document had done all that could have reasonably been expected of them in creating a (constitutional) life out of the materials that history provided them. Whether or not one embraces the deeply constitutive meaning of the ancient constitutional understanding, the Aristotelian distinction between a physical identity and a real identity requires, as Madison understood, that one withhold judgments about identity until after confirming that the codified hopes of the founders actually resonate in the practices and culture of the body politic. Words on paper, like the physical boundaries of a state, are only an introduction to the determination of identity, which in the end incorporates the beliefs and behavior of the governed as well as the content of their governing

125. This historical experience has been splendidly analyzed in Jens Meierhenrich, *The Legacies of Law: Long-Run Consequences of Legal Development in South Africa, 1652–2000* (Cambridge: Cambridge University Press, 2008). Meierenrich considers South Africa as a "dual state," a hybrid regime in which the "prerogative state" and the "normative state" have been locked in a competitive relationship that ultimately paved the way for the post-apartheid constitutional polity. His account fits squarely within my understanding of the development of constitutional identity, as it presents a path-dependent analysis of "interacting adversaries" that served to connect past and present in the constitution-making process.

126. Appiah, *Ethics of Identity,* 18.

127. For a provocative discussion of the two-stage constitution-making process in South Africa and elsewhere, see Andrew Arato, *Constitution Making Under Occupation: The Politica of Imposed Revolution in Iraq* (New York: Columbia University Press, 2009).

document.[128] The dialogic process is an ongoing one in which constitutional identity is shaped in the manifold political and private activities that happen over time in multiple and varied arenas.[129]

India

As we have seen in the previous chapter, the Indian Supreme Court has been unusually self-conscious in its use of the concept of constitutional identity. The Court has done so mainly through elaboration of the controversial doctrine of "Basic Structure," in which it has designated a number of constitutional features to be of such importance that it would be prepared to challenge any action, including an amendment to the Constitution, perceived as a threat to their existence. Moreover, in the spirit of the multilateralism that serious engagement with the problem would seem to require, it has upheld extraordinary actions by other institutions that were arguably motivated by a proper regard for constitutional identity.

Understandably, much of the debate in India over judicial enforcement of the basic structure doctrine has concerned its application to the issue of secularism. The Indian Constitution was adopted against a backdrop of sectarian violence that was only the latest chapter in a complex centuries-old story of Hindu-Muslim relations on the Asian subcontinent. Much of that history had been marked by peaceful coexistence; nevertheless the bloodbath that accompanied Partition reflected ancient contestations and ensured that the goal of communal harmony would be a priority in the constitution-making process.[130] But it was not the only priority. If not as urgent, then certainly as important, was the goal of social reconstruction, which could not be addressed without

128. For an interesting discussion of identity in relation to content and behavior see Larry Alexander, "Introduction," in Alexander, *Constitutionalism,* 1.

129. As Erik Erikson pointed out, "Identity is safest . . . when it is grounded in activity." Erik H. Erikson, *Dimensions of a New Identity,* 105. In the case of a written constitution, the first stage of this evolution is one of establishing a correspondence between the words of a document and the behavior of those who fall under its jurisdiction.

130. "We have accepted [secularism] not only because it is our historical legacy and a need of our national unity and integrity but also as a creed of universal brotherhood and humanism. It is our cardinal faith." S. R. Bommai v. Union of India, 3 SC 1 (1994), 148.

constitutional recognition of the state's interest in the "essentials of religion."[131] So deep was religion's penetration into the fabric of Indian life, and so historically entwined was it in the configuration of a social structure that was by any reasonable standard grossly unjust, that the framers' hopes for a democratic polity meant that state intervention in the spiritual domain could not be constitutionally foreclosed. The design for secularism in India required a creative balance between socioeconomic reform that could limit religious options and political toleration of diverse religious practices and communal development.[132] Taken together, the ameliorative and communal provisions evince a constitutional purpose to address the social conditions of people long burdened by the inequities of religiously inspired hierarchies.

Over the years this constitutional equilibrium has come under repeated assault from different locations on the political spectrum, with the greatest challenge issuing from the Hindu right. The Supreme Court's main response has been to declare secularism a "part of the basic structure of the Constitution and also the soul of the Constitution."[133] Describing the

131. Gary Jeffrey Jacobsohn, *The Wheel of Law: India's Secularism in Comparative Constitutional Context* (Princeton, NJ: Princeton University Press, 2003).

132. This balance is inscribed in several constitutional provisions that express the limits and possibilities of secularism in India. Thus the ameliorative aspiration of Indian secularism is embodied in Article 25, which, after providing for religious freedom, declares that the state shall not be prevented from "regulating or restricting any economic, financial, political or other secular activity which may be associated with religious practice." "Providing for social welfare and reform" is explicitly included within the parameters of the guaranteed freedom. This constitutional strand underscores the transformative dimension of Indian nationalism, the commitment to social reconstruction as the path to creating one nation out of a multiplicity of peoples. In this commitment, "India," as Subrata Mitra points out, "is virtually alone among post-colonial states in Asia to have adopted secularism as a key feature of her constitution and the cornerstone of her strategy of nation-building." Subrata Mitra, "The Limits of Accommodation: Nehru, Religion, and the State in India," 9 *South Asia Research* (1989), 107. Additional provisions are designed to accommodate the other principal facet of Indian social reality, the entrenched character of communal affiliation. Under Article 26, religious denominations are granted the right to establish and maintain institutions for religious and charitable purposes, and the same right is extended to the creation and administration of religiously based educational structures in Article 30.

133. *Bommai,* at 143. This is the leading Indian case on secularism. In it the Court upheld the authority of the Central Government to dismiss the elected governments in three

commitment to secularism in this dramatic way added a notable rhetorical flourish to a landmark decision in Indian jurisprudence, but it also suggested that the same concern with constitutional identity that lay behind the Court's earlier rulings on unconstitutional amendments generated the outcome in the secularism case. To be sure, there is no reason to think that a judicial reference to the "soul of the Constitution" was used with any awareness of debates in the seventeenth and eighteenth centuries (or indeed as far back as Plato) over the significance and place of the soul in determining personal identity, but there is every reason to suppose that its usage was intended to mark secularism as critical to Indian constitutional identity.

Indian secularism, however, poses an interesting challenge for a theory of identity. We might call it the "presumption in favor of settled practice" problem, adverted to earlier in connection with Burke and the prescriptive constitution. We want to retain the idea of prescription without having to embrace a correspondence logic that requires us to extend the legitimacy of the constitution to the society of which it is a part. Burke's opposition to the status quo—especially in India—related to his opposition to policies involving external intrusions into local settled practices. But when reviewing the debates about religion and politics at the Constituent Assembly and the various judicial pronouncements on the subject over the years, one sees very clearly that a principal purpose behind the Indian commitment to secularism was to challenge an entrenched way of life and to modify it in the direction of a democratic way of life rooted in equality. As is elaborated more fully in Chapter 5, in a very real sense the constitutional "soul" was intended to be ornery, projecting an identity that was at once confrontational and emblematic of the document's abiding commitments. In both the early philosophical ruminations about consciousness and the Burkean reflections on nationhood

states because of the alleged failures of their administrations in implementing and respecting the constitutional commitment to secularism. By upholding the deployment of emergency powers under Article 356, the Court agreed that these governments had not acted "in accordance with the provisions of the Constitution." Article 356 had been modeled after the American Guaranty Clause (Article IV, Section 4), but the willingness of the Indian Court to confront the question of identity contrasts sharply with the American Supreme Court's reluctance to engage it.

and prescription, the concept of identity is associated with the idea of continuity rather than transformation. How then are we to explain the expansive ambitions of the soulful concept at the core of Indian constitutional design?

There are two points to be made in response. First, constitutional identity can accommodate an aspirational aspect that is at odds with the prevailing condition of the society within which it functions. Burke's prescriptive constitution might suggest that what is must be (identity as pure discovery), but, as MacIntyre demonstrated, a strictly positivistic inference need not be drawn from the principle of inheritance. In the case of India's constitutional framers, the prevailing social structure, while deeply rooted in centuries of religious and cultural practice, was contestable in accordance with sources from within the Indian tradition that are also a part of the prescriptive constitution.[134] History revealed disharmony within established traditions and between the dominant strand and the society. "One of the remarkable developments of the present age," wrote Jawaharlal Nehru shortly before independence, "has been the rediscovery of the past and of the nation."[135] Nehru was one of several delegates at the Constituent Assembly to invoke the name of Ashoka, the third king of the Mauryan Dynasty in the third century B.C., and a legendary figure whose famous edicts have endured as a source of moral and ethical reflection for more than a millennium. Used both as an emulative model for behavior toward society's destitute and as a basis for criticizing the Hindu nationalist rejection of Indian nationhood as rooted in a composite culture, the Ashokan example shows how continuity in the construction of a constitutional identity can draw upon alternative (and even dissenting) sources within one tradition, and then

134. As H. Patrick Glenn observes, "Opposition to a tradition may be . . . conducted within the tradition itself, using both its language and its resources (the struggle from within)." Glenn, *Legal Traditions,* 17. This is particularly the case in Hinduism, which stands out among the world's religious traditions for the heterodox character of its teachings. "What distinguishes Hinduism from other traditions, religious and other, is that informal tradition is recognized generally as having priority even over the sacred texts" (ibid., 269).

135. Jawaharlal Nehru, *The Discovery of India* (Oxford: Oxford University Press, 1997), 515.

re-constitute them to serve at times as a reproach to other strands (and their societal manifestations) within the same tradition. In MacIntyre's terms, it exemplifies "continuities of conflict."

The second point speaks directly to the authenticity-existentialism polarity. A defense of secularism as a central feature of the Indian Constitution's basic structure inevitably finds people differing in the meanings they assign to this consensus fundamental commitment. For example, the Hindu right has often assured Indians that it accepts the constitutional centrality of secularism, which it embraces as a version of the strict separationist model endorsed by many in the United States, and which it contrasts with the "pseudo-secularism" championed by its political opponents.[136] The latter include the justices on the Supreme Court, most of whom have incorporated the differing perspectives of Gandhi, Nehru, Ambedkar, and others to articulate a uniquely Indian understanding that has been aptly described by Rajeev Bhargava as "contextual secularism." At the core of this position is the strategy of "principled distance" that, according to Bhargava, means that "[T]he State intervenes or refrains from interfering, depending on which of the two better promotes religious liberty and equality of citizenship."[137] Thus the specific forms that secular states take should reflect the particular constitutive features of their respective polities. In India this means (as is so enshrined in the Constitution) that for certain purposes—for example, establishing separate sectarian electorates—the state cannot recognize religion, but for others—for example, establishing a limited regime of personal laws—it may do so. The state need not relate to all religions in the same way; the bottom line, however, is that public policy regarding intervention, noninterference, or equidistance be guided by the same nonsectarian principle of equal dignity for all.

136. This position has been often espoused by Arun Shourie, perhaps the leading ideologue of the Hindu right, who insists, in explicit reference to American church/state separatism, that the state must take no formal cognizance of religion. See Arun Shourie, *A Secular Agenda* (New Delhi: Harper Collins, 1997). In the Indian context this view has the effect of advancing the cultural religious beliefs and practices of the majority, which of course in India is represented overwhelmingly by its Hindu population.

137. Rajeev Bhargava, "What Is Secularism For?" in Rajeev Bhargava, ed., *Secularism and Its Critics* (New Delhi: Oxford University Press, 1998), 515.

The process by which this concept of secularism emerged as a mark of constitutional identity, then to be extended protected status under the Court's basic structure jurisprudence, is roughly analogous to the dialogical formation of personal identity, which is developed—recall Charles Taylor's account—"only against the background of things that matter." Much as a self evolves interactively within the specific contours of its environment, India's constitutional identity, as refracted through the determinative lens of secularism, is the product of historically conditioned circumstances in which choices are limited by the dual realities of complex communalism and religiously inspired societal inequality.[138] The nation as an "idea of continuity," in which, as Burke said, a constitution discloses itself "only in a long space of time," can go far to explain how the main outlines of a secular identity are discoverable as a contingent part of the political and moral order. But within these broad outlines is considerable space for inventive statesmanship, as is illustrated not only in the work of the Constituent Assembly, but also in the earlier efforts of the Indian National Congress culminating in such documents as the Nehru Constitutional Draft of 1928 and the Karachi Resolution of 1931.[139]

Secularism's designation as a basic structure makes it, in the words of a former Indian chief justice, "immutable in relation to the power of Parliament to change the Constitution."[140] The constitutional theorist, Jed

138. As Anthony D. Smith observes, "A national identity is fundamentally multidimensional; it can never be reduced to a single element. . . ." Smith, *National Identity,* 14. The same applies to constitutional identities. Thus, Smith's discussion of the Indian case appropriately invokes the communal question as one of the relevant dimensions. "The Indian example reveals the importance both of manufactured political identity and of preexisting ethno-religious ties and symbols from which such an identity can be constructed" (ibid., 113).

139. These documents addressed in particular the rights of minorities to their own culture and religion. But the prescriptive constitution is not inscribed only in official documents. A constitutional identity expresses as well important—and continuous—developments in the private sphere that are integral to the dialogical process of identity formation. In India this includes the very long tradition of reform movements within the various Hindu communities that helped shape the Constitution's commitment to socioeconomic reconstruction. See in this regard, Charles H. Heimsath, *Indian Nationalism and Hindu Social Reform* (Princeton, NJ: Princeton University Press, 1964).

140. M. N. Venkatachaliah, "There Are Some Things of Eternal Verity," interview in *Frontline,* V. 17, February 19, 2000.

Rubenfeld, has described "[r]adical interpretation . . . [as] a new interpretation of the basic principles or purposes behind a constitutional provision."[141] In relation to Indian constitutional secularism, a radical move is one that seeks to replace the commitment underlying this basic structure with something fundamentally different. The chief justice's comment in 2000 was made in response to an initiative of the BJP-led government to establish a National Commission to review the Constitution and to make recommendations for change within the constraints of basic structure. For those who suspected the intentions of the Hindu nationalists in power, the concern was not that the Commission would consign secularism to oblivion, but that the commitment would in effect become a victim of identity theft. If, for example, it were denuded of its ameliorative content, or rendered incompatible with public policies protective of religious minorities, then there would be reason to worry about a fundamental transformation in the concept's essential meaning.[142] Were secularism to be redefined to implement the principle of non-cognizance of religion (in other words, strict separation), this development would mark a substantial change in constitutional identity.

Opposition to such a contemplated change might again bring Burke to India, this time embodied in the following points: (1) There ought to be a strong presumption on behalf of continuity in the prevailing contextual understanding of secularism. Such a presumption is rooted in the prescriptive constitution and is consistent with a view of identity (or personality), according to which the distinctive character of a constitution (or person) is bound up in a specific set of characteristics that is constant (and contestable) over time; (2) This presumption can be overcome only by a showing of substantial changes in the polity of the sort that would clearly indicate that the extant secular identity no longer conforms to

141. Jed Rubenfeld, *Revolution by Judiciary*, 9.

142. In fact, the Union law minister, Ram Jethmalani, suggested reviewing the "misguided secularism" that had emerged in the Supreme Court's church/state jurisprudence. It would have been consistent with the Commission's terms of reference to seek an amendation to existing constitutional language concerning secularism that explained exactly what this unamendable basic structure meant.

the requirements of the newly constituted fundaments of the regime.[143] So, for example, if the social injustices resulting from religiously mandated practices were addressed through internal communal reform (a nearly impossible eventuality given the radically heterodox and nonhierarchical character of the major religions in India), then the ameliorative identity of constitutional secularism should be permitted to fade or perhaps even disappear; and (3) Absent such a demonstration, be wary of those who "have some change in the church or state, or both, constantly in their view."[144] Their advocacy likely flows either from the anticipation of some direct and particular political gain or from a theoretically driven agenda whose goal is to achieve a more satisfactory compliance with the mandate of principle. The attempt to reconfigure a constitutional model of spiritual-temporal relations should therefore not be undertaken absent compelling evidence that doing so is essential to the pursuit of the constitution's unique historically rooted vision of development.

Conclusion

There is of course much more that could be said about these cases. That they are both commonly viewed as success stories is no doubt partly attributable to the enormity of the challenges confronting their respective constitutional experiments. Like so much else in India and South Africa that is jarring in the magnitude of their incongruities, the histories of intercommunal hostility and conflagration in these polities coexist with stories of democratic constitutionalism that are remarkable for having unfolded as impressively as they have within such distinctly inhospitable environments. But the conflicts out of which the constitutional identities of these nations have come into being are exceptional only in their extremity; their emergence conforms to the model of disharmonic contestation that is present in the shaping of all such identities.

143. If, in other words, "the fixed form of a constitution whose merits are confirmed by the solid test of long experience and an increasing public strength and national prosperity," no longer accurately describes the situation. Edmund Burke, *Reflections on the Revolution in France* (Indianapolis: Bobbs-Merrill, 1955), 66.

144. Ibid., 73.

The intensity of the contestation may not be present in many places, and even when it is, it may not manifest itself in quite the same way as in the above instances. Thus there are two dimensions along which conflict fuels the development of constitutional identity: the first is internal to the document (assuming one exists) and includes alternative visions or aspirations that may embody different strands within a common historical tradition; the second entails a confrontational relationship between the constitution and the social order within which it operates. Most constitutions are fundamentally acquiescent in the sense that their framing is not likely to culminate in a document antagonistic to the very societal structures of stability that provide ballast for the constitutional enterprise. But even these constitutions—the American being a good example—may take on a militancy at some point in its history, as the tensions within the first dimension create a dynamic of change that proves ultimately transformative in the evolution of the nation's constitutional identity.

As we saw in the previous chapter, the debate over the post-Civil War amendments, a debate that was all about the substance of American constitutional identity, implicated both of these dimensions of disharmonic contestation. Those who have held that the amendments essentially completed the Constitution, that they represented, in Frederick Douglass's famous metaphor, the removal of the scaffolding surrounding the "magnificent [basic?] structure" of constitutionally designed liberty, must nevertheless acknowledge the tensions remaining in the document after the additions had been incorporated. These discordant parts—involving mainly the locus of power within a federal system of governance—have provided occasions for institutional conflict in which political actors (including judges) have pursued their competing aspirational agendas. Writing about American constitutionalism, George Thomas contends that it is "primarily about countervailing power and not about the legal limits enforced by courts."[145] He rightly views this as a result of constitutional planning: "In attempting to balance agonistic principles, which furnish the

145. George Thomas, *The Madisonian Constitution* (Baltimore: Johns Hopkins University Press, 2008), 2.

basis for a workable and contained political order, the Madisonian framework necessarily invites struggles over constitutional meaning and identity."[146] The second dimension of contestation—confrontation between constitution and social order—came into play in the course of the ongoing struggle to apply the amended document to the massive problem of racial inequality, either by efforts to denude it of any real significance or to enable it to begin the process of social reconstruction.

The channeling of conflict in the American Constitution around a set of agonistic institutions and principles may, as Thomas suggests, reflect a calculated feature of constitutional design, but one may also understand it as a refined and carefully crafted version of a phenomenon that presents itself—if in less structured ways—in the experience of other nations as well. As the African statesman, Julius K. Nyerere, observed, "[A]ny constitution must take into account of divisions within the society without entrenching them—or it must allow the institutions it establishes to do these things."[147] To describe a specific constitutional identity requires familiarity with the history and culture of a given society, for it is out of custom and tradition that a people acquire the materials from which the rules and aspirations that shape future governance spring. As I discuss in the next chapter, it is a concern for the integrity of these materials that the movement of constitutional ideas across borders has aroused controversy in some political circles. Yet there is nothing immutable in what emerges from this history; the past always remains a part of the present, and identity develops as a dialogically unfolding process of adaptation, appropriation, and overcoming of the past. The imperfection of all constitutions, a point also developed in the next chapter,

146. Ibid., 38.

147. Mwalimu Julius K. Nyerere, "Reflections on Constitutions and African Experience," in Thomas J. Barron, Owen Dudley Edwards, and Patricia J. Storey, eds., *Constitutions and National Identity* (Edinburgh: Quadriga, 1993), 19. This understanding, in which disharmony is both necessary and troubling, parallels Jonathan Marks's interpretation of Rousseau's political thought, in which "the human good [is viewed] not as a unity but as a set of disharmonious attributes or tendencies that must somehow be arranged in a life so as not to tear the human being apart." Jonathan Marks, *Perfection and Disharmony in the Thought of Jean-Jacques Rousseau*, 87.

leaves their identities open to contestation. This imperfection includes the presence of contradictory aspirations, some of which can coexist in a tenuous balance and others of which cannot. In the end, constitutional identity will be fashioned—and refashioned—through the struggle *over* constitutional identity.

CHAPTER 4

The Permeability of Constitutional Borders

> [T]he science of jurisprudence, the pride of the human intellect, which with all its defects, redundancies, and errors is the collected reason of ages, combining the principles of original justice with the infinite variety of human concerns. . . .
>
> —Edmund Burke

> You can translate a word by a word, but behind the word is an idea, the thing which the word denotes, and this idea you cannot translate if it does not exist among the people whose language you are translating.
>
> —Bankim Chandra Chatterji

Introduction

The U.S. Supreme Court often delivers its most controversial decisions on the last day of its term, a custom followed in 2003 when a bitterly divided Court ruled that a Texas homosexual sodomy statute was unconstitutional. The division over the case's substantive issue was exacerbated by the justices' contrasting positions on judicial methodology, specifically the citation of foreign legal sources. Writing for the majority, Justice Anthony Kennedy referred to several decisions of the European Court of Human Rights in support of its landmark judgment.[1] "The

1. Lawrence v. Texas, 539 U.S. 558 (2003).

right the petitioners seek in this case has been accepted as an integral part of human freedom in many other countries."[2] In response, Justice Antonin Scalia dismissed "[t]he Court's discussion of these foreign views" as "meaningless [but "dangerous"] dicta,"[3] repeating what had become a familiar refrain, namely that "this Court . . . should not impose foreign moods, fads, or fashions on Americans."[4] The dismissal was scathing but neither path breaking nor uniquely American. For example, in 1951 an Indian judge had written: "The craze for American precedents can soon become a snare. A blind and uncritical adherence to American precedents must be avoided or else there will soon be a perverted Constitution operating in this land under the delusive garb of the Indian Constitution. We are interpreting and expounding our own Constitution."[5]

In the latter case the Constitution had been in existence for only a very short time, but deploring the use of legal materials from other places originated from a set of concerns similar to those that had provoked the American justice's denunciation. In both instances the worry was that foreign ideas and practices would undermine the efforts to establish (as in India) and maintain (as in the United States) a constitutional identity expressive of each nation's commitments and experience. The Indian jurist's comment intimates that a formal written document is an unreliable indicator of constitutional identity; the real meaning of a constitution could, for better or worse, turn out to be something quite different from what was delineated by the printed word.

Given the momentousness of the legal change wrought by the *Lawrence* decision, the Kennedy-Scalia exchange received only a passing glance in the extensive commentary immediately following its announcement. It has since received more attention; Robert Bork, for example, cited the references to foreign sources in Lawrence v. Texas (along with Grutter v. Bollinger)[6] as episodes in an "absurd turn in our jurisprudence"

2. Ibid., at 577.

3. Ibid., at 598.

4. Ibid., quoting Justice Clarence Thomas in a denial of certiorari in Foster v. Florida, 537 U.S. 990, n. (2002).

5. Mahadeb Jiew v. Dr. Sen, AIR 1951 Cal. 563 (1951).

6. Grutter v. Bollinger, 539 U.S. 306 (2003).

that reflects the arrogance of power of the modern judiciary.[7] "[E]ven Scalia at his gloomiest did not foresee [how a new Constitution] might be designed bit by bit from European, Asian, and African models."[8] He connected this jurisprudential turn with one of his long-standing concerns, "the transnational culture war."[9] Along similar lines, Ken Kersch discovered in the "seemingly benign references" to foreign sources "a vast and ongoing intellectual project," part of a "sophisticated effort to transform American constitutional law and its interpretation."[10] As a result, "Eventually, and perhaps sooner than we think, the nature and path of American constitutional development will be radically altered."[11]

These reactions may very well exaggerate the influence of external sources in the outcomes of these cases, and arguably they overstate the broader jurisprudential significance of the infusion from abroad. They do, however, address important issues of constitutional identity and the role of constitutional theory in comparative law, both evident in Justice Scalia's objection to the judicial deployment of comparative examples by the Court in overturning Bowers v. Hardwick.[12] That case had withheld the status of "fundamental right" to consensual sexual relations between homosexuals (as well as others who perform acts of sodomy in their intimate associations) on the ground that the behavior in question was not "deeply rooted in this Nation's history and tradition."[13] Scalia underscored the words "this Nation's," and observed that the *Bowers* majority opinion, contrary to the implication in Justice Kennedy's opinion, had

7. Robert H. Bork, "Whose Constitution Is It, Anyway?" *National Review,* December 8, 2003, 37.

8. Ibid.

9. Robert H. Bork, *Coercing Virtue: The Worldwide Rule of Judges* (Washington, DC: AEI Press, 2003), 11.

10. Ken I. Kersch, "Multilateralism comes to the Courts," 154 *The Public Interest,* Winter 2004, 4, 5. For examples of the thinking that concerns Kersch, see generally Anne-Marie Slaughter, *A New World Order* (Princeton, NJ: Princeton University Press, 2004), 65–203, and Harold Hongju Koh, "International Law as Part of Our Law," 98 *American Journal of International Law* 43 (2004).

11. Kersch, "Multilateralism," 16.

12. Bowers v. Hardwick, 478 U.S. 186 (1985).

13. Ibid., at 192.

not relied on "values we share with a wider civilization."[14] His own implication was that, in contrast with *Lawrence,* the strength of *Bowers* was evident in the local ingredients that went into its making. Thus a homegrown product is superior to one built with the help of imported materials.

In debunking interpretive approaches that utilize cross-national sources, Scalia was doing more than trumpeting American exceptionalism in constitutional matters. He was, in effect, implicitly raising serious doubts about the whole project of theorizing coherently about constitutions and constitutionalism. Thus his attachment to local tradition and history involves more than just a preference for a particular approach to substantive due process analysis; it bespeaks as well hostility toward any judicial reliance on transnational norms of constitutional understanding. "Scalia the judge roots himself in an America whose values he purports to be able to identify. If the job of the judge is to identify and then apply these distinctive values, why would it be relevant to study how other cultures approach similar questions?"[15] As a way of limiting judicial discretion in the designation of fundamental rights, privileging those with historical roots in American experience is an understandable way of pursuing the Court's business in a complex and contested area of the law. It need not, in fact, have anything to do with a principled choice for "legal particularism," an interpretive stance that emphasizes a nation's history and political culture in addressing constitutional questions.[16] It is only when, as in the case of Scalia, the commitment to particularism requires a categorical rejection of all sources outside of the tradition that theorizing about *a* constitution to theorizing about constitutionalism is rendered suspect.

14. *Lawrence,* at 598.

15. Sanford Levinson, "Looking Abroad when Interpreting the United States Constitution: Some Reflections," 39 *Texas Journal of International Law* (2004), 361.

16. Sujit Choudry, "Globalization in Search of Justification: Toward a Theory of Comparative Constitutional Interpretation," 74 *Indiana Law Journal* 801 (1999), 830. Take Justice Kennedy, for example, the author of the *Lawrence* opinion. He is often an ally of Justice Scalia. For instance, in Michael H. v. Gerald D., he joined Scalia's judgment for the Court that included a preference for "the most specific level at which a relevant tradition protecting, or denying protection to, the asserted right can be identified." 491 U.S. 110, 127 (1989).

Ultimately the goal of constitutional theory is to attain understanding of what it means to be governed by something called a constitution. But the variability in what that something is cannot help but strike even the most casual observer. The differences on display—in text, but more importantly in practice—are mainly attributable to the diversity of social and political life around the world. A sensible reaction to this diversity is to counsel caution in the assimilation of foreign materials into the indigenous constitutional matrix of one's country. The widely held assumption that a constitution is rooted in the way of life of a given society creates an understandable predisposition to resist the temptations of legal transplantation. For example, Frederick Schauer suggests "[o]ne need not slide into an unacceptable relativism to acknowledge that perhaps American constitutionalists can perform a great service by helping other countries to understand that constitutional constraints rest on culturally contingent social categories."[17] His demonstration that a category such as "political speech" will vary according to cultural history and national differences supports what we might call a policy of *constitutional protectionism,* in which national courts are jurisprudentially committed to the defense of their legal borders.

But if this condition "militates against cross-cultural assimilation of constitutional categories," even Schauer acknowledges (albeit in a brief footnote) that there are also "factors of internalization militating in exactly the opposite direction."[18] One of these factors surely must be the natural desire to learn from others in order to improve one's own circumstances. Including the American Constitution, I know of no example of a country whose constitution making avoided examining and often incorporating promising features from the governing experience of distant lands. "American reflection on the pathologies of political power exemplifies a larger feature of the American constitutional mind, to wit, its absorption in the best available comparative political science."[19] While

17. Frederick Schauer, "Free Speech and the Cultural Contingency of Constitutional Categories," 14 *Cardozo Law Review* 865 (1993), 880.

18. Ibid., 879 n. 71.

19. David A. J. Richards, "Revolution and Constitutionalism in America," in Michel Rosenfeld, *Constitution, Identity, Difference, and Legitimacy* (Durham: Duke University Press, 2004), 92.

there is a difference between constitution making and constitutional interpretation that might indicate the wisdom of distinct standards for incorporation, in principle the logic of self-improvement argues for an open border policy for both activities.

Open, however, does not necessarily mean unmonitored. As William Alford reminds us, "we need to approach foreign subjects with an even greater tentativeness of theoretical construct and with an even greater self-consciousness than we would subjects closer to home."[20] Just as responsible advocates of free trade insist on rigorous standards to assess the impact of economic traffic on vital national interests such as working conditions and the environment, comparativists (scholars and judges) should consider how the free flow of commerce in constitutional ideas could affect valued political and legal assets. Alford's worries about the dangers of "grand theory" are rooted in the belief that what Clifford Geertz referred to as "thick description" is critical to how we form judgments about foreign societies and how we use this knowledge to inform our own self-understanding. Only a "careful, contextualized consideration of a society" can enable one to appreciate why "a gesture that might be quite innocent in one cultural setting may be fraught with meaning in another."[21] If we are to study the criminal justice process in imperial China, we need to focus on the cultural context from which it emerged, rather than due process norms that reveal its deficiencies as an instrument of justice rightly considered.

In this chapter I argue for taking seriously the concerns raised by Schauer and Alford, but distinguishing them from the position articulated both by Scalia on the Court and supporters of his from the sidelines. Thus, I share the particularist perspective on constitutional arrangements as manifestations of key attributes of national identity, but contend that this should not preclude courts from seeking to strengthen the supports for constitutionalism while remaining attentive to the requirements and development of their respective polities' distinctive

20. William P. Alford, "On the Limits of 'Grand Theory' in Comparative Law," 61 *Washington Law Review* 945 (1986), 947.

21. Ibid.

constitutional identities.[22] Although advocates of an extreme protectionist constitutional policy will find the admonitory arguments of Schauer and Alford congenial to their case, a less categorical stance on the use of comparative materials will ensure that these arguments are not taken to be the exclusive preserve of the rejectionists. In making this argument I rely mainly on my own experience exploring constitutional domains beyond American shores, in which I have sought to develop contextually informed thick accounts of the unique features of local political/constitutional cultures without embracing a rigidly deterministic view of the constraints this imposes on constitutional actors.

In the next section I argue that aspirational considerations are critical to how one should theorize about the use of comparative materials in constitutional adjudication. All constitutions establish rules for the conduct of public business and the protection of private rights. But as we have seen, only the most crabbed understanding of what constitutions do would stop there; equally common to the genre is a conception, implicitly or explicitly incorporated in the document, of the kind of polity the constitution seeks to preserve and to become. This conception, or vision, will consist of a mix of attributes reflecting what is distinctive in the political culture as well as what are taken to be shared features of a universal culture of constitutionalism. Inevitably, contradictions within a given set of constitutional principles, or between those prescriptions and the societal status quo, will stimulate efforts—judicial and others—to achieve greater consistency. This disharmonic jurisprudential context establishes the incentives, opportunities, and costs inhering in the practice of looking abroad for interpretive inspiration.

I rely on three judicial settings—Israel, India, and Ireland—for suggestive examples in thinking about constitutional identity and the permeability of constitutional borders. The Israeli case focuses on a judiciary whose challenge has been to provide legal coherence to the unresolved political contradictions of an evolving constitutional order. The absence

22. I follow in this regard the cautionary advice of Vicki Jackson: "Learning from elsewhere . . . is always limited by the need to be mindful of institutional and other contextual differences." Vicki Jackson, "Constitutional Comparisons: Convergence, Resistance, Engagement" 119 *Harvard Law Review* 109, 122 (2005).

of a constitutional consensus presents judges with attractive incentives for assimilating the experience of courts in other nations, but it also highlights the risks of doing so. The deep division over the most basic questions of national identity, which is responsible in large measure for having impeded the process of constitutional design (including the adoption of a formal comprehensive written document), has encouraged members of the Supreme Court to complete the task of constitutional closure with the aid of examples taken from places where constitutional development has progressed less problematically in fulfillment of liberal democratic aspirations. But the identification of one side of the cultural divide with these transnational efforts, and the resistance to them emanating from the other side, threatens to undermine the Court's ability to function as an effective arbiter of constitutional questions.

The Indian case presents us with a different picture of constitutional disharmony. Here the Constitution, while by no means free of internal tension, is committed to a specific sociopolitical agenda involving major reform of an essentially feudal society. The free trade in legal ideas that has accompanied constitutional development since the inception of the independent republic has also been used freely by actors with sharply diverging agendas for India's future. Judges who are committed to realizing the *constitutionally* mandated agenda have had to be careful to adapt philosophically appealing ideas of external origin to the particular cultural context within which the work of the Court is done. Interests opposed to this agenda have been very clever in employing liberal ideas that resonate favorably within international circles to advance their cause. In this section I look at several landmark cases that reveal the pitfalls of failing to situate the universal in the particular while seeking guidance from abroad, as well as the constitutional benefits accruing from judges sensitive to the need to direct the light of foreign experience through the filter of their own cultural condition.

Finally, the Irish case is instructive in further illuminating the problem of translation in comparative constitutional theory, particularly as it relates to the realization of universalist aspirations that do not require abandoning the connection to moorings in a specific moral code of conduct. The Irish Supreme Court has confronted a number of issues concerning matters of personal freedom that have been made more difficult in light of secularizing trends that have created a widening gulf between societal mores and a constitutional tradition rooted in precepts of Catholic theology. The focus of jurisprudential concern has been on the question of natural law, which in Ireland possesses a meaning quite different from what the term conveys in many of the places that secularizing societies often draw upon for models of constitutional emulation. For example, with respect to the right of privacy, which contemporary accounts typically associate with a natural desire for individual autonomy, the Irish Court has struggled to achieve a balance between the need for constitutional adaptation and respect for traditional institutions of civil society. The penultimate section of this chapter reflects on how this effort has contributed dialogically to enhancing the self-understanding of the constitutional culture.

The Disharmonic Gap

The United States, Israel, India, and Ireland share a common preconstitutional experience as extensions of British imperial governance. That experience produced similarities in postindependence constitutional evolution; inevitably, for example, these polities have, to one degree or another, been engaged in a process of legal de-Anglicization. At the same time they have also sought to preserve ties with inherited traditions as an important component of their respective nation-building projects. But the textual constitutional differences—in length and specificity, in comprehensive or cumulative adoption, in configuration of spiritual and temporal domains, to name just a few—are much more obvious than the similarities.[23] Underlying these differences is a characteristic that unites

23. For a good discussion of similarity and difference in comparative case selection see Gerhard Dannemann, "Comparative Law: Study of Similarities or Differences?" in Mathias Reimann and Reinhard Zimmermann, eds., *The Oxford Handbook of Comparative Law* (Oxford: Oxford University Press, 2006). Dannemann points out that "Comparative scholarship might profit from an approach which ventures beyond different legal systems with a similar context by adding at least one legal system with a different context" (ibid., 411). Regarding the selection of Israel, India, and Ireland, the first two are similar in the challenges they confront from multicultural populations and ethnic tensions, and distinguishable from the latter, which is relatively free from these problems.

them and indeed all constitutions: their state of imperfection. The gap between the ideal and the actual expresses itself in various ways; in most cases a constitution will accurately reflect local circumstances; but it would be unusual to find a constitution that was not in some way committed to the achievement of things seemingly beyond its immediate reach.

The first great student of comparative constitutionalism pointed out that "The attainment of the best constitution is likely to be impossible for the general run of states; and the good law-giver and the true statesman must therefore have their eyes open not only to what is the absolute best, but also to what is the best in relation to actual conditions."[24] Aristotle scholars have long contested the meaning of this teaching from Book IV of *The Politics*.[25] Resolution of the debate, however, is not essential to appreciating the relevance of the philosopher's observation to the constitutional experiences of diverse nations. To wit: the creation of the American Constitution was accompanied by Publius's announcement in the last paper in *The Federalist* that "I am persuaded that it [the Constitution of 1787] is the best which our political situation, habits, and opinions will admit."[26] That this focus on "actual conditions" was not all that could be said about the document whose ratification was being sought is the theme of Martin Luther King Jr.'s famous "I Have a Dream" speech. "When the architects of our republic wrote the magnificent words of the Constitution and the Declaration of Independence, they were signing a promissory note to which every American was to fall heir."[27] Following Lincoln and others who apprehended an aspirational dimension in American constitutional development, he, in effect,

24. Aristotle, *The Politics*, trans. Ernest Barker (New York: Oxford University Press, 1962), 155.

25. See, for example, R. G. Mulgan, *Aristotle's Political Theory: An Introduction for Students of Political Theory* (Oxford: Clarendon Press, 1977), 113; and John B. Morrall, *Aristotle* (London: G. Allen & Unwin, 1977), 86–87.

26. *The Federalist*, 85, Henry Cabot Lodge, ed. (New York: G. P. Putnam's Sons, 1888), 547.

27. Martin Luther King Jr., "I Have a Dream," Keynote Address of the March on Washington, DC, for Civil Rights (August 28, 1963), in James M. Washington, ed., *A Testament of Hope: The Essential Writings of Martin Luther King, Jr.* (San Francisco: Harper & Row, 1986), 217.

attached three additional words to the Publius comment: "at this time." The framers might not have dwelled on "the absolute best," but in King's persuasive account their intentions encompassed more than the achievement of what was immediately possible.[28]

This distinction between the actual and the ideal is sufficiently familiar that it prompts one to consider if it is not (in different ways) endemic to the constitution-making process. Perhaps the most distinctive feature of the Indian Constitution is its inclusion of a section of Directive Principles of State Policy, which found their way into the document "in the hope and expectation that one day the tree of true liberty would bloom in India."[29] The Principles are nonjusticiable, although through judicial interpretation they have acquired more than simply hortatory significance in informing the meaning of enforceable fundamental rights provisions.[30] Included are commitments embodying the idea of the Indian state as constitutionally mandated to realizing radical social reconstruction. The model for the Indian framers was the Irish Constitution, whose authors were part of a nationalist movement with ties to Indian nationalists dating back to the nineteenth century. The Irish framers established a clear rationale for their innovation: "They will be there as a constant headline, something by which the people as a whole can judge their progress in a certain direction; something by which the representatives of the people can be judged as well as the people judge themselves as a whole. We will judge our progress in a certain direction by asking how far we have advanced

28. I develop this argument at length in Gary J. Jacobsohn, *The Supreme Court and the Decline of Constitutional Aspiration* (Totowa, NJ: Rowman and Littlefield, 1986).

29. Granville Austin, *The Indian Constitution: Cornerstone of a Nation* (Delhi: Oxford University Press, 1999), 50. Other examples of constitutionally inscribed directive principles may be found in the constitutions of Nigeria, Spain, Portugal, and Namibia. See Nigeria Constitution chap. 2, arts. 13–24; Constitucion tit. I, chap. 3, arts. 39–42 (Spain); Constituicao Da Republica Potuguesa Sec. I (Portugal); Namibia Constitution, chap. 11, arts. 95–101. The practice has also been incorporated in international agreements, such as the International Covenant on Economic, Social, and Cultural Rights. See G.A. Res. 2200A, U.N. GAOR, 21st sess. Sopp. No. 16, at 49. U.N. Doc. A/6316 (1966).

30. Part IV of the Constitution (Articles 36–51) contains the Directive Principles of State Policy.

in that direction."[31] The framers were intent on affirming that the new Constitution was both an aspirational document as well as a strictly legal charter, that while nonjusticiable, the value of the directive principles lay in the role they were projected to play in placing moral and political obligations on the state.[32]

In India this was made even more explicit, and the jurisprudence surrounding Part IV of the Constitution has, as is elaborated in Chapter 5, developed further than it has in Ireland. Article 37 says of the Directive Principles that they are "fundamental in the governance of the country and it shall be the *duty* of the State to apply these principles in making law."[33] As an Indian constitutional scholar points out, the potential impact of this provision is quite extraordinary when juxtaposed with another that provides that "It shall be the *duty* of the *Union* . . . to ensure that the government of every State is carried out in accordance with the provisions of this Constitution."[34] So despite their unenforceability in the courts, the failure by a state to comply with the constitutional directives would, under a plausible interpretation of the relevant language, justify the central government's determination to require enforcement by the states. The comparative lesson in this is clear, especially in its implications for Americans, whose predominant inclination has been to view the judiciary as exercising a monopoly over constitutional interpretation.

31. *Constituent Assembly Debates,* May 11, 1937, 69, www.oireachtas-debates.gov.ie/D/0067/D.0067.193705110029.html.

32. The Irish and Indian experience with directive principles was carefully studied by the framers of the South African Constitution. One South African scholar writing at the time of the drafting of the transitional constitution concluded that the Irish, unlike the Indians, had not derived as much benefit from their directive principles as they could have. Thus "the moral and political role they might have fulfilled has not materialized." Bertus De Villiers, "Social and Economic Rights," in David Van Wyk, John Dugard, Bertus De Villiers, and Dennis Davis, eds., *Rights and Constitutionalism: The New South African Legal Order* (Oxford: Oxford University Press, 1995), 618. The reference is to the minimal exploitation of the principles by the courts as an instrument for creating new rights (despite the fact that a landmark case—Ryan v. Attorney General, I.R. 294 (Ir. S.C., 1965)—had ruled that certain rights not explicitly mentioned in the document could be derived from the Directive Principles).

33. India Constitution, Part IV, Article 37 (emphasis added).

34. Durga Das Basu, *Introduction to the Constitution of India,* 18th ed. (New Delhi: Prentice-Hall of India, 1998), 142.

When the aspirational dimension of constitutionalism is made explicit, as in the case of those constitutions that include directive principles, the collaborative role of other political institutions in the realization of constitutional norms is also made more apparent.[35] The lesson is not that others consider adoption of similar provisions; rather it is that they take seriously the existence of implicit constitutional commitments (promissory notes if one likes) that create obligations—political, moral, and legal—extending beyond the jurisdiction of courts.

While the Irish enumeration of Directive Principles has not figured as prominently in constitutional jurisprudence as has its Indian counterpart, in both cases the list confers upon officials responsible for constitutional development (i.e., more than just judges) a mandate to diminish the gap between actual conditions and political ideals. Although it is easy to characterize such principles as "pious aspirations,"[36] or perhaps mischievous generalities, as "moral precepts for the authorities of the State . . . they have," in the words of an influential Indian constitutional framer, "at least an educative value."[37] Their effectiveness is dependent on context. Thus in speculating on the differing experiences of India and Ireland with their respective sets of Directive Principles perhaps most pertinent is that the Indian section represents a more direct and explicit challenge to the status quo than does its Irish counterpart. Indeed the latter was consciously based on staples of the Catholic social tradition, which had a close connection to the predominant political culture of the nation. In contrast, to the extent that the political culture in India mainly reflected the practices and traditions of its Hindu majority, the Constitution in that country was designed expressly to *reconstitute* a way of life that was viewed as no longer defensible within dominant elite circles. The magnitude of the challenge is suggested in the comment of India's "Madison," Dr. B. D. Ambedkar, as he anticipated

35. This is not to say that the Directive Principles are unrelated to the Court's own interpretive powers. As the Indian example illustrates, they can be relied upon to influence judicial interpretation of enforceable provisions (especially fundamental rights), and they can be a source to be drawn upon to assess the constitutionality of legislative enactments.

36. Such was the characterization of Sir Ivor Jennings, as quoted in Basu, *Constitution of India,* 143.

37. B. N. Rau, as quoted in Ibid., 14.

the commencement of the new constitutional republic: "On the 26th of January 1950, we are going to enter into a life of contradictions. In politics we will have equality and in social and economic life we will have inequality. In politics we will be recognizing the principle of one man one vote and one vote one value. In our social and economic life, we shall, by reason of our social and economic structure, continue to deny the principle of one man one value. How long shall we continue to live this life of contradictions?"[38]

While the question possesses a special poignancy in India, it can be asked of all polities. The salient contradictions will vary from place to place, but inherent in the constitutional condition, whether subtle or dramatic, is a disharmony manifest either in the disjuncture between a constitution and a society or between commitments internal to a constitution, for example, between positive and negative rights. Indeed, in India, as Yash Ghai notes, "[T]he dialectic between Fundamental Rights, made supreme by the Constitution, and Directive Principles of State Policy" has been an ongoing reality "at the heart of the regime."[39]

38. *Constituent Assembly Debates,* vol. 12, 979, November 25, 1949 (Government of India). This will not surprise those scholars who perceive the increasingly familiar constitutionalization of rights as enabling ruling elites to rely on judicial empowerment to protect their interests in majoritarian political settings. This phenomenon "is often not so much the cause or the reflection of a progressive revolution in a given polity, as it is a means by which preexisting and ongoing sociopolitical struggles in that polity are carried out." Ran Hirschl, "The Political Origins of Judicial Empowerment through Constitutionalization: Lessons from Four Constitutional Revolutions," 25 *Law and Social Inquiry* 91 (2000), 139. To be sure, Indian support for this claim is complicated by the fact that the evidence suggests, in Granville Austin's apt phrase, that the judiciary was envisioned as "an arm of the social revolution," a role it initially performed in dutiful fashion by standing aside as the Nehru government endeavored to implement its ideas for far-reaching socioeconomic transformation. It was only years later that the Supreme Court began to resist these changes, although since the end of the dictatorial interregnum of Nehru's daughter in 1977, the judiciary spearheaded the effort to redress the massive inequities plaguing Indian society since time immemorial. Unlike in the formative years, its behavior in pursuing this role is more active than passive, so much so that the Indian Court's reputation as the most activist bench in the world is widely accepted. Much of its current popularity at home stems from its determination to narrow the distance between the animating ideals of constitutional design and the realities of social failure.

39. Yash Ghai, "Universalism and Relativism: Human Rights as a Framework for Negotiating Interethnic Claims," 21 *Cardozo Law Review* 1095 (2000), 1107.

The pursuit of a compelling unity becomes an important and predictable part of much of the activity of constitutional politics. This as well is the context from whence much of the initiative to explore constitutional possibilities abroad comes. Finding "an alternative to less congenial domestic law"[40] is a reasonable way to understand the strategic appeal to foreign sources, but one might view such activity with less suspicion if it is connected to a broader effort to address the imperfections of the local order. Precisely because it sometimes expresses a fundamental contradiction, what is "deeply rooted in [a] Nation's history and tradition" may be as much a problem as a solution for constitutional decision makers. Under these conditions seeking guidance from the experience of others presents attractive possibilities for achieving constitutional coherence. As the examples explored in the sections below suggest, being open to the lure of these possibilities is not incompatible with being very cautious about acceding to them.

Israel: External Sources and the Unresolved Dilemma of Constitutional Identity

By the mid-1990s the Israeli Supreme Court under the leadership of its president, Aharon Barak, had signed on to the judicialization of politics that is now so evident in India, Europe, and many other places. It is a development that has not pleased all observers, including Robert Bork, for whom the Barak-led judiciary has become "the most activist, antidemocratic court in the world and . . . may, unless a merciful Providence intervenes, foreshadow the future of all constitutional courts in the Western world."[41] Bork makes clear that one of the forms such intervention would no doubt take is the divine curtailment of a judge's ability to cite foreign constitutional rulings.

The temptation on the Israeli Court to look abroad for guidance and/or validation is readily comprehensible in light of its unique constitutional predicament, beginning of course with the absence in Israel of a formal comprehensive written charter. The series of Basic Laws that

40. Kersch, "Multilateralism," 5.

41. Bork, *Coercing Virtue*, 13.

cumulatively provide Israel with a framework for governance is inherently incomplete and provisional, which means that judges have often found themselves in uncharted constitutional waters, carried by interpretive currents to places where "real" constitutions might yield answers to difficult questions. Thus, for example, it is not surprising that in the absence of any textual constitutional guidance for solving free speech issues, the Court would find useful (if not controlling) the First Amendment jurisprudence of the American Court.[42] But two enactments in 1992—most notably the Basic Law on Human Dignity and Freedom—had important implications for the practice of constitutional jurisprudence, including the Court's use of foreign materials. Its importance is implicit in Justice Barak's repeated invocation of the term "constitutional revolution" to describe the new state of affairs, not so much for the actual substantive changes introduced by the enactments than for the possibilities latent within them for creative judicial intervention in the unresolved dilemma of regime definition.[43]

What is unresolved is the contradiction highlighted in Israel's Declaration of Independence between the particularist (the commitment to a Jewish State) and universalist (the commitment to a liberal democratic polity) filaments in the existent constitutional constellation. The resulting—and perhaps inevitable—constitutional project is to bring clarity and unity of purpose to the polity by resolving the inner tensions of these dual aspirations, and to move into a constitutional future that resembles the experience of other liberal democracies. Judicial interpretation, in Justice Barak's view, must be "purposive," with the goal "of achieving

42. See Ibid., chap. 6, where I consider the Israeli Court's application and modification of American free-speech doctrine to several cases in Israel involving allegedly dangerous speech.

43. My account of this development is in Gary Jeffrey Jacobsohn, "After the Revolution," 34 *Israel Law Review* 139 (2000). Much of the early commentary on substantive changes emphasized their connection to the pursuit of a neoliberal economic agenda. In addition to the aforementioned article by Ran Hirschl, see also his "Israel's 'Constitutional Revolution': The Legal Interpretaion of Entrenched Civil Liberties in an Emerging Neo-Liberal Economic Order," 46 *American Journal of Comparative Law* 427 (1998); Aeyal Gross, "The Politics of Rights in Israeli Constitutional Law," 3 *Israel Studies* 80 (1998); and Michael Mandel, "Democracy and the New Constitutionalism in Israel," 33 *Israel Law Review* 259 (1999).

unity and constitutional harmony."[44] For example, the Basic Law on Human Dignity requires upholding "the values of the State of Israel as a Jewish and democratic State."[45] How is this to be done? "The content of the phrase 'Jewish State' will be determined by the level of abstraction which shall be given it. In my opinion, one should give this phrase meaning on a high level of abstraction, which will unite all members of society and find the common ground among them. The level of abstraction should be so high, until it becomes identical to the democratic nature of the state."[46]

Controversy surrounding the Barak agenda has focused on whether it could undermine the long-term influence of the Court in Israeli political life. One of the justice's predecessors, Moshe Landau, gave voice to these concerns by predicting that "If questions of great political import are left to be finally settled by the Supreme Court of Israel, it will lead to the politicization of the Court. . . ."[47] Reliance on a high level of abstraction to achieve a unified view may indeed fuel the anxiety of powerful constituencies that the "enlightened" opinion from which guidance in values is to be found is likely to be a liberal, generally secular intellectual

44. "The Constitutional Revolution has led to a change in the judiciary's status. Great responsibilities have been imposed upon it. It must fill the mould created by the 'majestic generalities' in the new Basic Laws. The judiciary must be aware of the fundamental values of the people. It must balance them in accordance with the values of the 'enlightened general public' in Israel. It must reflect the general public's conscience, the social consensus, the legal ethics and the value judgments of society with regard to acceptable and unacceptable behaviour. Constitutional interpretation should not be formalistic or pedantic. It should be purposive. It should be done from a wide perspective and adopt a substantive approach. A constitution is a living organism, and its interpretation must express the deep 'I believe' of the society. This interpretation must base itself on the historical continuance of the nation's creation, with the intention of achieving unity and constitutional harmony." Aharon Barak, "The Constitutionalization of the Israeli Legal System as a Result of the Basic Laws and Its Effect on Procedural and Substantive Criminal Law," 31 *Israel Law Review* 3 (1997), 5.

45. Basic Law: Human Dignity and Liberty, sec. 1, 1992, S.H. 150 (Isr.).

46. Aharon Barak, "The Constitutional Revolution: Protected Human Rights," 1 *Mishpat Umimshal* 9 (1992–1993), 30.

47. Moshe Landau, "The Limits of Constitutions and Judicial Review," in Daniel J. Elazar, ed., *Constitutionalism: The Israeli and American Experiences* (Lanham, MD: University Press of America, 1990), 202.

elite, widely perceived as unrepresentative of Israeli public opinion.[48] A constitutional vision imposed on a deeply rifted society has the potential to backfire, particularly if done in a clumsy, heavy-handed way.[49] Whether a prudent imposition should occur depends, in part, on the answer to a question posed by Wiktor Osiatynski in considering the subject of constitutional borrowing: "Which should be attended to first? Should we undertake a broad educational attempt to create a constitutional culture and adopt a constitution only after such a culture is formed? Or should we enact a constitution first and then use it to form a constitutional culture?"[50]

Justice Barak has chosen the second option, which, given the extended delay in formalizing a constitution in Israel, is understandable, if controversial. The evolution of the constitution is a process that includes the justice and his colleagues; interpretation on "a high level of abstraction" is the vehicle through which the liberal constitution comes into being. From that point "[i]t is possible that the constitutional transformation will be internalized; that human rights will become the 'daily bread' of every girl and boy, and that the awareness of rights . . . will prevail, and that we will be more sensitive to the rights of a human being as a human being."[51] There is, then, (at least the hope of) something profoundly transformative in the constitutionalization of rights, with the most important change awaiting the incorporation of the evolved constitutional identity in the behavior of the people. Anticipating such a culture of rights will inevitably incur resistance from those

48. Barak's notion that the Court should seek guidance from "enlightened" opinion was criticized in Israel. The criticism has been echoed elsewhere; thus Bork writes that "Barak's enlightened community is not a community at all; the phrase is a metaphor for a particular set of values, which is to be made dominant by judicial decision." Bork, *Coercing Virtue,* 130. In May 2001, Barak expressed regret for having used the concept of the "enlightened public." *Haaretz,* May 15, 2001.

49. See Ruth Gavison, "The Role of Courts in Rifted Democracies," 33 *Israel Law Review* 216 (1998), 218. "The deeper the rifts in society, the more cautious the courts should be, because there is a greater danger of a serious break-down in the cohesion of society" (ibid., 253).

50. Wiktor Osiatynski, "Paradoxes of Constitutional Borrowing," 1 *I-Con: International Journal of Constitutional Law* 244 (2003), 266.

51. United Mizrachi Bank plc v. Migdal Cooperative Village, 49 (iv) P.D. 221 (1995), 448.

with a stake in the entrenched culture. These opponents will insist on rejecting any methods and sources that are not consistent with a defense of the cultural status quo; any foreign importations will be immediately suspect. As Osiatynski points out, "Culture usually tends to resist borrowing."[52]

It follows that Barak is the anti-Scalia. His jurisprudence, unsurprisingly, is distinguished by an affinity for foreign sources, especially Canadian and American. "Comparative law can help judges determine the objective purpose of a constitution. . . . A common basis of democracy is, however, a necessary but insufficient condition for comparative analysis. As judges, we must also examine whether there is anything in the historical development and social conditions that makes the local and the foreign system different enough to render interpretive inspiration impracticable. But when there is an adequate similarity, interpretive inspiration is proper."[53] Some of Justice Barak's opinions are vulnerable to the criticism that, in their reliance on comparative materials, they are too open to such inspiration in the face of critical differences between borrower and borrowee in historical development and social conditions.[54] While the merits of such criticism must be evaluated on a case-by-case

52. Osiatynski, "Paradoxes of Constitutional Borrowing," 261.

53. Aharon Barak, "Foreword: A Judge On Judging: The Role of a Supreme Court in a Democracy," 116 *Harvard Law Review* 16 (2002), 112–113.

54. For Bork, the Israeli Court under Barak's leadership is a principal target for this sort of criticism. "[J]udges on national courts have begun to confer with their foreign counterparts and to cite foreign constitutional decisions as guides to the interpretation of their own constitutions. One telling indication of the judicial activism and uniformity of outlook among judges is the way that legal interpretations of constitutions with very different texts and histories are now giving way to common attitudes expressed in judicial rulings." Bork, *Coercing Virtue,* 10. My own review of Barak-led Israeli Supreme Court decisions suggests that their frequent references to American sources have contributed to the failure of the Court to develop a jurisprudence, at least in the free-speech domain, that reflects the character of the larger pluralist democracy of which it is a part. But this still leaves open the question of whether this is necessarily a bad thing. One might argue, for example, that the Israeli political culture is sufficiently supple to accommodate a range of constitutional possibilities, and that the direction that may initially possess the greatest "fit" with the broader sociopolitical culture is not the best way to go. Bork's criticism would therefore be more persuasive if he presented more evidence than the simple fact that constitutions have different texts and histories.

basis, the best general defense against reliance of this kind starts with skepticism over the justice's own criteria for appropriating foreign sources. The appeal of these sources for Barak lies in their potential for bridging the gap between the liberal and illiberal commitments of the Jewish State. Promoting the harmonies of constitutional unity means muting the discordant notes in the Zionist political composition; this means that "a common basis in democracy" cannot be the predicate for constitutional borrowing or transplantation. Rather, it is the aspiration *for* democracy that renders the foreign inspirational.

The case against using foreign sources has been most forcefully made by the Israeli constitutional scholar (and frequent critic of Barak) Ruth Gavison, who insists "it is wiser to seek solutions to our legal disputes by looking for guidance to local norms rather than to international law or to other legal systems."[55] Gavison's concerns relate to questions of "collective identity," and her arguments are similar to those made by Scalia and others in the United States.[56] But she is careful to distinguish the American and Israeli cases; unlike her own country, the former's "self-identity is that of a civic nation, not an ethnic one."[57] In contrast, Israel's "unresolved conflict" creates "a special challenge to law as an agent of social and political cohesiveness."[58]

If for Barak this unresolved conflict becomes the predicate for aligning Israeli law with standards prevailing elsewhere, for Gavison it pulls in the opposite direction. "[W]hen the law does not provide an answer, the supplementary materials in Israel should not be universal or comparative or rational. They should be connected to particularistic Jewish heritage."[59] This heritage, she acknowledges, does not refer to the rules and arrangements of Jewish religious law, but rather to the principles of that tradition, which are "the universal values of peace, equity, and

55. Ruth Gavison, "Law, Adjudication, Human Rights, and Society," 40 *Israel Law Review* 13, 25 (2007).

56. Ibid. "[I]f we . . . take our law and legal tradition seriously as affirmations of our distinctive society, it follows that we must see the problem as something we want to resolve within our own culture" (ibid., 26).

57. Ibid., 28.

58. Ibid., 31.

59. Ibid., 34.

justice."[60] While "the special way that Judaism articulates basic universal values"[61] might seem to leave an opening to sources external to the indigenous Israeli legal tradition, Gavison grudgingly allows only for inspirational support as a reason for judges to consider these sources. What is clear, however, in the positions taken by both Barak and Gavison is that the disharmonic nature of the Israeli legal and constitutional tradition provides opportunities for the dialogical engagement that drives the development of constitutional identity. Their differences are not as significant as they may first appear; the lines they draw between the universal and the particular diverge, making them more or less receptive to the migration of constitutional ideas.

Indeed, the Israeli example is so suggestive because it invites us to consider the import of disharmony in comparative constitutional theory. If one were to imagine a continuum of constitutional polities that distributed regimes according to the degree to which their governing principles were internally coherent, Israel would doubtless be located at or near one of the endpoints. The other endpoint would be occupied by a nation whose constitutive principles manifested a high degree of consistency, such that an observer would have very little difficulty in characterizing the essential political character and commitments of the country. It is difficult to imagine, though, that even this country's principles would be perfectly consistent in all respects, to say nothing of its harmony between principles and practices. This is especially notable in the United States, which Samuel P. Huntington once characterized as "the modern disharmonic polity par excellence."[62] According to this account, in nations with a high degree of value consensus, the gap between promise and performance—for example, when the commitment to equality coexists with prominent inequality—is the phenomenon most responsible for generating political change and social reform. The argument is also applicable to tensions within constitutional principles (even if they are not the outright contradictions found on the opposite end of the continuum),

60. Ibid.

61. Ibid., 36.

62. Samuel P. Huntington, *American Politics: The Promise of Disharmony* (Cambridge, MA: Harvard University Press, 1981), 12.

in this case stimulating efforts to achieve internal consistency. Those efforts may not get very far, in part for a lack of urgency, perhaps also because prudent actors may view the situation as a "creative tension" better left unresolved. But the impulse to achieve *constitutional* harmony is rarely neutral in its directional tendency; the predominant thrust is to push from the particular to the universal.

The point can be put more emphatically. Alexis de Tocqueville famously declared that "The gradual development of equality of conditions is . . . a providential fact, and it has the principal characteristics of one: it is universal, it is enduring, each day it escapes human power; all events, like all men, serve its development."[63] I would be less inclined to invoke divine sanction to affirm democratic inevitability, and were I to do so, I might still find the path to democracy a more vexed and hence open question than did Tocqueville. But one cannot ignore the fact that even when the forces of particularism are in political ascendancy—as we have seen in India in the recent past—the success of their constitutional claims often hinges upon how clever they are in advancing principles that, in Justice Barak's terms, are put forward on "a high level of abstraction."[64] If history tells us anything it is that the democratic

63. Alexis de Tocqueville, *Democracy in America,* trans. Harvey C. Mansfield and Delba Winthrop (Chicago: University of Chicago Press, 2000), 6.

64. This is most evident in the debate in India over adoption of a uniform civil code. The principal advocates of such a code, which is prescribed in Article 44 as one of the Constitution's Directive Principles, are the Hindu nationalists, whose political base is in the Bharatiya Janata Party (BJP), the party that directs the nation's governing coalition. As they see it (and they are not alone in this regard), abandoning the system whereby different groups exercise a measure of legal autonomy over the lives of their adherents, is crucial to achieving the goal of a more communal—which is to say *Hindu*—state. See Susanne Hoeber Rudolph and Lloyd I. Rudolph, "Living with Difference in India: Legal Pluralism and Legal Universalism in Historical Context," in Gerald James Larson, ed., *Religion and Personal Law in India: A Call to Judgment* (Bloomington: Indiana University Press, 2001), 52–54; and Martha C. Nussbaum, "India: Implementing Sex Equality through Law," 2 *Chicago Journal of International Law* 35, 40 (2001). But rather than present the case for the code in terms that honestly convey their aspirations, they have, in effect, appropriated a liberal discourse that allows them to assume the rhetorical high ground of liberal universalism. Whether this strategy will ultimately prevail is yet to be determined, but the chosen terms of debate are a tacit recognition of the globally evident presumption in favor of *liberal* constitutionalism.

argument has won, even if in practice it is often notoriously honored in the breach.[65]

But of course local circumstances matter. If "[a]rguments from political culture are so often, in the end, sophisticated forms of a mystical fatalism"[66]

65. Sometimes, however, particularist forces are in such a dominant position that they need not compromise at all, especially in regard to how they frame their arguments. In such places—Iran, for example—ruling clerics may, as we have seen in the events surrounding the presidential election of 2009, ultimately have to accede to pressures from below, but then again they could do what now seems unlikely and overplay their hand, finding themselves carried away by a rising tide of liberal sentiment. An Iranian "constitutional revolution" is already imaginable, and ironically its model, as one student of that country's politics has noted, is Israel rather than the United States. "Over the past two decades, academics, reformist theologians and liberal clerics in Iran have been struggling to redefine traditional Islamic political philosophy in order to bring it in line with modern concepts of representative government, popular sovereignty, universal suffrage and religious pluralism. What these Iranians have been working toward is 'Islamic democracy': that is, a liberal, democratic society founded on an Islamic moral framework." Reza Aslan, "Why Religion Must Play a Role in Iran," *New York Times,* July 18, 2003, A21. If this revolution were successful it would not necessarily result in the triumph of a new paradigm, for indeed "the Jewish version of this ideal currently exists in Israel" (ibid). So while judicial revolutionaries in Israel are attempting to steer the constitutional politics in that country in a more secular Western direction, many Iranians would find the contradictions of an Israeli-style "religious democracy" a quite desirable and tolerable place to be." Of course, given the pariah status of Israel within the region, it is unlikely that a future Iranian Supreme Court will be too eager to include Israeli precedents in its opinions. But if one were to imagine the collapse of the Islamic Republic and its replacement with a constitutional polity rooted in democratic and indigenous cultures, then in theory at least the jurisprudence of the Jewish state would have much to offer such a fledgling regime. The interpretive premises underlying this imagined Court's borrowing from abroad bears a similarity to what Choudhry calls "universalist interpretation," but is distinguishable from it in at least one important respect. Universalists "posit that constitutional guarantees are cut from a universal cloth, and that all constitutional courts are engaged in the identification, interpretation, and application of the same set of principles. In seeking a transcendence of national boundaries, they exhort "courts to pay no heed to national legal particularities when engaging in constitutional interpretation." Sujit Choudhry, "Globalization in Search of Justification: Toward a Theory of Constitutional Interpretation," 74 *Indiana Law Journal,* 819, 833 (1999). If this were true, however, then surely it would make more sense for the Iranian Court to find in some other foreign jurisprudence—for example, American, German, or Canadian—a better source for constitutional emulation than the incompletely realized Israeli democracy.

66. Baruch Susser, "A Proposed Constitution for Israel," in Elazar, *Constitutionalism,* 181.

that obstruct the path of needed change, they are also the necessary, if not sufficient, condition for intelligent change.[67] An Iranian judge who finds himself attracted to the American model of separation of church and state would be well-advised to question its constitutional importation absent assurances that religion plays a comparable role in the two nations. We might imagine the ideal arrangement for achieving the perfect balance between church and state, and therewith the maximum protection for both spiritual and temporal concerns. But just as, in Aristotle's discussion of the best practicable constitution, the lawgiver and statesman should be attentive to "actual conditions," so must the jurist ruling in matters of religion and politics. The analysis of constitutional possibilities for addressing this relationship requires sensitivity to the "facts on the ground," especially the manner in which religious life is experienced within any given society and how this experience affects the achievement of historically driven—if not determined—constitutional ends. As Michael Walzer points out, "[T]here are no principles [beyond a basic respect for human rights] that govern all the regimes of toleration or that require us to act in all circumstances, in all times and places, on behalf of a particular set of political or constitutional arrangements."[68] For example, "[W]e [cannot] say that state neutrality and voluntary association, on the model of John Locke's 'Letter on Toleration,' is the only or best way of dealing with religious and ethnic pluralism. It is a very good way, one that is adapted to the experience of Protestant congregations in certain sorts of societies, but its reach beyond that experience and those societies has to be argued, not simply assumed."[69]

67. On this point see, Roger Cotterell, "Comparative Law and Legal Culture," in Mathias Reimann and Richard Zimmermann, eds., *The Oxford Handbook of Comparative Law* (Oxford: Oxford University Press, 2008), 713.

68. Michael Walzer, *On Toleration* (New Haven, CT: Yale University Press, 1997), 2–3. Walzer proceeds "to defend . . . a historical and contextual account of toleration and coexistence, one that examines the different forms that these have actually taken and the norms of everyday life appropriate to each." He continues, "It is necessary to look both at the ideal versions of these practical arrangements and at their characteristic, historically documented distortions" (ibid).

69. Ibid., 4. A good example of Walzer's point may be found in the Indian practice of state support for public events of a religiously celebratory nature. As Rajeev Dhavan observes, "This is where Indian secularism is vastly different from American or any other kind of secularism." Rajeev Dhavan, "The Kumbh," *The Hindu,* February 26, 2001.

Consider in this regard the controversy generated in Israel over the Qa'adan v. The Israel Land Administration et al. case.[70] In this troubling and painfully vexing case, an Arab couple (the Qa'adans) living in a poorly developed Arab settlement had sought to relocate and build a home in Katzir, a better-endowed Jewish communal settlement established in 1982 in the north of Israel. "We feel," said the husband, "that as citizens of this country we have a right to build our house where we choose."[71] But their application was rejected by the Katzir Cooperative Society, which, in collaboration with the Jewish Agency, had established the settlement on state land in 1982. The refusal to accept the couple was based upon the Society's policy of accepting only Jewish members. The Arabs' claim that the policy illegally discriminated against them on the basis of religion and nationality was upheld by the Supreme Court.

In its ruling the Court decided that, as a general rule, the state was prohibited by the principle of equality from allocating land to its citizens on these ascriptive grounds. Justice Barak's opinion (which he characterized as one of the most difficult of his career)[72] derived its conclusion from the values inherent in both the Jewish and democratic character of Israel. "We hold that the State of Israel was not permitted by law to allocate State Land to the Jewish Agency for the purpose of establishing the communal settlement of Katzir on the basis of discrimination between Jews and non-Jews."[73] For all but one of the five judges, the law prevented the state from discriminating directly in its land allocation, as well as indirectly through the instrumentality of the Jewish Agency. The majority also was careful to limit its ruling to the facts of this particular case, indicating that there are different kinds of settlements whose special problems would in each instance require separate arguments. "[I]t is important to understand and remember that today we are taking the first step on a difficult and sensitive path. It is therefore appropri-

70. Qa'adan v. The Israel Land Administration et al., 54(1) P.D. 258 (2000). All citations are taken from the English translation published in the *Israel Law Report.*

71. Michelle Chabin, "This Land Is Whose Land?" *The Jewish Week,* March 17, 2000, available at www.thejewishweek.com.

72. Serge Schmemann, "Israeli Learns Some Are More Israeli Than Others," *New York Times,* March 1, 1998.

73. *Qa'adan,* at 182.

ate that we proceed carefully from one case to the next case according to the circumstances of each case."[74]

Despite this gesture to incrementalism, the Court's judgment quickly became a political *cause célèbre.* On the right it was viewed as "effectively defin[ing] Israel as a democratic country only,"[75] and "a blow to the Zionist ideal of a Jewish state."[76] Thus, "It supports the post-Zionist secularist view that Israel is a state of all its citizens but not with a specific Jewish identity."[77] Elsewhere it was hailed as "one of the most powerful and positive decisions to come in decades."[78] The director of the Association for Civil Rights in Israel, which brought the case to the Court, could not have been more Barakian in the effusiveness of his response: "The acceptance of the petition by the Court and the prohibition of the transfer of state-owned land to bodies whose purpose is to enable settlement by Jews only, is nothing short of a revolution, crucial to the very essence of Israel as a democratic state, based on human rights values."[79]

If the intensity of the reactions (to say nothing of the issue itself) reminds Americans of Brown v. Board of Education, Barak's opinion

74. Ibid., at 180.

75. Yair Sheleg, "Katzir and a 'State of All Its Citizens,'" *Israel Religious Action Center,* www.irac.org (accessed March 14, 2000).

76. Yedidya Atlas, as quoted in the *Jewish Week,* March 17, 2000.

77. Ibid. While it may further the post-Zionist view in this way, post-Zionists, as we have seen, would see the *Qa'adan* decision as fundamentally incoherent to the extent that its derivation is linked to the alleged democratic values of the state. Indeed, the crux of the ethnocratic interpretation is to be found in Israel's land policies, and particularly in the ceding of authority to such extraterritorial organizations such as the Jewish National Fund and the Jewish Agency. The Court's incremental decision in the *Qa'adan* case leaves the logic of these policies essentially intact, which is hardly a post-Zionist victory. As one commentator has written, "The verdict itself leaves a loophole for the court to avoid supporting equal rights for Arab citizens if the mere specter of national security is raised." Baruch Kimmerling, *Clashing Identities: Explorations in Israeli and Palestinian Societies,* 180 (New York: Columbia University Press, 2008). In Chapter 6, we have an opportunity to revisit this critique in the context of another landmark decision, specifically relating to immigration policy and family unification.

78. Aliza Mazor, associate director of the New Israel Fund, as quoted in the *Jewish Week,* March 17, 2000.

79. The association for Civil Rights in Israel, "The Right of an Israeli Couple to Build Their Home in Katzir," at www.acri.org.il (homepage of the Association for Civil Rights in Israel [ACRI]), quoting ACRI Executive Director Vered Livne.

made the connection quite clear in specifically invoking the school segregation case with his declaration that "separate is inherently unequal."[80] "[S]eparation is insulting to the minority group being removed from the general public, stressing the difference between it and the others, and perpetuating feelings of social inferiority."[81] Also echoing the American decision was the Court's directive to the government to proceed with "deliberate speed" in implementing the ruling.[82] And as a further parallel, there was the subsequent activity within the legislative branch to nullify the Court's controversial judgment.

In 2002 the National Religious Party sponsored a bill designed to overturn *Qa'adan* by expressly giving the government the authority to allocate land for Jews only. The bill initially received overwhelming support in the Israeli Cabinet, but ultimately the firestorm precipitated by this incendiary legislation led to its burial in a Knesset committee. Even some supporters of the bill had worried that its passage would reignite the worldwide effort to delegitimize Israel as a racist apartheid state. To be sure, they agreed with the bill's proponents that a law designating state land for sole occupancy by Jews was faithful to honored and enduring Zionist settlement ideals, but they were persuaded that the international repercussions of such a codification were not worth the gains to be had. In short, their legislative retreat in no way signaled any diminution in the contempt they felt for a Barak-led Court that had flagrantly abandoned what they held to be the constitutive commitments of the Israeli polity.[83]

80. *Qa'adan,* at 170. After citing Brown v. Board of Education, Justice Barak explained its underlying reasoning.

81. *Qu'adan,* at 170. Barak then went on to point out how complicated an issue this is, acknowledging that there may be situations where separate but equal treatment might be legally permitted (as, for example, with reference to the Bedouin community). But he was emphatic that in this case the reasoning of *Brown* is applicable.

82. Interestingly, after prolonged delay by the Israel Land Administration and an apparent refusal to obey the Court's order in *Qa'adan,* the Administration finally—after four years—agreed to allocate a parcel of land to the Qa'adan family. See Yuval Yoaz and David Ratner, "ILA to Allow Israeli Family Build in Jewish Town," *Haaretz,* May 10, 2004.

83. The movement to formally adopt a constitution for Israel has always been associated with liberal political interests, but *Qa'adan* has prompted thinking on the other side of the

Those commitments, as we know, are deeply contested. Although *Qa'adan* was, in Cass Sunstein's terms, a minimalist holding in the purported narrowness of its reach, it was anything but minimalist in the depth of its theorizing.[84] Moreover, its "color-blind" reasoning presented an awkward fit with the realities of Israeli pluralism, however benignly or not those realities are viewed. When, in 1978, the Court upheld the exclusion of an Arab from the Jewish Quarter in the Old City of Jerusalem, the Court said, "We have a distinguished rule that we should never give our assistance in any matter that amounts to discrimination between persons on grounds of their religion or nationality. But . . . we must not close our eyes to reality and to actual conditions."[85] Justice Meir Shamgar added, "Automatic transfer from place to place of all the varied forms and ways in which the rule of equality has been applied, without taking into account special conditions and circumstances, can be misleading to no small extent; for example compulsory integration of school children there, which forces the English language and Anglo-Saxon culture on each and every student and is regarded there as the height of equality, could be considered here to be compulsory assimilation if an Arab student were to be forced because of it to forego a separate school system in which studies are conducted in his own language and in accord with his own

---

spectrum to reassess its opposition to the idea. With a Court that is viewed as hopelessly secular and liberal, some conservatives have figured out that the best way to safeguard Jewish identity is to entrench their ideology in fundamental law. For example, in response to Justice Barak's "first step on a difficult and delicate path" to nondiscrimination, one passionate critic of the decision wrote, "The conclusion to be drawn from this new path should be that the 'conservative' circles (from both a religious and nationalist perspective) are actually the ones who today should have an interest in formulating a binding constitution which would not only specifically define Israel as a Jewish and democratic state, but would also bindingly define the practical significance of such a balance." Sheleg, "Katzir," www.irac.org.

84. See Cass Sunstein, *One Case at a Time: Judicial Minimalism On the Supreme Court* (Cambridge, MA: Harvard University Press, 1999). One should note that Sunstein disputes the notion that *Brown* was a maximalist decision. "[I]t can even be taken as a form of democracy-promoting minimalism" (ibid., at 39). Despite its great importance, Sunstein views it as the culmination of a series of minimalist decisions. In that sense *Qa'adan* should probably be understood as less restrained in its minimalism.

85. Muhammad Sa'id Burkaan v. Minister of Finance, 32 (2) P.D. 800 (1978), at 805.

culture."[86] However incompatible with liberal ideals, separate (but equal?) communal development is plausibly consistent with principles of justice of a society in which group autonomy with respect to important domains of personal law takes precedence over social assimilation.[87]

It may be, of course, that attitudes and assumptions are changing, and that it is now misleading to say of Israel, "The pluralistic, integrationist approach that has been the standard for American society has no relevance here."[88] Alternatively, one would not be surprised to learn that such description is more timely than ever. In either case it is questionable whether an issue as critical as this—one that goes to the very core of the nation's identity and meaning—should be resolved by the Supreme Court. The manner of its resolution in *Qa'adan* conforms to the jurisprudential strategy for "achieving unity and constitutional harmony." Thus, the state's Jewish and democratic commitments are made to converge upon a shared principle of formal equality according to which constitutional meaning is assigned. Had the Knesset responded to this

86. Ibid., at 808. In an in-depth study of the *Qa'adan* case, Steven V. Mazie did extensive interviewing of different population groups in Israel to gauge their reactions to the decision. His summary of Arab reaction is quite relevant here. "These subjects' strong resistance to transplanting their lives to another locale is a consideration wholly absent from Chief Justice Barak's transplantation of *Brown* into the *Ka'adan* decision. In leaning on the concept of 'separate but equal is inherently unequal,' he ignores the prevalent Arab preference for state recognition and improved state funding of Arab towns rather than integration rights into Jewish towns. And he fails to address the parallel attitude among many Israeli Jews. As the comments of the subjects illustrate, even Jews who support the result in *Ka'adan* dispute the notion that equality requires Arabs and Jews to live in mixed localities." Steven V. Mazie, "Importing Liberalism: Brown v. Board of Education in the Israeli Context," 36 *Polity* 389 (2004), 400s.

87. Interestingly, it is not only critics on the left who point out the glaring inequality of conditions that characterize the separate development of the Jewish and Arab communities. Thus, the critique on the right of the Court's invocation of *Brown* in the *Qa'adan* case cleverly included a condemnation of the failure to provide equality to Arab citizens. "If the concept of 'separate but equal' has not been implemented until now—and indeed the lack of equal facilities extended to the Arab sector should be deplored—the Supreme Court should have ordered that this concept be implemented, rather than in effect canceling it." Sheleg, "Katzir," www.irac.org.

88. David K. Shipler, *Arab and Jew: Wounded Spirits in a Promised Land* (New York: Penguin Books, 1986), 273.

provocation with an egregious enactment that for the first time since the Law of Return explicitly discriminated by statute against non-Jews, the Court's ability effectively to counter such a challenge would have been severely tested. When the American Supreme Court was challenged in response to *Brown,* the justices could rise up in righteous indignation and point out in Cooper v. Aaron that "Article VI of the Constitution makes the Constitution 'the supreme Law of the Land.'"[89] The Court's further claim that its interpretation of the Fourteenth Amendment *is* the supreme law of the land perhaps went too far; the point, however, is that the judiciary was the unambiguous winner in this confrontation because, however controversial the issue, its ruling was seen as the product of constitutional rather than ordinary politics. In Israel the absence of a genuine constitutional settlement that denies the Court the political capital to withstand the charge of politics exposes the principles it wishes to defend to a perfunctory and dismissive hearing in the only arena that ultimately matters, the public at large. If the proposition that separation is inherently unequal is to be embraced as a key element in the wider political culture, arguably it should emerge from the crucible of constitutional negotiation and compromise, rather than the abstract theorizing of judges.

Does this mean that the specific outcome in this case was misguided? Is it valid to say that, as Robert Bork does in a brief reference to *Qa'adan,* "once again, universalistic principles were deployed . . . without adequately weighing Israel's particular circumstances and needs"?[90] Is the reliance on *Brown* illustrative of the judicial misuse of foreign precedent? Are there lessons here to illuminate the question of when and how such materials should be used?

The other two judges in the *Qa'adan* majority simply affirmed in two words their agreement with Justice Barak's opinion; the third, Justice Mishael Cheshin, wrote two sentences, but they intimated significant disagreement with the opinion's reasoning. "In the division of the general resources amongst the individuals of Israeli society, the petitioners were discriminated against and are therefore entitled to the remedy to

89. Cooper v. Aaron, 358 U.S. 1, 18 (1958).

90. Bork, *Coercing Virtue,* 125.

which the person discriminated against is entitled. For this reason I agree with the ruling of my colleague, President Barak."[91] This is consistent with Justice Cheshin's reluctance to address difficult questions of principle[92] and can be taken to mean the following: The Qa'adans were deprived of their legal right to equality, not because separate is inherently unequal in principle, but because under the conditions prevalent in Israeli society separate is in fact unequal.[93] Thus their effort to improve their living conditions is constrained by the unconstitutional manner in which the resources of the society are allocated in relation to the Arab and Jewish communities. This argument leaves unresolved the question of whether a color-blind society is constitutionally mandated in the Jewish State. Had Cheshin elaborated further, however, he might have (1) indicated how the objective inequalities between Arabs and Jews

91. *Qa'adan,* at 182.

92. Justice Cheshin's deferential position in *Qa'adan* is consistent with his deferential, practical approach in other cases concerning discrimination claims raised by Arab Israelis in the context of intentional underfunding of non-Jewish religious institutions or enrichment educational programs in non-Jewish school districts. In a few such cases that he adjudicated, Justice Cheshin was primarily responsive to concrete, almost mathematical manifestations of discrimination in funding, while being reluctant to address the more principled and difficult questions such as the very constitutionality of the separate but equal doctrine raised by the lawyers representing the claimants, let alone the Jewish and democratic issue. There are two main examples of this approach: Adalah v. Minister of Religious Affairs, 52 (2) P.D. 167 (1998); and Adalah v. Municipality of Tel Aviv, 56 (5) P.D. 167 (1998). In the latter case, Cheshin's opinion was highly deferential, advocating in a sensitive majority-minority case that the Court allow the legislature and executive to decide. He recommended a minimalist, practical solution very much like the line he later took in *Qa'adan.* His alternative to Justice Barak's "grandiose" approach is a tilt toward judicial restraint in politically charged cases. I wish to thank Ran Hirschl for his assistance in illuminating this issue. In Chapter 6 there is a fuller discussion of these contrasting approaches in a case that directly implicates the question of Israeli constitutional identity.

93. Again, Mazie's conversations with Arabs about the decision is worth considering. "Majjed, Muhammad, Nadia, Youssef and Omer all grew up in all-Arab towns, but they do not view that experience as one of stigmatization or oppression. They do not feel that living in separate towns is 'insulting' or makes them into 'social inferiors'—the negative effects of separation Barak identifies in his ruling. Far from it. These Arab respondents object to their villages and cities receiving 'unequal' state care and investment, but not to their being 'separate' from Jewish areas." Mazie, "Importing Liberalism," 405.

that stem directly from state policies are inconsistent with egalitarian norms that enjoy a broad consensus among Israelis; (2) considered how the invalidation of the Katzir policy was consistent with universal aspirations such as are described in the Israeli Declaration's injunction to "uphold the full social and political equality of all its citizens"; and (3) invoked decisions in other countries—for example, Canada and South Africa—to illustrate constitutional approaches supportive of the pursuit of these aspirations.[94]

This position allows one in turn to steer a middle course between Barak and Bork. The latter denounces the constitutional jurisprudence of the Israeli Court for redefining Israeli values so that "Jewish particularism disappears into the mists of abstract universalism."[95] He sees peril in "the Supreme Court's promulgation of the abstract universalisms of equality, radical individualism, and rationalism," believing that its actions endanger "Israel's survival."[96] But the "Cheshin alternative" makes clear that it is possible to accommodate particularism (or at least leave its fundamental commitments unchallenged) while pursuing those universalistic aspirations that are compatible with both the nation's own promises and the increasingly predominant internationally held view on equal treatment under law. From this perspective *Brown*'s integrationist norm was indeed an unfortunate invocation, in that it prematurely proclaimed a contestable constitutional norm with insufficient grounding in either sociological reality or an inclusively generated constitutional agreement. As one observer noted, "Despite Barak's footnotes, the reasoning in *Brown* is largely inapposite to the Israeli case. *Qa'adan* imports a principle into Israeli law that enjoys little support in any sector of the Israeli population."[97] But Barak's overreaching

94. In correspondence with the author (May 19, 2007) Justice Cheshin explained his views on quoting from constitutional judgments in other states: "[T]he intimacy between a constitution and the people of the state should put us on guard. . . . [I]nternational standards should be taken into account but at one breath not forgetting even for a second that [it] is for the Israeli people [that] we are laying norms and rules. We live in Israel, not in any other state."

95. Bork, *Coercing Virtue,* 130.

96. Ibid., 132.

97. Mazie, "Importing Liberalism," 405.

is matched by Bork's ideologically driven retreat to the narrowest jurisprudential articulation of culture. The excesses of the former do not justify the rigidities of the latter. Nor do they call into question judicial appeal to foreign sources that illuminate and advance those universalist aspirations that are firmly situated within the context of a prevailing constitutional consensus. Moreover, both positions preempt the process of interinstitutional engagement within which an Israeli constitutional identity can develop under the legitimating cover of a broad political agreement.

India: Universalism, Particularism, and the Transformational Constitution

If in Israel the presence of such aspirations—as well as the particularist commitments to which they are attached—must be gleaned from rather spare constitutional materials, the situation in India is dramatically different. The world's longest constitution is remarkably consistent in its embrace of a fairly coherent transformational agenda, but its interpreters need not strain to find in their document ample opportunities for balancing universalist and particularist commitments. The conceptual model of disharmonic politics illuminates the intriguing challenge of their task. "Traditional India with its caste system was a harmonic society because its social inequalities were considered legitimate."[98] By contrast, according to Huntington, the commitment to equality in the United States is disharmonious with the widely perceived reality, which historically has led, as pointed out earlier, to campaigns for political and social reform. But of course India's postcolonial constitution was carefully designed to dismantle traditional structures of inequality, much of which was associated with religious practices that had deeply penetrated and were firmly entrenched in the body politic. In this new environment, the juxtaposition between the ideal and the actual produced a constitutional agenda that, in comparative terms, was distinctive in the degree to which it directed political actors (including judges) to pursue the goal of social recon-

98. Huntington, *American Politics*, 12.

struction. One technique involved looking abroad for guidance. As Ruti Teitel points out in a different context, "[C]omparative analysis [has] allowed states to move beyond indigenous law in pursuit of legal transformation."[99]

It is in this decidedly disharmonic political context that judicial choices must be made. While the judiciary has not always performed (especially in the early years), in Granville Austin's depiction of the Indian framers' intent, as an "arm of the social revolution,"[100] its authority to interpret the law in the service of the political and social vision inscribed in the Constitution has interesting implications for the standard "democratic" critique of judicial activism. Thus Robert Bork's denunciation of "the worldwide rule of judges" is based on the observation that increasingly courts around the world have diminished the power of the people "to choose the moral environment in which they live."[101] They have preempted these choices often by making one of their own, choosing the universal over the particular. "Particularities are usually more difficult to defend than universals"; what's more, this "search for the universal and . . . denigrat[ion of] the particular" is manifest in "the insidious appeal of internationalism" and the practice of "justices of the Supreme Court . . . look[ing] to foreign decisions . . . for guidance in interpreting the Constitution."[102]

But making choices in relation to the universal and the particular is a very complicated matter. Bork contends "[t]he American Constitution . . . was framed and amended in the light of specific American history, culture, and aspirations."[103] For that reason it makes no sense, he argues, for an American court to take guidance from courts in countries with different histories, cultures, and aspirations. If, however, America's specific aspirations include the progressive realization of principles of justice that are expressive of what its founding document declares to be the self-evident truth of human equality, then it must be the case that the particular

99. Ruti Teitel, "Comparative Constitutional Law in a Global Age," 117 *Harvard Law Review* 2570, 2588 (2004).

100. Austin, *Indian Constitution*, 164.

101. Bork, *Coercing Virtue*, 1.

102. Ibid., 12, 22.

103. Ibid., 137.

history and culture of the United States are in large measure explicable in terms of certain universals. Similarly in India, the aspiration for a more egalitarian society emerges out of the unique circumstances of that nation's millennia-old experience. The challenge in both countries is to situate the universal in the particular rather than to dichotomize them as if they presented political actors with mutually exclusive options. In the judicial context it means, among other things, remaining open to the possibilities of illumination from abroad while maintaining a realistic sense of how that light needs to be filtered through the prism of local experience.[104]

Much as Indian national identity is often defined with reference to a composite culture, with its constitutional borders having been left open to the importation of foreign ideas, so too is that an apt description for its constitutional jurisprudence. As Dr. Ambedkar told the Constituent Assembly, "there was nothing to be ashamed of in borrowing because nobody holds any patent rights in the fundamental ideas of a constitution."[105] Yet as studies of the Indian Court's borrowing practices have shown, early judicial experience tended to avoid reliance on foreign sources.[106] This behavior was perhaps less attributable to the concern

104. In his famous speech on Fox's East India Bill, Edmund Burke suggested that Western charters of liberty could, if prudently managed, be transplanted to India and adapted to local experience: "Of this benefit, I am certain, their condition is capable of more, my vote shall most assuredly be for our giving to the full extent of their capacity of receiving; and no charter of dominion shall stand as a bar in my way to their charter of safety and protection." Edmund Burke, "Speech On Fox's East India Bill," in David Bromwich, ed., *On Empire, Liberty, and Reform: Speeches and Letters* (New Haven: Yale University Press, 2000), 293.

105. Soli J. Sorabjee, "Equality in the United States and India," in Louis Henkin and Albert Rosenthal, eds. *Constitutionalism and Rights: The Influence of the United States Constitution Abroad* (New York: Columbia University Press, 1990), 97. Sorabjee points out that the openness to ideas from abroad was also consistent with the spirit of Vedic prayer, to wit: "Let noble thoughts come to us from all sides" (ibid., 101).

106. The most systematic analysis is Adam M. Smith, "Making Itself at Home: Understanding Foreign Law in Domestic Jurisprudence: The Indian Case," 24 *Berkeley Journal of International Law* 218 (2006). Also valuable is, Arun K. Thiruvengadam, "'The Common Illumination of our House?': Foreign Judicial Decisions and Competing Approaches to Constitutional Adjudication: A Study of Trans-Judicial Influence in Six Jurisdictions" (Doctoral diss., New York University School of Law, 2006).

that such reliance in new and developing states "may work to stifle the development of a richly organic indigenous constitutional culture,"[107] than to the judiciary's support of entrenched interests. Unlike in the United States, where external legal sources were more frequently consulted in the early days of the nation's history than in contemporary times,[108] the Indian Court's behavior has more closely followed broader political trends in which the justices' use of comparative law has tracked political elites' decisions to expand and curtail rights.[109] Still, any reader of Indian Supreme Court opinions cannot help but be struck by the copious use of foreign judgments in the adjudication of domestic cases. Indeed, this use includes a potentially landmark ruling of the Delhi High Court in 2009, in which, citing *Lawrence* and other foreign decisions, the Court struck down a colonial-era ban on sodomy as a violation of privacy rights and constitutionally guaranteed equality.[110] There was no discussion of "impos[ing] foreign moods, fads, or fashions" on Indians.

107. Ken I. Kersch, "The New Legal Transnationalism, the Globalized Judiciary, and the Rule of Law," 4 *Washington University Global Studies Review* 345, 368 (2005).

108. See, for example, Harold Koh, "International Law as Part of Our Law," 98 *The American Journal of International Law* 43 (2004); and Sarah Cleveland, "Our International Constitution," 31 *Yale Journal of International Law* 1 (2006). H. Patrick Glenn argues that the reception of foreign law "has been an indispensable element in what we know today as law, and . . . it has occurred invariably in the primary stages of the development of a legal tradition or field of law." H. Patrick Glenn, "Persuasive Authority," 32 *McGill Law Journal* 261, 264 (1987). This makes sense given the logic that a court that has not yet accumulated a body of its own precedents will rely on those of other polities, but it flies in the face of the counter-logic that says that a fledgling legal system will make every effort to place the stamp of its newly independent status upon its early developing law. On the other hand, as the South African example illustrates, a transitional regime may find international and comparative materials to be valued legitimating assets in its constitutional jurisprudence.

109. Smith, "Making Itself at Home," 259, 265. For a different reading of the Court's behavior see Manoj Mate, "The Origins of Substantive Due Process in India: The Role of Borrowing in Personal Liberty and Preventive Detention Cases" (paper presented at the Midwest Political Science Association Conference, Chicago, April 2006). Mate argues that judicial borrowing has also been associated with the effort to maintain the status quo on certain issues related to fundamental rights.

110. *Naz Foundation Case* (2009).

Recipient Court

Judges have relied extensively on these materials without viewing their actions as necessarily transgressive of their history and culture. Thus in applying American decisions they "would not be incorporating principles foreign to [their] Constitution."[111] Interestingly, while Hindu nationalists have vigorously critiqued the idea of a composite culture, their interests nevertheless also lie in allowing the transmission of at least some liberal ideas through these constitutional borders. Indeed, their attraction to, and appropriation of, the theorizing of Western intellectuals (and the decisions that connect to it) contain lessons for those engaged in constitutional borrowing.

Case in point: John Rawls. In *Political Liberalism,* Rawls tackled the pluralist conundrum of "how [it is] possible for there to exist over time a just and stable society of free and equal citizens, who remain profoundly divided by reasonable religious, philosophical, and moral doctrines[.]"[112] While Rawls rightly assumed that all societies with aspirations to political justice confront this vexing dilemma, it is of course a question with special significance for India, arguably the most diverse society in the world. Not surprising, then, are the occasional references to Rawls and his arguments in the opinions of Indian judges.[113] When asked about the use of Rawls in judicial opinions, one of them—an ex-chief justice of India—explained, "It is entirely appropriate to use concepts from Western philosophical liberalism in Indian constitutional cases, because there are universals that apply to all societies."[114]

The occasion for raising the question was a discussion of the so-called *Hindutva Cases,* a series of Supreme Court decisions in the mid-1990s involving application of the Representation of the People Act, the foundational 1951 enactment that governs Indian elections. One of its key provisions details a number of "corrupt practices," including the inappropriate use of religious speech to advance one's electoral

111. Air India v. Nergesh Meerza, AIR 1981 SC 1829, 1852 (as quoted in Soli J. Sorabjee, Ibid., 79).

112. John Rawls, *Political Liberalism* (New York: Columbia University Press, 1993), 4.

113. See, for example, Faraqui v. Union of India, 6 S.C.C. 360, 404 (1994).

114. Author's interview with Chief Justice Venkatachaliah, New Delhi, March 10, 1999.

prospects.[115] In these cases, the Court was asked to address both the constitutionality of the provision and the reach of its statutory application. In the end, it upheld the constitutionality of the section while vindicating, through a narrow construction of the law's meaning, most of the Hindu nationalists charged with its violation.[116] The cases are noteworthy in India for addressing core issues of constitutional identity. Of less concern for most Indians is that the philosophical edifice upon which the Court's argument to sustain the law was built is taken from the pages of John Rawls.[117] Thus the Court's understanding of a "corrupt practice" relied on a normative view of politics in which the presence of procedurally correct reasoned deliberation becomes the measure of viable secular democratic institutions. Those activities that depart from this defining norm are therefore corrupt in their tendency to undermine the essential principles of secular democratic governance. "In order that the democratic process should thrive and succeed, it is of utmost importance that our elections to Parliament and the different legislative bodies must be free from the unhealthy influence of appeals to religion, race,

115. The relevant section defines corruption as "The appeal by a candidate or his agent . . . to vote or refrain from voting for any person on the ground of his religion, race, caste, community, or language or the use of, or appeal to, religious symbols . . . for the furtherance of the prospects of the election of that candidate or for prejudicially affecting the election of any candidate."

116. Findings against politicians were reversed in the case of one Hindu nationalist who had pledged in his campaign to turn Maharashtra into India's "first Hindu state," and in the case of another who had appealed to voters on the basis of the candidate's support of "Hindutva," a term widely held to signify the religious faith of Hindus, but which the Court chose to interpret as referring to the culture and ethos of the people of India.

117. Although there is no citation of Rawls in the Court's judgment, the author of the opinion, Justice J. S. Verma, was familiar with the argument of *Political Liberalism,* having cited it two years earlier in his majority opinion in the *Ayodhya Reference Case.* His opinion there quotes a speech of a judicial colleague, in which the latter said, "In a pluralist, secular polity law is perhaps the greatest integrating force. A cultivated respect for law and its institutions and symbols; a pride in the country's heritage and achievements; faith that people live under the protection of an adequate legal system are indispensable for sustaining unity in pluralist diversity. Rawlsian pragmatism of 'justice as fairness' to serve as an 'overlapping consensus' and deep seated agreements on fundamental questions of basic structure of society for deeper social unity is a political conception of justice rather than a comprehensive moral conception." Dr. Ismail Faruqui and Others v. Union of India and Others, 6 SCC 360 (1994), at 36.

caste, community, or language."[118] The Court's argument bears a striking resemblance to formulations advanced in contemporary liberal political theory, which, as Ronald Thiemann aptly puts it, "grant virtual axiomatic status to the belief that religious convictions must be limited solely to the realm of the private."[119] This segmentation is essential for a "liberalism of reasoned respect," the goal of which is a structured society that places a premium on the virtue of civility.

Not long after the judgments in the *Hindutva Cases* were announced, the justice who had authored the Court's opinions received some unsolicited praise for his efforts from Ronald Dworkin, who happened to have been in India at the time of the decisions.[120] As perhaps our preeminent Rawlsian legal philosopher, Dworkin's approval of the rulings is perfectly understandable.[121] For Justice J. S. Verma, whose opinions in these cases (reversing most of the convictions) prompted some observers to question his liberal credentials and to suspect him of harboring anti-Muslim views, this approval from a pedigreed and disinterested "enlightened" source was quite welcome.[122] But however useful Rawls and Dworkin were in affirming judicial bona fides, their teachings (Rawls in this instance) were arguably misplaced in the context of the Indian socioeconomic environment and constitutional

118. Prabhoo v. Kunte, 1 Sup Ct 130 (1996), at 160.

119. Ronald F. Thiemann, *Religion in Public Life: A Dilemma for Democracy* (Washington, DC: Georgetown University Press, 1996), 89.

120. Author's interview with J. S. Verma, former chief justice of India, Ghaziabad, India, February 28, 1999.

121. In *Taking Rights Seriously,* Dworkin called for "a fusion of constitutional law and moral theory." He then reminded his readers that "Professor Rawls of Harvard . . . has published an abstract and complex book about justice which no constitutional lawyer will be able to ignore." Ronald Dworkin, *Taking Rights Seriously* (Cambridge, MA: Harvard University Press, 1977), 149.

122. Justice Verma became a lightning rod for criticism for failing to distinguish between Hinduism and Hindutva. Many observers felt that this played into the hands of the anti-Muslim Hindu right, for whom Hindutva is not so much about religion as it is about racial, national, and cultural phenomena for constituting a regime of political domination by the majority over the nation's minorities. See, for example, Brenda Kossman and Ratna Kapur, "Secularism's Last Sigh?: The Hindu Right, the Courts, and India's Struggle for Democracy," 38 *Harvard International Law Journal,* 113, 114 (1997).

culture.[123] The application of public reason-based arguments to sustain the constitutionality of restrictions on religious speech was, in a setting where religion is a constitutive reality for most people, inadequate to the task of convincingly placing such rhetoric beyond the arena of public disputation.

The ameliorative aspirations of Indian constitutionalism are critical to the interpretive choices faced by judges. In construing "corrupt practices" this means attending to those constitutive principles that establish a polity's constitutional identity, and then in specific instances drawing the appropriate conclusions from Montesquieu's teaching that "The corruption of every government generally begins with that of its principles."[124] The constitutional essentials of the Indian polity were forged out of the tension between religion and equality. If political corruption is best represented as an erosion of the core commitments of a given polity, then the most compelling argument for allowing limitations on religious speech in an Indian electoral setting is that they might advance constitutive egalitarian goals. This is not to say that such limitations are advisable, only that their legality should be appraised in accordance with the constitutional essentials of the Indian experiment, rather than Rawlsian "constitutional essentials," which do not specifically include principles of socioeconomic justice.[125]

This claim might appear on first glance to be premised on purely particularist assumptions. In effect it says that the norms of public reason must be framed in such a way that culturally specific iterations are given their due. It argues that constitutional restrictions on religious speech, to be legitimate, must be shown as necessary to defend core principles of *this* secular regime, that a defense based on the logic of an ideal secular democracy fails in India, whether or not it succeeds elsewhere. It emphasizes the distinctiveness of the Indian example, rooted in the transformational

123. See Chapter 6 in Gary Jeffrey Jacobsohn, *The Wheel of Law: India's Secularism in Comparative Constitutional Context* (Princeton, NJ: Princeton University Press, 2003).

124. Baron de Montesquieu, *The Spirit of the Laws* (New York: Hafner, 1966), 109.

125. For Rawls, constitutional essentials are of two kinds: (1) fundamental principles specifying the general structure of government and the political process, and (2) equal basic rights of citizenship, including rights connected to voting and political participation conscience, thought and association, and the rule of law. Rawls, *Political Liberalism*, 227.

agenda of Indian nationalism, in which the democratization of a social order inhabited by a thickly constituted religious presence provides a special logic for managing the constitutional affairs of church and state.

But upon closer examination the attention to the specific interpretive requirements of the Indian constitutional context suggests, as mentioned earlier, that distinguishing universals and particularities is not a simple matter for clear-cut delineation. In India today, liberal content-neutral principles are invoked most insistently by political interests who understand that faithful adherence to such principles will advance the cause of an ethnically conceived nationalism that by definition exalts the partial over the whole. Moreover, as many students of Indian politics have noted, this ascriptively based nationalism is associated with the protection of upper caste and class interests, which means that one challenge to substantive equality is compounded by another.[126] The commitment to formal equality—to some of the constitutional essentials of liberal constitutionalism—is fundamentally strategic, in other words, an investment in political calculation not political principle. At this stage in the realization of Indian constitutional aspirations, judges who integrate formal norms of universal justice into their constitutional discourse may actually be (in some cases inadvertently) aiding the forces of regressive cultural particularity. The implication that follows from this is not that judges should avoid looking abroad for constitutional guidance; rather it is that they should exercise careful discretion in selecting their instructional sources. At least in the short term, Indian jurists may make more progress in realizing their ultimate goals by exploring jurisprudential options gleaned from, say, the contemporary South African constitutional experience, than from the philosophical literature of the United States.[127]

126. See, for example, Thomas Blom Hansen, *The Saffron Wave: Democracy and Hindu Nationalism in Modern India* (Princeton, NJ: Princeton University Press, 1999); Christophe Jaffrelot, *The Hindu Nationalist Movement in India* (New York: Columbia University Press, 1995); Madhu Kishwar, *Religion at the Service of Nationalism and Other Essays* (New Delhi: Oxford University Press, 1998); and Achin Vanaik, *The Furies of Indian Communalism* (London: Verso, 1997).

127. Accompanying this attention to the particulars of constitutional context should be an awareness of how the achievement of local constitutional aspirations can serve the

Consider again the landmark case S. R. Bommai v. Union of India, the ruling that upheld the central government's dismissal of three state governments that had been implicated in the violence in Ayodhya in 1992. The justices decided that the failure to act in accordance with the substantive provisions of the Constitution, in this case the commitment to secular rule, was sufficient to trigger the emergency powers of the union government. "Secularism is a part of the basic structure of the Constitution. The acts of a State Government which are calculated to subvert or sabotage secularism as enshrined in our Constitution, can lawfully be deemed to give rise to a situation in which the Government of the State cannot be carried on in accordance with the provisions of the Constitution."[128]

In *Bommai,* unlike in the subsequent *Hindutva Cases,* the Court was careful to respect the secular ideal of religious freedom while focusing on actual conditions, religion's constitutive role in the social order. The dominant theme of most of the opinions invokes one of the oldest Indian traditions—*sarva dharma sambhava* (equal treatment of religions)—which is also at the core of any serious account of the essentials of secular governance. "We hold that no one religion should be given preferential status, or unique distinction, that no one religion should be accorded special privileges . . . for that would be a violation of the basic principles of democracy."[129] But presented in this rather formal way, the equal treatment principle provides only limited insight into the underlying commitments of those in India who have espoused it. Some who voice the ideal of equality, insisting, for example, on the immediate enforcement

---

ends of a transcendent ideal of constitutionalism. David Beatty, for example, has argued that "For ordinary people, who believe in the idea of human rights, the good news is that the judgments that have been written by courts around the world point very strongly to the existence of universal principles of law." David Beatty, "Law and Politics," 44 *American Journal of Comparative Law* 131 (1996), 141. His point speaks more to means than to ends, to "a universal method of constitutional validation," but an analysis of how nations at different stages of political development and with different social and cultural circumstances address common problems of constitutional import, can also engender a more textured account of what the substantive liberal democratic ideal might look like in practice.

128. S. R. Bommai v. Union of India, 149 (1994).

129. Ibid., at 76.

of the constitutionally directed goal of a uniform civil code, were directly implicated in the violence against Muslims, whom they stridently and provocatively describe as unfair beneficiaries of Indian law. Their purpose in doing so is to advance their ambitious agenda of creating a Hindu State, which, as we saw in the election cases, benefits from the appropriation of a liberal constitutional discourse whose legitimacy inheres precisely in its universal appeal to human rights.[130]

At least several of the justices in *Bommai* correctly understood that the pursuit of the ideal of *constitutionalism* required an incremental approach to *constitutional* adjudication in order to establish the identity of the ideal in the actual. For these judges, the jurisprudential challenge was to work within the constraints of the existing social reality without allowing it to obscure the secular vision of the transcendent ideal. They endeavored to adjudicate within the broad sociological configurations of the Indian people, while protecting the ideal of greater democracy for which that people had been constitutionally dedicated. The ideal was familiar within the Indian tradition (nowhere better exemplified than in the Emperor Ashoka), but not always evident in the path of precedent established by judicial decisions. To clarify the ideal, several of the opinions in *Bommai* discuss decisions of other national courts without reflexively transplanting them to Indian soil. In doing so, the judges were attempting to show (in contrast to the tendentious and simplistic renderings of the Hindu revivalists) how the commitment to secularism embedded in the concept of equality is meaningful only if equality is situated within the context of the Indian Constitution's specific transformative aspirations. "Our object," as one of the justices explained, "is to ascertain the meaning of the expression 'secularism' in the context of our Constitution."[131]

Two of the justices used the term "positive secularism" to supply this meaning. It was designed to remedy the deficiencies of the formal equal treatment model, which, while compatible with the liberal ideal often

130. See, especially, the work of Brenda Cossman and Ratna Kapur. As an example, "Secularism: Bench-Marked by the Hindu Right," 38 *Economic and Political Weekly*, September 21, 1996.

131. *Bommai*, at 232.

reflected in the judgments of foreign courts, strengthens existing socio-cultural structures in a society where the impact of the dominant religion is pervasive, encompassing, and unacceptably inegalitarian. The principle of equal treatment needed to be loosened from its secure moorings in procedural justice and situated more proactively within the context of the Constitution's broader substantive objectives. Sameness in the state's interactions with different religious communities was not therefore a virtue and certainly not a constitutional requirement. Under the term "positive secularism," government policies were therefore acceptable if their purpose was to eradicate social injustices, even if these policies targeted specific communities.

Political support for the destructive campaign waged by Hindu activists in Ayodyha had assumed a significance that extended beyond the immediate and obvious details associated with that event. As one of the positive secularists wrote in his opinion: "The interaction of religion and secular factors . . . is to expose the abuses of religion . . . by purely partisan, narrow or selfish purpose to serve the economic or political interest of a particular class or group or country. The progress of human history is replete with full misuse of religious notions in that behalf."[132] Thus a judge looking objectively at the political dynamic at work in the mobilization around Ayodhya could plausibly have concluded that the most profound threat to secularism resided not so much in the immediate damage to communal relations so vividly on display in the rubble of the mosque, but in the long-term consequences of unchallenged ethno-religious nationalism for the prospects for social reform and reconstruction.[133] In invoking the "basic structure" doctrine and applying it to the particulars of Indian secularism, this judge could then have expected that his actions would help sustain and develop the constitutional identity imagined by the Constitution's framers.

132. Ibid., at 164.

133. Other scholars have recognized the Ayodhya incident as a threat to the movement toward a secular, pluralistic society and an example of how ethno-religious nationalism could undermine long-term social reform. See, for example, Jaffrelot, *Hindu Nationalist Movement,* 457–468.

Donor Court

While the distinctiveness of constitutional regimes persists in the face of the harmonizing effects of liberal globalization and international law, increasingly apparent in the rising prominence of these phenomena are certain common attributes of constitutional organization that transcend national boundaries. If constitutional borders are to remain permeable to transcendent ideals, then the aforementioned distinctive feature of Indian constitutional jurisprudence that speaks to the relationship of the particular to the universal—the "basic structure" doctrine—warrants consideration. As first discussed in Chapter 2, it is the foundation for the Supreme Court's extraordinary power to declare a constitutional amendment unconstitutional on substantive grounds, and among the features deemed essential for constitutional government—and hence unamendable—is the commitment to secularism.

Since these secular commitments have a deeply contextualized meaning that defies casual transnational mobility, skepticism in South Asia about emulating Western arrangements in church/state matters has long been entrenched in the political and legal culture.[134] Such skepticism applies not only to long-distance borrowing, but also to the kind that takes place among nations sharing a closer geographical proximity. While contiguity may suggest—particularly to the distant observer—greater incentives for cross-national constitutional appropriation, those closer to the scene and possessing a more refined sense of relevant political and cultural differences may, in contrast, find themselves impressed by the obstacles to successful legal transplantation.[135] Indeed, to

134. Ashis Nandy is the most insistent and eloquent critic of Western secularism. His categorical rejection of the liberal secular worldview, with its embrace of a Gandhian, antimodernist suspicion of the state, places him at odds with mainstream secular opinion in India. But even among many of the latter group who find his critique too sweeping in its wholesale rejection of the Western model, there remains doubt about the prospects of constitutional transplantation. For a concise sample of Nandy's position, see Ashis Nandy, "The Politics of Secularism and the Recovery of Religious Tolerance," 13 *Alternatives* (1998).

135. In this regard it is worth reflecting on the American-Canadian constitutional relationship. See, for example, Seymour Martin Lipset, *Continental Divide: The Values and Institutions of the United States and Canada* (New York: Routledge, 1990).

the extent that fundamental concerns about the character of the polity are implicated in decisions about the use of foreign sources in constitutional adjudication, geographic contiguity should in principle be irrelevant to questions centering on the wisdom or advisability of constitutional borrowing.[136]

That Indian jurisprudence would present judges in neighboring South Asian countries with precedents and ideas for addressing their own church/state issues is not surprising. The constitutional status of religion in India is in various ways unique to that nation, but its dominant position on the subcontinent—politically, economically, and militarily—ensures that the legal configuration of its spiritual and temporal domains will receive serious attention in non-Indian South Asian courts. In the case of Sri Lanka, the direct intervention of the larger nation in the internal constitutional affairs of its island neighbor (the Thirteenth Amendment case discussed in Chapter 2 is a prime example) creates the further likelihood that the Sri Lankan judiciary's scrutiny of Indian constitutional approaches may, at least for some issues, have as much to do with political necessity as it is does with jurisprudence.

Whatever the motivation for incorporating foreign ideas and approaches into a nation's constitutional settlements, one will want to know if these moves are likely to materially threaten its constitutional identity. If they do, should that necessarily preclude borrowing? If a particular (basic) structural attribute—such as secularism in India—is critical to a polity's constitutional identity, should courts in nations where that attribute is differently constituted—for example, Sri Lanka—pursue an indigenous orientation to the exclusion of the foreign? Or, to the extent

136. Responding to criticism that the draft of the Indian Constitution borrowed heavily from other constitutions at the expense of India's indigenous village system, B. N. Rau (the author of the original draft) said that "so long as the borrowings have been adapted to India's peculiar circumstances, they cannot in themselves be said to constitute a defect. . . . To profit from the experience of other countries or from the past experience of one's own is the path of wisdom. There is another advantage in borrowing not only the substance but even the language of established constitutions; for we obtain in this way the benefit of the interpretation put upon the borrowed provisions by the courts of the countries of their origin and we thus avoid ambiguity or doubt." B. N. Rau, *India's Constitution in the Making* (Bombay: Orient Longmans, 1960), 360.

that constitutional identities are at least in part mutable, what is to be gained from a judicial decision to seek instruction from the jurisprudence of another judiciary?

One of the more contentious issues in South Asia over which the meaning of secular identity has been adjudicated concerns the problem of multiple marriages. The landmark American polygamy cases of the nineteenth century figured prominently in the leading Indian cases on that subject, sometimes through rejection of the American approach, but also to reach the conclusion that lies at the core of Indian constitutional secularism, namely that "religious practices must give way before the good of the people of the State as a whole."[137] The exercise contributed to a result consistent with Christopher McCrudden's claim that constitutional borrowing is much more likely to be practiced by judiciaries in transformative regimes than in preservative ones.[138] It is a claim, however, that requires qualification, as the following illustration from Sri Lankan constitutional jurisprudence makes clear. It also suggests that, as manipulative as the application of foreign precedents can be (although that hardly distinguishes them from their domestic counterparts), judges who indulge in the practice have an incentive to do so in order to maintain the status quo, much as do judges whose objective is its transformation. Or to put it differently, the conservative aspirations of a nation's constitutional identity does not mean that the members of its judiciary will find the use of foreign materials to be an unattractive jurisprudential option.

The case raised the question of whether a Roman Catholic man could, consistent with a law that prohibited polygamy, maintain two marriages on the basis of his having converted to Islam before marrying his second wife. Christopher Abeysundere and his first wife, both Roman Catholics, had been married under the Marriage Registration Ordinance, which, among other things, made polygamy illegal. Subsequently, Christopher married Ms. Edirisinghe under the Muslim

137. State of Bombay v. Appa, AIR Bombay 84 (1952), 86. The leading cases are discussed at length in Jacobsohn, *Indian Secularism,* 95–103.

138. Christopher McCrudden, "A Common Law of Human Rights?: Transnational Judicial Conversations on Constitutional Rights," 20 *Oxford Journal of Legislative Studies* 499 (2000), 524.

Marriage and Divorce Act. His first wife brought legal action against him on charges of bigamy, to which Christopher responded that he and Edirisinghe had embraced Islam before their second marriage. The Magistrate's Court convicted Christopher for bigamy, but the ruling was reversed by the Provincial High Court on the basis of a Privy Council precedent.[139] Subsequently the Supreme Court reinstated the conviction and voided the second marriage, arguing that the defendant could not "cast aside his antecedent statutory liabilities and obligations" incurred by his first marriage. The five justices interpreted the Marriage Registration Ordinance as requiring a statutory obligation on the part of Christopher and his first wife to remain in a monogamous relationship. In the judgment, the justices emphasized the public policy of Sri Lanka to support monogamy by citing an earlier judgment, King v. Perumal: "It is thus clear that, except in the case of Muhammadans, *polygamy is as obnoxious to the public policy of Ceylon as to that of European States*. . . . In view of the circumstance that polygamy is *expressly prohibited* by the Municipal law of the Colony (except in the case of Muhammadans) I am clearly of opinion that a polygamous marriage between persons who are not Muhammadans is void in Ceylon."[140]

The judgment quoted extensively from the reasoning of the Indian Supreme Court in Sarla Mudgal v. Union of India, where the issue was whether a Hindu husband, married under Hindu law, by embracing Islam could solemnize a second marriage. The 1994 case concerned one of the ingenious ways in which Hindu men have endeavored to circumvent the ban on polygamous marriages. Under Section 494 of the Indian Penal Code, a Hindu who marries while still married to someone else is acting illegally, an act that could result in the voiding of the second marriage and the imprisonment of the guilty party. By contrast, the same restriction did not apply to Muslims, who were free

139. In Attorney General v. Reid, the facts of the case were similar to the Abeysundere situation. The Privy Council ruled that in a country like Ceylon, there must be an inherent right in the inhabitants domiciled there to change their religion and personal law and contract a valid polygamous marriage if recognized by the laws of the country notwithstanding an earlier marriage. Only a statute could abrogate such an inherent right.

140. King v. Perumal, (1912) 14 NLR 496 (Full Bench).

to have multiple spouses. This disparity in legal treatment had led to a rise in the number of apostates in India, with many polygamy-minded Hindus having figured out that conversion to Islam was a solution to their problem. Describing the *Sarla Mudgal* ruling as one of "decisive importance," the Court agreed with the Indian Justice Kuldip Singh, who had held that the second marriage must be voided because of contractual obligations of monogamy under the first marriage. "In my view," wrote the chief justice, "the reasoning of Justice Kuldip Singh . . . is cogent and valid, and is clearly applicable to the facts before us. . . ."[141]

Of particular persuasive power were the Indian jurist's reflections on the family: "Marriage is the very foundation of the civilized society. The relation once formed, the law steps in and binds the parties to various obligations and liabilities thereunder. Marriage is an institution in the maintenance of which the public at large is deeply interested. It is the foundation of the family and in turn of the society without which no civilization can exist."[142] Where the Privy Council had gone wrong was in failing to appreciate that the family, upon which so much depends, was an exclusively monogamous structure.

But the invocation of *Sarla Mudgal* does not reveal what made that case so controversial in India. Justice Singh's opinion was notable as much for its passionate call for compliance with the unequivocal mandate of Article 44 to achieve a uniform civil code as for its ringing affirmation of the institution of marriage. It went further than the Court had ever gone in the urgency of its insistence on implementing the constitutionally prescribed directive of uniformity. "There is no justification whatsoever in delaying indefinitely the introduction of a uniform personal law in the country."[143] The Court, according to Justice Singh, should be actively engaged in seeing that the regime of personal laws came to an end. "Inevitably, the role of the reformer has to be assumed by the Courts because, it is beyond the endurance of sensitive minds to

141. Natalie Abeysundere v. Christopher Abeysundere and Another, SC Appeal No. 70/96, 1997, 200.

142. Ibid., at 200.

143. Sarla Mudgal v. Union of India, 1538 (1995).

allow injustice to be suffered when it is so palpable. But piecemeal attempts of Courts to bridge that gap between personal laws cannot take the place of a common Civil Code."[144] As the Justice has since affirmed, a critical component in Indian constitutional identity is "the power of judicial review given to the judiciary which gives it the authority to enforce the Directive Principles."[145]

Singh's opinion was criticized not only for its robust assertion of judicial power, but also for its majoritarian implication, which, fairly or unfairly, was interpreted by some as anti-Muslim. As one critic wrote, "[*Sarla Mudgal*] is not exactly a legal judgment but more of a political sermon on how the Muslim community should learn to behave and what ought to be its relationship to the Indian State."[146] Hindus, Sikhs, Buddhists, and Jains had all accepted the priority of national unity over sectarian attachments to religious practices regarding marriage, succession, and like matters; "other communities" [translation: Muslims] needed to get on board.

These sentiments were *obiter dicta,* and thus the Sri Lankan Court was surely not remiss in ignoring them in its judgment in *Abeysundere.* Moreover, it is difficult to see what profit there would be in antagonizing the local Muslim community, whose exceptional legal status regarding plural marriages enjoyed long-standing recognition in Sri Lanka. It is, however, also clear that the constitutional borrowing in this instance was consistent with support for an indigenous constitutional identity that had as one of its cardinal assumptions the primacy of the nation's majority community.[147] Here the borrowing from Indian case law reflected substantive concerns about how another country facing similar

144. Ibid., at 1539.

145. Author's interview with Justice Kuldip Singh, New Delhi, June 15, 2006.

146. Kishwar, *Religion,* 235.

147. By saying that the borrowing was consistent with the commitment to maintaining the primacy of this community I do not suggest that it was so motivated. Indeed the Sinhalese Buddhist community was not directly involved in the case. The judges also drew upon a ruling in a Privy Council case (King v. Perumal) to show that monogamy and the prohibition against polygamy (except in the case of Muslims) were part of public policy and the law since 1847. Strict legal interpretation of marriage rather than deference to cultural norms is a recurring theme in the Court's jurisprudence even where the majority community is involved.

issues involving clashes between personal laws had resolved the matter. It demonstrates judicious borrowing where the circumstances were such as not to impact the Buddhist nature of Sri Lankan identity.

In doing so it is easy to see why the animating vision behind the Indian precedent might have appealed to the Sri Lankan Court. That vision is one of "legal universalism," which "treats individuals as the basic unit of society and the state and imagines homogeneous citizens with uniform legal rights and obligations."[148] This idea, of course, is a staple of political liberalism, but in contemporary India it has, as we saw in the *Hindutva Cases,* come to be associated as well with the communal interests of the Hindu majority—at least as those interests have been articulated by the Hindu right, who seek to equate Hinduism with Indian national identity. As noted earlier in the Thirteenth Amendment case, a consensus on the Supreme Court is discernible in the broad acceptance of the primacy of Sinhalese Buddhism in Sri Lankan identity and the firm judicial intention to defend the unitary state, which is the structural attribute of constitutional design most closely associated with that defense. Any judicial outcome that secures the philosophical underpinnings of the unitary state—and therefore the predominant position of the constitutionally favored majority—is to be seen as welcome indeed. To be sure, most advocates of a uniform civil code for India—and this includes justices such as Kuldip Singh—are not motivated by ethnonationalist concerns. But just as surely, their arguments provide appealing sources for constitutional borrowing by those who may be so motivated.

To the objection, then, that judicial appropriation of comparative legal sources will compromise constitutional identity, the Sri Lankan example shows how the practice can become part of a judicial strategy to reinforce critical components in the home country's constitutional identity.[149] Constitutional borrowing can be unambiguously opportunistic

148. Rudolph, "Difference in India," 37.

149. There are other examples of Sri Lankan borrowing of Indian precedents that allow us to reach the same conclusion. For example, in another important secularism case, this time concerning the issue of conversion, the Court drew upon a much-contested Indian decision to advance the ethnic dimension of Sri Lankan constitutional identity. This was done with a clear appreciation of the distinctions in the multicultural premises underlying

without being unprincipled. The choices made on the Sri Lankan Court—to borrow and not to borrow—were consistent with the larger judicial effort to secure the constitutional moorings upon which the identity of the Sri Lankan state was tethered. Foremost here is the preferred position of Sinhalese Buddhism. Attentiveness to Indian experience led the Court to invoke just those structural features of Indian constitutional design that allowed them to advance their arguments for preserving the ethno-religious identity of the polity without acknowledging the very different ideological context within which these structural attributes are situated. So the borrowing by Sri Lankan justices was opportunistic in the sense that it was resourceful in its tendentious application of Indian constitutional materials, but principled to the extent that its advantage lay in potential reinforcement of essential—if controversial—regime principles.

Ireland: Constitutional Adaptation, the Claims of Culture, and the Virtue of Prudence

To travel from Delhi to Dublin is to open oneself up to the shock of recognition. To be sure, expectations of jarring discontinuities will not go unfulfilled. Thus, moving from an immense, impossibly diverse country to one that is in these respects its opposite cannot but help produce a dizzying sense of unfamiliarity. But if one looks beyond the obvious (and important) differences, some commonalities appear that are quite suggestive for constitutional borrowing and the problem of balancing the universal and the particular that is vital to the identity question.

In the case of religion, for example, religious identity figured prominently in the two nations' struggles for independence from the same empire. More specifically, Articles 25 and 26 of the Indian Constitution, which concern the nature of the state's relations with religious life, are

---

the neighboring polities. Far from evincing a deficit in comparative/constitutional understanding on the part of the justices in Sri Lanka, the strategic calculations underlying the borrowing in this instance succeeded in large part because of the sure grasp of the different constitutional identities in play. The Sri Lankan case: *Provincial of the Teaching Sisters of the Holy Cross of the Third Order of Saint Francis in Menzigen of Sri Lanka,* SC: 19/2003; the Indian case: Stanislaus v. State of Madhya Pradesh, AIR 908 (SC), 1977.

based for the most part on Article 44(2) of the Irish Constitution of 1937 (much like, as previously mentioned, the Indian section on Directive Principles is modeled after Article 45). More generally, religion in both places penetrates deeply into the fabric of society, and while the differences between Hinduism and Catholicism matter greatly in terms of the sorts of problems this penetration creates for their respective polities, it offers us a shared jurisprudential challenge to consider: how to realize the Constitution's democratic aspirations while respecting the existence of an entrenched and countervailing religious presence.

As suggested earlier in relation to the Directive Principles of both countries, when compared to India, this religious presence in Ireland does not represent as massive an obstacle to the achievement of constitutionally inspired political and social goals. Indeed, with regard to questions of social and economic justice, mainstream Catholic theology was to a large extent quite compatible with reform-minded policy objectives. But that same theology was difficult to reconcile with a whole host of rights-related concerns—abortion, birth control, homosexuality, among others—that, particularly in the context of increasing integration into the larger European community, presented a substantial judicial dilemma.

Justice Barak would surely recognize the problem, as there are some glaring similarities between the Irish and Israeli experiences. For example, references in Irish Supreme Court opinions to the "Christian and democratic nature of the State"[150] will resonate with students of Israeli jurisprudence. Neither of the majority faiths in Israel and Ireland is an established religion; however, each enjoys a constitutional recognition that far exceeds mere symbolic significance. The Irish Constitution's preamble commences "In the Name of the Most Holy Trinity, from Whom is all authority and to Whom, as our final end, all actions both of men and States must be referred," and then "Humbly acknowledg[es] all our obligations to our Lord, Jesus Christ, Who sustained our fathers

150. See, for example, Ryan v. Attorney General, I.R. 265 (1965), 317. The full quote is "The personal rights which may be invoked to invalidate legislation are not confined to those specified in Article 40 but include all those rights which result from the Christian and democratic nature of the State."

through centuries of trial. . . ."[151] Although the language in a preamble is widely assumed to have limited (if any) legal standing, it can hardly be dismissed as irrelevant when cited, as it was, in the following manner: "It cannot be doubted that the people, so asserting and acknowledging their obligations to our Divine Lord Jesus Christ, were proclaiming a deep religious conviction and faith and an intention to adopt a Constitution consistent with that conviction and faith and with Christian beliefs."[152] This led the Chief Justice (in the majority) to conclude in a landmark case in 1984 that "the Christian nature of our State" supports the criminalization of homosexual conduct on the grounds that its practice is "morally wrong."[153]

Such reliance on the preamble, while revealing, is much the exception in Irish constitutional jurisprudence. More important to the judicial dilemma are the explicit natural law references in the body of the constitutional text. Thus the long-standing debate in the United States over the existence/relevance of natural rights or law to constitutional

151. Preamble, Constitution of Ireland, 1937. In addition, Article 6, Section 1 reads "All powers of government, legislative, executive and judicial. Derive, under God, from the people, whose right it is to designate the rulers of the State and, in final appeal, to decide all questions of national policy, according to the requirements of the common good." In 1972, however, a constitutional amendment deleted a provision from the 1937 document that had recognized the "special position" of the Catholic Church.

152. Norris v. Attorney General, I.R. 36 (1984), 64. One cannot help but compare this case with the American decision in Bowers v. Hardwick, decided two years later. There, too, a chief justice (Burger) cited "Judeo-Christian moral and ethical standards" to uphold an antisodomy statute. Bowers v. Hardwick, 478 U.S. 186, 196 (1986). The mention in this brief concurring opinion occupies a place of lesser prominence than does the reference in Chief Justice O'Higgins's opinion, but it is arguably a more controversial move by an American justice, who clearly lacks any textual justification for making it. The text of the Irish Constitution does not address the specific issue of homosexuality. Thus in Ireland, too, the Court's decision must be considered controversial as an example of interpretive excess.

153. *Norris,* at 64–65. There were two passionate dissents written in this case, whose positions were eventually vindicated by the European Court of Human Rights. The European Court found the Irish legislation to be in violation of the European Convention for the Protection of Human Rights. Norris v. Ireland (1991) 142 Eur. Ct. H.R. (ser. A) at 21 (1998). This was one of the cases cited by Justice Kennedy in *Lawrence* to support the majority's view that the right of homosexual adults to engage in intimate, consensual conduct had been accepted by the wider civilization.

adjudication is very much beside the point in Ireland. "For the purposes of constitutional interpretation, its existence is a positivistic fact which requires no justification."[154] As noted by an Irish Supreme Court justice, "A judge may be a legal positivist and have no use for natural law concepts, but if the Constitution (as it does) explicitly recognises the existence of rights anterior to positive law these jurisprudential views must yield to the clear conclusions which are to be drawn from the construction of the constitutional text."[155] So, for example, Article 41(1) reads: "The State recognises the Family as the natural primary and fundamental unit group of Society, and as a moral institution possessing inalienable and imprescriptible rights, antecedent and superior to all positive law."[156] Over the years, however, the Court's reliance on principles of natural justice has not required explicit textual specification, and the notion of unenumerated rights has flourished within Irish constitutional jurisprudence.

There is little ambiguity about the natural law source for the Court's invocations—the Thomistic philosophical tradition and its emphasis on duties rather than, as in the liberal version more familiar to American law, rights.[157] Until recently the Irish judiciary rather *faithfully* upheld the Catholic natural law position in constitutional adjudication. The initial break occurred in 1971 with the Court's establishment of a constitutional right to marital privacy in McGee v. Attorney General.[158] While known for being the first time the Supreme Court expressly ruled in a case contrary to Catholic teaching, the landmark decision is especially

154. Richard Humphreys, "Constitutional Interpretation," 15 *Dublin University Law Journal* 59 (1993), 70.

155. Ibid., quoting Justice Costello.

156. Also explicit in its invocation of natural right is Article 43, Section 1: "The State acknowledges that man, in virtue of his rational being, has the natural right, antecedent to positive law, to the private ownership of external goods."

157. For an extensive treatment of natural law in Irish jurisprudence, see Desmond M. Clarke, *Church and State: Essays in Political Philosophy* (Cork, Ireland: Cork University Press, 1984). See also V. Bradley Lewis, "Liberal Democracy, Natural Law, and Jurisprudence: Thomistic Notes on an Irish Debate," in Timothy Fuller and John P. Hittinger, eds., *Reassessing the Liberal State: Reading Maritain's* Man and the State (Washington, DC: Catholic University of America Press, 2001).

158. McGee v. Attorney General, 1 I.R. 284 (1974).

notable for illuminating the problem of how one protects universal rights at the local level.

The problem has risen in intensity and urgency in the ensuing years with the well-documented changes that have been occurring in Irish society.[159] As one observer notes, "communal views of society are increasingly challenged by a growing emphasis on the rights of the individual."[160] This liberalizing trend is reflected in the most sensitive constitutional arena—abortion—with a series of decisions that have loosened, if not severed, the hold of traditional natural law teachings on personal behavior.[161] Nevertheless, the idea that the decline in influence of institutionalized religion means that the thickly constituted religious presence in Ireland is no longer of constitutional significance, is as questionable as a similar conclusion would be in regard to the major religions in India. "[The] cooling of religious zeal does not entail a complete rejection of Ireland's strong Catholic heritage; there is little doubt that the Church will continue its social, spiritual, and cultural mission in this revised context. . . ."[162] Catholic teaching may no longer dictate the substance of legislative and judicial activity, but the tension between Christian and democratic commitments remains a factor at the core of constitutional interpretation.

159. For an excellent empirical analysis of these changes, see Finola Kennedy, *Cottage to Creche: Family Change in Ireland* (Dublin: Institute of Public Administration, 2001). See also Diarnaid Ferriter, *The Transformation of Ireland* (New York: Overlook Press, 1986).

160. Gerard Whyte, "Religion and the Irish Constitution," 30 *John Marshall Law Review* 725 (1997), 725.

161. The most important of these decisions, Attorney General v. X, 1 I.R. 1 (1992), involved the efforts of a 14-year-old rape victim to obtain an abortion in England. The attorney general sought to prevent her travel abroad in order to uphold the Constitution's ban on abortion. While the Court's decision left the meaning of the constitutional provision in some confusion, it did hold that in view of the substantial risk to the life of the mother (who had threatened suicide), the injunction against the girl's travel would have to be lifted. In the wake of the Court's decision, two constitutional amendments—one protecting the right to travel and the other to receive information about abortion—were adopted after approval by the electorate. The latter is discussed shortly.

162. Christine P. James, "Cead Mile Failte? Ireland Welcomes Divorce: The 1995 Irish Divorce Referendum and the Family (Divorce) Act of 1996," 8 *Duke Journal of Comparative and International Law* 175 (1997), 255.

In *McGee,* the Court heard a married woman's claim that restrictions on access to contraception (a ban on the selling or importation into Ireland of any birth control device) violated her constitutional rights, most importantly the right to lead her private life in accordance with the dictates of her own conscience. In the main opinion by Justice Brian Walsh, there are two references to the Constitution's preamble that underscore the interpretive challenge for the Court. The first is to the language quoted earlier to the effect that "the Constitution acknowledges God as the ultimate source of all authority." The second is to the constitutional intention to "promote the common good, with due observance of Prudence, Justice and Charity, so that the dignity and freedom of the individual may be assured. . . ." In the face of these dual (if not contradictory) commitments, the reference in the opinion to Griswold v. Connecticut was doubtless tinged with envy, since the American Constitution, Justice Walsh pointed out, is not "governed by the precepts of Christianity."[163] According to the justice, the discovery in *Griswold* of a right to privacy still required a rejection of legal positivism, but without the competing tug of Christian doctrine, the result was more straightforwardly attainable through a process of reasoning driven by principles of universal application.[164]

At several places in the opinion mention is made of Aristotle and the "virtue of prudence."[165] These appear in a paragraph declaiming judicial responsibility for determining the substance of natural law in a pluralist society. The broader context is this. On the one hand, there is the petitioner, who asserts a right of privacy as a matter of individual conscience; on the other, the State, which imposes a restriction consistent with the theological precepts of the religion of the majority and its church. The Court's solution is indeed an exercise in prudence. The woman's right is upheld, but not as a matter of conscience, rather as a vindication of the family "as the natural primary and fundamental unit

163. *McGee,* at 319.

164. For Justice Walsh, the Irish Constitution clearly indicates that "justice is placed above the law and acknowledge[s] that natural rights, or human rights, are not created by law but that the Constitution confirms their existence and gives them protection" (ibid., at 310).

165. Ibid., at 318–319.

group of society."[166] "[T]he rights of a married couple to decide how many children, if any, they will have are matters outside the reach of positive law where the means employed to implement such decisions do not impinge upon the common good or destroy or endanger human life. . . . It is outside the authority of the State to endeavour to intrude into the privacy of the husband and wife relationship for the sake of imposing a code of private morality upon that husband and wife which they do not desire."[167] Thus by appealing to the Catholic-inspired provisions of Article 41 to upset a Catholic-inspired policy, the Court was able to secure a right that was in progressive step with the movement for globalization of rights while legitimating it under the local mandate of traditional Catholicism.[168]

McGee is only one decision, which is not cited as illustrative or representative of a distinctive Irish constitutional jurisprudence. Rather, the point is to call attention to an interpretive approach with suggestive possibilities for comparative constitutional theory and the effort to understand the concept of constitutional identity. In this regard, one should note a similarity between the judgment here and the *Bommai* decision in

166. Ibid., at 310.

167. Ibid., at 313.

168. There is a substantial literature on the political effects of Catholicism on the success of liberal democratic institutions. Most familiar, perhaps, is Robert Putnam's argument that Catholicism in its traditional form discourages the formation of a civic culture supportive of liberal democracy. Robert Putnam, *Making Democracy Work: Civic Traditions in Modern Italy* (Princeton, NJ: Princeton University Press, 1993). On the other hand, there is another argument that extends back at least as far as Tocqueville, which is that religion (including Catholicism) can, and has, played a civilizing role in fostering values that are useful for civic responsibility. It is interesting to note, apropos the above discussion, that Tocqueville, after mentioning that "Ireland began to pour a Catholic population into the United States," observes that Catholics "form the most republican and democratic class there is in the United States." This, he acknowledges, will be surprising to those who wrongly "regard the Catholic religion as a natural enemy of democracy." He then goes on to explain that the reason for Catholicism's compatibility with democracy has to do with its favorable predisposition to equality of conditions. Tocqueville, *Democracy in America,* 275–276. How much of this is relevant to the constitutional question in contemporary Ireland is uncertain, but the egalitarian theme seems at least to resonate with the language of the Constitution's Directive Principles, which was inspired by Catholic doctrine. This of course is relevant to my earlier contrast between Catholicism and Hinduism and the extent to which they pose a challenge to the existing social order.

India. In the latter case, the Court provided content to Indian secularism in a manner that carefully crafted a meaning consonant with the ameliorative aspirations of the larger constitutional project of which it was a "basic structural" part. Within their respective political contexts, both the Indian and Irish courts achieved their outcomes essentially by drawing upon constitutional sources expressive of the particular realities of the local culture. Both took notice of developments in other places—notably the United States—to advance their arguments, but then, in contrast with the American Court, pursued these arguments in quite different directions.[169] In the case of India, the basic structure doctrine provided cover for negotiating a constitutional understanding of secularism that balanced the specific concerns of the *Indian* Constitution with the aspirations of liberal constitutionalism, the latter most sharply defined by the American model. In Ireland, natural law sustained a constitutional right to privacy, not so much as a support for individual autonomy but to advance the authority of the family "as the necessary basis of social order."[170]

Interpreting natural law in this way is a means of harmonizing the dual influences on the Constitution adopted by the people of Ireland in 1937: the inherited liberal democratic tradition of the free state and the teachings of the Catholic Church. But this harmonizing process, in its emphasis on specific, if selective, features of Catholic natural law, is distinguishable from Justice Barak's interpretive method of moving the focus to the highest level of abstraction, and thus, in effect, reconciling the tension between the Jewish and democratic contents of the polity through artful transvaluation of the meaning of the more particularist of the nation's twin

169. In *McGee,* for example, Justice Walsh wrote, "Three United States Supreme Court decisions were relied upon in argument by the plaintiff: Poe v. Ullman (1961) 367 U.S. 497; Griswold v. Connecticut (1965) 381 U.S. 479; and Eisenstadt v. Baird (1972) 405 U.S. 438. My reason for not referring to them is not because I did not find them helpful or relevant, which indeed they were, but because I found it unnecessary to rely upon any of the dicta in those cases to support the views which I have expressed in this judgment." *McGee,* at 319. By contrast, other justices in the case did invoke these cases, and in so doing no doubt aroused the concerns of the Church, which surely knew that the American Court had used them to undergird its "proabortion" decision in Roe v. Wade.

170. Ibid., at 311.

philosophical commitments.[171] (In India, as was pointed out, the dynamic of abstraction may actually work to the benefit of those pursuing illiberal ends.) Yet if the goal in Ireland is, as in Israel, the achievement of constitutional harmony, judges will continue to be tested in ways that will challenge their jurisprudential imagination in progressively perplexing ways. This is nowhere better illustrated than with the issue of abortion. Here the constitutional politics of disharmony that is increasingly manifest

171. An extreme version of Barak's methodology as applied to Ireland may be found in the work of the Irish constitutional theorist, Richard Humphreys, who proposes that "the natural law conception of the Constitution . . . be regarded as effectively a secular one." Humphreys, "Constitutional Interpretation," 69. For Humphreys, "We are not engaged in an exercise of deciding what was meant in 1937. We are rather searching for the best contemporary understanding of the natural rights which the constitution mandates the State to protect." Richard Humphreys, "Interpreting Natural Rights," 28–30 *Irish Jurist* 221, 227–228 (1993–1995). Students of American jurisprudence may be reminded of Benjamin Cardozo's discussion of natural law in *The Nature of the Judicial Process*, where, for reasons similar to Humphreys', Cardozo advocates understanding the concept "in a different sense from that which formerly attached to the expression 'natural law.'" Benjamin N. Cardozo, *The Nature of the Judicial Process* (New Haven, CT: Yale University Press, 1969), 122. That the Irish theorist's view is anti-Scalia with a vengeance is confirmed by Humphrey's designation of recommended sources from which to draw the contemporary understanding. "[The] task involves an attempt to determine the extent to which the international community has recognised the right sought to be protected, and the result of that enquiry goes directly to the question of whether the right concerned, or the aspect of it at issue, deserves protection as a natural right under the Constitution of Ireland." Humphreys, "Constitutional Interpretation," 227. Such a proposal for determining the scope of fundamental rights represents Justice Scalia's worst nightmare, combining as it does a rejection of both originalism and indigenous constitutional evolution. Going abroad for constitutional inspiration is not simply a matter of obtaining analogical perspective on contested meanings, but of direct transplantation. To be sure, the Irish Constitution (Article 29) explicitly affirms a connection to the European Union, and the increasing importance of the European Court of Justice in the laws of even the most independent minded of Union members is undeniable. This perhaps mitigates somewhat the radical quality of the proposal, although Humphreys specifies the American Constitution ("as interpreted by the United States Supreme Court") as a source equal in usefulness to that of the case law emerging from the European Convention on Human Rights. In the end, however, Humphreys's call is for "a fundamentally internationalist reorientation of our constitutional law." Humphreys, "Constitutional Interpretation," 77. To the extent that Justice Scalia is successful in casting the opposition to his rejection of comparative materials in terms of such a commitment, he will doubtless be vindicated in his struggle to exclude cross-national references from American constitutional law.

in the disjuncture between constitution and society has become centered in the document itself, one consequence of which is that debate in Ireland over an unconstitutional constitutional amendment is, as we have seen, no longer a matter of purely academic interest.

Recall from Chapter 2 that under Article 26 of the Irish Constitution, any bill passed by both houses of the legislature (Oireachtas) may be referred to the Supreme Court for a decision on whether it is repugnant to the Constitution. In 1995 this provision was invoked to allow consideration of a bill passed in order to execute the terms of a recently adopted constitutional amendment. The Information (Services outside the State for the Termination of Pregnancies) Bill prescribed conditions for providing individual women or the general public information relating to abortion services lawfully available outside of Ireland. It followed upon the Fourteenth Amendment to the Constitution, which had granted the "freedom to obtain or make available in the State, subject to such conditions as may be laid down by law, information relating to services lawfully available in another State." While there were a number of questions for the Court to consider, perhaps the most interesting had to do with whether this amendment was itself constitutional in light of the Eighth Amendment, which declares: "The State acknowledges the right to life of the unborn and, with due regard to the equal right to life of the mother, guarantees in its laws to respect, and, as far as practicable, by its laws to defend and vindicate that right."[172]

That the consistency of the two amendments would come before the Court was not a surprise given the attention to the question that had surfaced before adoption of the latter amendment. Opponents had contended that provisions contrary to the natural law content of the Constitution (in this case pertaining to the right to life of the unborn) could not legally be added to the document. Supporters saw these objections as an effort by the defenders of sectarian politics to contain the secularizing trends of

172. In its judgment the Court indicated that, absent the Fourteenth Amendment, the bill would be in clear violation of the Eighth Amendment. *In re Art. 26 of the Constitution and the Regulation of Information (Services Outside the State for Termination of Pregnancies) Bill 1995* (1995) 2 I.L.R.M. 81, 24.

liberal democracy. As presented to the Court by the "counsel for the unborn," "any provision in the Constitution or in any legislation which would permit or render lawful the giving or obtaining of such information was contrary to the natural law right to life of the unborn which right is acknowledged in the Eighth Amendment to the Constitution." In addition, "[T]he natural law is the foundation upon which the Constitution was built and ranks superior to the Constitution."[173] The judicial response was succinct and direct: "The Court does not accept this argument."[174]

Earlier this nonacceptance was considered in the context of the unconstitutional amendment puzzle and found disappointing. It is also interestingly vague. After going on at considerable length about the supremacy of the Constitution with respect to lawmaking powers, the Court pointed out that the two amendments would appear to be in direct conflict "as decided by this Court" in several cases. "The People in enacting this Amendment were aware of this conflict because they specifically decided that the freedom to obtain or make available such information [about abortion] should not be limited by the provisions of the Eighth Amendment."[175] In effect, then, in upholding the ultimate authority of the people to amend the Constitution, the Court was acknowledging its own subordination to the supremacy of the document. In contrast with what the American Court said in Cooper v. Aaron—that "the interpretation of the Fourteenth Amendment enunciated by this Court in the *Brown* case is the supreme law of the land"—the Irish Court's interpretation of its own Fourteenth Amendment was distinguishable in theory from the meaning of that amendment as understood by its sovereign authors.

But more was involved here than judicial humility. The Court relied very heavily on Justice Walsh in *McGee.* It quoted from a lengthy excerpt in that opinion:

> In a pluralist society such as ours, the Court cannot as a matter of constitutional law be asked to choose between the differing views, where they exist, of experts on the interpretation by the different

173. Ibid., at 37.
174. Ibid., at 38.
175. Ibid., at 45.

> religious denominations of either the nature or extent of these natural rights as they are to be found in the natural law. . . . The judges must . . . interpret these rights in accordance with their ideas of prudence, justice, and charity. It is but natural that from time to time the prevailing ideas of these virtues may be conditioned by the passage of time: no interpretation of the Constitution is intended to be final for all time. It is given in the light of prevailing ideas and concepts.[176]

Or stated differently, judges must be sensitive to the increasing diversity of opinion in society concerning fundamental moral questions. The natural law basis of the proscription against abortion is, as it was in the case of birth control, theological. To the extent that this particular commitment is inscribed in the document it must be respected—at least by judges. After all, the Constitution *is* supreme. But in relation to matters not specifically addressed in the text, the sovereign will of the people, which stands for the rule of the universal over the particular, must be respected and be permitted to infuse the fundamental law with prevailing ideas and concepts. The Court may disagree that "the equal right to life of the mother" requires information about abortion options outside of Ireland, but the Eighth Amendment's protection of the right to life of the unborn cannot nullify a subsequent amendment adopted under prevailing popular assumptions that such information is required.[177]

To comprehend the seeming paradox of the Court's rejecting the idea that natural law was superior to the Constitution while concurrently affirming the proposition that "justice is not subordinate to law," one might envision these moves as an attempt to steer Irish constitutional identity more in the direction of the prevailing norms of the European (and American) Economic Community (EEC) with regard to the role of religion in civil affairs.[178] Thus the subordination of

176. Ibid., at 41–42.

177. Ibid., at 44.

178. This effort, it has been pointed out, has met considerable resistance. "[C]onservative constructions of an 'Irish' national identity have been strategically deployed as a means to resist progressive law reform, facilitated by European human rights discourse, in the

natural law effectively means the channeling of Catholic theology to its proper place within the constitutional polity, a place that, implicitly in the Court's opinion, still respects the uniqueness of Irish history and culture. For example, in overturning the previously discussed *Norris* case, the European Court of Human Rights suggested that the Irish Supreme Court majority's explicit invocation of Christian theology to uphold the criminalization of homosexual conduct represented an inappropriate elevation of sectarian natural law within the scheme of constitutional enforcement. In the absence of any constitutional provision on homosexuality, the Court's interpretive reliance on Catholic theology to determine the scope and substance of civil rights was arguably a distortion of the proper relationship between temporal and spiritual authority demanded by principles of liberal constitutionalism. This may be distinguished from the Constitution's explicit protection of unborn life, in which the Court's enforcement of a general ban on abortion is normatively unproblematic as an exercise of judicial power. To be sure, the ban has historic roots in Catholic natural law; its codification within the provisions of the supreme law of the land symbolizing the intimate relationship between the state and the religion of the nation's majority. But the very act of constitutional inscription and incorporation means that natural law is subordinate to the Constitution; judges do not appeal from the document to some higher law in order to establish the terms or dimensions of legal obligation.

The Court's lengthy opinion in the *Abortion Information* case made no references to any foreign materials. That provokes one to ask why, with a major component of the case—the balancing of competing rights claimed on behalf of the unborn and the mother—having been much adjudicated in the United States, Germany, Canada, and other jurisdictions, the Court would not seek guidance from abroad. One factor "militat[ing] against cross-cultural assimilation of constitutional

---

area of abortion and gay rights. . . . European rights have sometimes been interpreted in an oppositional fashion to national identity, with arguments grounded in localism and the rights of political communities to make laws which are tailored to national social mores." Carl F. Stychin, "Relatively Universal Globalization, Rights Discourse, and the Evolution of Australian Sexual and National Identities," *Legal Studies* (2006), 553.

categories" is, as Schauer and other particularists emphasize, the problem of translation; simply put, the difficulty in assigning legal significance to critical terms and concepts whose meaning is culturally determined. When, for example, an issue has not traditionally been framed in terms of a discourse of rights, the utility of borrowing from locations where the opposite is true may not be deemed worth the effort.[179] In Irish jurisprudence generally, and specifically in regard to abortion, the idea of natural law has exerted a powerful sway over the decision making of the Court. In most other constitutional polities (especially the United States) it occupies a much less prominent place in constitutional adjudication, and to the extent that it matters at all, its meaning is philosophical, not theological. Its judicial application is generally associated with expansion of personal freedoms, not, as in Ireland, with limitations placed upon them. What is "deeply rooted in [the Irish] nation's history" is a sectarian worldview increasingly questioned and challenged by inhabitants who find their cultural borders readily penetrated by the secularizing forces of "a wider civilization."[180] To expect that their constitutional borders will not be similarly penetrated is unrealistic.

179. Mary Ann Glendon has written at length about the transferability of rights discourse in constitutional law. "So far as constitution-making and judicial interpretation of rights are concerned . . . there is little evidence that, thus far, oversimplified rights ideas in the current American dialect are displacing nuanced and complex interpretations more suited to conditions elsewhere." Mary Ann Glendon, *Rights Talk: The Impoverishment of Political Discourse* (New York: Free Press, 1991), 168. It is interesting to contrast Glendon's views with Bork's. They are in agreement on most constitutional issues, and while Bork quotes Glendon approvingly for her critique of rights discourse, their positions on constitutional borrowing are widely disparate. Bork attacks the excesses of borrowing in the context of a critique of the "liberal wing of the Court" and its proclivity for rights and universals at the expense of culture and particulars. Bork, *Coercing Virtue,* 22. Glendon, on the other hand, deplores the insularity of American courts, urging them to explore approaches from abroad so that they will come to appreciate the alternatives to a rights-based jurisprudence. Whereas Bork imagines exercises in cross-national constitutional assimilation as a liberal strategy for gaining influence on the Court and thus opposes it, Glendon believes such techniques to be of potential benefit to conservatives as well and heartily supports them.

180. Justice Scalia tried to distinguish between forces from "a wider civilization" and something "deeply rooted in this Nation's history" in *Lawrence,* at 598.

But what the Court seems to have understood (at least in *McGee* and *Abortion Information*) is that the monitoring of these constitutional borders is critical, that whatever the ultimate extent of integration into the cultural and constitutional mainstream of advanced liberal democratic polities, the balance between the universal and the particular needs to be carefully calibrated. For centuries the Irish had been concerned about the penetration of English law into their legal domain, an apprehension that perhaps has stood them in good stead in the time of their constitutional independence. Mary Ann Glendon observes: "[A]wareness of foreign experiences does lead to the kind of self-understanding that constitutes a necessary first step on the way toward working out our own approaches to our own problems."[181] Her point is an example of "dialogical interpretation," that is to say, "comparative jurisprudence [as] an important stimulus to legal self-reflection."[182] With respect to natural law in Irish jurisprudence, one might point out in this connection that the Supreme Court appears to have accepted that the declining efficacy of such moral argument in the contemporary culture requires a diminution in its role in determining constitutional outcomes. Also, however, the Court understands that for critical institutions of civil society—in particular, family and church—that have evolved in significant ways through the precepts of natural law thinking, any radical departure from traditional moorings could be damaging to these institutions, and perhaps to its own legitimacy as well. The Court's decisions in these sensitive areas have been criticized for being too tentative and too bold, no doubt a commentary in part on an institution seeking to work out, as suggested by Glendon, its own approach to the nation's unique problems. It is in this circumstance that looking abroad (without necessarily bringing anything home) may be most helpful—if only to sharpen the awareness of constitutional difference.[183]

181. Mary Ann Glendon, *Abortion and Divorce in Western Law* (Cambridge, MA: Harvard University Press, 1987), 142.

182. Choudhry, "Globalization," 836.

183. For an interesting discussion of the Irish Supreme Court's response to rulings from abroad (mainly Europe), see Bruce Carolan, "The Supreme Court, Constitutional Courts and the Role of International Law in Constitutional Jurisprudence: The Search for Coherence

To sum up: "From the foundation of the State to the enactment of the 1937 Constitution a broad consensus existed regarding the values that should inform laws and policies. This led to a close similarity . . . between the teaching of the Catholic Church and the laws of the State."[184] For a number of years thereafter this collaboration only intensified, as would not have surprised anyone who reflected on the much more explicit connection between church and constitution codified in the 1937 document. Nor, however, would any reflective observer of the Irish scene have failed to appreciate the significance of the loosening of this relationship—in both law and society—that has dramatically occurred in the last several decades. This emerging disharmony is a driving force in the evolution of Irish constitutional identity, although a fair account of the nation's prescriptive constitution must acknowledge that Catholic and democratic commitments have had long-standing ties that constitute an ongoing tradition embodying, in MacIntyre's phrase, "continuities of conflict." As foreign ideas and legal precedents—those at least that bear upon this constitutive conflict—migrate across constitutional borders and enter the arena of Irish juridical contestation, they confront the shifting winds of these identity-shaping forces and are processed accordingly.

Conclusion: Permeability and Imperfection

To complete this journey I return to the concerns raised at the time of departure. As disparate as the places visited in this chapter are, a characteristic that unites them, and indeed all constitutions, is their state of imperfection. While the gap between the ideal and the actual is omnipresent, it expresses itself in a variety of ways. In most cases a constitutional text will accurately reflect local circumstances and project, in Publius's words, "the best which [the] political situation, habits, and opinions will admit."[185] Sometimes, as in the case of India,

---

in the Use of Foreign Court Judgments by the Supreme Court of Ireland," 12 *Tulsa Journal of Comparative and International Law* 123 (2004).

184. Kennedy, *Cottage to Creche,* 156.

185. *Federalist* 85, Clinton Rossiter, ed., *The Federalist.* I include the qualification to account for constitutions—perhaps best exemplified by the old Soviet constitution—that

the framers will make explicit their founding constraints with the inclusion of provisions (the Directive Principles) that say, in effect, that our constitutional ideals are immediately unenforceable and must rely for their fulfillment upon the eventual arrival of propitious political and social conditions. Sometimes, as in the case of Israel, the gap will be implicit in the contradictions that lie at the core of constitutional arrangements, leading bitter antagonists to concur on only one main point, that however fundamentally flawed the status quo is, it may be worth maintaining for at least the short term. And sometimes, as in the case of Ireland, the space between what a constitution is and what it ought to be is manifest in the normative code embraced in the document, but obscured by a fundamental ambivalence over the changing status of traditional institutions of civil society governed by that code.

Constitutional imperfection is, then, the setting within which constitutional interpretation, especially as it looks outward, takes place. "The migration of constitutional ideas across legal systems," Sujit Choudhry notes, "is rapidly emerging as one of the central features of contemporary constitutional practice."[186] Judges in the Indian, Israeli, and Irish Supreme Courts all regularly consider judgments and approaches from the courts of other nations. They do this presumably to determine what might profitably be transplanted to native constitutional soil. Yet much of what judges do when they scrutinize the work of foreign judiciaries may simply enable them to better comprehend the scope and substance of constitutional imperfection. Comparative inquiry can illuminate the jurisprudential challenge inherent in the gap between actual and ideal conditions. Whether to catch a glimpse of the future in anticipation of judicially imposed constitutional improvements at home, or to get a better appreciation for the limits of reform through exposure to alternative legal contexts abroad, expanding

---

bears no resemblance to the realities on the ground. Whether a sham constitution may be considered a constitution is best left for another discussion.

186. Sujit Choudhry, "Migration as a Metaphor in Comparative Constitutional Law," in Sujit Choudhry, ed., *The Migration of Constitutional Ideas* (New York: Cambridge University Press, 2006), 13.

the scope of constitutional sources expands the available options for judicial problem solving.[187]

Indeed, for critics of borrowing the additional options made possible through these endeavors is exactly the problem. In his classic text on American politics, E. E. Schattschneider wrote that "[t]he most important strategy of politics is concerned with the scope of conflict."[188] All efforts to expand or contract the scope of conflict, he argued, have a bias attached to them, with "socialization of conflict" associated with liberal causes and privatization the defense of the status quo. In the judicial context, this model conforms to the debate over constitutional protectionism in the United States, as evidenced by Robert Bork's insistence that the appeal of going abroad for judicial guidance is a phenomenon associated with the liberal wing of the Court. Bork's denigration of universals in favor of "[c]onservative pragmatism [and] its concern with particularity—respect for difference, circumstance, tradition, history, and the irreducible complexity of human beings and human societies,"[189] is consistent with Schattschneider's account of the political dynamics of scope management. "Universal ideas in the culture, ideas concerning equality, consistency, equal protection of the laws, justice, liberty, freedom of movement, freedom of speech and association, and civil rights tend to

187. See Cheryl Saunders, "The Use and Misuse of Comparative Constitutional Law," 13 *Indian Journal of Global Legal Studies* (2006). As for Justice Scalia's position on the irrelevance of foreign jurisprudence for American constitutional interpretation, it can mean one or both of two things. Either Americans have nothing to learn from abroad because perfection has been attained, or, however imperfect our attainment, judges should not allow themselves to be the instruments of convergence between the ideal and the actual. The first position could reflect an extreme particularist perspective in which the ideal is to be understood in purely relativistic or positivistic terms, entailing a collapse of any distinction between the is and the ought in constitutional jurisprudence. The second could reflect an extreme posture of self-restraint, requiring a commitment to judicial abnegation with respect to any aspirational role for the Court. Both positions, I would argue, undermine constitutional theory, an enterprise whose vitality requires confronting the problem of constitutional imperfection.

188. E. E. Schattschneider, *The Semisovereign People: A Realist's View of Democracy in America* (Hinsdale, IL: Dryden Press, 1975), 3.

189. Bork, *Coercing Virtue,* 3.

socialize conflict."[190] As the South African Justice Albie Sachs wrote in his country's gay marriage case, "It would be a strange reading of the Constitution that utilized the principles of international human rights law to take away a guaranteed right."[191] To understand Justice Scalia's aversion to the comparative moves of some of his colleagues on the American Court, one need only reference his constitutional orientation on questions of federalism, where his state sovereignty stance manifests, in Schattschneider's framework of analysis, a clear preference for privatizing conflict in the interest of nonuniversalist ends. As Ken Kersch, a supporter of Scalia's views on borrowing, argues, "Just as the New Dealers transcended an outmoded localism and pioneered a constitutionalism for a newly interconnected nation, so too the new legal multilateralists would transcend, in the words of Justice Ginsburg, the outmoded 'island or lone ranger mentality' of the nation-state."[192]

In this chapter I have offered oblique reactions to this criticism; now I respond more directly—albeit briefly—by addressing the two most serious elements of the critique, what may be referred to as the *cultural* objection and the *juridical* objection. The first argues that constitutional interpretation must be grounded in the legal and political culture within which it operates, that the infusion of foreign sources into the process of domestic adjudication undermines the constitution's role in sustaining a viable sense of national identity. In Justice Scalia's words, "We must never forget that it is a Constitution for the United States of America that we are expounding."[193] The second asserts that the expansion of the geography from which constitutional sources may be drawn encourages judges to assume an increasingly active role in the inappropriate adaptation of constitutional meaning to changing social realities and intellectual currents of opinion. Moreover, this activity undermines the authority of the courts.

190. Schattschneider, Semisovereign People, 7.

191. *Minister of Home Affairs v. Fourie,* CCT 60/04, 66.

192. Kersch, "Multilateralism," 18.

193. Thompson v. Oklahoma, 487 U.S. 815, 868 n. 4 (1988).

The Cultural Objection

The cultural objection has both normative and empirical parts. "If our constitutional system and its underlying culture is significantly different from that of countries we seek to borrow from, the decision to borrow from those countries is on the weakest normative grounds."[194] Critiques of this kind are embedded in a broader concern that is particularly acute in connection with public, as opposed to private, law. "Public law reflects an inner relationship—a sort of spiritual and psychical relationship—with the people over whom it operates. This historical contact between public law and national identity is not readily transplantable from one country to another."[195] Even if it were, Judge Richard Posner is doubtful that, at least as far as his own countrymen are concerned, it should be attempted. "[F]oreign decisions emerge from complex social, political, cultural, and historical backgrounds of which Supreme Court justices, like other American judges and lawyers are largely ignorant."[196]

The cultural objection should not be taken lightly, especially in the United States. It has become a commonplace (which is not to diminish its relevance to the issue at hand) that the American Constitution, as the embodiment of the political ideas that provide definition to the nation, is constitutive of the society. Other polities, as is often pointed out, are more dependent on such factors as ethnicity, race, religion, or language to establish a secure basis for national unity, identity, and membership. Therefore, to trifle with indigenous constitutional sources by exposing them to the importation of transnational materials is potentially to compromise the integrity of the American national experiment.

But this presumes a result that is empirically contestable. The question of whether such exposure invites a threat of compromise is by no means obvious. As the dialogic approach to the use of comparative law suggests, going outside one's constitutional borders may actually result

194. Kersch, "New Legal Transnationalism," 383.

195. Christopher Osakwe, "The Problem of the Comparability of Nations in Constitutional Law," 59 *Tulane Law Review* 875, 876. For further elaboration of this view, see Roger Cotterrell, "Comparative Law and Legal Culture."

196. Richard Posner, "Forward: A Political Court," 119 *Harvard Law Review* 31 (2005), 86.

in an enhancement of national self-understanding. Moreover, as Cheryl Saunders argues, "[W]here a court is using foreign law in a dialogical manner, the demands of context will be less and will vary from instance to instance."[197] Certainly experience elsewhere indicates that *how* judges choose to make use of foreign case law matters much more than the fact that they permit themselves to be instructed by it in the first instance. The fact, too, that increasingly the American model has been used by judges elsewhere as an "anti-model" should give pause to those who depict the permeability of constitutional borders as a threat to the constitutional essentials of the receiving nation.[198] Judges in all three of our constitutional settings could (as some of them did) inspect the equal treatment principle in American church/state jurisprudence and recognize that it incorporates a widely held and respected precept of liberal constitutionalism. But the principle might also ordain practices with problematic implications for certain societies in their current circumstances, which then would require creative adaptation of the precept to conform to the specific needs of the judge's constitutional polity. This is what happened in the *Bommai* case when some Indian judges, after reflecting on the anti-redistributive social implications of the American solution,[199] reconfigured the equal treatment norm in a way that addressed local needs consistent with the spirit and history of their constitutional tradition.[200]

197. Saunders, "Comparative Constitutional Law," 73.

198. Heinz Klug, "Model and Anti-Model: The United States Constitution and the 'Rise of World Constitutionalism,'" 2000 *Wisconsin Law Review* 597 (2000).

199. See Richard A. Epstein, "Religious Liberty in the Welfare State," 31 *William and Mary Law Review* (1990), 391.

200. From a non-American perspective one needs to consider that the desirability of permeable constitutional borders may sometimes lie in the possibilities inhering therein for *changing* important cultural attributes of the local constitutional scene. In his study of the Indian Constitution, Granville Austin points out that "the most frequently expressed fear, and the most easily understandable, was that the largely foreign origin of the Constitution would make it unworkable in India." Austin, *Indian Constitution*, 325. The fear was well-grounded given the pointed efforts of the framers to borrow from other systems. As Andrzej Rapacznski notes, "It is one of a few cases of a massive borrowing by a country with a vastly different tradition that has had lasting effects on the legal and political culture of the borrowing country. . . ." Andrzej Rapacznski, "Bibliographical Essay: The Influence of U.S. Constitutionalism Abroad," in Henkin, *Constitutionalism and Rights*, 447. To say that this was a bad thing, however, would be to deny the surprising success of the Indian constitutional experiment.

On the other hand, in the *Hindutva Cases,* the judicial deployment of Rawlsian theory could have been better attuned to the immediate Indian political context. Contrary to Schattschneider's analysis of the socialization of conflict in American politics, the appeal in those cases by Justice Verma to universal ideas crafted in the West actually advanced (whether inadvertently or by design) the cause of non-egalitarian, illiberal interests. In the *Qa'adan* case, Justice Barak's incorporation of *Brown*'s colorblind principle into his reasoning for the Court represented an attempt to identify the Israeli approach to equal treatment with an American solution that was both politically and sociologically at odds with the reality at home. Arguably in both of these instances political conditions had not reached the point where the judicial insinuation of universalist concepts into the local constitutional equation had much chance of achieving results comparable to what was attainable in settings where a tighter fit existed between aspirations and actualities. In contrast, Justice Walsh's opinion in *McGee* demonstrated a sensitivity to the claims of culture by providing a constitutional path that led to a more expansive field of personal freedom without severing or obscuring the connection to "the Nations's history and tradition." To the extent that a natural right of privacy as developed in the United States and elsewhere was to be a positive source for legal change, it had to be adapted to Ireland's natural law environment, its prescriptive constitution.

The Juridical Objection

The juridical objection is closely related to the cultural objection. Judges will expand the scope of their constitutional field of vision in order to legitimate outcomes that would otherwise be defeated if confined to domestic sources. Judges who open their constitutional borders to the importation of foreign legal materials are, it is claimed, activists who have discovered yet another means to avoid the constraints of text and intention. Of their borrowing practices, "Its naked focus is on judges as policymakers, searching the globe for expert advice and experience on the best means of solving public policy problems. . . ."[201] For Judge Posner, "The

201. Kersch, "New Legal Transnationalism," 385.

citation of foreign decisions is opportunistic, . . . best understood as an effort to mystify the adjudicative process and disguise the political decisions that are the core of the Supreme Court's constitutional output."[202]

Thus in *Lawrence,* Justice Scalia viewed the citation of decisions by the European Court of Human Rights as an additional quiver in an expanding arsenal of weapons of judicial activism (to say nothing of mass destruction).[203] As Justice Clarence Thomas observed in a denial of certiorari opinion challenging the use of foreign precedents: "[W]ere there any support [for the arguments advanced by the foreign citations] in our own jurisprudence, it would be unnecessary for proponents of the claim to rely on the European Court of Human Rights, the Supreme Court of Zimbabwe, the Supreme Court of India, and the Privy Council."[204] Interestingly, Judge Bork has criticized an Israeli decision concerning the adoption of a child by a lesbian couple for its reliance on a California law to "normaliz[e] homosexual conduct." "Israel has lost the authority to define what constitutes a legal family on its soil whenever a foreign country recognizes some other arrangement as a family."[205]

That the citation of foreign sources opens up possibilities for judicial activism is irrefutable; but like many other possibilities already in use, the technique is in principle unrelated to instances of activism or

202. Posner, "Political Court," 88.

203. There is another way of understanding Justice Scalia's rejection of constitutional borrowing. In Sarah Harding's insightful comparative analysis of judicial reasoning in the United States and Canada, Scalia personifies what she calls the "enforcement model," a distinctively American approach to constitutional decision making that emphasizes finality and judicial supremacy. "Its refusal to engage foreign legal systems arguably stems from similar concerns about maintaining a tight grip on authority." Harding, "Comparative Reasoning and Judicial Review," 451. This she contrasts with the more "dialogical" model prevailing in Canada, in which the Supreme Court's willingness to engage with foreign courts is of a piece with its internal dialogical perspective vis-à-vis other political institutions. Seen in this way, Scalia's hostility to constitutional borrowing is not so much a testament to his parochialism as it is an extension of his understanding of the proper exercise of judicial review. "The enforcement model tends to enshrine the past, marking it as the source of principled, definitive, and closely tailored legal norms. Not only does this legal past hold out the promise of virtue and integrity in legal reasoning . . . it also can be cast as a uniquely local experience" (ibid., 462).

204. Knight v. Florida, 528 U.S. 990 (1999).

205. Bork, *Coercing Virtue,* 126.

restraint. Thus in *Lawrence* the Court overturned a sodomy statute in Texas, but in *Grutter*, the contemporaneous affirmative action case that displayed the Court again referring to developments in other countries, a Michigan program was upheld. This reminds us of the *Hindutva Cases* in India, which validated the Representation of the People Act section on corrupt practices in part on the basis of its consistency with principles famously articulated by an American philosopher. It also brings to mind the Sri Lankan experience with Indian precedents.

In practice, however, as the Schattschneider model predicts, judicial appeals to law in other places are surely correlated positively with challenges to the status quo. But the important question to be asked is how one should evaluate the activity or passivity of courts, for which there is no one generally applicable answer. A court in Israel that expands the geographic scope of its resource base beyond its own borders invites a different level of scrutiny for its actions than its counterpart in India. Assuming that the goal of each is to use foreign case law as an instrument of change, assessments of the wisdom or propriety of doing so must account for the different constitutional contexts within which the two courts operate. So it must matter that the Israeli Court's appropriation of a foreign case will be understood as an effort by the judiciary to advance the prospects of one side of a constitutional debate that has raged since the inception of the state. In contrast, a similar appropriation by the Indian Court may be immunized from most attacks because of two historically specific reasons: (1) as an "arm of the social revolution," the judiciary can claim a constitutional mandate to emulate "progressive" developments in other places; and (2) as an institution functioning within a society that accentuates and values syncretistic development, the assimilation of foreign materials into the native jurisprudence enjoys the legitimacy of an action that, in cultural terms, appears perfectly natural. To the extent, then, that the juridical objection is expressed as a concern over the maintenance and best use of institutional power, the evaluation of the efficacy of constitutional borrowing will require detailed analyses of the political and cultural assets and liabilities of a given national judiciary.

How permeable constitutional borders should be is in the end a question directly implicating constitutional identity. Once one gets beyond the polemics that often, especially in the United States, accompany the migration of constitutional ideas, we can, whatever our assessment of any given exercise of comparative incorporation or non-incorporation, appreciate the heuristic possibilities these occasions offer. As dialogical interactions, they highlight the dynamics that exist in efforts to maintain and transform constitutional identity. Engagements with sources external to the domestic constitutional environment invite us to consider which features of that setting represent prescriptive elements of the local constitutional culture and which are essential to a regime of constitutional governance. Certain characteristics may fall into both categories, serving as variations on a theme of generic constitutionalism while embodying idiosyncratic characteristics of a particular constitutional tradition. As judges evaluate the relevance of foreign materials to the immediate task at hand, their focus will (or should) be drawn to the possible interactive effects that integrating such materials into the home environment could have with regard to these first- and second-order constitutive features.[206]

For example, in the next chapter I discuss two models of constitutionalism expressive of different constitutional orientations—acquiescent and militant—toward the social order. These orientations do much to establish the constitutional identities of the polities in which they are situated. Judges in one of these polities might opt to borrow from the jurisprudence of the other in the hopes of contributing to the modification of their constitutional identity in the direction of the contrasting model. Criticism would doubtless follow if such a move were seen as inappropriate, and just as assuredly defended by those sharing the judges' sense of the shortcomings of the extant constitutional order. To the extent that these differences reflected the ongoing disharmony within the constitutional tradition of the society, it could generate a salutary occasion for deliberation and further internal dialogic engagements about perfecting

206. David A. J. Richards has shown how the American founders used the ideas of Montesquieu and Hume to illuminate their specific predicament without becoming "hostage to Montesquieu's and Hume's own preferences for the British Constitution." Richards, "Revolution and Constitutionalism," 93. Another way of putting this is that they appropriated the philosophers' ideas about constitutionalism without following them in their partiality toward the specific constitutional identity that had materialized in Great Britain.

constitutional conditions. Not so salutary, however, would be a scenario in which critics and respondents perceived the positions of their adversaries as threatening the very essentials of constitutionalism. Such a clash would be symptomatic of a deeper infirmity for which the closing of constitutional borders would do precious little to address.

CHAPTER 5

The Sounds of Silence: Militant and Acquiescent Constitutionalism

Family policy is no one's business at present.
—Daniel Patrick Moynihan

Political tyranny is nothing compared to social tyranny and a reformer, who defies society, is a much more courageous man than a politician, who defies government.
—B. R. Ambedkar

Introduction: Fundamental Law and the Fundamental Unit of Society

Among the questions that might be asked in an exploration of constitutional identity, one stands out in importance: how should we understand the connection between a constitution and the social order within which it is situated? Accustomed as we are to identifying constitutionalism with written limits on power, a reasonable response would be to see a predominantly preservative role in the relationship of the first to the second. Thus the institutions that provide order to a society—for example, church, property, family—should be protected from hostile acts threatening to their essential continuity. Moreover, the framing of governing charters is not likely to culminate in a document antagonistic to the very societal structures of stability that provide support for the constitutional experiment. This is not to say that constitutionally governed polities typically immunize the institutions of civil society from change, rather that the constitution itself is not the direct source of major revisions. A constitution provides protected space for institutional transformation in accordance with the actions and desires of private actors and, on occasion, of its own public standards. But the manner in which this occurs will ultimately be supportive of the existing social order, whose preservation requires an adaptive capacity to meet the needs of a changing environment.

An alternative perspective on this connection may be less familiar. In this version the constitution is a potentially subversive presence in the social order. Here the institutions of civil society are vulnerable to transformative attacks emanating from a constitution that is fundamentally antagonistic to the status quo. These institutions are not left totally unprotected, and their defenders will find ample political and legal (including constitutional) resources with which to secure them from the ravages of radical reconstruction. But to the degree that the preservative presumption is absent from constitutional design, defending the social order will be a more formidable task than in circumstances where the imprimatur of constitutional legitimacy extends to the prevailing configurations of that order. As we have seen, inherent in the constitutional condition is a gap between foundational ideals and existing realities; in this alternative understanding much more is involved than just an implicit reminder of the inevitable disharmonies between law and society, namely the constitutional obligation assigned the state to resolve the severest of these contradictions.

These approaches represent two distinctive—but not mutually exclusive—constitutional orientations reflecting contrasting constitutional identities. In this chapter I concentrate initially on the Indian and American cases, both of which contain preservative and transformative elements, the latter predominant in India and the former in the United States. I then look to the Irish case as a classic instance of an evolving constitutional identity in which the disharmonic tension between preservation and transformation is strikingly evident. My specific focus is on one bastion of civil society—the family—an institution variously described in constitutional provisions around the world as "the fundamental unit of society," "the basic nucleus of social organization," "the natural and fundamental cell of society," "the basis of society," "the foundation of society," "the foundation of the preservation and improvement of the nation," "the main center for the growth and edification of the human being," and "a moral institution possessing inalienable and imprescriptible rights, antecedent and superior to all positive law."[1] None of these encomia are to be found in the Indian and American constitutions, which are among the small minority of such documents without any explicit reference to the family.[2] Yet, the centrality of the family to all societies—a fact recognized in political philosophy as well as practice—ensures the institution's constitutive prominence even where documents are silent about its societal significance. As Jean Bethke Elshtain observes, "The question of the family and its relation to the broader social and political order has bedeviled Western political discourse from its inception."[3] And within this discourse is an issue of signal importance: "[Are] the social relations of the family, with their competing loyalties and standards of human conduct, a threat to political order and authority or a constituent feature of that order . . . ?"[4]

1. These characterizations are taken from the constitutions of Afghanistan, Iran, Nicaragua, Angola, Armenia, Oman, Paraguay, Turkey, Greece, Iran, and Ireland.

2. The other constitutions that do not reference the family at all are Australia, Austria, Canada, Denmark, Finland, France, Lebanon, Nepal, Netherlands, New Zealand, Norway, Russia, Singapore, and Yemen. There are also a group of countries, for example, South Africa, Italy, and Sweden, whose constitutions make incidental references to the family without guaranteeing them any real protection. In the South African case the Supreme Court has suggested one reason for the Constitution's lack of specificity: change in the definition of the family. Thus in its landmark gay marriage case, the justices agreed that "family as contemplated by the Constitution can be constituted in different ways and legal conceptions of the family and what constitutes family life should change as social practices and traditions change. . . ." Minister of Home Affairs v. Fourie, CCT 60/04 (2005).

3. Jean Bethke Elshtain, "Introduction: Toward a Theory of the Family and Politics," in Jean Bethke Elshtain, ed., *The Family in Political Thought* (Amherst: University of Massachusetts Press, 1982), 7.

4. Ibid., 7. In either case, the constitutional order has always needed to take the measure of the family, even when, as famously regarded by Aristotle, it was a subordinate institution, albeit one essential to the existence of any polis no matter the specifics of its constitution.

The question of "a threat to political order" is critical to the contrasts drawn in this chapter. My purpose is not to present another iteration of the often-considered distinction between constitutions of negative (or "first generation") and positive (or "second generation") rights. Many modern constitutions include provisions for social and economic entitlements whose enforcement would require extensive state intervention within the private realm. Whether these constitutions have a transformative mission of the kind I am interested in cannot be determined solely on the basis of such inclusions. Thus, even when it is difficult to dismiss their positive rights commitments as window dressing or as part of a calculated strategy of "hegemonic preservation,"[5] it does not follow that a subversive posture to the social order lies behind these commitments. As illustrated by Franklin D. Roosevelt's support for a "second Bill of Rights," these constitutional rights are just as likely to embody a preservative intent as a fundamentally transformative one.[6]

Nor does it follow that the absence of these entitlements is indicative of a comfortable fit between constitution and social order. The Indian Constitution, my example of a confrontational document, does not include them.[7] By "confrontational" I refer to a particular kind of transformative constitution, one whose identity is in large measure defined by its commitment to reshape key structures of the social order. It is these structures that need to be confronted as threats to the new order envisioned in the constitutional experiment. To the extent that family structure in India

5. The reference is to the thesis in Ran Hirschl's, *Towards Juristocracy: The Origins and Consequences of the New Constitutionalism* (Cambridge, MA: Harvard University Press, 2004). Hirschl argues that the best explanation for judicial empowerment through constitutionalization is that it serves the interests of political, economic, and legal power holders. It is "a form of self-interested *hegemonic preservation*" (ibid., 11). With regard to inequalities in society, Hirschl does not find much empirical support for the idea that constitutionally guaranteed socioeconomic rights lead to meaningful change on the ground.

6. See Cass R. Sunstein, *The Second Bill of Rights: FDR's Unfinished Revolution and Why We Need It More Than Ever* (New York: Basic Books, 2004).

7. A section on Directive Principles of State Policy is now being interpreted to provide it with more than hortatory significance, which is not to say that it creates judicially enforceable rights. See Mark Tushnet, *Weak Courts, Strong Rights: Judicial Review and Social Welfare Rights in Comparative Constitutional Law* (Princeton, NJ: Princeton University Press, 2007).

reflects the entrenched inequalities and arbitrariness of an ancient feudal order whose passing is constitutionally ordained, its protected status must yield to the urgency of the mission at hand. The salient features of this *militant constitutionalism* will be contrasted with a more *acquiescent constitutionalism,* the hallmark of which is a basic satisfaction with things as they are.

In the sections to follow I pursue the meanings of these contrasting approaches within a consideration of the family in constitutional jurisprudence. Readers may wonder about my use of the terms "acquiescent" and "militant" to distinguish the two kinds of constitutionalism. To the best of my knowledge, neither of these words has ever been attached to constitutions, no doubt for good reason as both suggest behavior at odds with conventional ideas about the functions of a constitution. A more obvious terminological choice would be the aforementioned "preservative" and "transformative." But these words do not quite convey what it is I want to emphasize in the relationship between constitutional and social orders. Thus it is not so much the distinction between change and no change that interests me, but rather the deeper commitments that underlie the desire to preserve or transform. For example, transformation might occur in the absence of the strongly confrontational relationship that is implied by the notion of militancy. Similarly, preservation need not involve the level of satisfaction with the status quo that is associated with acquiescence.

Finally, the terminology used in this chapter is not intended to convey a judgment or a prediction about constitutional outcomes. It is, for example, quite possible that as much, if not greater, change will emerge from the activity of courts in the acquiescent setting than in its militant counterpart. The very notion of a confrontational constitution hints at the magnitude and daunting nature of the challenge of reconstruction; what an eminent Indian jurist has called a "militant environment"[8] is unlikely passively to submit to the transformative designs of a hostile constitution. For that reason the success of such a constitution in delivering

8. V. R. Krishna Iyer, "Towards an Indian Jurisprudence of Social Action and Public Interest Litigation," in Indra Deva, ed., *Sociology of Law* (New Delhi: Oxford University Press, 2005), 308.

on its promise of radical reform is by no means assured. Moreover, as Christopher Lasch has written, "Of all institutions, the family is the most resistant to change."[9] On the other hand, the friendlier environs of acquiescent constitutionalism may ironically be conducive to significant change; with the institutions of civil society enjoying general constitutional legitimacy, innovative efforts to improve their performance—while not threatening their basic structure—may experience a similar presumption of legitimacy.

Born Equal . . . or Not

Implicit in the widespread constitutional recognition extended the family is a general acknowledgment of its societal standing as a basic structure. For John Rawls, too, "The family is part of the basic structure, since one of its main roles is to be the basis of the orderly production and reproduction of society and its culture from one generation to the next."[10] By some accounts this designation means that it is an institution to which principles of justice should apply. Following John Stuart Mill's argument in *The Subjection of Women* that the family—at least as constituted in his time—was a school for gendered despotism, some feminist theorists have faulted Rawls for not following through sufficiently on his appraisal of the institution's constitutive significance. "Without just families," observes Susan Moller Okin, "how can we expect to have a just society?"[11] Hard, then, was it for her to agree with Rawls's assertion that "We wouldn't want principles of justice—including

9. Christopher Lasch, *Haven in a Heartless World: The Family Besieged* (New York: Basic Books, 1977), 4.

10. John Rawls, *The Law of Peoples with "The Idea of Public Reason Revisited"* (Cambridge, MA: Harvard University Press, 1999), 157.

11. Susan Moller Okin, *Justice, Gender, and the Family* (New York: Basic Books, 1989), 135. Martha Nussbaum describes the family as "a, if not the, major site of the oppression of women." Martha Nussbaum, *Women and Human Development* (Cambridge: Cambridge University Press, 2000), 243. Not surprisingly, then, when addressing Rawls's argument, she argues that the family is "an institution . . . to which principles of justice most especially ought to apply, if our goal is to promote justice for all citizens." Nussbaum, *Women and Human Development*, 245.

principles of distributive justice—to apply directly to the internal life of the family."[12]

The debate within liberal political theory over how far the state should intrude itself into the domestic sphere is of course directly implicated in the constitutional question at hand. Yet important as it is to evaluate how the structure and mores of the family shape the relations among persons in the wider society, so too is it critical to consider how the family is shaped by that society and its political culture. However one finally sorts out the relative strengths of these two vectors of influence, if constitutionally encouraged and empowered actors view the latter as fundamentally unjust, the state will doubtless be less inclined to restrain itself in observing a rigid boundary protective of the family's autonomy. For surely a family structure long ensconced within a social order premised on morally compromised practices would not have escaped the taint of that order's injustice, thereby making it an obvious target for remedial politics and jurisprudence.

In the nineteenth century such a social order caught the attention of Alexis de Tocqueville, whose observations about India are less well-known than his commentaries on other places. Although Tocqueville never visited India, he grasped the enormity of the challenges confronting it. "India cannot be civilized as long as she conserves her religion and her religion is so intermingled with the structure of its social state, of its customs and of its laws, that one does not know how to destroy it. Religions of this sort survive long after people stop believing in them. It is a vicious circle."[13] His account of a religiously based feudalism was tinged with a dark pessimism, the poignancy of which is underscored by his experience as a direct observer of a feudal order that had been destroyed. "The immense majority of Hindus belong to the lower castes.

12. Rawls, *Law of Peoples,* 159. Rawls does, however, argue that these principles "do impose essential constraints on the family as an institution and so guarantee the basic rights and liberties, and the freedom and opportunities, of all its members" (ibid., 159). In this respect he held the family to the same standard as other associations, for example, the church. Not so Okin: "Rather than being one among many co-equal institutions of a just society, a just family is its essential foundation." Okin, *Justice, Gender, Family,* 17.

13. Alexis de Tocqueville, *Oeuvres Complétes, vo. 3 Ecrits et Discours Politiques,* ed. J.-P. Mayer (Paris: Gallimard, 1962), 480.

No matter what happens, their birth has placed them poor and always on the lowest rungs of the social ladder where one has little to hope from the government and little to fear from it."[14]

Tocqueville had not imagined a constitutionally based deliverance from this vicious circle. Ironically, one who many years later did was B. R. Ambedkar, the principal architect of Indian constitutional design, and a member of his society's most degraded class: the untouchables. Understanding that his country's social structure was entwined with religion in a way that rendered meaningful social reform unimaginable without the state's direct intervention into the spiritual domain, he provided the intellectual rationale for India's militant constitutionalism. Where faith and piety were widely and directly inscribed in routine social patterns, a viable constitutional approach to church/state relations would require greater attention to the substance of religious belief than in places where social conditions bore a less theological imprint.[15] Like Tocqueville, he was very clear about the connection between the religion of the majority and India's unjust caste-based social order: "The Hindus hold to the sacredness of the social order. Caste has a divine basis. You must therefore destroy the sacredness of the social order."[16] And so, consistent with this view and in anticipation of his efforts at the Constituent Assembly a decade later, Ambedkar wrote: "[U]nless you change your social order you can achieve little by way of progress. . . . You cannot build anything on the foundations of caste."[17]

14. Ibid., 448.

15. I have discussed this in great detail in Gary Jeffrey Jacobsohn, *The Wheel of Law: Indian Secularism in Comparative Constitutional Context* (Princeton, NJ: Princeton University Press, 2003). The ameliorative aspiration of Indian secularism is embodied in Article 25, which, after providing for religious freedom, declares that the state shall not be prevented from "regulating or restricting any economic, financial, political or other secular activity which may be associated with religious practice." "Providing for social welfare and reform" is explicitly included within the parameters of the guaranteed freedom. This constitutional strand underscores the transformative dimension of Indian nationalism, the commitment to social reconstruction as the path to creating one nation out of a multiplicity of peoples.

16. B. R. Ambedkar, "The Annihilation of Caste," in Valerian Rodrigues, ed., *The Essential Writings of B. R. Ambedkar* (New Delhi: Oxford University Press, 2002), 291.

17. Ibid., 287. As André Bétaille rightly observes, "[Ambedkar] saw more clearly than the others the pervasive contradictions between the hierarchical social structure inherited

For Ambedkar, "a caste may be defined as a collection of families or groups of families bearing a common name. . . ."[18] He argued that "[t]he real remedy for breaking caste is inter-marriage. Nothing else will serve as the solvent of caste."[19] Families give definition to a caste, and through the custom of endogamy, the maintenance of the structure of which it is a part is dependent on particular family practices such as sati (the burning of a widow on the funeral pyre of her deceased husband), enforced widowhood, and the marriage of young girls to adult men.[20] While these notorious practices effectively dramatize the degraded condition of the family within a social structure of religiously based caste hierarchies, a multitude of lesser indignities were, as an extension of the logic of feudal arrangements, similarly sanctioned for family life. Some of them, such as the burdens and horrors of dowry demands, discriminated against women in ways largely unfamiliar to the Western experience; others involving gender inequities associated with divorce (or the lack thereof), polygamy, succession, and adoption, were not tethered to the unique customs of a particular social structure. It was, however, a particular feudal structure of power that confronted India's constitution makers and challenged their democratic aspirations. "The result," as Robert D. Baird notes, "is that for those who want to promote the principles of traditional systems of law, their systems of religious values are in a head-on collision with the system of values promoted in the Constitution of India."[21]

---

from the past and the urge for a democratic legal and political order. . . ." André Bétaille, "Constitutional Morality," *Economic and Political Weekly,* October 4, 2008, 35.

18. B. R. Ambedkar, "Castes in India," in Rodrigues, *Writings of Ambedkar,* 243.

19. Ibid., 289.

20. These practices are "principally intended to solve the problem of the surplus man and surplus woman in a caste and to maintain its endogamy" (ibid., 252).

21. Robert D. Baird, "Gender Implications for a Uniform Civil Code," in Gerald James Larson, ed., *Religion and Personal Law in Secular India: A Call to Judgment* (Bloomington: Indiana University Press, 2001), 146. Or stated more directly: "Instead of being seen as a vital source of India's strength, the Constitution regards [society] as an enemy who needs to be disarmed and dismantled. . . . [If] carried through to its logical conclusion, [it] would bring about the destruction of Indian society in any form." Peter G. Sack, "Constitutions and Revolutions," in Indra Seva, ed., *Sociology of Law* (New Delhi: Oxford University Press, 2009), 354.

The presence of a rigidly defined hierarchically organized society may be a necessary condition for militant constitutionalism; obviously it does not make it inevitable. Indeed, the purest form of acquiescent constitutionalism should logically be found where the constitution functions as a shield against the overthrow of divinely sanctioned entrenched privilege. Nathan Brown points out that "Arab constitutions proclaim the importance of the family with a frequency and vagueness that might even make an American politician blush."[22] Where constitutions confer authority upon the *shari'a* for the allocation of rights and privileges, the family in effect becomes a site for the enforcement of extreme inequality in the relations between men and women.[23] However vague may be the constitutional references to the family, in many of these documents the accompanying injunction to the state to protect it signals that the religiously prescribed configuration of that institution is also to be its constitutionally sanctioned form.

Viewed comparatively, both the caste system of the Indian subcontinent and the social setting of Islamic constitutionalism seem far removed from the American experience. There has, of course, been a lively debate concerning the fluidity and openness of the social structure in the United States. Tocqueville's famous insight that Americans possessed the distinct advantage of having "arrived at a state of democracy without having to endure a democratic revolution," that they were "born equal, instead

22. Nathan J. Brown, *Constitutions in a Nonconstitutional World: Arab Basic Laws and the Prospects for Accountable Government* (Albany: State University of New York Press, 2002), 92.

23. For example, Chapter 3, Article 9 of Saudi Arabia's Constitution: "The family is the kernel of Saudi society, and its members shall be brought up on the basis of the Islamic faith, and loyalty to and obedience to God, His Messenger, and to guardians; respect for and implementation of the law, and love of and pride in the homeland and its glorious history as the Islamic faith stipulates." The extent to which the family is protected as a site for religiously based inequality in Muslim countries is a complex phenomenon. Mounira M. Charrad's wonderfully insightful study of women's rights in Tunisia, Algeria, and Morocco suggests that despite the cultural similarities shared by these neighboring countries in the Maghreb, the status of family law differed as a function of the differences in their respective processes of state formation. The critical variable was the degree of autonomy of the state in relation to kinship solidarities. Mounira M. Charrad, *States and Women's Rights: The Making of Postcolonial Tunisia, Algeria, and Morocco* (Berkeley: University of California Press, 2001).

of becoming so,"[24] has not gone unchallenged. Rogers Smith, for one, has countered with a powerful denial meant to correct Tocqueville as well as his latter-day disciples, most notably Louis Hartz: "[A]merica was not born equal but instead has had extensive hierarchies justified by illiberal, undemocratic traditions of ascriptive Americanism. . . ."[25] Smith points out that the law has "strengthened rather than weakened the nation's ascriptive hierarchies. . . ." This appraisal applies to the Constitution itself, explicitly with regard to racial hierarchies, but also as interpreted with respect to gender-related issues.

Yet, Tocqueville's comparative perspective should not be slighted, even if one ultimately is persuaded by Smith's revisionist account. Emphasizing "the social goals [the American Revolution] did not need to achieve,"[26] Hartz and the consensus historians may very well have exaggerated the extent of the equality into which Americans had been born. Nevertheless, the ascriptive hierarchies that prevailed (slavery excepted) were of a different order of magnitude than those that characterized the *ancien régime,* to say nothing of India.[27] They were neither so severe that one should expect a constitution would be written as a charter of opposition to the manifest injustices contained within them, nor so inconsequential that one could think that the beneficiaries of the existing order would be oblivious to their protection. Tocquevillian comparisons may leave some readers

24. Alexis de Tocqueville, *Democracy in America, Vol. II* (New York: Vintage Books, 1945), 108.

25. Rogers Smith, *Civic Ideals: Conflicting Visions of Citizenship in U.S. History* (New Haven, CT: Yale University Press, 1997), 36.

26. Louis Hartz, *The Liberal Tradition in America* (New York: Harcourt, Brace and World, 1955), 50.

27. With regard to the issue of race, specifically African Americans, the original Constitution tolerated their legally enforced subordinate condition. In that sense it was a form of acquiescence, although one cannot infer that all those who were a party to the compromises attendant its adoption were reconciled to the resulting inequities. I would argue that the post–Civil War amendments exemplify militant constitutionalism in the American context; in other words, they were adopted with the express purpose of directly confronting well-entrenched elements of the social order that had lost the support necessary for their preservation. Americans, according to Louis Hartz, had not had the experience common to many other places, namely, "the effort to build a new society on the ruins of an old one" (ibid., 66). In many ways, however, that is exactly the effort begun in the South after the end of the war.

unconvinced by the portrayal of all aspects of American life as expressive of the equality of condition, but the comparative dimension of the undertaking may to a degree compensate for perceived descriptive inaccuracies by showing them to be revealingly significant in the context of a broader universe of possibilities.[28]

In the case of the American family, Tocqueville's depiction of relations between men and women furnishes ample material for those supportive of applying principles of justice to the domestic sphere. While he noted "a sort of equality being established around the domestic hearth,"[29] Tocqueville also was quick to observe that Americans had "carefully divided the functions of man and woman in order that the great social work be better done."[30] "Neither have Americans ever imagined that democratic principles should have the consequence of overturning marital power and introducing confusions of authority in the family. They have thought that every association, to be efficacious,

28. Consider France, which like the United States and India, has no protection for the family in its constitutional text. This absence is arguably traceable "[t]o the French revolutionaries, [for whom] the old feudal statuses, the Church, the guilds, and even some aspects of family organization were seen both as oppressive to individuals and as threats to the nation-state." Mary Ann Glendon, *The Transformation of Family Law* (Chicago: University of Chicago Press, 1989), 298. As Jonah D. Levy has pointed out, "Tocqueville lamented the preponderance of the State and the weakness of organizational life in France." Jonah D. Levy, *Tocqueville's Revenge: State, Society and Economy in Contemporary France* (Cambridge, MA: Harvard University Press, 1999), 9. Another way of telling the French story as it pertains to the institutions of civil society is as an example of militant constitutionalism. The absolute devotion to the state demanded by French nationalism precluded strong commitments to competing subordinate entities. As Liah Greenfield notes, "Certainly [the State] had no tolerance for the plethora of lesser loyalties and identities which constituted the fabric of traditional French society." Liah Greenfield, *Nationalism: Five Roads to Modernity* (Cambridge, MA: Harvard University Press, 1992), 119. "There are no rights except those of individuals and the State," may no longer be embraced with the ideological fervor that possessed its earliest proponents, but surely a complete rendering of contemporary French constitutional identity would reveal the imprint of this profoundly decisive historical affirmation. And one significant manifestation of this identity is the constitutional de-emphasis on competing identities within civil society, including those facilitated by the family.

29. Alexis de Tocqueville, *Democracy in America,* trans. and ed. Harvey C. Mansfield and Delba Winthrop (Chicago: University of Chicago Press, 2000), 561.

30. Ibid., 574.

must have a head, and that the natural head of the conjugal association is the man."[31] To be sure, he famously attributed American prosperity to "the superiority of women," but it was in his depiction of women's happiness in the "voluntary abandonment of their wills"[32] that he perhaps earned the enmity of many subsequent proponents of gender equality.[33]

Is this depiction compatible with the enjoyment by all members of the family of their basic rights as equal citizens? Rawls insisted that as long as this condition held, the internal life of the family should be immune from state enforcement of principles of justice. He might, then, have been swayed at least partially by what Tocqueville said of men and women in the United States, but which the Frenchman would clearly not have said about India: "[A]mericans do not believe that man and woman have the duty or the right to do the same things, but they show the same esteem for the role of each of them, and they consider them as beings whose value is equal although their destiny differs."[34] While Rawls's tolerance for the division of labor between the sexes could hardly be equated with Tocqueville's, his acquiescence in prevailing family practices (not necessarily those of nineteenth-century America) reflected a willingness to accept some departure from egalitarian norms in order to protect other freedoms. Thus, he wrote: "[A] liberal conception of justice may have to allow for some traditional gendered division of labor within families—assume, say, that this division is based on religion—provided it is fully voluntary and does not result from or lead to injustice."[35]

What one can say, then, is that where gender distinctions result from and lead to rank injustice—for example, in India's caste system—the fact

31. Ibid.

32. Ibid., 576, 575.

33. Okin, for example, cites Tocqueville as follows. He (as well as others) "bifurcated public from private life to such an extent that [he] had no trouble reconciling inegalitarian, sometimes admittedly unjust, relations founded upon sentiment within the family with a more just, even egalitarian, social structure outside the family." Okin, *Justice, Gender, Family,* 19.

34. Tocqueville, *Democracy in America,* 576. To the extent, though, that their differing destinies did not include broader civic membership for women, Rawls could not have agreed that their value as people were equal to that of men.

35. Rawls, *Law of Peoples,* 161.

that religion may at the deepest level have caused the predicament should not obviate the need to confront and possibly dismantle the implicated institutions. When "connected with basic liberties, including the freedom of religion,"[36] the inequities of role differentiation within the family should, according to Rawls, be protected from radical legal intervention—assuming, that is, the basic justice of the system as a whole. But where these assumptions are undeserved, the argument for not acquiescing in the status quo is compelling, and thus so too is the rationale for militant constitutionalism. In this political environment maintaining the integrity of basic structures of civil society will likely be thought an indulgence too costly to embrace and too difficult to reconcile with a strong commitment to principles of a just social order.

Americans may not, as suggested by Tocqueville, have been born equal, but neither were they born so unequal as to have pursued this rationale. In contrast with India, theirs was a constitution fundamentally hospitable to the surrounding social order. In the next section I show how this nonconfrontational constitutionalism reveals itself in the constitutional jurisprudence of the family. I then turn to India for the alternative model of militant constitutionalism, followed by a consideration of the family in the Irish constitutional scheme. Unlike India and the United States, the Constitution in Ireland is not silent on the family; indeed it is notable for loudly proclaiming the institution's centrality in the life of the nation and, more particularly, its constitutional identity. It also highlights the mutability of this identity, which I will situate within the polarities of acquiescence and militancy embodied in the experiences of the other two polities.

Acquiescent Constitutionalism

A constitution's failure directly to address a subject can mean different things. One possibility is reflected in Chief Justice Marshall's famous denial that the absence of constitutional language authorizing Congress to establish a bank means that the power to do so does not exist: "[The Constitution's] nature . . . requires, that only its great outlines should be

36. Ibid., 162.

marked. . . ."[37] To comport with the kind of document "we are expounding," the Constitution should not "partake of the prolixity of a legal code."[38] Another take on constitutional silence is suggested in Justice Douglas's opinion in Griswold v. Connecticut: "We deal with a right of privacy older than the Bill of Rights—older than our political parties, older than our school system."[39] Here what has gone unmentioned in the Constitution—privacy in relation to marital relations—is attributable to its historic centrality; if Marshall's minimalism explains why "minor ingredients which compose . . . [important] objects" need not be "designated," Douglas's opinion would have us accept constitutional recognition of *major* ingredients whose significance is acknowledged in their non-enumeration.

In the American constitutional tradition these are not mutually exclusive possibilities; further, the striking brevity of the document underscores their coterminous plausibility in a way that would be difficult to assert were we speaking of a book-length constitution such as exists, for example, in India. Where the governing charter is unsparing in its attention to detail, constitutional silence cannot so easily be accounted for on the basis of the above interpretive positions. Especially with regard to the family, which, in Martha Minow's apt formulation, "carries an implicit claim of universality"—"we are all members of families"[40]—the lack of attention in a constitution that is otherwise attentive to matters of much less import suggests very strongly that something else is going on. But before considering what this might be, I want to argue that the American silence with respect to the family, while consistent with the Marshall and Douglas positions, is also a mark of what I am referring to in this chapter as acquiescent constitutionalism.

37. McCulloch v. Maryland, 17 U.S. 316 (1819), 407.

38. Ibid., at 407.

39. Griswold v. Connecticut, 381 U.S. 479 (1965), 486. The importance of marriage and the family has long been recognized by the Court. "[Marriage] is an institution, in the maintenance of which in its purity the public is deeply interested, for it is the foundation of the family and of society, without which there would be neither civilization nor progress." Maynard v. Hill, 125 U.S. 190 (1888), 209.

40. Martha Minow, "We, the Family: Constitutional Rights and American Families," 74 *Journal of American History* 959 (1987), 982.

To acquiesce in something is to give silent or passive assent to it. For one who is silently acquiescent, inattention should not be equated with indifference. Leaving the family constitutionally unaddressed need convey neither neglect nor agnosticism. In William Galston's account of the Constitution's inattention to the family—and, we might add, the *Federalist Papers'*—none of the following three explanations advanced requires one to equate silence with indifference:[41] (1) The family (as well as other formative institutions) was perceived by the framers of the Constitution as having performed well, and "they assumed (or at least hoped) that [it] would remain healthy of [its] own accord";[42] (2) As a matter of constitutional design, social questions—including those involving the family—were to be addressed at the subnational level;[43] and (3) With the clearer separation of the public and private realms that accompanied the ascendance of liberal democracy over classical republicanism, "[t]he formation of character . . . was left to institutions such as families and religious communities. . . ."[44]

While Galston's first explanation is the only one that explicitly invokes the acquiescence theme, his other two should be viewed as its corollaries.[45] Standing alone, these latter two points are consistent with the idea

41. William A. Galston, "Liberal Virtues and the Formation of Civic Character," in Mary Ann Glendon and David Blankenhorn, eds., *Seedbeds of Virtue: Sources of Competence, Character, and Citizenship in American Society* (Lanham, MD: Madison Books, 1995), 55–56.

42. Ibid., 55.

43. Federalism may suggest a third model of constitutionalism, one in which the constitutional order is neither actively hostile to the social order nor actively supportive. Accordingly, the variation—for example, with regard to the configuration of the family—that the federal solution makes possible means that the constitution in effect avoids social-order questions. My view, however, is that the choice of leaving such issues for ultimate determination at the subnational level is at least indicative of an unwillingness to challenge existing social institutions. It may not indicate active support of them, but it is consistent with the idea that there is sufficient approval of the social order that some measure of variation and experimentation is tolerable at the local level. That said, I would acknowledge that there could be such deep division over a prominent social structure—slavery comes to mind—that for the sake of constitutional peace the document may be neither acquiescent nor militant with regard to it.

44. Galston, "Liberal Virtues," 56.

45. His third point, however, should not be understood to mean that the family was left to develop outside the domain of law and public scrutiny, for that would belie the obvious,

that the Constitution took no position on the family, that its silence connotes a stance of neutrality; but in conjunction with the evaluative assessment in (1), they represent a tacit expression of support for and satisfaction with the status quo. Had the structure and configuration of the family been perceived as antithetical to founding societal aspirations, their constitutional choices would, in retrospect, have to be seen as misconceived. As E. E. Schattschneider famously argued nearly fifty years ago, both federalism and the public/private distinction provide important political resources to support the existing social order.[46] Limiting the Constitution's scope of conflict is in this view consistent with the idea of a document that does not include among its principal purposes the bringing about of major reform in the institutions of civil society. Such reforms, as might occur in the course of time, would instead be either limited in their impact (the federalism effect) or expressive of an evolving societal consensus crystallizing beyond the parameters of constitutional direction (the privacy effect).

It would of course matter a great deal if Galston's characterization of the framers' family performance assessment was wrong. But there is very little evidence to think that it is, that the family, or for that matter the larger social order (slavery again excepted), was a source of concern requiring explicit constitutional delegitimation and/or dismantling. "When the United States was founded," Gretchen Ritter points out, "the law governing citizens in their daily activities drew upon English common law."[47] The common law governing family relations was most assuredly hierarchical and paternalistic, and in that way "central to the establishment and maintenance of social order."[48] However problematic this familial order may have been later perceived, Tocqueville's claim that

---

that it is an institution very much a creature of the law. As Stephen Macedo has noted, "Public norms do not simply shield but penetrate and shape the relations of persons even in the sphere of family life." Stephen Macedo, *Liberal Virtues: Citizenship, Virtue, and Community in Liberal Constitutionalism* (Oxford: Oxford University Press, 1990), 264.

46. E. E. Schattschneider, *The Semi-Sovereign People: A Realist's View of Democracy* (Hinsdale, IL: Dryden's Press, 1975).

47. Gretchen Ritter, *The Constitution as Social Design: Gender and Civic Membership in the American Constitutional Order* (Stanford, CA: Stanford University Press, 2006), 68.

48. Ibid., 70.

"Americans [n]ever imagined that democratic principles should have the consequences of overturning marital power," has, at least for the formative period in American history, not been contradicted.

In time, as Ritter shows, "the centrality of marriage to civic status and [its] importance . . . as a social-ordering tool in a democracy,"[49] became increasingly important to American constitutional politics, inspiring efforts to widen the circle of effective membership in the political community. Over an extended period of time these efforts were incrementally effective in altering—or at least unsettling—relations within the family and beyond.

Much of this story has unfolded in the judgments of the Supreme Court. From the late nineteenth century to the present, the Court developed a constitutional jurisprudence of the family that, as scholars of family law have noted, served multiple purposes, including, importantly, the reinforcement of various forms of traditional authority. Martha Minow argues that "family rights have sometimes been announced to shore up patterns of authority that strengthen the forms of social stability preferred by the state or by groups in power."[50] Robert Burt finds the Court in its family jurisprudence to be "fundamentally concerned with addressing conflicting claims of individual and community, of liberty and authority."[51] Eva Rubin discerns a common theme in the many family-related judgments of the Court: reliance on "the traditional ideology of the family," which is present even in its more innovative rulings.[52]

Thus, even when the Court has not supported the family structure "preferred by the state," as, for example, in providing constitutional protection to the extended family as against a governmental policy favoring the nuclear model, it draws upon sources "deeply rooted in the Nation's history and tradition."[53] That explains, according to the Court, why "the Constitution protects the sanctity of the family." In addition, according

49. Ibid., 71.

50. Minow, "We, the Family," 978.

51. Robert A. Burt, "The Constitution of the Family," 1979 *Supreme Court Review* (Chicago: University of Chicago Press, 1979), 331.

52. Eva R. Rubin, *The Supreme Court and the American Family* (New York: Greenwood Press, 1986).

53. Moore v. East Cleveland, 431 U.S. 494 (1977), 502.

to Justice Lewis Powell's opinion in Moore v. East Cleveland, "It is through the family that we inculcate and pass down many of our most cherished values, moral and cultural."[54] Tradition both establishes the family's claim on constitutional recognition and in turn is maintained through the authority of the family. Powell was not presenting a philosophical argument, but his observation embodies an idea critical to acquiescent constitutionalism: the development of moral character, what once was referred to as the "salvation of souls," is to occur with minimum intervention by the state, or, as Harvey Mansfield puts it, the "intent [of modern constitutionalism was] . . . to restore the balance of society and enable it to function on its own with only minimum regulation and without being ruled by government."[55]

Mansfield's specific concern with this societal balance is with religion. "[T]he religious issue *was* the social issue in its first appearance, and . . . the social issue as it appears today is the consequence of the religious issue. If politics is defined by its issues, the religious issue at the origin of modern constitutionalism is still at the heart of modern constitutionalism."[56] The "cherished values" on behalf of which the family, in the Court's depiction, is the principal conduit, are nested within historical and traditional sources heavily imbued with religious overtones. As Minow notes, "the sphere of family was . . . regulated, not by the state, but by religion,"[57] a point that underscores the integrated nature of the social order and hence the need to connect the traditions associated with discrete institutions (i.e., church and family) of civil society. The judicial invocation of "history and tradition" in conjunction with the family implicitly directs the Court to do the same with regard to the broader

54. Ibid.

55. Harvey C. Mansfield Jr., "The Religious Issue and the Origin of Constitutionalism," in Robert A. Goldwin and Art Kaufman, eds., *How Does the Constitution Protect Religious Freedom?* (Washington DC: American Enterprise Institute for Public Policy Research, 1987), 3.

56. Ibid., 2.

57. Minow, "We, the Family," 967. See also Steven Mintz, "Regulating the American family," in Joseph M. Hawes and Elizabeth Nybakken, eds., *Family and Society in American History* (Urbana: University of Illinois Press, 2001), 9: "Early colonial New Englanders conceived of family law as moral pedagogy in which law's primary function was to articulate a religious ideal of hierarchy and patriarchy."

American religious experience of which the family is a vital part. Constitutional acquiescence in the traditional family is in this respect an extension of a more fundamental acquiescence in the structure of the social order.

This is evident in a number of the famous religion cases that implicate the family, such as Pierce v. Society of Sisters and Wisconsin v. Yoder, but most tellingly perhaps in the early and very controversial polygamy case of Reynolds v. United States. Its standing as a respectable precedent has been compromised by the aura of intolerance that surrounds it, but as a source of insight into the relationship between the Constitution and social order, and as a point of departure for comparative reflection about constitutionalism, it warrants careful attention. *Reynolds* was one of several cases in the latter half of the nineteenth century involving the efforts of the United States to curtail the activities of the Mormon Church. While the activity that was expressly targeted was plural marriages, the religiously sanctioned practice provided the Court an opportunity to affirm the supremacy of the civil law and to frustrate the determination—real or imagined—of an ecclesiastical hierarchy to wield sovereignty over territory within the United States.[58]

At first glance the polygamy cases may seem an odd fit with the argument about acquiescence. For example, in *Reynolds* the Court was considering the constitutionality of the Morrill anti-bigamy act, which was a federal statute criminalizing polygamy in the territories of the United States. Not only does this reveal national-level concern with social-order questions related to the family, it also is in tension with the commitment to having the government leave family matters to the private realm, including religious communities. As we shall see, in India the absence of constitutional language about the family is expressive of a very different sensibility and intention—to encourage the implementation of a

58. Marital practices were just one element—albeit the most notorious—in a regulative culture whose domain extended well into the temporal side of human experience. The Mormons made it easy for people to believe that the religion's geographic base in Utah was expected to serve as a home for illegitimate sovereign ambitions. For good discussions of this perceived threat, see Klaus J. Hansen, *Mormonism and the American Experience* (Chicago: University of Chicago Press, 1981); and Richard S. Van Wagoner, *Mormon Polygamy: A History* (Salt Lake City, UT: Signature Books, 1989).

nationally directed reform of the religiously configured family as part of a broader assault on the more flagrantly inegalitarian characteristics of the social order. What, then, is different about the American government's far-reaching intrusion into the most intimate of familial relationships among members of a particular religious community, an intervention given constitutional sanctification in the Mormon polygamy cases?[59]

The national government's direct involvement may initially be accounted for by the urgency of the perceived threat to its authority embodied in the Mormon Church's political and territorial ambitions. The Court framed the question by deflecting attention from religion to politics. "Marriage while from its very nature a sacred obligation is nevertheless in most civilized nations a civil contract, and usually regulated by law."[60] Emphasizing its secular motivations, the Court declared the polygamous family undemocratic. "According as monogamous or polygamous marriages are allowed, do we find the principles on which the Government of the People, to a greater or lesser extent, rests."[61] As Nancy Rosenblum notes, "Plural marriage rested on a theory of male sexuality as the key to apotheosis, and to social order, which explains Mormon insistence on congruence among sexuality, family structure, and ecclesiastical and political community. In this sense the *Reynolds*

59. Just to be clear, the law was one of general applicability and not directed specifically against Mormons, although it was obvious that this was the group being targeted by the ban. The general proscription meant that the constitutional objection to the law's enforcement was predicated on the failure to grant the Mormons a religiously based exemption. Chief Justice Waite's rejection of this claim was framed as a defense of the rule of law in a democracy and is still prominently referred to (see Justice Scalia's opinion for the Court in Employment Division v. Smith) in contemporary Free Exercise cases. "Can a man excuse his practices . . . because of his religious belief? To permit this would be to make the professed doctrines of religious belief superior to the law of the land, and in effect to permit every citizen to become a law unto himself. Government could exist only in name under such circumstances." Reynolds v. United States, 98 U.S. 145 (1878), 167.

60. *Reynolds,* at 164. This assertion was one of several made by the Court that rested on questionable "civilizational" assumptions. In many other countries marriage was regulated by the laws of the religious communities, which were granted significant autonomy in matters related to personal status. Whether they were "civilized" is beyond the scope of this paper. But certainly today, countries that would surely be deemed as such, including Israel, are legally structured in this way.

61. Ibid., at 166.

decision can be said to be hostile to polygamy as a tenet of Mormon religion. . . . But the reasons had more to do with political ideology than heterodoxy. . . ."[62] In other words, in this particular instance—the Mormons "were not a tiny separatist community claiming toleration and free exercise exemption from laws," but a religion whose "goal was statehood"[63]—the political and social issues in play resembled more the conditions associated with militant constitutionalism than with its acquiescent counterpart. Thus, the Court ruled, "Congress . . . was left free to reach actions which were in violation of social duties or subversive of good order."[64]

This particular instance also lays the jurisprudential foundation for a constitutional model predicated on a family that serves as the cornerstone of good order. The Court's intention to protect Mormon wives from the harm that flows from patriarchal authority has been properly described by Rosenblum as "disingenuous."[65] After all, it is not as if traditional marriage was untainted by patriarchal dominance, and yet this standard familial power differential is not generally viewed as antagonistic to the democratic project. There is, however, an important difference according to the Court. The patriarchal principle in polygamy "fetters the people in stationary despotism, while that principle cannot long exist in connection with monogamy."[66] One is reminded again of Rawls's view that the traditional gendered division of labor within families is to be acquiesced in so long as it can reasonably be described as voluntarily entered into, but where, as with polygamous relationships, the pattern of domination moves the question to a different order of magnitude, the inability to reconcile the more extreme practice with a strong commitment to principles of a just social order can culminate in a more confrontational, if exceptional, constitutional

62. Nancy L. Rosenblum, "Democratic Sex: Reynolds v. U.S., Sexual Relations, and Community," in David Estlund and Martha Nussbaum, eds., *Sexuality and the Law* (Oxford: Oxford University Press, 1997), 74.

63. Ibid., 75.

64. *Reynolds,* at 164.

65. Rosenblum, "Democratic Sex," 77.

66. *Reynolds,* at 166.

moment.[67] "An exceptional colony of polygamists under an exceptional leadership may sometimes exist for a time without appearing to disturb the social condition of the people who surround it; but there cannot be a doubt that, unless restricted by some form of constitution, it is within the legitimate scope of the power of every civil government to determine whether polygamy or monogamy shall be the law of social life under its dominion."[68]

How exceptional is the practice of polygamy? "Polygamy has always been odious among the northern and western nations of Europe, and, until the establishment of the Mormon Church, was almost exclusively a feature of the life of Asiatic and African people. At common law, the second marriage was always void, and from the earliest history of England polygamy has been treated as an offence against society."[69] This answer is what is often remembered about *Reynolds,* that its support for the government's marital policy manifested a scarcely concealed hostility toward Mormonism rooted in what today would be called Eurocentric prejudice. We should note, however, that embedded in the response is a cruder version of the substantive due process formula (as in *Moore*) for establishing the favored family order; it is the "nation's history and tradition," here cast in terms of the cultural superiority of the West, that in effect delegitimates polygamy and leaves it bereft of constitutional protection. When seen against the appropriate historical background, the institution of plural marriage represents "an offence against society," or in the language of later cases, an attack on the nation's "cherished values, moral and cultural."

Had the practice of polygamy not been entwined in the political challenge of a geographically concentrated church with theocratic ambitions triggering national concerns, and instead been associated with a more

67. The different order of magnitude is better captured in the Court's other momentous polygamy case, Davis v. Beason. There the practice is described as one that tends "to destroy the purity of the marriage relation, to disturb the peace of families, to degrade woman, and to debase man. Few crimes are more pernicious to the best interests of society, and receive more general or more deserved punishment." Davis v. Beason, 133 U.S. 333, 341 (1890).

68. *Reynolds,* at 166.

69. *Reynolds,* at 164.

scattered pattern of aberrant marital behavior expressive perhaps of no more than fringe beliefs, it is likely that the "offence against society" would have been addressed differently, if at all. Inasmuch as the hypothetical society offended against in this way would be the dominant Judeo-Christian social order, whose history and tradition would provide it with sufficient resources to fend for itself without the assistance of the central government, we might speculate that if there were any legislative efforts to eliminate the offence, they would occur at the local level. To speculate further, the Supreme Court's review of such legislation would rely on history and tradition to affirm the constitutionality of the ban.[70]

This hypothetical society is of course not difficult to imagine, since it mirrors the normal workings of the American sociopolitical order as it pertains to marriage and the family. Somewhat more difficult to imagine would be a society in which the polygamous family was at least tolerated by the country's dominant religion, and where the tolerance was consistent with other commitments of the faith that were in direct conflict with constitutional design and purpose. Family structure and functioning might in this setting be considered and evaluated within a social order heavily invested in constitutionally incorrect feudal modes of organization. "Each realm [of feudal society]," Karen Orren argues, "exhibit[s] its own particularized morality within the larger feudal ethic of hierarchy."[71] In such a society, according to Orren, we might expect that the dismantling of the order would be marked by a major shift from a system of governance centered in the judiciary to one centered in the national legislature.

70. In doing so, however, it is possible to envision the Court accepting an exemption for a certain group on religious grounds. In Wisconsin v. Yoder, the Court upheld the claim of the Old Order Amish to be exempt from a state's compulsory school attendance law. As is now widely believed, the Amish commanded the deference of the Court precisely because they exemplified those traits that define a good American. The *Yoder* opinion, with its unabashed enthusiasm for good old-fashioned American values, is as much a vindication of authority as it is a victory for group rights. In this sense it is hard to see how it could be duplicated in a polygamy case, where the behavior in question is in blatant repudiation of those American (family) values. But the focus on an otherwise benign group's actual plural marriage experience could reveal it to be insufficiently different from the normal American family so as to justify, in the eyes of the Court, a constitutional exemption.

71. Karen Orren, *Belated Feudalism: Labor, the Law, and Liberal Development in the United States* (Cambridge: Cambridge University Press, 1991), 41.

"The change [is] registered as much through what [is] lost in the abandonment of government by common law—by tradition, intellect, entrenched privilege—as through the positive gains made on behalf of legislation."[72]

We will recognize change of this kind when we turn to India and reflect on the significance of the codification of Hindu law in the decade following the establishment of independence. But before leaving the United States, we should consider that, consistent with Rawls's view that radical legal intervention into the family to rectify the inequities of role differentiation should not occur unless these disparities are manifestly unjust, the family has not, for the most part, been an object of national legislative attention. It has, of course, been a frequent object of national judicial attention, and the jurisprudence that has developed, principally under the rubric of substantive due process, reflects the assumptions of acquiescent constitutionalism.[73] Thus the judicially enacted privacy right has both facilitated reform and loosened the bonds of traditional authority within the family (e.g., decisions regarding abortion and sexual activity); and concurrently, as Ritter has shown, provided a constitutional means for adapting traditional family ordering to a new legal reality in which common-law status relations were no longer available to the courts.[74] "The household that had previously contained

72. Ibid., 211.

73. "The Court has long recognized that freedom of personal choice in matters of marriage and the family is one of the liberties protected by the Due Process Clause of the Fourteenth Amendment." Cleveland Board of Education v. LaFleur, 414 U.S. 632 (1974), 639. The leading cases stem from the 1920s: Meyer v. Nebraska: affirming under due process a "right of the individual to . . . marry, establish a home and bring up children. . . ." 262 U.S. 390 (1923), 399; Pierce v. Society of Sisters: invalidating a state law that "unreasonably interferes with the liberty of parents and guardians to direct the upbringing and religion of children under their control." 268 U.S. 510 (1925), 534; and a case from the 1940s: Prince v. Massachusetts: affirming "the private realm of family life which the State cannot enter." 321 U.S. 158 (1944), 166. To this must be added Justice Harlan's famous dissent in the 1961 case Poe v. Ullman, which argued in what proved to be profoundly important ways: "The home derives its pre-eminence as the seat of family life. And the integrity of that life is something so fundamental that it has been found to draw to its protection the principles of more than one explicitly granted Constitutional right." Poe v. Ullman, 367 U.S. 497 (1961), 552.

74. Ritter, *Constitution as Social Design*, 97. Ritter argues that the old common-law doctrine of coverture, according to which "[b]y marriage, the husband and wife are one

a master who governed over his wife, children, servants, and wards according to legal prescription, was now a home in which the free man apparently was left to re-create those private authority relations without government intrusion."[75]

In Orren's terms this court-centered incrementalism could mean that the feudal family structure has yet to undergo the sort of fundamental restructuring that has been the experience of American labor (her focus), or that the story of the American family is one that should not be told as a progression from dismal feudal past to happier non-feudal present. We are, then, in essence, back to the "born equal or not" question, although for our purposes a final judgment need not be rendered on that particular conundrum. One could, for example, place the family within a rigidly hierarchical ascriptive historical account and nevertheless conclude that for the framers this state of affairs did not warrant constitutional opposition. Or, with the Indian experience in mind, one could read into their acquiescence a caution that prior to labeling things "feudal," one ought to pursue the implications of a comparative consideration of familial inequality.

Militant Constitutionalism

During the discussion at the Indian Constituent Assembly of the Interim Report on Fundamental Rights, Rev. Jerome D'Souza, a delegate from Madras, made this observation:

> We have nothing in these fundamental rights that safeguards or encourages or strengthens the family in an explicit way, and indeed I do not think this is necessary at this stage, because that is not a justiciable right. There are certain constitutions where the wish of the State to protect and encourage the family is explicitly declared. I

person in law" (Blackstone's *Commentaries*), and under which the woman's rights and duties are placed under the "cover" of the man, was at least partly reproduced in a privacy right that better reflected the emergence of new normative ideals in the twentieth century. Apropos the connection between family and religion, Ritter points out that "The moral content of that relationship [coverture] was governed by the church" (ibid., 68).

75. Ibid., 97.

> hope in the second part, among these fundamental rights, which are not justiciable, some such declaration or approbation of the institution and rights and privileges associated with family life will be introduced.[76]

Much later, while reflecting on the draft Constitution, this same delegate returned to the earlier topic:

> Now, Sir, if one thing characterizes our people more than anything else, it is the power and the sanctity of the family tie, the sacredness which we have been accustomed to attach to the sanctities that go to make up the spirit and the atmosphere of home life. Therefore, I am sure that every section of this House will feel that it is in the fitness of things that this strong and traditional spirit of our nation and race might somehow be expressed in our Constitution. Sir, I venture to say that if the virtues, the strength and manhood of our people have survived so many centuries of invasion and subjection, it is because, in spite of external and political changes, the strength of the family, its protective power, its capacity to inspire and maintain virtue and moral strength, have never been diminished, have never been completely overcome in our land. Whatever is best in the Caste system—and nobody will say that it is an unmixed evil—I venture to say is an extension of the family spirit, and the attachment to family ties that has come out of it is its best and most admirable characteristic.[77]

He went on:

> Sir, in a Constitution, we undertake legislation for the organization of society. We are speaking of villages, of provinces and the Centre, of tribes and Communities, and every other forms of society. Now, the primary unit of society, one whose limits and characteristics are fixed by nature itself, is the family. The varieties and forms of

76. Constituent Assembly of India. Constituent Assembly Debates: Official Report, 9.12.1946–24.1.1950 (New Delhi: Lok Sabha Secretariat, 1966–1967), Vol. 3, 496.

77. Ibid., Vol. 7, 513.

> external civil society may vary and change, but the limits, the characteristics, the fundamental features of the family, are fixed by nature And it is within the bosom of the family that the social virtues, on the basis of which we are making this Constitution, and the firmness of which will be responsible for the carrying out of the Constitution, those fundamental virtues are developed and most lastingly founded in the family circle—mutual dependence, respect for authority and order, foresight and planning, and even the capacity for negotiating with other units,—qualities which would be required on a wider scale and in a wider theatre in our political and public life. Nay, Sir, patriotism itself is but the extension and the amplification of the love of the family. We call our country Fatherland or Motherland. . . . Therefore, I feel that this house will not reject this plea that in some form our respect and love for family traditions, may be reflected in this Constitution.[78]

He concluded:

> I would, as a last idea which should accompany this notion of the sanctity and permanence and stability of the family, plead for respect for the rights of parents, the recognition of all reasonable authority on the part of parents in regard to their children, particularly, the right of the parent to see that his child is brought up in the traditions and in the beliefs, which are dear to him. . . .[79]

D'Souza's speech evoked no response whatsoever. Nor did the Assembly's final product reveal evidence that his remarks had had any effect on the course of the subsequent deliberations. Thus, the Indian Constitution was adopted without provision for the protection of the family.

As a Jesuit, delegate D'Souza surely knew of the incorporation of Catholic doctrine on the family into the provisions of the Irish Constitution. His references to the "sanctity of the family tie" and the "sacred-

78. Ibid.
79. Ibid.

ness" of the institution of the family in Indian history and tradition are suggestive of a desire on his part to inscribe a similar commitment into the Indian Constitution, albeit one that reflected the specific religious profile of his country. His description of the family as "the primary unit of society" closely resembles the Irish document's recognition of that institution as "the natural primary unit group of Society."[80] Unlike in Ireland, however, where protection and encouragement of the family are "explicitly declared" as rights enforceable by the courts, in India, according to D'Souza, it will suffice to provide for such commitments in aspirational terms by anchoring them in an entrenched enumeration of nonjusticiable rights. They should be placed, in other words, in a distinctively crafted corner of the document that the framers directly copied from the Irish, the Directive Principles section of the Constitution.

Why was D'Souza's recommendation given such short shrift, indeed totally ignored in the Assembly? Some reflection on these Directive Principles is instructive, as it is among them that one finds an articulation of the animating spirit of the Constitution, formulated in a series of aspirational directives intended by their authors to instruct governing bodies in the achievement of a more just and egalitarian society. For example, the state is directed to pursue policies toward securing "that children are given opportunities and facilities to develop in a healthy manner and in conditions of freedom and dignity and that childhood and youth are protected against exploitation and against moral and material abandonment."[81] This pursuit, one might think, should not incur significant opposition. But what if in compliance with the directive, the state should

80. Article 41 of the Irish Constitution describes the family as the "necessary basis of social order . . . indispensable to the welfare of the Nation and the State." Understandably, then, the state "guarantees to protect the Family in its constitution and authority." What precedes this guarantee—a description of the family as "a moral institution possessing inalienable and imprescriptible rights, antecedent and superior to all positive law"—expresses uniquely Irish circumstances, but the legally mandated protection is an increasingly familiar feature of modern constitutional governance.

81. Article 39 (f). This language was added by the Forty-second Amendment in 1976. It follows naturally from paragraph (e) in the original document, which says that children and other citizens should not be forced by "economic necessity to enter avocations unsuited to their age or strength."

intrude upon prerogatives traditionally associated with the family and nurtured by the legal and cultural requirements of religious communities? What happens when the exploitation of which the Constitution speaks turns out to be, in D'Souza's words, "an extension of the family spirit and the attachment to family ties" that embodies the caste system's "most admirable characteristic"?

Again, there is no recorded response to D'Souza's proposal, but it is easy to imagine one built around the idea that its implementation would complicate, if not render incoherent, the central thrust of Indian constitutionalism. Indeed it could begin with a nod to Cicero: *silent enim leges inter arma,* the idea being that in the battle to be waged against the existing social order the law of the Constitution should choose its silences carefully.[82] Or stated otherwise, "The stronger the presence of constitutional morality, the less need to put everything in black and white."[83] Thus, the message of the Directive Principles expresses the thematic content of the document as a whole: civil society must be dramatically transformed to accommodate the underlying mission of the Constitution. As affirmed by Jawaharlal Nehru from a jail cell in 1944: "Between these two conceptions [the caste system and much that goes with it and political and economic democracy] conflict is inherent and only one of them can survive."[84]

Nehru's incarceration stemmed from activities related to his leadership role in the campaign for national independence. That movement was about many things, not the least of which was reform of the Indian family. As part of a calculated colonial governing strategy, the British had largely avoided intervening in the domestic circumstances of the many

82. The metaphor of war should not be considered far-fetched. Consider this comment by the English jurist, Edward Jenks, writing in 1898: "The two institutions, the Clan and the State, stand . . . free to face each other. Linked together against external attack, they are pledged to the deadliest internal warfare. . . . The leading characteristics of the Clan are a caste organization, a respect for the autonomy of its constituent groups, and exclusiveness. The principles of the State are precisely the opposite. . . ." Quoted in Robert Nisbet, "Foreword," in Joseph R. Peden and Fred R. Glahe, eds., *The American Family and the State* (San Francisco: Pacific Research Institute for Public Policy, 1986), xxi.

83. Bétaille, "Constitutional Morality," 36.

84. Jawaharlal Nehru, *The Discovery of India* (New Delhi: Penguin Books, 2004), 277.

groups subject to its rule in India.[85] This policy of nonintervention was one of the major grievances animating the early participants in the nationalist movement. To be sure, over time concerns about the inequities of family life were often subordinated to other considerations, but "[f]rom [1887] the reform of the legal foundations of the traditional Indian family could not be dissociated from the struggle for national independence."[86] Indeed the same arguments from Mill's *Subjection of Women* that were later prominently to figure in the West in feminist critiques of the family, were often taken verbatim and used to good effect by nineteenth-century Indian advocates of social reform.[87]

The family, then, was not a subject notable for any lack of attention in the years preceding the drafting of the Constitution; there was, in other words, no pre-constitutional silence. That may in fact help to explain why the Constitution *is* silent, why it turned out not to be one of those documents "where the wish of the State to protect and encourage the family is explicitly declared." Rather, implicitly stated is constitutional encouragement for a family different from what had long existed, and attainable only if the old social order was left unprotected from state intervention. Such a commitment is prominently reflected in the documentary history of the drafting of the Constitution. For example, Raj Kumari Amrit Kaur, a woman delegate and social reformer, wrote to B. N. Rau, a leading figure in the writing of India's Constitution: "As we are all aware there are several customs practiced in the name of religion e.g. *pardah*, child marriage, polygamy, unequal laws of inheritance, prevention of inter-caste marriages, dedication of girls to temples. *We are naturally anxious that no clause in any fundamental right shall make impossible*

85. The exception to this was in regard to such practices as sati and female infanticide, abuses so horrific as to reflect badly on the British themselves. For the most part, however, as has been noted in India: "The Indians were left to live [by the British] in the cobweb of their own social superstitions, because they knew that the social emancipation of the Indians meant the end of the foreign rule in India." Haripada Chakraborti, *Hindu Intercaste Marriage in India* (Delhi: Sharada Publishing House, 1999), 134.

86. Richard Lardinois, "India: The Family, the State and Women," in André Burjuiere, Christiane Klapisch-Zuber, Martine Segalen, and Francoise Zonabend, eds., *A History of the Family—Vol. Two: The Impact of Modernity* (Cambridge: Polity Press, 1996), 274.

87. Charles Heimsath, *Indian Nationalism and Hindu Social Reform* (Princeton, NJ: Princeton University Press, 1964), 48.

future legislation for the purpose of wiping out these evils."[88] Within the constitutional silence that flowed from such anxieties is a sociological insight of universal application but particular relevance to the politics of constitutional identity in India: "[T]he family plays a crucial if not decisive role in the reproduction of the social structure, including the structure of inequality."[89] Militant constitutionalism emerges from this insight's incorporation into the argument for independence and its later absorption into the dynamic of constitutional politics.[90]

Consider again the polygamy issue. The legal focus in India has not been on the practices of a fringe religion, even one that may have secured a local power base from which to launch a theologically inspired assault on constitutional government. Instead, the targeted group has been the Hindu majority. In the Indian analogue to *Reynolds,* the 1952 decision of the Supreme Court of Bombay cited in the previous chapter that applied the provisions of the new Constitution to uphold a statute forbidding bigamous marriages by Hindus, the Court concluded: "If religious practices run counter to . . . a policy of social welfare upon which the State has embarked, then the religious practices must give way before the good of the people of the State as a whole."[91] There are, to be sure, similarities between the early Indian and American polygamy cases—the

88. Government of India Press, *The Framing of India's Constitution: Select Documents* (New Delhi: Indian Institute of Public Administration, 1967), Vol. 2, 146 (emphasis added).

89. André Bétaille, "The Family and the Reproduction of Inequality," in Patricia Uberoi, ed., *Family, Kinship, and Marriage in India* (Delhi: Oxford University Press, 1993), 436.

90. Elsewhere Bétaille suggests another way in which the family has posed a threat to constitutionalism in India. Reflecting on the emergency, he considers the tension between dynasty and democracy, illustrated in the 1970s by the baneful influence of Prime Minister Gandhi's thuggish son, Sanjay, on the authoritarian policies adopted by the government at that time. "The ascendance of Sanjay Gandhi showed how fragile constitutional properties are in the face of personal loyalties and family attachments." Bétaille, "Constitutional Morality," 38. He argues that these loyalties and attachments are fundamental to Indian society, "aris[ing] out of moral compulsions that are deeply rooted in Indian social values. . . . [T]he moral basis of these obligations is different from the basis of constitutional morality" (ibid). What we might say, then, is that the family in India is one of the factors that engenders militant constitutionalism, but it is also one of the elements that explain the occasional excesses associated with that constitutional orientation.

91. State of Bombay v. Appa, AIR Bombay 84 (1952), 86.

former, for example, explicitly rely on the latter for the importance of distinguishing religious belief and action—but there is a key difference. In *Reynolds,* Congress was left free to regulate because, as the Court put it, polygamy was "subversive of good order." In *Appa,* the state's intervention was sanctioned as part of an official program designed to create good order. The juxtaposition of the defensive rationale of the American Court and the proactive reasoning of its Indian counterpart directs our attention to the contrasting ways in which the two constitutions relate to their respective social orders.

Polygamy in India, of course, was also deemed subversive of good social order, but—and this is what lies at the heart of militant constitutionalism—for many of the framers a social order worth defending represented an aspiration not a reality. The *Constitution*, therefore, is the subversive datum to be reckoned with (and ultimately celebrated) as it confronts a social structure whose inequities are ingrained in behavior that the dominant ethno-religious group encourages, mandates, or acquiesces in.[92] The upshot is that in India, "the nation's history and tradition" represent a dubious source from which to draw upon in protecting the sanctity of the family. Or more precisely, and with MacIntyre's critique of Burke in mind, that history and tradition, while deeply conflicted, had been dominated by its non-egalitarian strand. To appreciate what is jurisprudentially at stake comparatively, substitute the word "Christian" for "Hindu" in the enactment under judicial review in the Indian case and then transpose the Court's observation to an American setting. "The Hindu Bigamous Marriages Act is attempting to bring about social reform in a community which has looked upon polygamy as not an evil institution, but fully justified by its religion."[93]

Under the terms of this hypothetical one might wonder, for example, whether the family would find constitutional protection under the umbrella of a right to privacy. Religion's relegation to the private realm may

92. Hinduism is a famously fragmented religion lacking an ecclesiastical hierarchy, which means that these practices have varied widely in use. The Constitution, however, appears to endorse the view that intolerance for such practices as polygamy is insufficiently widespread among Hindus so as to justify sole reliance on internal reform to eradicate the associated injustices.

93. *Bombay,* at 88.

very well lie at the core of modern constitutionalism, but to accommodate it requires, as we have seen, a comfort level sufficiently high as to justify acquiescence in what transpires within that realm. But this separation is a much costlier indulgence when, as in India, it serves to legitimate an unjust status quo. That explains why Indian justices routinely wander into the thickets of theological disputation to ascertain whether morally questionable behavior is an essential part of religious identification. In polygamy cases they have determined that the sanctioning of plural marriages by "Hindu tradition" is in fact not "an integral part of Hindu religion."[94] They have, in other words, expressly renounced tradition as obstructive of the state's pursuit of a just social order. They have gone where justices in our acquiescent model have studiously avoided—to an interrogation of the essentials of religion.[95]

Such avoidance is understandable not only for the obvious benefit of minimizing awkward judicial intervention into the spiritual domain, but also for maintaining an appropriately modest profile for the Court as a governing institution. There are prudential considerations that might impel Indian judges to embrace a similarly passive role in adjudicating at the borders of law and religion, but worries about being denounced for their "activism" need not weigh heavily upon them. Militant constitutionalism does not so much encourage judicial activism as it alters how we conceptualize behavior commonly associated with it. Thus, the Indian Constitution, as Granville Austin notes, makes the judiciary "an arm of the social revolution."[96] Often this requires only standing aside to

94. Ibid., at 86. See also Ram Prasad v. State of U. P., AIR Allahabad 411 (1957), at 413 for the same assertion.

95. As Laurence Tribe argues, "[T]he most clearly forbidden church-state entanglement occurs when institutions of civil government use the legal process in order to discover religious error or to promulgate religious truth." Laurence H. Tribe, *American Constitutional Law* (Mineola, NY: Foundation Press, 1988), 1232. The heterodox character of Hinduism facilitates the different orientation of Indian judges. Max Weber once commented that "the concept of 'dogma' is entirely lacking" in Hinduism. Max Weber, *The Religion of India: The Sociology of Hinduism and Buddhism* (Glencoe, IL: Free Press, 1958), 21. This flexibility leaves the interpretation of foundational scriptural texts arguably open to all, including judges.

96. Granville Austin, *The Indian Constitution: Cornerstone of a Nation* (Oxford: Oxford University Press, 1966), 80.

allow other institutions to attempt an "extreme makeover" of the social order, but frequently the courts find themselves actively engaged in this effort. When they do, they can be seen as performing the judiciary's "mission as a radical fiduciary and redemptive institution of the people."[97] The remedial jurisprudence that flows from this role is constitutionally driven; the militancy of the document extends an aura of legitimacy to an intrusive judiciary engaged in the pursuit of its inscribed agenda.

We need, however, to look beyond the judiciary to take the full measure of militant constitutionalism. Since there is in India, in contrast with the United States, less ambiguity surrounding the use of "feudalism" as a descriptive term applicable to the social order, Orren's argument that the dismantling of feudal institutions involves a shift from a judicial to a legislative-centered approach should, if accurate, resonate in the Indian setting. We need also to consider her (and Schattschneider's) further point that a national focus is required to eliminate the particularized moralities of the various realms that exist within the broader feudal ethic of hierarchy. This is especially pertinent to the family, which in India has been subject to a regime of personal law, laws that are the creations of the various religious communities, establishing legally enforceable obligations in accordance with the individual's communal affiliation. But unlike some other countries that have such group-differentiated rights (e.g., Israel), matters of personal law in India do not fall under the jurisdiction of religious courts.[98] One result is that these communally generated

97. Iyer, "Indian Jurisprudence of Social Action," 297. The author was a prominent Indian Supreme Court justice, who was one of the leaders of the effort to remove legal barriers to judicial involvement in social and economic issues. The Indian Court is widely recognized as one of the world's most powerful judiciaries, a reputation largely attributable to the elimination of such procedural obstructions.

98. In Israel there is a regime of personal laws that survived the transitions from the Ottoman Empire to the Zionist State. It is a more entrenched arrangement than exists in India, leading to a less interventionist state vis-à-vis the autonomy of religious communities and their determination of family policy. To be more precise, as Marc Galanter and Jayanth Krishnan note, the state in Israel, in the rulings of the Supreme Court, has become increasingly interventionist with regard to personal status issues of the majority Jewish community. It has, on the other hand, scrupulously avoided such issues as they apply to the minority communities, including the Muslim population. The key difference between the regimes of

laws are in a constant state of tension with the policies of the state, which often finds its ambitions undercut or thwarted by competing communal agendas.

These state policies, particularly relating to the family, receive the constitutional imprimatur of Article 44, the Directive Principle that proclaims, "The State shall endeavor to secure for the citizens a uniform civil code throughout the territory of India." Judges who have sought to accelerate the achievement of this goal have found their efforts entangled in the combustible politics of religious nationalism.[99] On the polygamy issue, the early judicial tolerance of Muslim exemption from the ban on plural marriage has been steadily eroded by impatience with the state's unhurried progression in realizing legal uniformity. In the 1995 polygamy case—Sarla Mudgal v. Union of India—discussed in the previous chapter, the Court affirmed what the Constitution had left unspoken: "Marriage is the very foundation of the civilized society. . . . [I]t is an institution in the maintenance of which the public at large is deeply interested. It is the foundation of the family and in turn of the society without which no civilization can exist."[100] Referring to Article 44 as "an unequivocal mandate," the Court then declared: "When more than 80% of the citizens have already been brought under the codified personal law there is no justification whatsoever to keep in abeyance, any more, the introduction of [a] 'uniform civil code' for all citizens in the territory of India."[101]

The mandate may not have been as unequivocal as the Court suggested, but it did represent, in Schattschneider's scheme, a constitutional commitment to socializing conflict, to transferring a significant amount of the decisional focus for family policy from the private to the

---

personal law in Israel and India is "In Israel, personal laws are administered by qualified religious specialists in courts that are part of, or attached to, religious institutions. By contrast, in India, personal law is applied by common-law-trained judges in the regular state courts." Marc Galanter and Jayanth Krishnan, "Personal Law Systems and Religious Conflict: A Comparison of India and Israel," in Gerald James Larson, ed., *Religion and Personal Law in Secular India: A Call to Judgment* (Bloomington: Indiana University Press, 2001), 284.

99. I have considered these efforts at length in Gary Jeffrey Jacobsohn, *India's Secularism,* 104–119.

100. Sarla Mudgal v. Union of India, AIR SC 1531 (1995), 1533.

101. Ibid., at 1532.

public domain. Moreover, a reasonable inference from the Court's observation is that the failure thus far to enact a uniform civil code has not left the social order unattended and untransformed. The 80 percent figure perhaps overestimates the number of Hindus who have actually experienced a changed legal condition with respect to the personal law, yet "For the first time, the bulk of the world's Hindus live under a single central authority that has both the desire and the power to enforce changes in their social arrangements."[102]

The reference is to the Hindu Code laws of the 1950s. Ambedkar and Nehru had long envisioned a radical overhaul of Hindu personal law to conform to the spirit of the Constitution's strong emphasis on social reform. In 1951 an omnibus Hindu Code Bill was put together, essentially secularizing various areas of the personal law—marriage, divorce, succession, inheritance, property, and women's rights.[103] The bill foundered over communal politics and the disagreement between Prime Minister Nehru and President Prasad on the wisdom of the proposal, the latter arguing that the legislation, which did not include Muslims in its coverage, discriminated against Hindus.[104] Ambedkar, then the law minister in Nehru's government, resigned from the Cabinet in protest over what he considered to be the prime minister's inadequate efforts

102. Marc Galanter, *Law and Society in Modern India* (Delhi: Oxford University Press, 1989), 30.

103. In seeking passage of the legislation, Ambedkar sought to understate its reach. Thus he concluded his speech in Parliament with this appeal: "I hope that the clarification which I have given on the various points will allay the fears of members who are not well disposed towards this measure. They will realize that this is in no sense a revolutionary measure. I say that this is not even a radical measure." Rodrigues, *Writings of Ambedkar,* 516.

104. In his extended commentary on the Hindu Marriage Act, Jaspal Singh makes the argument that the legislation is both nondiscriminatory and in pursuance of constitutional aspiration. "The Act, introducing as it does, the principle of monogamy is undoubtedly a law providing for social welfare and reform as contemplated by Art. 25(2) of the Constitution. . . . [I]t is a step towards the establishment of a uniform Civil Code, the cherished goal of Article 44 of the Constitution. True, the Muslims were left out but the persons governed by the Hindu law were ripe for the social reform and in choosing them for the reform it cannot be said that Parliament was discriminating against them." Jaspal Singh, *Law of Marriage and Divorce in India* (Delhi: Pioneer Publications, 1983), 95.

on behalf of the bill.[105] Eventually, however, components of the omnibus bill were separately enacted into law, first the Special Marriage Bill of 1954 (applying to all Indians), and followed in 1955 by the Hindu Marriage Act, and in 1956 the Hindu Succession Act, the Hindu Minority and Guardianship Act, and the Hindu Adoptions and Maintenance Act.

These laws were imperfect in design, and their implementation has over the years met with mixed success. Feminist scholars, in particular, have been outspoken in detailing their deficiencies. "The codified Hindu law was hailed as providing greater legal rights to women. In reality it failed to do so."[106] Moreover, the codification arguably commenced a problematic trend for women's rights. As Flavia Agnes notes, "During the decades that followed, the state moved further away from its declared objective of a uniform and secular family law. In several instances the vested patriarchal and community interests of the influential sections superseded the rights of women and children."[107] Such critiques follow upon others, for example by the noted scholar of Hindu law J. Duncan M. Derrett, who long ago had depicted many of the Hindu Code's weaknesses and failures. But Derrett also suggested that his reservations should not "obscure the magnitude of the achievement effected in codifying the former

105. Valerian Rodrigues, a prominent Indian authority on Ambedkar, says that the law minister's efforts on the Hindu Code Bill were an attempt "to effectively transform the hierarchical relations embodied in the Hindu family and the caste system and bring them in tune with the values embodied in the Constitution." Rodrigues, *Writings of Ambedkar,* 15. Given the failure of the omnibus bill, Rodrigues characterizes Ambedkar's work as a "vain attempt." The subsequent piecemeal adoption of much of the original bill suggests, however, that all was not in vain.

106. Nandini Azad, "Gender and Family: State Intervention in India," in Margrit Pernau, Imtiaz Admad, and Helmut Reifeld, eds., *Family and Gender: Changing Values in Germany and India* (New Delhi: Sage Publications, 2003), 205. "All that can be said [of the Code] in its favour is that it did to an extent help to establish the notion of women's equality as a desirable ideal to which the Indian polity became committed" (ibid., 208). In fairness, however, it accomplished much more than that, not the least of which was the abolition of the requirement that a husband and a wife come from the same caste for a Hindu marriage to be recognized as valid. Recall that for Ambedkar intermarriage among castes was the key to destroying the caste system itself.

107. Flavia Agnes, "Law and Gender Equality," in Mala Khullar, ed., *Writing the Women's Movement: A Reader* (New Delhi: Zubaan, 2005), 115.

system and amending it comprehensively."[108] Indeed, according to Derrett, one is obliged to recognize "India's momentous experiment, which for width of scope and boldness of innovation can be compared only with the *Code Napoleon*."[109] This evaluation has been echoed by Marc Galanter, the leading American scholar of Indian law, who wrote: "The Code marks the acceptance of Parliament as a kind of central legislative body for Hindus in matters of family and social life. The earlier notion that government had no mandate or competence to redesign Hindu society has been discarded."[110]

This, of course, is critical to the argument in this chapter. The idea of a mandate to redesign society lies at the core of the militant model of constitutionalism. When he introduced the Draft Constitution to the Constituent Assembly, Dr. Ambedkar responded to several questions that had arisen in regard to the document, including the worry that the Directive Principles had no legal force behind them. He readily conceded the validity of the concern, but then proceeded to argue that the Constitution was, in effect, a political instrument that did in fact create obligations, though in a strictly legal sense they were not directly enforceable. "What are called Directive Principles is merely another name for Instrument of Instructions. The only difference is that they are instructions to the Legislature and the Executive." Those in power "may not have to answer for their breach in a Court of Law. But [they] will certainly have to answer for them before the electorate at election time. What great value these directive principles possess will be realized better when the forces of right contrive to capture power."[111]

108. J. Duncan M. Derrett, *Religion, Law and the State in India* (New York: Free Press, 1968), 326. Such a comprehensive change met with considerable resistance. For example, the ban on polygamous marriages in the Hindu Marriage Act aroused the objection that "if a man is healthy and wealthy he should be allowed to marry again" and "why should he be deprived of a right which has been enjoyed by him for three thousand years." Quoted in Singh, *Marriage and Divorce in India,* 29.

109. Derrett, *Religion in India,* 326.

110. Galanter, *Law in Modern India,* 30. Galanter, like Derrett, was keenly aware of the Code's various deficiencies in addressing the needs of its purported beneficiaries. The feminist critique has been particularly severe.

111. Rodrigues, *Writings of Ambedkar,* 490.

Such contrivances are often unsuccessful, a fact that goes a long way to explain why in India, at least, the militant constitution has fallen short in delivering on its promise of far-reaching social reconstruction. But even when the electoral stars are in alignment, the intractability of the environment renders improbable any smooth translation of constitutional aspiration into social reality. The adoption of the Hindu Code laws—and the jurisprudence that followed in its wake—exemplifies several key elements of militant constitutionalism: the socialization of conflict, the blurring of the line separating public and private sectors, and the ascendance of legislation over adjudication as the institutional focus for societal regulation. But the modest success of these laws in actually transforming the social order only underscores the inherent limits of all power—whether constitutionally sanctioned or not.

Within the Constitutional Polarities

"Com[ing] to Terms with These Changing Circumstances"

The intractability of the social order to the transformational aspirations embodied in constitutional documents may be contrasted with a social order whose transformation has outpaced the commitments of its fundamental law. To the extent that those commitments represent a textual template of a nation's constitutional identity, that identity will have to adapt to the changing societal realities, or else the widening disharmonic gap between the text and the facts on the ground could present the prospect of a crisis in constitutional legitimacy.

Among the locations where the tension between text and changing social mores is most interestingly on display is Ireland. Its 1937 Constitution is a textbook example of acquiescent constitutionalism; in particular its provisions on the family were intended to embrace the extant practices and attitudes associated with that institution. These in turn derived from—or at least were consistent with—the teachings of the Catholic Church, which, as is now well-known, had played a prominent role in the drafting of the Constitution. But in the last several decades of the century it had become apparent that the Church's theologically driven prescriptions for family structure and behavior were increasingly out of step with popular ways of thinking under the sway of forces more material than spiritual. A state whose family policies had been, consistent with prevailing constitutional philosophy, protective of "the natural and fundamental cell of society's" traditional configuration, could no longer comfortably acquiesce in the antiquated conceptions embodied in a minimally amended text.

The constitutional pendulum has not swung to the pole of militancy, but a discernible movement away from its opposite is evident in an evolving constitutional identity that has left the state positioned to confront aspects of family life once sanctioned by conventional thinking and the expectations of the Catholic Church. As Gerard Hogan and Gerry Whyte, authors of the leading treatise on the Irish Constitution, observe: "Articles 41 and 42 were originally informed, in part at least, by Catholic social teaching that prized the status of the marital family, defined marriage as life-long, reflected a patriarchal view of society and provided strong protection for the autonomy of the family in its relationship with the State. This value-system has been increasingly challenged in recent decades, and, indeed, the influence of a more liberal perspective is already evident in the repeal of the constitutional ban on divorce in 1995."[112] One year later this challenge was also reflected in the recommendations of the Constitution Review Group, a high-profile body established by the government and charged with the task of suggesting changes in the 1937 document. It called for a substantial overhaul in the Constitution's traditional conception of the family's role in Irish society.[113]

By the mid-1990s, however, much in the legal landscape had already changed. One turning point was the Supreme Court's decision in *McGee,*

112. Gerard Hogan and Gerry Whyte, *J. M. Kelly: The Irish Constitution,* 4th ed. (Dublin: Lexis Nexus Butterworths, 2003), 1967.

113. For our purposes its most important recommendation concerned the Constitution's characterization of the rights of the family as "inalienable" and "imprescriptible." It recommended the deletion of these references in light of the fact that they had acquired a meaning that provided the family with a degree of autonomy that prevented the state from intervening on behalf of individual members of the family unit. These terms, of course, were originally included in the document as explicit evocations of Catholic natural law theology, and so their deletion (as yet unachieved) would have a significance much broader than the public policy options it would make possible.

which has been aptly described as "a first step . . . on the path towards judicial freedom from ecclesiastical constraints."[114] Equally apt was the perception of the ruling as "a threat to Roman Catholicism's power to mark national identity."[115] But one could cite other critical moments as well, including the entry of Ireland into the EEC one year earlier in 1973. Membership in the EEC "hastened the emergence of a different model of the family, one based on equality legislation and the participation of both partners in the workforce. . . ."[116] While Ireland remained sensitive to the distinctiveness of its cultural identity—particularly with respect to the question of abortion—its integration into Europe provided both economic incentives for transforming the institutions of civil society (including the family), and an increasing awareness of the ways in which the lives of its people were similar to their counterparts on the continent. Demography may not be destiny, but a heightened sense of how a population's statistical profile resembles that of others with whom there has been only minimal contact, can doubtless lead to the sort of collective introspection that could have transformative consequences.

On a more individual introspective level one should also include in the list of critical moments, the Second Vatican Council (specifically Pope John XXIII's encyclical, *Mater et Magistra*), which, beginning in the mid-1960s, led to considerable soul-searching on the part of Catholics who had previously given little thought to questioning the Church's right to maintain a protective shield over the conduct of family life. Implicated in this reconsideration was a feature of Irish constitutional identity that holds great significance for the pendulum swing away from

114. Christine James, "Cead Mile Faitte? Ireland Welcomes Divorce: The 1995 Irish Divorce Referendum and the Family (Divorce) Act of 1996," 8 *Duke Journal of Comparative and International Law* 175, 188. The decision, decided one year after Roe v. Wade, also aroused fears within Ireland's antiabortion community that, much as Griswold v. Connecticut established a constitutional path to affirming a right to an abortion, the contraception judgment would produce the same result in Ireland. Indeed, the adoption of the Eighth Amendment was in significant part a response to those concerns.

115. Ruth Fletcher, "'Pro-Life' Absolutes, Feminist Challenges: The Fundamentalist Narrative of Irish Abortion Law 1986–1992," 36 *Osgoode Hall Law Journal* 1 (1998), 19.

116. Finola Kennedy, *Cottage to Creche: Family Change in Ireland* (Dublin: Institute of Public Administration, 2001), 114.

acquiescent constitutionalism. Thus the constitutional presumption that had assumed the status of unassailable orthodoxy—that the family, the only institution endowed with moral rights, was protected from interference by the state—began to crumble as the whole idea of protection assumed a fundamentally different meaning in the changed reality of late-century Ireland.

The old presumption had been incorporated in the principle of *subsidiarity,* which held that the state should not intervene in the affairs of the family, that it should support an environment in which the family as traditionally constituted would develop and prosper essentially in accordance with Catholic standards. The principle had been set forth in a 1931 papal encyclical, and in a few years it informed the constitution-drafting process of 1937. That process resulted in a document that more than made up for the 1922 Free Constitution's silence on the family with the boldest of pronouncements on the centrality of the institution for Irish society. If the earlier charter had been, as it was described by the influential constitutional advisor, Father Edward Cahill, "exotic, unnatural and quite foreign to the native tradition,"[117] then the new one surely vindicated Eamon de Valera's triumphant assertion: "Since the coming of St. Patrick, fifteen hundred years ago, Ireland has been a Christian and Catholic nation . . . She remains a Catholic nation."[118]

And so she has remained, but the lesson of Vatican II is that the substance of what that means is changeable. In 1984 Bishop (and later Cardinal) Cathal Daly expressed the new reality of the Church's role in

117. Quoted in Sean Faughnan, "The Jesuits and the Drafting of the Irish Constitution of 1937," 26 *Irish Historical Studies* 79 (1988), 82. Cahill advice to the framers of the Constitution included the following declaration: "The Holy Roman Catholic Church . . . occupies in the social life and organization of the Irish nation a unique and preponderant position, which is recognized by the state" (ibid., 94). While Cahill and other Catholic activists would have preferred a heavier theological imprint on the document than what eventually emerged from the constitutional deliberations, they and the hierarchy in the Vatican were generally pleased with the outcome, affirming "the wonderful Christian spirit which animates the whole Constitution" (ibid., 97). Or as a justice of the Supreme Court once put it, "The political philosophy of our Constitution owes infinitely more to Thomas Aquinas than to Thomas Paine." Quoted in Hogan, *Irish Constitution,* 1827.

118. Quoted in Basil Chubb, *The Politics of the Irish Constitution* (Dublin: Institute of Public Administration, 1991), 27.

Ireland, saying, "We . . . in no way seek to have the moral teaching of the Catholic Church become the criterion of constitutional change or to have the principles of Catholic faith enshrined in the civil law."[119] No doubt this concession to the pressures of secularization (and some scandalous excesses of the Church) makes perfect sense, but the story of the Church's engagement with civil authority is a more complicated one. As Finola Kennedy suggests, the Church's retreat from the principle of subsidiarity and its condemnation of state interference in the family reflected a Vatican-inspired shift in its social thought; hence its newfound support for such laws as a guaranteed minimum income for every household served to reinforce the economic-inspired pressures for interventionist family policies.[120] Such policies would at an earlier time have violated the principles of Catholic faith, but theological interpretation is not entirely unlike constitutional interpretation in its remarkable adaptive capabilities.[121]

Consider, for example, what today is arguably the Constitution's most unfashionable provision, its recognition in Article 41(2) that a woman's life in the home should be protected by the state. The provision's lack of attention by the judiciary for most of its history is hardly surprising and consistent with the acquiescent commitments of the 1937 document and the religious views underlying them. In the current cultural climate it has attracted more attention in the Court and elsewhere, including, as one might expect, sentiment directed at its removal from the Constitution. But social legislation seeking to liberate women from the intimate surroundings of hearth and home is no longer likely to encounter either serious constitutional or ecclesiastical resistance. "In the Ireland of the Celtic Tiger," as a justice—female, one is obliged to note—pointed out, the article needs to be construed in a manner compatible with the socio-

119. Quoted in ibid., 51. This sentiment was echoed in an official pronouncement of the Church hierarchy. "The Catholic Church in Ireland totally rejects the concept of a confessional state. We have not sought and we do not seek a Catholic State for a Catholic people." Quoted in Kennedy, *Cottage to Creche,* 236.

120. Ibid., 179.

121. See, for example, Sanford Levinson, *Constitutional Faith* (Princeton, NJ: Princeton University Press, 1988).

economic realities of the prevailing Irish condition.[122] Doing so, moreover, does not require countenancing the violation of the constitutional text (the original intent is another matter); thus the provision's recognition of the domestic role played by women need not preclude efforts to expand the possibilities for their additional productive contributions to the welfare of society.

This interpretive move should be placed within the broader context of the textual possibilities offered by the preceding, more general, section in the article. It reads: "The State, therefore, guarantees to protect the Family in its constitution and authority, as the necessary basis of social order and as indispensable to the welfare of the Nation and the State." When read in the spirit of the times in which these words were adopted, the family's "constitution and authority" refers to a model of domestic relations that includes the role for women that is made explicit in Section 2 of the article. Protection, therefore, means that the state is to be committed to the traditional family structure endorsed by the framers and their ecclesiastical benefactors. But de Valera's Constitution, as has been often chronicled, was a document written for a simpler time, one dominated by the mores and sensibilities of a largely agrarian society. "As economic factors change, new opportunities lead to a transformation in the interests of individuals, and behavior changes accordingly. Government and politicians tend to reflect what the people want in family matters."[123] What the people may come to want is a somewhat different understanding of state protection, in which the family is conceived of in terms of the needs of its specific members, rather than as a collectivity organized in accordance with traditional gendered role assumptions, and so requiring a more interventionist and less acquiescent interpretive framework for constitutional legitimation. "The provisions of Article 41 create not merely a State interest but a State obligation to protect the family."[124] In the changed environment of late-century

122. Sinnott v. Ireland, 2 IR 545, 665 (2001).

123. Kennedy, *Cottage to Creche,* 17. Kennedy subscribes to the view that cultural factors, including religion, can at best slow down the dominating forces of economic change but that in the end the latter will always prevail. One need not fully accept the full determinist sway of her claim and yet find that it resonates quite accurately in the Irish context.

124. O'B v. S, IR 316, 336 (1984).

Ireland, this declaration from a 1984 case assumes a markedly different meaning than would have a similar assertion by the Court two-score earlier.[125]

What does this mean for Irish constitutional identity? According to Mary Robinson, the former president of Ireland, "Our identity must be constantly rediscovered, or re-created, if we are to come to terms with . . . changing circumstances. . . ."[126] The choice she poses reminds us of Chapter 3's detailing of the contrasting philosophical approaches to the question of personal identity. Discovery—the idea that a life's meaning is to be gathered from what is inscribed in the makeup of the individual—and creation—the idea that such meaning is essentially what one chooses it to be—each provided insight into, but not a comprehensive account of, the elusive phenomenon. More persuasive was the Mill-Appiah notion that an identity can be defined and crafted by the individual but only against a background of things that matter. Or as MacIntyre put it, "To create a life is to create a life out of the materials that history has given you."

On the constitutional level, understanding the effect of changing circumstances on identity begins, in Robinson's terms, with "rediscovery" and the articulation of those signal characteristics of the polity that already exist, and then moves on to "re-creation" and the emergence of an evolved identity that exists in a significantly adapted form: think of Burke's prescriptive constitution and MacIntyre's dynamic tradition. The dynamism of tradition is rooted in the conflicts internal to it; in Ireland Catholicism is the looming omnipresence both politically and constitutionally, but the religion carries multiple meanings, theologically and politically. Historically, conservative social teachings coexisted with a radical political agenda that culminated in the achievement of indepen-

125. As Finola Kennedy notes, "The focus of Article 41 is on the rights of the family as a unit and on the protection of the family from intervention by the State, rather than on the rights of individual members of the family." Kennedy, *Cottage to Creche,* 123. Her reference is to the article as conceived by the authors of the 1937 Constitution. For an American case that features the same sort of distinction, see Wisconsin v. Yoder, 406 US 205 (1972). Defending the constitutional rights of children, Justice William Douglas was alone in articulating a vision of the family as a collection of individuals.

126. Quoted in James, "Cead Mile Faitte?" 179.

dent nationhood.[127] As a vehicle for political transformation the civic ambitions connected to the faith of the majority were not always at odds with the prevailing theology, but they provided valuable experience and resources for reconstructive efforts when the stresses of societal change became increasingly evident. Played off against the dissonance within the spiritual domain—for example, the pre- and post-Vatican II encyclicals—and the temporal domain of constitutional identity has taken on a decidedly twenty-first century cast, but one that bears the disharmonic imprint of the past.

Abortion and Identity

Change has occurred across a broad range of issues concerning the family. The spiritual and temporal domains in Ireland have come to be characterized by significantly less overlap, and through both the formality of constitutional amendment (divorce, abortion) and the more informal process of constitutional interpretation (abortion, contraception, gender equality), the landscape of domestic relations experienced appreciable change. The latter processes include human rights judgments from the continent, which, as in the case of homosexual rights, have reversed judicial outcomes in Ireland when such rulings have veered in an apparently theologically driven antilibertarian direction.[128] These judgments constitute an integral part of the dialogical process of identity modification, a process that has played out dramatically in the abortion issue.

127. "If the Constitution differed from its predecessor in introducing religious values into constitutional law for the first time, it was also a return to the democratic ethos of the 1922 document, which had been inspired by very radical ideas." Bill Kissane, "Eamon de Valera and the Survival of Democracy in Inter-War Ireland," 42 *Journal of Contemporary History* (2007), 218. Eamon de Valera embodies this coexistence in modern times, but perhaps the figure who best evinces the nationalist politics of Catholicism is the great early nineteenth-century political leader Daniel O'Connell, widely known as The Liberator. His dying wish, which was honored, is telling in this regard—to have his heart buried in Rome and the rest of his body in Dublin.

128. The 1984 decision that upheld the criminalization of homosexual conduct (Norris v. Attorney General, 1 I.R. 36) was based on an understanding of "the Christian nature of our State" (ibid., at 65). The European Court of Human Rights found the Irish legislation to be in violation of the European Convention for the Protection of Human Rights. Norris v. Ireland, 142 Eur. Ct. H. R. (ser. A) at 21 (1998).

Protection for fetal life was not included in the 1937 Constitution but was added in 1983 (pursuant to a referendum) in response to concerns provoked by developments on and off of the Court, in particular, the Supreme Court's decision in *McGee.* As one observer noted, the worry was that "Ireland might follow the path of other European and North American states in liberalizing access to abortion, as a threat to Roman Catholicism's power to mark national identity."[129] That Roe v. Wade was so fresh in the minds of the readers of *McGee* only heightened the anxiety over a ruling that came to be identified as the first decision in Ireland expressly to challenge a central teaching of the Catholic Church. But though a benchmark in the secularization of society, it was, as we saw in the previous chapter, an achievement linked to a natural law jurisprudence with which it was in significant tension.

It was the policy result, of course, that troubled opponents of abortion and led them to take action in response to the decision. But the constitutional path to greater access to birth control is instructive as well for the larger story about constitutional identity and change. The Court-facilitated change in constitutional thinking about these controversial matters produced an outcome that was substantively inconsistent with the views and expectations of those who first formally stamped the Constitution with an identity, but an outcome that nevertheless was in its construction respectful of that identity. Had the Court accepted McGee's claim that the contested restrictions violated her constitutional right to lead her private life in accordance with the dictates of her conscience, nothing would have been materially different with respect to the status of the law in question. But such an alternative scenario might have embodied a different set of implications for subsequent legal evolution; in embracing a constitutional argument for a right not sanctioned by the church that was also not rooted in a church-friendly jurisprudence, the Court would have affirmed the weakened state of Irish constitutional identity, thereby pointedly marginalizing it as a factor in constitutional change.

Had such an affirmation been forthcoming, how might it have found expression? One possibility that bears directly on the interface between

129. Fletcher, "Irish Abortion Law," 19.

Irish and European constitutional development involves the transvaluation of natural law jurisprudence. For example, Richard Humphreys, a prominent Irish constitutional scholar, proposes "the natural law conception of the Constitution . . . be regarded as effectively a secular one."[130] "We are not engaged in an exercise of deciding what was meant in 1937. We are rather searching for the best contemporary understanding of the natural rights which the Constitution mandates the State to protect."[131] To this end he has sought a convergence between rights protection in the international community and under the Constitution of Ireland. This "internationalist reorientation of our constitutional law"[132] would also facilitate a convergence between the secularizing trends in society and the course of constitutional development, such that the document would, for the most part, not stand as an impediment to the Europeanization of constitutional identity.

The adoption in 1983 of the amendment acknowledging "the right to life of the unborn" ("with due regard to the equal right to life of the mother") complicated hopes for any such convergence.[133] Based on this

130. Richard F. Humphreys, "Constitutional Interpretation," 15 *Dublin University Law Journal* 59, 69 (1993). Another variant of this kind of constitutional transvaluation can occasionally be observed in Irish Supreme Court opinions. In a case arising under Article 41, one of the justices (Hardiman) noted that the presumption in favor of parental authority was a strongly held view of Jeremy Bentham: "I would endorse this as a description of the Irish constitutional dispensation, even if any reflection of the views of Jeremy Bentham is coincidental. I do not regard the approach to the issue in the present case mandated by Articles 41 and 42 of the Constitution as reflecting uniquely any confessional view." North Western Health Board v. W. (H.), IESC 70 (2001), www.bailii.org/ie/cases/IESC/2001/70.html, at 74. This was a response to another justice's observation that Article 41.1 was the provision in the Constitution that came closest to accepting that there is a natural law in the theological sense.

131. Richard F. Humphreys, "Interpreting Natural Rights," 28–30 *Irish Jurist* 221, 227–228 (1993–1995).

132. Humphreys, "Constitutional Interpretation," 77. This reorientation is, as Humphreys points out, consistent with the prevailing jurisprudence of the European Convention on Human Rights. "The European Court of Human Rights has described the Convention as 'a living instrument,' which 'must be interpreted in the light of present-day conditions'" (ibid., 64). (The quotation is from Tyrer v. United Kingdom, 2 E.H.R.R. 1, 10 (1978).

133. Prior to 1983 abortion had been illegal under an 1861 statute known as the Offences Against the Person Act.

amendment, a series of cases in the 1980s concerning abortion referral services resulted in victories for antiabortion proponents.[134] But given Ireland's membership in the EEC, these victories were tinged with uncertainty, as the general practice and expectation of member states to accede to rulings from the continent when they clashed with local judgments was well established. Indeed, in short order supranational legal regulation reversed the referral decisions, leaving the status of abortion law in considerable doubt.

This in turn led the Irish government to seek and eventually obtain in the 1992 Maastricht Treaty on European Unity a protocol exempting the constitutional ban on abortions in Ireland from any decision affecting its application. The efficacy of the protocol with respect to the specific issue of traveling abroad to secure abortion services was cloudy; moreover, the actual need for it in relation to the fundamental question of maintaining the illegality of abortion (consistent with the life of the mother) was questionable, since the evidence suggested a disinclination on the part of the EEC to harmonize national abortion laws throughout the community.[135] But apart from those considerations, the larger meaning of the protocol lies in the effort to isolate an area of domestic law, specifically one uniquely expressive of constitutional identity, from external forces. Irish identity was constructed in no small measure to resist an external threat centered in Great Britain; years hence it was thought to require, much in the spirit of the earlier nationalist efforts, a defense against an internal threat—secularization—that would again focus on a perceived external menace.[136]

Yet, later in 1992 a referendum was held that approved the inclusion of new paragraphs in Article 40 on abortion, guaranteeing freedom to

134. See, for example, The Attorney General (Society for the Protection of Unborn Children (Ireland) Ltd. v. Open Door Counselling Ltd., IR 593 (1988), and The Society for the Protection of Unborn Children (Ireland) Ltd. v. Grogan, IR 753 (1989).

135. "[T]here is no possibility whatsoever of the Community legislature (or indeed the Court of Justice in Luxembourg) acting to legalise abortion itself *in Ireland.* The question of whether abortion should be legal or otherwise in a given Member State is a moral value judgment outside the scope of Community law and within the sphere of sovereign decision-making by Member States." *Irish Times,* March 2, 1992.

136. On this point see Fletcher, "Irish Abortion Law," 23, who casts it somewhat differently than I do here.

travel and freedom of information. It thus also effectively guaranteed that with respect to these freedoms there would be no conflict between Irish law and European supranational obligations. Then, as discussed in Chapter 2, in 1995 the Supreme Court affirmed the legitimacy of these amendments against the charge that they contradicted the constitutional obligation to protect unborn life. Perhaps surprisingly, it did so in part by declaring natural law subordinate to the Constitution.[137] So how are we to understand this somewhat strange sequence of events?

One way is to see it as an ongoing debate in the formation of constitutional policy. In this story a polity determined to accommodate significant social change seeks to do so under the restraining sway of the prescriptive constitution. What appear as discrete and occasionally inconsistent developments (e.g., privileging Thomistic natural law in one case, putting it in its place in another) are best understood as moments in a dialogical unfolding of identity refinement and calibration. In the end the resulting policy makes sense as a modest adjustment—in this case in the practice of abortion—that more closely aligns Irish constitutional jurisprudence with prevailing norms in many Western democracies, without abandoning the distinctive character of the local constitutional culture. At the same time it points to a similar adjustment in the evolution of constitutional identity.

The benchmarks of this narrative as outlined above are (1) Abortion is illegal under the laws of a state whose Constitution was strongly influenced by a powerful ecclesiastical authority; (2) At a time of changing sexual mores and a weakened church, the Supreme Court affirms a right to birth control access under a constitutional theory rooted in traditional Catholic natural law doctrine; (3) The Constitution is amended to codify protection for unborn life, something previously thought safely shielded under statutory law; (4) Concerns over the finality of abortion judgments in Irish courts lead to a grant of immunity from possible EEC overruling; and (5) A referendum leads to additional abortion amendments

137. A brief submitted by "the counsel for the unborn" had argued that "the natural law is the foundation upon which the Constitution was built and ranks superior to the Constitution." Recall the judicial response: "The Court does not accept this argument." *Abortion Information Case,* In Re [1995] IESC 9 (1995), at 38.

protecting the freedom to travel and to receive information related to abortion services in another state, and the validation of these changes is accompanied by a pointed judicial downgrading of the constitutional significance of Catholic theology.

Missing from this list is the landmark Supreme Court case, Attorney General v. X, decided in 1992 (chronologically between Nos. 4 and 5). It is the "litmus test for determining when abortions may lawfully be carried out in Ireland."[138] It is also a case, much like Planned Parenthood v. Casey in the United States, which left partisans on both sides of the abortion divide dissatisfied with key elements of the result. The fourteen-year-old victim of an alleged rape was permitted to go abroad to terminate her pregnancy, but this was allowed only because the Court judged her threat to commit suicide to be a substantial risk to the life of the mother. Dicta in the opinions revealed a judicial lack of sympathy, absent compelling evidence of a threat to the mother's life, for permitting travel outside Ireland to obtain an abortion. To the extent that this commitment did not comport with changing mores and external political realities—in relation to the continent, but also Northern Ireland—the amendments of No. 5 were designed and approved to redress the incongruity.

From this it appears that abortion law in Ireland has moved toward more flexibility and accommodation in the procedure's availability, without appreciably disturbing the polity's underlying constitutional commitment to maintaining its illegality. Despite the steeply declining influence of the church in the affairs of state, the constitutional identity it was instrumental in shaping helped forestall a parallel decline in its doctrinally supported moral order. In the process, however, this identity was itself modified; much as abortion policy was forged incrementally and interactively in response to an environment where religion, state, and family have all been in flux, so too was constitutional identity.[139] While the Trinitarian

138. Hogan, *Irish Constitution,* 1513.

139. In Walter Murphy's important work on constitutional democracy, there is a fictional dialogue concerning the abortion question, in which one of the characters—who happens to be named Jessica Jacobsohn—refers approvingly to the process by which the abortion-related changes in the Constitution occurred: "[I]t is critical to understand that neither Ireland nor Germany followed a rigid moral or legal course. Rather, these constitutional

cast of the original document (itself an outgrowth of centuries of constitutional development) remains, it has become less specifically Catholic in content. In *McGee,* Justice Walsh affirmed the religious character of family rights that were "superior or antecedent to positive law," but stipulated, "In a pluralist society such as ours, the Courts cannot as a matter of constitutional law be asked to choose between the differing views, where they exist, of experts on the interpretation by the religious denominations of either the nature or extent of these natural rights as they are to be found in the natural law."[140] They were Judeo-Christian, if not specifically Catholic. Twenty years later, in the *Abortion Information Case,* the Court took pains to assert the superiority of positive law over natural law. The shift need not be downplayed, but in practical terms the Irish Constitution's explicit incorporation of natural law within the folds of its positive law renders somewhat academic the question of superiority.

More to the point at hand, that incorporation—and the jurisprudence extending from it—may be likened to the thread of consciousness that sets apart one individual from another, that is critical, as the philosophers were fond of writing, to the discernment of personal identity. To borrow from one of them, Thomas Reid, it connotes a "continued uninterrupted existence," which, elevated to the national level, brings us to Burke's prescriptive constitution. Specific constitutional provisions such as those in Articles 40 and 41 are in themselves not as important as the larger phenomenon they call to our attention: an inheritance embodying a unique history that over time shapes the constitutional aspirations of a people. Seen in this light, the theological underpinnings of the law's antiabortion policy are perhaps better conceptualized as an expression of the "prejudices of the community" that happen to be rooted in religion. These prejudices are distinguishable from public opinion,

---

democracies acted through thoughtful deliberations in which judges were helpful participants." Walter F. Murphy, *Constitutional Democracy: Creating and Maintaining a Just Political Order* (Baltimore, MD: The Johns Hopkins University Press, 2006), 137. The fictional Jacobsohn is in agreement, then, with this Jacobsohn's account, as both emphasize the dialogical interaction between the judiciary and other political institutions in the incremental development of abortion policy.

140. McGee v. Attorney General, IR 284 (1974), 318.

which is not to say that they are immutable, or that they guarantee particular legal and constitutional outcomes. They establish, in other words, a strong presumption in favor of practices deeply engrained in constitutional experience that ought not to be overcome by a simple showing of present popular inclination. In the Irish abortion rights narrative they establish a presumption (even before the 1983 amendment) in favor of fetal protection, but not one so impervious to shifting currents of public opinion as to remain untouched by them.[141]

Conclusion: Back to the United States

The contrasts drawn in this chapter between two models of constitutionalism (and three cases) represent a preliminary effort to highlight some of the differences in the ways constitutions imagine the relationship between the legal and social orders. This relationship lies at the core of a polity's constitutional identity, which, depending on the circumstances, may be relatively fixed or poised for modification. The focus, however, on just three countries can only begin to establish a basis for identifying the features that distinguish acquiescent from militant constitutionalism. Constitutional provisions that are important in one setting may not perform the same role elsewhere. Indeed, they might not exist in other places. There are no directive principles, for example, in the South African Constitution, a document that must be considered an obvious candidate for inclusion in any grouping of nations where the constitution confronts a social order hostile to the document's fundamental commitments. On the other hand, the directive principles in the Irish Constitution served as a model for the framers of the Indian Constitution, but they have had practically no influence on the substance of jurisprudential thinking, even as the priorities once surrounding Ireland's acquiescent constitution began to evolve.[142]

141. As seen in the nonlinear progression of post-*McGee* policy development, the result is to change things at the margins of what is allowable and what is not; important too, but more difficult to determine, is the cumulative effect that the experience has had on the texture and substance of constitutional identity.

142. Anthony Coughlan's characterization of these principles would not describe their role in India: "The directive principles belong to what Bagehot might have regarded as the

Of equal importance are the anomalies and discontinuities that exist within specific constitutional settings. It would be surprising to find constitutional arrangements that did not include both preservative and transformational attributes. In India social reform must always be balanced against the demands of multiple cultures, whose resistance to changes threatening to their way of life finds support in constitutional provisions that explicitly endorse cultural preservation. Such provisions are as much an expression of political reality as they are a measure of constitutional acquiescence, but they do serve in arguably salutary ways to moderate and restrain the radical transformational impulse. Or stated otherwise, the presence of these preservative commitments in a predominantly confrontational document means that the enforcement of the constitution's militant agenda should occur within the parameters of feasibility. That is perhaps the best way of understanding the placement of the uniform civil code within the nonjusticiable section of Directive Principles.

In the United States, the non-acquiescent parts of the Constitution are largely embodied in the post–Civil War amendments. Acquiescence in a social order that tolerated slavery was itself an anomaly in a Constitution predicated on principles opposed to that institution.[143] It took a bloody war to destroy slavery, but to eradicate the racial hierarchies that were engrained in the social order required a new constitutional militancy. This militancy may be seen in commitments implicit (perhaps even explicit) in the three amendments—to nationalizing the issue of racial equality, to penetrating the barrier separating public and private realms, and to promoting legislative solutions to the challenge of social reconstruction.

Tellingly, however, the enforcement and interpretation of these provisions bear the imprint of a prior and more pervasive constitutional embrace

---

ornamental part of the Constitution." Anthony Coughlan, "The Constitution and Social Policy," in Frank Litton, ed., *The Constitution of Ireland 1937–1987* (Dublin: Institute of Public Administration, 1988), 149.

143. For a different view see Mark Graber, *Dred Scott and the Problem of Constitutional Evil* (Cambridge: Cambridge University Press, 2006). Graber criticizes the aspirational account of the Constitution; thus for him the acquiescence in slavery is not an anomaly but an essential component of the document's complicity in evil.

of an acquiescent mindset. As Robert Post, echoing Alasdair MacIntyre, points out, "At any given moment in time, American constitutional culture, like all culture, is typically etched with deep divisions."[144] The controversies generated by these divisions are less the mark of incoherence than they are the engine for adjustment and clarification in the meaning of constitutional identity. The words of the Fourteenth Amendment—"The Congress shall have power to enforce, by appropriate legislation, the provisions of this article"—may not be an American precursor of a directive principle, but there is in that declaration something like an "instrument of instruction" regarding national legislative engagement in dismantling the structures of racial subordination. As early as 1873, relying on different sources within the broader constitutional tradition, the Supreme Court's decision in *The Slaughter-House Cases* began to denude the amendment of its militancy, an effort that became even more evident ten years later in the *Civil Rights Cases,* in which the federal government's attempt to confront the harsh legacy of slavery was declared unconstitutional. All of this was too much for Justice John Marshall Harlan, who wrote in his dissent:

> [I]f the recent Amendments are so construed that Congress may not, in its own discretion, and independently of the action or non-action of the States, provide, by legislation of a primary and direct character, for the security of rights created by the National Constitution; if it be adjudged that the obligation to protect the fundamental privileges and immunities granted by the Fourteenth Amendment to citizens residing in the several States, rests, primarily, not on the Nation, but on the States; if it be further adjudged that individuals and corporations exercising public functions may, without liability to direct primary legislation on the part of Congress, make the race of citizens the ground for denying them that equality of civil rights which the Constitution ordains as a principle of republican citizenship,—then, not only the foundations upon which the national supremacy has always rested will be materially disturbed, but we shall enter upon

144. Robert C. Post, "The Supreme Court, 2002 Term—Forward: Fashioning the Legal Constitution: Culture, Courts, and Law," 117 *Harvard Law Review* (2003), 8, 54.

> an era of constitutional law, when the rights of freedom and American citizenship cannot receive from the nation that efficient protection which heretofore was accorded to slavery and the rights of the master.[145]

That era of constitutional law did not abruptly end, as the denial of direct and primary legislative power, with the accompanying constraints of the "state action" doctrine, has persisted well into the modern period of American jurisprudence. Thus the Court's upholding of the Civil Rights Act of 1964 was based on the indirect and circuitous methodology of commerce rather than, as Justice William Douglas preferred, a "construction [that] would put an end to all obstructionist strategies and finally close one door on a bitter chapter in American history."[146] These constitutional landmarks might be construed as illustrative of the kind of friction that results when militant constitutionalist threads are woven into a preexisting constitutional fabric whose overall design represents a wholly different conceptual structure and organization.

It is this overall design that is decisive in how we evaluate the workings of the courts in a constitutional democracy. Debates in the United States over judicial activism long ago became tedious and predictable, in part, I would argue, because they avoided genuine engagement with alternative models of constitutionalism. An American court that found unconstitutional state action when school authorities allowed their policies to reflect racial patterns in the community, that argued that purely private discrimination was no longer private when manifested in the most important policies of a public institution, would be viewed as activist by most observers. These observers might disagree about whether such activism was a good thing, but fail to appreciate how the basic constitutionalist framework establishing the relationship between the legal and social orders shaped their characterization of judicial behavior and their evaluation of it. A constitutional predisposition to acquiesce in the existing social order naturally puts judicial activism in a normatively defensive posture, but where militant assumptions dictate the constitution's relationship

145. *The Civil Rights Cases,* 109 U.S. 3 (1883), 57.

146. Heart of Atlanta Motel, Inc. v. United States, 379 U.S. 241, 286 (1964).

to the social order—where, for example, affirmative action is an explicit constitutional obligation (as in India)—neither the activist label nor its accompanying normative defensiveness need be the focus of heated debate or agonized reflection. Thoughtful and productive consideration of the judicial role begins, then, with the recognition of constitutional democracy's contrasting conceptual possibilities and the distinctive set of institutional expectations that extend from them.

There are, of course, other ways to understand these developments, but I end the chapter in this way to underscore the potential of the comparative approach in illuminating questions that may be of interest only to those concerned with constitutional matters pertaining to one nation, usually their own. The meaning and significance of the "state action" doctrine in the United States are accessible to American constitutional scholars directly through resources located within the four corners of their local political and jurisprudential history, but placing the doctrine within a comparison of alternative understandings of constitutionalism enables one to appreciate the broader significance of the doctrine.[147] Still, the payoff from such analysis will be disappointing if we rely on casual, superficial understandings of the individual cases included in any comparative set, particularly one involving inquiry into complex questions of identity. Such, of course, was the assumption underlying the Tocquevillian model, which presumed that whatever lessons might be transferable from one nation to others required intense and sustained engagement with specific places and their distinctive political cultures. In the spirit of this commitment to a richer, more textured appreciation of alternative models whose experience might yield useful comparative insight, I turn in the next chapter to a detailed study of a single case from one nation that can arguably illuminate the general dynamics of constitutional identity and its development.

147. For instance, the South African Constitution "made clear that the provisions of the Bill of Rights could apply not only vertically (protecting the individual against the state) but also . . . diagonally (protecting individuals against a variety of semi-private actors sufficiently linked to the state to count as part of it) and horizontally (controlling private actors' relations with each other)." Stephen Ellmann, "A Constitutional Confluence: American 'State Action' Law and the Application of South Africa's Socio-Economic Rights Guarantees to Private Actors," 45 *New York Law School Law Review* 21 (2001).

CHAPTER 6

"The First Page of the Constitution": Family, State, and Identity

One of the most basic elements of human dignity is the ability of a person to shape his family life in accordance with the autonomy of his free will, and to raise his children within that framework, with the constituents of the family unit living together; the family unit is a clear expression of a person's self-realization.

—Justice Aharon Barak

[T]he strong and decisive intent of the state in protecting the identity of society in Israel is capable of overriding . . . the strength of the right to family life in so far as the immigration of a foreign spouse into Israel is concerned.

—Justice Mishael Cheshin

Introduction

Disharmony is endemic to the constitutional condition but more apparent in some places than in others. One way to think of the difference is in background and foreground terms. Thus we might imagine one polity in which a tension or inconsistency in the constitutional order may lie largely dormant, occasionally emerging to establish the contours within which a difficult issue gets addressed, only to recede from prominence after it passes from scrutiny; and another where the contradiction lives as a lurking omnipresence that dominates the discourse of ordinary politics, intermittently threatening to undermine the societal equilibrium that makes such politics possible, but just as likely serving to forestall the advent of an enduring constitutional settlement. A paradigmatic instance of the latter is the state of Israel, in which the competition between seemingly irreconcilable visions of national identity has shaped the course of that nation's unconventional constitutional development.

In this chapter I pursue the issue of identity in Israel through a case study in radical disharmonic constitutional politics. Most conflict in Israeli society runs along a definitional fault line emphasizing one fundamental question: is the essential character of the state comprehensible mainly as the embodiment of democratic—basically Western—attributes, or as the fulfillment of the national ambitions of a particular people? Radiating in multiple directions, the question is posed differently depending on the context at hand, but ultimately centers on the same vexatious uncertainty as to whether constitutionalist principles can tolerate any official subordination in the treatment of particular groups. Thus, non-Jews, particularly Palestinian Arabs, are confronted with many reminders—both symbolic and material—that their status as full and effective citizens is something less than what is enjoyed by the favored majority; but, the majority is itself divided in a way that leads its numerically stronger part to chafe at the restrictions on its choices made by a smaller part possessing potent political assets and a claim to greater ascriptive authenticity.

My focus is on the first of these rivalries, even if it is the second that has had more to do with the absence in Israel of a comprehensive constitutional document. The divisions over how to understand the Jewishness of the state have probably played a larger role in derailing and delaying the adoption of an all-encompassing governing text than the presence of two contentious peoples in the same land with deeply antagonistic national outlooks.[1] Yet, it is the policies pertaining to this latter division that is responsible for the most intense and troubled internal agonizing over the meaning of Israeli constitutional identity. If the legitimacy of the

1. The hostilities generated by this duality have certainly not advanced the constitutional project, but other ethnic nation-states—for example, Malaysia and Sri Lanka—have managed not to allow their entrenched tribal loyalties stand in the way of achieving entrenched constitutional provisions. The success of these achievements is of course another matter.

Jewish State is rooted in the chronicle of a particular people, its legitimacy as a constitutional state may be determined by its capacity to deliver on the promise of the Independence Proclamation to "uphold the full social and political equality of all its citizens." While this promise represents a clear and substantial commitment to democratic values, the accompanying invocation of "the natural and historic right of the Jewish people" to their own state has guaranteed endless disputation over the genuineness and efficacy of the commitment.

Not surprisingly, much of this disputation has focused on the most basic of regime questions: membership in the political community. The Israeli Law of Return offers to most Jews who desire it automatic and nearly immediate citizenship. Others may, of course, become citizens, but the raison d'être of the state as a homeland for the Jewish people ensures that citizenship (in the fullest meaning of the term) and nationality will possess distinctive meanings and legal significance.[2] Unlike many countries—for example, the United States—where membership in the political community establishes nationality, the opposite obtains in Israel, with, to be sure, varying opinions about the magnitude of the constitutive implications attendant thereto. Those implications are increasingly controversial to the degree that they affect the status of citizens of the state who are not in the favored group for immigration. The underlying assumption of the Law of Return, however, is that immigrating Jews are simply returning to their native soil; moreover, the law, in not differentiating between Jews born in Israel and those who have arrived from other lands, assumes that all Jews acquire their citizenship from the right of return.[3] "Strictly speaking, the Law of Return incapacitates the Israeli

2. Disputes over what exactly it means to be a homeland for the Jewish people have led to bitter divisions over who can claim eligibility under the Law of Return. Thus the demographic imperative of maintaining a Jewish majority exerts political pressure in the direction of generous criteria for determining entry qualifications under the law, but this in turn poses a threat to the orthodox definition of "Who is a Jew?" Struggles in the 1990s surrounding the immigration to Israel of Soviet and Ethiopian Jews revealed the intense passions that these crosscutting conflicts are capable of generating.

3. The Proclamation of the Establishment of the State of Israel declares: "The State of Israel will be open for Jewish immigration and the ingathering of the exiles." The "ingathering of the exiles" should be considered in the context of the failure to adopt a constitution after independence. Where the essence of the regime is so entwined with the issue of *who*

State from restricting Jewish immigration and thus reveals the state to be the property of all Jews in the world, and not of the state's citizens."[4]

A related assumption is that Jews are linked to one another by familial-like ties that ideally aim at a condition of unification culminating in residency in the state of Israel.[5] Conceived in this way, the Law of Return embodies an idea that is an accepted feature in the immigration policies of most nations.[6] For example, family reunification accounts for approximately two-thirds of permanent immigration to the United States each year.[7] Such policies mirror the prominence accorded the institution of the family in international law and the constitutional law of the large majority of nation-states.[8] In many countries, the selection criterion of family unification is in competition with other criteria—such as job skills

---

the majority of the citizens are, the postponement of a formal constitution is not without a compelling logic. Thus it makes sense to want to leave the future relatively unfettered by principled constraints until more people can participate in defining the substance of the principles.

4. Christian Joppke, *Selecting by Origin: Ethnic Migration in the Liberal State* (Cambridge, MA: Harvard University Press, 2005), 162. According to Joppke, the Law of Return embodies the "strongest ethnic immigration policy in any state today" (ibid., 223). For some in Israel this mark of Jewish identity should not carry over into the substance of policy within the state. Such minimalism is one of the goals of the "constitutional revolution." Yet as Joppke points out, the Law of Return "has remained the last vestige of Jewish particularism in the constitutional revolution" (ibid., 197).

5. As Alexander Yakobson and Amnon Rubenstein argue, "At base, the phenomenon of the kin-state flows from the fact that in many cases the borders of modern countries do not coincide with the borders of national ethnic and cultural groups." Alexander Yakobson and Amnon Rubenstein, "Democratic Norms, Diasporas, and Israel's Law of Return," www.policyarchive.org/bitsream/handle/10207/13685/Democratic%20Norms.pdf?sequence=1, 13. They point out: "[I]srael's laws of 'kinship repatriation' differ little, if at all, from those of many European states . . ." (ibid., 1).

6. As Michael Walzer has written, "[W]e can think of countries as neighborhoods, clubs, or families." Michael Walzer, *Spheres of Justice* (New York: Basic Books, 1983), 36. "Clearly, citizens often believe themselves morally bound to open the doors of their country—not to anyone who wants to come in, perhaps, but to a particular group of outsiders, recognized as national or ethnic 'relatives.' In this sense, states are like families rather than clubs . . ." (ibid., 41). See also, Craig Calhoun, *Nationalism* (Buckingham: Open University Press, 1997).

7. Ramah McKay, "Family Reunification," *Migration Information Source,* May 2003, www.migrationinformation.org.

8. While most nations extend special privileges of entry, residence, and naturalization to family members of citizens residing in the country, recognition of a right to family reuni-

or educational attainment—that are unrelated to the ethnic background of the majority population. In Israel, however, family reunification policy is folded into the fundamental disharmony that defines the constitutional predicament and thus poses a real dilemma involving two conceptualizations of the family. The jurisprudence spawned by the issue of family reunification of Palestinians living in the occupied territories with their kin in Israel speaks powerfully to this dilemma.

In this chapter I explore the jurisprudential dimensions of constitutional identity in the context of a case in Israel that has become one of that nation's most controversial legal disputes. As in the American and Indian instances, the family is unmentioned in Israeli constitutional text, and this silence, as in those countries, has inspired the Supreme Court creatively to indulge and deploy its interpretive instincts and powers. The approaches of the principal judicial antagonists in the family reunification case were launched from common constitutional ground; but, in their quite distinctive methodologies they highlighted both how formidable an obstacle the polity's disharmonic tradition remains to achieving clarity in constitutional identity, and how critical the dialogical interaction between them is to a further clarification of that issue.

Dignity, Family, and the Paths of the Law

In an extensive empirical study of collective identity in Israel conducted in the mid-1990s, researchers concluded that the family as a factor in constituting social identity had different significance for the Jewish and Arab populations. One of the differences was described as follows. "If being family-oriented has the same meaning for Jews and Arabs, then the means to achieve family goals is the exact opposite for the two groups: For the Jews, maximizing life opportunities means living in Israel; for the Arabs, it means leaving Israel."[9] Examining this more closely, the study found that "Arabs who rank family as their major identity component

fication is far from universal. See Elahu Frank Abram, "The Child's Right to Family Unity in International Immigration Law," 17 *Law and Policy* 397 (1995), 401.

9. Baruch Kimmerling, *Clash of Identities: Explorations in Israeli and Palestinian Societies* (1997), 45. This book is a collection of essays written at different times. The essay in which the study appears was originally published in 1997 and coauthored by Dahlia

are less committed to living in Israel and show a greater willingness to emigrate."[10]

Sociology is one thing, individual behavior quite another. In 2000 an Arab citizen of Israel, a resident of Kefar Lakia in the Negev, was attending a Canadian university where he met a Palestinian woman from Bethlehem. He, a lawyer, and she, a social worker, eventually married in 2003 in a ceremony conducted in Israel. Aside from the week that coincided with the marriage ceremony, she was not allowed to enter Israel. Like many others with similar stories, this couple was effectively prevented from living together as a family in one of the spouses' home country. For all of these citizens the common obstacle to family reunification was the Citizenship and Entry into Israel Law, which prevented residents of the occupied territories, subject to qualifications, from entering and remaining in Israel.[11]

The various petitioners in the cases before the Supreme Court argued that the law was blatantly unconstitutional. They claimed it violated rights guaranteed by the Basic Law: Human Dignity and Liberty; moreover, it did so on the basis of inappropriate ethnic and national considerations. While the law prevented the spouse of any Israeli citizen who resided in the territories from reuniting with his or her family in Israel, for obvious reasons the implementation of its terms fell exclusively on Israeli

---

Moore. It was written up in the *International Review of Sociology* (v. 7, 25–50) under the title, "Collective Identity as Agency and Structuration of Society: Tested by the Israeli Case."

10. Kimmerling, *Clash of Identities*, 45.

11. The Citizenship and Entry into Israel Law was enacted during the height of the second intifada as a temporary measure (one year) and later extended. It consists of five sections, including authorization for the Minister of the Interior to approve at his discretion permits to stay in Israel for individuals who met certain age requirements and other criteria concerning medical and employment conditions. These qualifications represented concessions to the governmental policy that were added as amendments to the law passed originally by the Knesset on August 6, 2003. Even in this more lenient form, however, the blanket prohibition against allowing Palestinians between the ages of 14 and 35 (for males) or 25 (for females) from entering the country to unify their families was challenged as a violation of constitutional rights. One of the rationales for the law was that Palestinians from the territories were using family unification as a backdoor to implement the "right of return." Needless to say, this claim was hotly disputed.

Arabs. This, it was alleged, constituted a breach of equality forbidden by the Basic Law. But in their view the Knesset law's biggest problem was that it violated their right to personal freedom, specifically the natural right of a family to live together as a functioning unit of society. These related infirmities, they insisted, transgressed not only the entrenched provisions of Israeli fundamental law, but also those requirements of international law that recognized rights of marriage and family life.

In response, the government defended the law's constitutionality by emphasizing the security situation that had led to its enactment and continued necessity. Thus it cited evidence of terrorist attacks committed by residents of the territories who had received a status in Israel as the result of the family reunification process. Consistent with the duty of the state to protect its citizens, preventing persons of the territories from entering Israel and perhaps remaining was deemed an entirely appropriate and lawful policy.[12] With regard to the Basic Law, the respondents denied that the right to family life was included in its basic meaning, or indeed that the right to equality should be folded into a dignity guarantee that had not been so conceived when adopted into law. The law, it was argued, would in any case be consistent with a requirement of equality, since there was an absence here of improper discrimination, meaning legal distinctions based on irrelevant differences. As to international law, the government maintained that the right of nations to regulate immigration is—particularly when security is the issue—a well-accepted principle of sovereign authority and hence not subject to legal challenge.

The government's denial actually goes to a more fundamental point in connection with the public/private distinction in liberal political theory that we encountered in the previous chapter. Susan Okin's argument against John Rawls, to the effect that a just society requires just families, has a particular resonance in the debate over constitutional identity in Israel. Thus, viewed from an Arab perspective, the provision of human

12. For example, France's policy with respect to family reunification is among the most generous of such policies, but it allows for revocation of an alien family member's status where there is a grave threat to the *ordre public*. Abram, "Family Unity in International Immigration Law," 402.

dignity was not in its essence a matter of formal equality attainable through the realization of the state's nondiscriminatory legal obligations. Within the majority Jewish community, the very acceptance of security as a relevant difference by both sides to the family unification controversy mirrors the feminist critique of liberalism's acquiescence in male domination within the traditional family. As we will see shortly, the failure of the adversaries on the Court to consider the demographic argument as germane to the controversy over family unification policy, is, from this standpoint, a reflection of the larger liberal failure to embrace substantive equality as a necessary component of human dignity. Whatever importance is attached to equal citizenship rights between Arabs and Jews as the core of Israeli constitutional identity is mitigated by the unequal status of the two groups in Israeli national identity. As in Okin's critique of the autonomy extended the family in liberal political thought, Israel in this account will fall short in achieving justice as long as the separation of these two identities is preserved in its current form.

The ruling in Adalah v. Minister of Interior consisted of eleven separate opinions that lined up six to five for upholding the constitutionality of the contested law. The main opinions were delivered by the Supreme Court's intellectual leaders, Aharon Barak and Mishael Cheshin, two justices with decidedly different views of the role that the judiciary should play in the Israeli polity. In Chapter 4 we encountered Justice Barak's "purposive" understanding of judicial interpretation. As noted earlier, that purpose referred to the achievement of "unity and constitutional harmony," which was mainly about finding common ground on which to pursue, in the language of the Basic Law on Human Dignity and Liberty, "the values of the State of Israel as a Jewish and Democratic State."[13] In exercising this responsibility the Court was not slated to be a marginal player, but rather one centrally positioned to direct the future course of Israeli constitutionalism. The "constitutional revolution" heralded by Justice Barak envisioned a reconciliation of the competing particularistic and universalistic strands in the nation's founding aspirations, such that in the course of judicial consideration the discordant notes in that legacy would be muted if not totally eliminated. In this

13. Basic Law: Human Dignity and Liberty (1992).

calculus, revolutionary clarity obtains when these Jewish and democratic commitments come together in a constitutional settlement whose identity reflects a substantial level of coherence and integrity.

In United Mizrachi Bank v. Migdal Cooperative Village,[14] the landmark case of 1995 in which the Court asserted its authority to exercise judicial review over acts of the Knesset, Justice Cheshin had expressed a somewhat less rapturous view of the constitutional revolution, one that later found an echo in his disagreement with Justice Barak in *Adalah*. He viewed his colleague's celebration of this revolutionary moment as "filled with exaltation and elation," and he worried that "labels—in themselves—may sometimes be blinding and invite wishes to be perceived as reality."[15] Thus, for Cheshin, it is wishful thinking to expect that the inner tensions of Israel's dual constitutional aspirations can be happily resolved through a judicially led campaign to pave the way for a constitutional future more consonant with the reality prevailing in established liberal democracies. "We must remember that a court is not a classroom in ethics, and that it is not always that the court should have the last word."[16] If, for Barak, the judiciary "must fill the mould created by the 'majestic generalities' in the . . . Basic Laws,"[17] Cheshin's jurisprudential inclinations were more modest in scope, with the Court less prominently positioned to elaborate and instantiate regime principles.

In *Adalah* this more reticent approach made a dramatic initial appearance in the justice's opening remarks, which consist of a quite nonjudicial-like dream sequence featuring, of all people, Thomas More. After following "paths that were paved with basic principles" and ascending "mountains with summits of basic rights," Justices Cheshin and Barak encounter the great patron saint of politicians and statesmen

14. United Mizrachi Bank v. Migdal Cooperative Village, 49 (4) PD221 (1995).

15. Ibid., at 567.

16. Correspondence with Justice Mishael Cheshin and the author, May 19, 2007. A similar sentiment appeared in his opinion in the *Mizrachi* case. "The concept 'constitutional revolution' embraces more than the concept of change. Not only is it likely to lead to excessive enthusiasm, but by adding force and energy to one side of the equation, it simultaneously derogates from the power and energy of the other side, and *vice versa.* Is this how a constitution ought to be framed?" *Mizrachi,* at 567.

17. Aharon Barak, "The Role of the Supreme Court in a Democracy," 3 *Israel Studies* 6 (1998), 24.

in his island state, where they proceed to question him about the similarities between the legal systems of utopia and Israel. "I am sorry," the saintly man replies, "but there are vast differences between the two legal systems, and it will be a long time before Israel reaches the level of Utopia. At this time, you are fighting for your lives, for the existence of the state, for the ability of the Jewish people to have a communal and national life like all peoples. The laws of Utopia—in the position you find yourselves in at present—are not for you. Not yet. Take care of yourselves, do the best you can, and live."[18] Upon awakening, Justice Cheshin drew upon his reverie to delineate the judicial work of his conscious life from that of Justice Barak: "My path in the law is, in its essence, different from my colleague's path."[19]

What follows in Cheshin's opinion is an enumeration of the different conclusions to which these separate paths take the two justices. Playing on the utopian theme, he drew distinctions that emphasized the entitlements a people at war have at their disposal in addressing the immigration of foreigners into the nation: "The basic right to marriage and family life is a basic right that we all recognize as a right derived from human dignity. But I doubt whether it implies, in itself, a duty imposed on the state to allow the entry into Israel of enemy nationals merely because they married persons who are residents or citizens of Israel."[20] Viewed in this way the separate paths speak less to principle than to prudence; Barak is utopian in the sense that he does not take the security threat seriously enough. A detailed examination of the separate opinions reveals, however, that more is at stake in the choice of one path over another than a comparative assessment of the dangers to the public posed by alternative immigration policies. Rather, the different trails bring the traveler to varying destinations of constitutional identity. These destinations are only partially marked by their dissimilarities; indeed from certain vantage points they may appear indistinguishable. But viewed from within the great dualism that has framed the terms of political contestation, they occupy different locations along the landscape of Israeli constitutionalism.

18. Adalah v. Minister of Interior, HCJ 7052/03 (2006), 115.

19. Ibid., at 116.

20. Ibid., at 117.

Moreover, as I will argue, each destination is attainable by following a particular judicial methodology—the relationship between the process and substance of constitutional identity is an important component of the family reunification story.

On Not Doing Something Special

More often than not, controversy over the judicial power centers on the relative standing of the legislative branch. If, as Jeremy Waldron contends, "legislation and legislatures have a bad name in legal and political philosophy,"[21] then chiefly this is a consequence of the prominence courts have acquired as constitutional overseers of the lawmaking body's performance. In the case of Aharon Barak, the justice's historic role in establishing judicial review's importance in Israeli politics has made him very cognizant of the criticism that judges are insufficiently respectful of the prerogatives of the legislative branch. To counter this impression he offers reverent appreciation: "The foundation of democracy is a legislature elected freely and periodically by the people. . . . [M]y concept of the role of a judge in a democracy recognizes the central role of the legislature."[22]

The centrality of the legislative role was on display when the Twelfth Knesset adopted the Basic Law on Human Dignity and Liberty in 1992. Previous Basic Laws had addressed the structural details of constitutional governance, but it was not until the enactment of the 1992 legislation that provision for individual rights protection was actually included in the nation's evolving constitution.[23] When viewed, however, from the

21. Jeremy Waldron, *The Dignity of Legislation* (Cambridge: Cambridge University Press, 1999), 1.

22. Aharon Barak, *The Judge in a Democracy* (Princeton, NJ: Princeton University Press, 2006), 226.

23. One should note that while most of the Basic Laws were passed by overwhelming majorities in the Knesset, the 1992 law was approved by only 32 of its 120 members. The specific rights enumerated under Human Dignity and Liberty include protection against various invasions of privacy, property, and travel by Israeli nationals in and out of the country. Not included in the law were such cardinal rights as equality, speech, religion, and protest. The idea of an evolving constitution goes back to a compromise proposal—the Harari Resolution—adopted by the First Knesset, prescribing a process of incremental

perspective of the judiciary, the Knesset's importance in this historic development is a complicated story. Thus, according to Justice Barak, "For me, if there is anything about [Israeli] constitutional identity, it's this Basic Law on Human Dignity, which inspires and gives a vision of the human being, of the relationship between human beings . . . and the state."[24] But as crucial—indeed "revolutionary"—a moment as this legislative milestone has turned out to be in Israeli constitutional history, Barak, the justice most responsible for whatever momentous significance the enactment has thus far enjoyed, has also questioned whether the legislators in 1992 in fact understood the implications of their handiwork. "They didn't know what it mean[t], or at least they didn't think they were doing something special."[25] Ironically in this respect he is aligned with Justice Cheshin, who, in his *Mizrachi* opinion had wryly inquired "whether the Knesset members themselves were aware of the 'revolution' that they were generating."[26]

Yet this apparent agreement also conceals alternative jurisprudential meanings that bear directly on the question of the Supreme Court's role in shaping constitutional identity. On the one hand, it points to a quite modest judicial posture in which the constitutive significance of the Basic Law is diminished, thus leaving the Court constrained to operate within the limited reach of the Knesset's unpretentious ambitions. In contrast, it can be construed as an invitation to the Court, through its subsequent interpretive efforts, to build a grander and more authoritative meaning upon the bare legal foundations provided by the legislature. For the lawmakers who wrote the Basic Law, "it was a political move, it was not an aspirational move."[27] Therefore, "provid[ing] mean-

---

accumulation of individual chapters (or basic laws) that when terminated will together form the state constitution. See 5 Knesset Protocols, 1950. Thus every Knesset in effect serves concurrently as a constituent assembly with the power to enact both ordinary law as well as fundamental law.

24. Author's interview with Justice Aharon Barak, New Haven, CT, April 27, 2007.

25. Ibid.

26. *Mizrachi,* at 540.

27. Author's interview with Justice Aharon Barak, April 29, 2007. The question to which Justice Barak was responding was "Do you think that in writing the Dignity provision there was an expectation that you and the judges would provide meaning to it?"

ing [is] clearly our job."[28] But that meaning is not synonymous with constitutional identity, even if it is the idea of human dignity "from which constitutional identity may come from."[29] Thus, "It's not just dignity, it's richer than that; the Basic Law on Dignity also has the expression—the State of Israel is a Jewish and democratic state. So . . . it's dignity plus the basis of the State of Israel. This has in it tremendous power. It's the first time basically that Israel said we are a Jewish and democratic state."[30]

It was within this framework that the Court addressed the issue of family reunification. Is the right to live together as a family protected under the constitutional guarantee of dignity, and if so, does it preclude an immigration policy that denies a foreign spouse the privilege of moving to Israel to live with a citizen of the state as part of a family unit? The difference between the jurisprudential paths taken in the two main opinions relates only to the second question; with regard to the first there was a shared acceptance of the idea that the concept of human dignity requires recognition of the family as a protected societal institution. Whereas the immigration question called for responses that meant wrestling with the tensions in the Jewish and democratic strands of Israeli constitutional identity, the background and more basic question of family rights implicated concerns transcending that foundational dualism.

Indeed it was Justice Cheshin whose opinion was particularly strong in its reliance on transcendent values: "[I] accept that the right of a

28. Ibid.

29. Ibid. Elsewhere Justice Barak has observed, "Human dignity is . . . the freedom of the individual to shape an individual identity." Barak, *Judge in a Democracy,* 86. To the extent, then, that constitutional identity flows from human dignity, which in its substance consists of the freedom to form an individual identity, there is, as we shall see, a decisive connection between these two identities.

30. Ibid. According to Barak, however, even this important innovation was not the result of a carefully considered act of legislative draftsmanship. His understanding is that the initial draft of the law referred only to Israel as a democratic state. This reflected the fact that the Canadian limitations clause, which speaks of democracy, had been the model for this language. But then, he suggests, representatives of the observant Jewish community intervened, questioning whether the dignity requirement would affect such matters as business, marriage, and divorce. In other words, the final product manifested the same disharmonic tension that appears in the Proclamation of Independence.

person in Israel to have a normal family is a right that derives from human dignity. This is what we are taught by natural law, and the state merely embraces what is already there by wrapping natural law in the garb of law and constitution."[31] This law of nature is in his account connected to the law of nations: "The family unit is the basic unit of society, and society and the state are built on it. It is not surprising, therefore, that the right to a family life has been recognized in the international community as a basic right. This is also the law in Israel."[32] Implicit in this embrace of a universal principle is the assumption that a constitutional regime must recognize the family as an entity to which fundamental entitlements attach. At the most basic level these entitlements are unrelated to the specific identity of any given constitution; they inhere in the constitution as a generic form of human governance. That the legislature did not see fit explicitly to specify the right under its newly adopted Basic Law was no bar to its enforcement by the Court. Deriving the right to a normal family life from human dignity does not so much stem from a specific codification of Human Dignity as it does from the inherent logic of constitutional supremacy.

This was a point easily assented to by Justice Barak,[33] who found in his colleague's previous reflections on the family compelling arguments for both a core family right and one that extended from it to address the

31. *Adalah,* at 172. "We all agree—how could we do otherwise?—that a person, any person, has a right to marry and to have a family life. The covenant between a man and a woman, family life, was created before the state existed and before rights and obligations came into the world" (ibid., at 152). One might compare this affirmation to the text of the Irish Constitution, which states in Article 41: "The State recognizes the Family as the natural primary and fundamental unit group of Society, and as a moral institution possessing inalienable and imprescriptible rights, antecedent and superior to all positive law."

32. Ibid., at 153. As Christian Joppke points out, family ties are the only ascriptive criterion universally recognized in immigration law, in that "a consensus [exists] that the family is the fundamental building block of society." Joppke, *Selecting By Origin,* 2. For further elaboration, see Kate Jastrom, "Family Unification, Including Migration of Children," (discussion paper prepared for the International Legal Norms and Migration Project Conference, Geneva, May 2002).

33. "Indeed, the question is not whether there is a 'lacuna' in the Basic Law: Human Dignity with regard to the right to family life, and whether it is possible to fill this lacuna. The question is whether the interpretation of the right to human dignity leads to a conclusion that within the framework of this express right there is also included the aspect of the

specific issue raised in the *Adalah* case. "Every separation of a child from a parent," Justice Cheshin had written in an earlier case, "is a violation of a natural right."[34] But quoting his fellow justice to establish common ground on the core right was also a way of preparing the ground for separating himself from Cheshin on the peripheral right involving reunification of citizens and noncitizens of the same family. Thus, for Barak, the right to family life "is violated if the Israeli spouse is not allowed to have his family life in Israel with the foreign spouse."[35] To support this claim he went on again to quote his colleague, this time from a 1997 case involving the granting of citizenship to a foreign spouse in Israel, in which the latter wrote, "The State of Israel recognizes the right of the citizen to choose for himself a spouse and to establish with that spouse a family in Israel. . . . [I]srael has recognized—and continues to recognize—its duty to provide protection to the family unit also by giving permits for family reunifications."[36] Supported by this statement as well as numerous citations from international and comparative law, Barak went on to find Section 2 of the Citizenship and Entry into Israel Law unconstitutional as a violation of the constitutional right of the Israeli spouse to have a family life and to realize it in Israel. In so doing he parted company with Cheshin, whose willingness to apply the interpretive powers of his office to articulate and establish unenumerated rights extended only so far.

What accounts for the divergence? To answer we need to shift the focus from what both justices seemed to view as generic aspects of constitutional identity to the specifics of Israeli identity, that is, to the

---

autonomy of individual will that is directed towards having a family life and realizing it in Israel." *Adalah,* at 45.

34. *Adalah,* at 38, quoting from A. v. Biological Parents, LFA 377/05.

35. *Adalah,* at 39.

36. Ibid., at 39, quoting from Stamka v. Minister of Interior, HCJ 3648/97. In his opinion, Justice Cheshin responded to this citation: "I do not retract the remarks that I made, but I do not think that it is possible to deduce from them that an Israeli citizen has a constitutional right that his foreign spouse can enter Israel and take up residence in it" (ibid., at 170). Cheshin went on to point out that his remarks in *Stamka* were made more than a year before the serious armed conflict between the Palestinian Authority and Israel began. He noted that his comment about reunification was qualified by considerations of "national security, public safety and public welfare" (ibid., at 171).

significance of the Basic Law's stipulation concerning a Jewish and democratic state. A useful place to begin is the Cheshin opinion cited by Barak to affirm family unity as a "natural right," which includes the following elaboration:

> It is the law of nature that a mother and father naturally have custody of their child, raise him, love him and provide for his needs until he grows up and becomes a man. This is the instinct for existence and survival inside us . . . "the blood ties," the primeval yearning of a mother for her child—and it is shared by man, beast and fowl. . . . This tie is stronger than any other, and it goes beyond society, religion and state.[37]

While it is clear that the object of Cheshin's attention here is the nuclear family, a reader of the justice's *Adalah* opinion might be tempted to think more metaphorically and see in these reflections on the family a representation of the Israeli polity.[38] Such an image comports with an important filament in the political culture and often expresses itself in national moments of stress and danger. In 1985, for example, Israel exchanged 1,150 Arab prisoners who had been incarcerated for acts of terrorism for three soldiers captured during the 1982 war in Lebanon. The exchange came to be viewed as a mistake by many, but at the time it received overwhelming public support. "Calculations of prestige, future cost, responsibility, were all secondary to the communal quasi-familial sentiment that one does whatever possible for one's child without adding up costs. It was precisely what one expects of a family, not from a state."[39]

37. Ibid., at 153.

38. Lest there be any doubts as to Justice Cheshin's thoughts on this matter, while he views this as "a nice interpretation," he had "not thought of it" in this way. Correspondence with Justice Mishael Cheshin and the author, May 19, 2007.

39. Charles S. Leibman, "Conceptions of 'State of Israel' in Israeli Society," *Jerusalem Quarterly* 47 (1988), 101. Consider the finding reported in the sociological study of collective identity in Israel quoted earlier: "[F]or Jewish respondents, the most important component of social identity is . . . the family. Approximately 40 percent of Jewish respondents ranked it as the most important component and about 20 percent ranked it as their second choice." Kimmerling, *Clash of Identities*, 42.

Or stated otherwise, the priorities might have been differently assessed had, say, David Hume's understanding that "a nation is nothing but a collection of individuals" been closer to the operative political and social reality.[40]

A quarter of a century later, the same scenario was reenacted as the nation again confronted the agonizing decision of whether to free 1000 Palestinian prisoners for the return to his family of Staff Sgt. Gilad Shalit, an Israeli soldier seized several years earlier by the radical organization Hamas. The *family* in question may be understood in two senses, as was made clear by the Israeli Welfare Minister, who commented, "In this country, it is very difficult to differentiate between the personal and the political."[41] This difficulty lies at the core of the ongoing poignant debate in Israel over national security priorities.

The familial metaphor is not a stranger to the constitutional law of a country where the issue of civic identity has so often been on the docket of its Supreme Court.[42] "Blood ties," of course, are at the heart of the controversy over the "Who is a Jew?" question; currently, for example, the Law of Return defines a Jew as "a person who was born of a Jewish mother or has become converted to Judaism and is not a member of another religion."[43] "[T]he Jew living in Israel," it was once said in a landmark Supreme Court case, "is bound, willingly or unwillingly, by an umbilical

40. David Hume, "Of National Characters," in Thomas Hill Green and Thomas Hodge Gross, eds., *The Philosophical Works—Vol. 3* (Darmstadt, Germany: Scientia Verlag Aalen, 1964), 244.

41. *New York Times,* December 9, 2009, A6. Shalit was captured by Hamas militants in a cross-border raid on June 25, 2006. The Israeli public has been deeply divided over whether a deal should be negotiated to obtain his release. While strong sentiment exists to arrange a transfer of prisoners, intense opposition has focused on the possibility that such a move would provide Hamas with the incentive to kidnap more Israeli soldiers in the days ahead.

42. I discuss the major cases in *Apple of Gold: Constitutionalism in Israel and the United States,* Chap. 3. The metaphor's application also precedes the establishment of the state. "The regulation of children's lives . . . became a microcosm of colonial rule itself. Colonialism was often represented as a parent-child relationship, a period of temporary unselfish, paternalistic tutelage during which native 'children' were prepared for self-government." Assaf Likhovski, *Law and Identity in Mandate Palestine* (Chapel Hill: University of North Carolina Press, 2005), 85.

43. Law of Return (Amendment no. 2), section 4b, 1970.

cord to historical Judaism. . . ."[44] Thus the idea that it is only natural for parents to have custody of their children, and that they commit themselves to their offspring's "existence and survival," resonates clearly not only within the families of which most of us are a part, but also on a broader canvas in which a state tethered to the story of a particular people acts to preserve its distinctive identity.[45]

Significantly, Justice Cheshin introduced the question of identity in a passage addressing the key point of contention on the Court: whether, as a constitutional matter, a distinction should be made between the right to have a family life and the asserted corollary right of an Israeli citizen to bring a foreign spouse into the country. For Cheshin, incorporating the latter into the former would "change the *status quo ante* of Israeli society,"[46] although he did not specify exactly what the nature of that change would be. Further elaborating on this concern—without, however, clarifying very much of its meaning—Cheshin then argued, "[T]he strong and decisive interest of the state in protecting the identity of society in Israel is capable of overriding—and, it should be emphasized, on the constitutional, as opposed to the legislative level—the strength of the right to family life in so far as the immigration of a foreign spouse into

44. Rufeisen v. Minister of Interior [the "Brother Daniel case"], 16 P.D. 2428 (1962), 2438.

45. On the Jewish community as a family, consider this story: Avraham Burg is a member of one of Israel's iconic families. His father had been a long-serving minister in several governments, someone known in Israel for the fervor of his Zionist commitments. The younger Burg had himself once been on track to become prime minister, having served as speaker of his nation's Parliament and head of the World Zionist Organization. But for many readers of *The New York Times* he is known rather for "challeng[ing] his country's identity," as the headline in a lengthy piece in that newspaper declared in December 2008. Ethan Bronner, "Once a Political Riser, an Israeli Challenges His Country's Identity," *The New York Times,* December 20, 2008. Detailing Burg's controversial abandonment and denunciation of Zionism, it quoted him as saying, "If we do not establish modern Israeli identity on foundations of optimism, faith in humans and full trust in the family of nations, we have no chance of existing." His views have gained negligible traction in Israel, but the article reports that despite their unpopularity, Burg remains a beloved figure in his country. Ibid. "This may be because, despite it all, Avrum Burg is family. And whether he likes it or not, Israelis look out for family" (ibid).

46. *Adalah,* at 165.

Israel is concerned."[47] The "identity of society" doubtless referred to Israel as a "Jewish and democratic" state; whatever ambiguity there might be in this formulation would ultimately require clarification by the state, which of course includes the institution of which the justice had been an integral part.

Different Citizens

If the laws of utopia are not for Israel, those of Ruritania are at least worth considering. Or so Justice Cheshin believed when he referred to this mythical state to make the point that defending the state interest in identity is a prerogative available to all polities in the conduct of their immigration policies. In the justice's telling, Ruritania had decided to encourage immigration in order to address the problem of an aging population, but in time it found that the new immigrants "changed the image of the state" and "threaten[ed] the hegemony of the original citizens." The government, he concluded, was within its rights to suspend further immigration—"even for family reasons."[48]

Back in the real world the government of Israel had argued in a similar fashion before the Court: "Even if the predominant purpose of the [Citizen and Entry] law was demographic—which is not the case—this purpose would be consistent with the values of the State of Israel as a Jewish and democratic state. . . ."[49] So, despite its categorical assertion that security considerations were the sole basis of the contested policy on family reunification, the government conceded that had demographic concerns been advanced, they would have comported with the underlying values of the society.[50] Nevertheless, Justices Cheshin and Barak were

47. Ibid.

48. Ibid., at 166.

49. Quoted in ibid., at 257.

50. This was the position taken by some on the right. They denied any racist purpose behind the law while affirming that the demographic threat to Israel's Jewish nature, rather than the security threat, was the real motivation behind the legislation. According to Haim Misgav, a prominent member of the right-wing Professors for a Strong Israel, "We are entitled to defend the Jewish character of the country. . . . Israel is a Jewish state. That was established in the Declaration of Independence, and the Supreme Court itself has upheld the principle that the key to entering the Jewish state resides in Jewish hands." Quoted in Ina

both insistent that demography was not relevant to the case. Why they and the government would try to elide this issue has a plausible explanation: to do otherwise would convey to the Arabs already in the state that they constituted a "demographic threat," which is "an unacceptable message to citizens of a liberal democracy."[51] Thus, Cheshin wrote: "[T]he demographic issue was not considered at all by us and we were in any event not required to decide it."[52] As for Justice Barak: "The law is not based on any 'demographic' purpose of restricting the increase of the Arab population in Israel."[53] Not surprisingly, these disclaimers were skeptically received by many of the critics of the Court's ruling, who in

---

Friedman, "Three Groups Urge Supreme Court to Strike Down Citizenship Law," *The Jerusalem Report,* September 8, 2003, 6.

51. Na'ami Carmi, "Immigration Policy: Between Demographic Considerations and Preservation of Culture," 2 *Law & Ethics of Human Rights* 1 (2008), 26. From an institutional perspective, avoiding the topic also meant that the justices would not have to confront the state regarding the veracity of the latter's assertions respecting the law's predominant purpose.

52. Ibid., at 214. Justice Cheshin acknowledged, "I will not deny that questions of demography pestered me, but as a judge I made the best of efforts to dissociate myself from them and to concentrate on the real issue out before us." Correspondence with the author, May 19, 2007. According to one commentator, who, as the legal assistant to Justice Barak at the time of this decision was not a disinterested observer, demography *was* the real issue. "[I]t is difficult to explain the opinion of Justice Cheshin without assuming that to a large degree, it was guided by the very same demographic consideration from which he attempts to distance himself." Yaacov Ben-Shemesh, "Immigration and the Demographic Consideration," 2 *Law & Ethics of Human Rights* 1 (2008), 32.

53. *Adalah,* at 15. This understanding differed from the accounts of two other justices, Proccacia and Joubran. For example, according to the former, "[F]rom the debates in the Knesset it can be seen that the demographic issue hovered over the legislative process the whole time, and was a major issue in the deliberations of the Interior Committee of the Knesset and the House" (ibid., at 256). Of course, the statements of some legislators to the effect that demography was a principal factor in passing the law need to be placed in the context of a debate that featured many other statements emphasizing the security issue as the main legislative motivation. In an interview with the author, Justice Barak allowed as how "many of those who voted in favor of the law . . . voted in favor of it because of demography." Nevertheless, before the Court the state maintained "[W]e don't have a view on demography . . . ; this is not a demography case, and they gave us all the reasons why this is not a demography case and I am convinced that it is not. . . . I would write another judgment altogether if it would be a demography case. But still the demography question is there." Author interview with Justice Aharon Barak, April 27, 2007.

essence found the "Ruritania rationale"—that the state (including the Court) can legitimately act in response to a perceived "threat [to] the hegemony of the original citizens"—to have in fact driven the policy on family reunification.

To these critics, the avoidance of the demographic issue was a convenient way for the Court to sidestep the contradictions of Israeli national identity, but the justices' efforts could not conceal the underlying dilemma embedded within it. On the left, the decision was viewed as an ethnically motivated evisceration of family rights. "All the arguments [about security] are nonsense, it's all meant to prevent 'creeping right of return.' But don't ever admit racism."[54] To an Arab member of the Knesset, "The decision proves that a Jewish and democratic state is an error in logic and that these two values are inherently contradictory."[55] As amplified by the head of the organization that brought the case to the Court, "There is a deep-rooted consensus among [the justices] that Jewish dominance should be preserved in the State of Israel."[56] And on the right, the decision of the sharply divided Court aroused concern that the Basic Law on Human Dignity and Freedom had been cynically and baselessly interpreted, an impression underscored by the denial by a majority of the judges that demographic issues had been essential to the case. "On political issues, such as how to preserve the State of Israel as a Jewish and democratic state, decisions must be made by the state's elected organs, not by a group of appointed judges who were not elected by the people."[57]

A more neutral journalistic account simply pointed out that the decision "bears great constitutional significance with respect to the tension inherent in the character of the state as both Jewish and democratic." Its conclusion was that "the ruling . . . rests on a preference for the Jewishness of the state (the majority opinion) over the more democratic (the

54. Meron Benvenisti, "But Don't Ever Admit Racism," *Haaretz,* May 14, 2006.

55. MK Ahmed Tibi, as quoted in *Haaretz,* May 15, 2006. Not to be outdone by his Arab colleague, MK Ran Cohen said, "It is unbelievable that Israeli and Jewish judges have accepted a law rooted in racism."

56. Hassan Jabareen, *Adalah's Newsletter: The 10th Anniversary of Adalah: Identities, Jurisprudence and Politics* (2006).

57. MK Michael Eitan, as quoted in *Haaretz,* May 19, 2006.

minority opinion)."[58] This reading goes to the crux of the second dimension of human dignity raised by the Citizenship and Entry law: whether the policy on family reunification violated the constitutional right to equality of Arab citizens of Israel. It was addressed almost exclusively in terms of the security issue, but to the extent that the *status quo ante* of Israeli society occupied a place of some importance in the majority's lead opinion, the concept of security unavoidably contained both short- and long-term implications.[59] As a short-term issue it was all about the immediate threat to Jews in Israel who were the potential targets of Arab terrorists admitted into the country to join a family member already there as a citizen of the state. As a long-term problem it concerned the right of the Jewish people to national self-determination, a right often considered fundamental to the immigration policies of the state in general, and by extension to the specific exclusionary criteria of the family reunification legislation in the case at hand. "Security of the state is synonymous with security of the Jewish collective, and that is often seen as being dependent on promoting 'Jewish national goals.'"[60]

The collective rights of one people will most assuredly impinge on those of another; raising "the demographic issue" emphasizes the injustices experienced by the latter, presenting it in the more benign language of self-determination (Cheshin's *status quo ante?*) confers legitimacy on the former. As Chaim Gans notes, the liberal objection to nationality-based priorities in immigration is that they transgress the ideal of state neutrality and create two unequal classes of citizens. They "violate the principle of equality among individuals in the name of a collective right and thus conflict with the liberal principle of the moral primacy of indi-

58. *Haaretz editorial,* May 14, 2006.

59. In an interview with the author, Justice Barak acknowledged both of these understandings of security, but said, "When I'm talking security I mean security bombs." He went on to indicate that the drafters of the law intended it in the same way, and not as "a statement about immigration to Israel." Author's interview with Justice Aharon Barak, April 27, 2007.

60. David Kretzmer, *The Legal Status of the Arabs in Israel* (Boulder, CO: Westview Press, 1990), 136. According to Kretzmer, one of the problems associated with using the broad view of security is that it inevitably will be greeted by deep suspicion by those not sharing accepted national goals. As in the *Adalah* case, these decisions "may be seen purely as a means of legitimizing political decisions" (ibid., 139).

viduals over collective entities."[61] Gans himself does not believe that the incompatibility of such priorities with the liberal ideals of neutrality and equality render them inherently unjust, although he finds both the Israeli Law of Return and the family reunification law to be unjust in the particular ways they go about implementing these priorities.[62] "[T]he justification for nationality-based priorities in immigration derives from interests that individual human beings have in the existence and in the self-determination of their group."[63] To what degree this justification can be allowed to compromise the right to equality is, of course, precisely the sort of question that philosophers should and do reflect upon. But for a judge navigating the politically treacherous currents of Judaism and democracy, a different role in relation to the long-term security interest might be preferred, one more consistent with the idea that "a court is not a classroom in ethics." He might prefer to have the settlement of such deeply constitutive questions resolved within a dynamic of institutional interaction that, if permitted to run its course, could be expected to sacrifice a measure of moral clarity for a certain degree of political legitimacy.[64] This could perhaps explain why the judge would express an awareness of the salience of the identity issue—in other words national self-determination—without engaging it in a direct and systematic manner. What some will see as the disingenuousness of his effort, others will view as an act of prudence.

61. Chaim Gans, "Nationalist Priorities and Restrictions in Immigration: The Case of Zionism and Israel," 2 *Law and Ethics of Human Rights* (2008), 6.

62. "The principal injustice perpetrated by [the Law of Return] does not stem from the very fact that it grants priorities regarding immigration on a nationalist basis, but rather from the fact that it grants unlimited advantages to one national group while completely denying advantages to another national group." Chaim Gans, *The Limits of Nationalism* (Cambridge: Cambridge University Press, 2003), 125.

63. Gans, "Nationalist Priorities and Restrictions," 8.

64. According to one commentator, the constitutionality of the Citizenship and Entry into Israel law was a test of whether "Israel can be a home for the Jewish nation and a medium for the flourishing of Jewish culture without infringing the full equality of its Arab citizens." Daphne Barak-Erez, "Israel: Citizenship and Immigration Law in the Vise of Security, Nationality, and Human Rights," 6 *International Journal of Constitutional Law* 184 (2007), 191. One might share this assessment and yet feel that this is perhaps too high a burden for any given case to carry.

As it played out on the Court, the disagreement over equality focused on the short-term security question, but traces of the broader dispute are not difficult to discern. There is agreement, however, that is also important. To the question of the institutional roles of the judicial and legislative branches in the elaboration of Israeli constitutional identity, it is significant that there was a broad consensus on the Court regarding the existence of a constitutional right to equality as a fundament of the Basic Law's dignity provision. The identification of the Supreme Court with an unequivocal position on the legal obligation to provide equality is critical for any dialogical negotiation of the tensions between the universal and particular aspects of constitutional identity. In the two main *Adalah* opinions, for example, quick agreement was reached between Justices Barak and Cheshin on the right to equality as an integral part of the general right to human dignity.

On the facts of the case, too, there were shared perceptions. "We all agree (for how could we not?) that the Citizenship and Entry into Israel Law harms mainly and for the most part the Arab citizens of the state." Although the law did not distinguish between Arab and Jew, as pointed out by Justice Cheshin, "*de facto* it is Arab Israeli citizens who are harmed by the law, since it is only they . . . who find a spouse among the residents of the territories."[65] For Barak the differential impact was decisive: "[T]he . . . Law results in depriving Arabs—and only Arabs—who are citizens of Israel of the possibility of realizing their right of family life. A law that has this result is a discriminatory law. A law that causes an injury that focuses almost exclusively on the Arab citizens of Israel violates equality."[66] To the state's submission that no denial of equal treatment in a constitutional sense had occurred because the law was based on a relevant distinction—some foreign spouses are security risks and others are not—Barak responded that the law improperly prohibited entry of every Palestinian spouse regardless of whether that person presented a security danger or not. Moreover, on the basis of established precedents, the absence of any intention by the state to discriminate did

65. *Adalah,* at 184.
66. Ibid., at 58.

not save the law since the discriminatory outcome of its implementation was so clearly evident.

The "relevant equality" standard, which Justice Barak identified with the Aristotelian conception of discrimination as treating equals differently and treating persons who are different equally, was embraced as well by Justice Cheshin—but with very different results.[67] "The Citizenship and Entry into Israel Law was enacted against the background of the armed conflict and state of war between Israel and the Palestinians, and consequently there is a proper and permitted distinction between persons who married foreigners, who are Palestinian 'enemy nationals' that are presumed to constitute a potential security risk to the residents of the state, and persons who married foreigners who are not 'hostile nationals.'"[68] Cheshin thus relies on the conditions of war to exonerate the state in the enforcement of an immigration policy that prevents enemy nationals from entering its territory. "This ban does indeed harm a minority group of which the vast majority are Arabs, but this harm derives from the marriage to enemy nationals who are likely to endanger the public in Israel and not from the fact that they are Arabs. The decisive factor is national security and the lives of the residents of the state, and this factor outweighs the others."[69]

Most informed observers would doubtless agree that a nation at war with another nation could, consistent with generally accepted international standards, reach the same conclusion as Justice Cheshin. Whether the existential fact of armed conflict with residents of territories under

67. Justice Barak (and Justice Cheshin) cited an opinion by Justice Shimon Agranat (in Boronovski v. Chief Rabbis) for the Israeli acceptance of the Aristotelian standard: "[I]t will be a permitted distinction if the different treatment of different persons derives from their being, for the purpose of their treatment, in a state of relevant inequality, just as it will be discrimination if it derives from their being in a state of inequality that is not relevant to the purpose of the treatment" (quoted in ibid., at 59).

68. Ibid., at 187.

69. Ibid. Justice Cheshin first introduced the state-of-war argument shortly after his encounter with Thomas More. "We should always remember: Israel is not Utopia. Israel finds itself in a difficult armed conflict with the Palestinians. An authority against a state. One collective against another. And this armed conflict has become like a war. Not like the War of Independence; not like the Six Day War; not like the Yom Kippur War. But it is a war nevertheless" (ibid., at 118).

the military control of a nation renders these people "enemy nationals," and thus subject to international human rights criteria, is of course extremely controversial.[70] For my purposes, however, this important question need not be resolved here; rather, I want to consider the justice's position for its relevance to the issue of constitutional identity and the disharmonic sources of its meaning.

The specific substance and configuration of a nation's constitutional identity at any given time involves a balancing between particularistic and universalistic commitments—in the Israeli case, the two strands of the Proclamation of Independence—whose content in part reflects circumstances in the local and global environments. National self-determination for the Jewish people is rooted in a narrative with ancient and modern connections to the local geography, although much of the story has unfolded in very distant locales. The self-understanding of this people is inscribed in a corpus of rich and complex materials, some of which has been shaped by the struggle for survival that has been the constant motif in the historical progression of the national community.

It is in this sense that Justice Cheshin's anti-utopianism takes on significance for us; the enemy nationals to whom he attached such importance in *Adalah* may or may not be properly categorized, but they play a critical role in one of the disharmonic venues through which the constitutional identity of the polity continues to evolve. Thus, important as the aspirational component is to the development of constitutional identity, it is not a phenomenon fueled solely by the unencumbered targeting of constitutive priorities unilaterally established within a hermetic national environment. To be sure, much indigenously inspired goal setting is generated from within the Jewish tradition, but there is also a dynamic of negation, the objects of which can extend beyond the reach of domestic politics and law. In this regard, Anne Norton has written of "the

70. Thus, for example, Article 27 of the Fourth Geneva Convention stipulates that residents of occupied territories "are entitled, in all circumstances, to respect for their persons, their honor, their family rights, their religious convictions and practices, and their manners and customs." But, as David Kretzmer points out, "The Supreme Court has refused to regard Geneva Convention IV as part of customary international law enforceable in domestic courts." David Kretzmer, *The Occupation of Justice: The Supreme Court of Israel and the Occupied Territories* (Albany: State University of New York Press, 2002), 43.

constitutive power of contradiction, the order imposed on us by opposition."[71] Here enemies are indeed important. "In choosing what they will reject, nations determine what they signify and what they will become. The recognition that polities are defined in difference should teach them to choose their enemies with care. Their enmities define them."[72]

Pertinent as these differences are to the equality question posed explicitly in the family reunification controversy, they also illuminate the related question of identity. In Norton's scheme, "The presence of differences among a people will reveal to them, many times, the principle that unites them. . . . They will come to see their contradictions as their constitution."[73] Her account, however, emphasizes the liminal status of those to whom the state seeks to differentiate itself as it seeks to provide meaning for the nation and its people. "The recognition that liminars are at once other and like carries with it conscious recognition of the differences the nation can embrace."[74] Territorial liminars, she argues, are often identified with adjacent, usually antagonistic nations, producing an inordinate fear of the marginal group—even paranoia, as occurred in the United States with the internment of Japanese Americans.[75]

71. Anne Norton, *Reflections on Political Identity* (Baltimore: Johns Hopkins University Press, 1988), 55.

72. Ibid.

73. Ibid., 57.

74. Ibid., 55.

75. Ibid. This example is not irrelevant to the case at hand. Thus the American case of Korematsu v. United States was raised—and debated for its relevance—in the opinions in *Adalah.* Justice Barak quoted from the opinion of Justice Jackson to the effect that the judiciary must treat human rights seriously both in times of war and in times of peace. *Adalah,* at 35. Justices Procaccia and Naor differed sharply on the appropriateness of citing *Korematsu.* Said Proccacia: "The circumstances in that case are completely different from those in our case, but the wind that blows in the background of the constitutional approach that was applied there by the majority opinion is not foreign to the arguments that were heard from the state in the case before us. We must take care not to make similar mistakes" (*Adalah,* at 265). In response, Justice Naor wrote: "The cases are light years apart. If we wish to make a comparison, we should ask the following: would Britain, during the Second World War, have allowed the entry of thousands of Germans into Britain for the purpose of marriage with British citizens? Would the United States have allowed the entry of tens of thousands of residents of the Japanese Empire into the United States for the purpose of marriage with citizens of the United States after the attack at Pearl Harbor" (ibid., at 290)?

One need not rely on a familiar quip about the real enemies paranoids sometimes have, to distinguish between the morally compromised uses to which liminality may be put in Norton's troubling rendition from the majority judgment in *Adalah.* One might, in other words, view (or not) that judgment as excessively alarmist in its depiction of the security threat represented by the Palestinians who were seeking unification with their families, without ascribing to its author a cynical intention to exploit the vulnerability of this unfortunate minority for the benefit of the state's favored majority. Instead, the essentials of Norton's "we/they" representation of national identity construction can be incorporated within a standard, if controversial, Zionist narrative in which the focus on survival in a demonstrably hostile world has definitional significance for the identity of the nation. This is a story "of a common Jewish destiny of victimization and persecution, in which the Arabs had now emerged as the 'other,' the enemy that threatened Jewish life."[76] While reflecting the uniqueness of the Israeli/Palestinian circumstance, it is also arguably an extreme example of a more common phenomenon; as Charles S. Maier has said, "Group identity—whether national, religious, linguistic, class, or other—functions by constructing some sort of boundary condition, a cultivated awareness of qualities that separate 'us' from 'them.'"[77]

Not surprisingly, Israeli scholars have given extensive consideration to this problem. Pnina Lahav has distinguished between "catastrophe" and "utopian" Zionism, the theme of the first centering on defending against external threats to the Jewish people, which contrasts sharply with the liberal and messianic objectives of the second. "For catastrophe Zionists, Israel serves primarily as a safe haven from repetition of the various catastrophes that have befallen Jews in the past. In contrast, utopian Zionism stands for the proposition that Israel should be constructed

76. Pnina Lahav, *Judgment in Jerusalem: Chief Justice Simon Agranat and the Zionist Century* (Berkeley: University of California Press, 1997), 190.

77. Charles S. Maier, "'Being There': Place, Territory, and Identity," in Seyla Benhabin, Ian Shapiro, and Danilo Petranovic, *Identities, Affiliations, and Allegiances* (Leiden: Cambridge University Press, 2007), 68.

as a model state."[78] While this opposition suggests two contradictory visions traceable to the dichotomous set of principles embedded in the nation's founding, they often coexist within the worldviews of specific judges struggling to come to terms with Israeli identity.

Another Israeli scholar, David Kretzmer, an expert on the legal issues related to Israel's occupation of Arab territory, has grappled with these alternative visions in connection with a deeply perplexing question: "How can one explain the fact that a court that has played such a dominant role in forging a democratic and essentially liberal body of jurisprudence has consistently displayed a government-minded approach in decisions related to the Occupied Territories?"[79] Among the decisions he scrutinizes are several that involved West Bank and Gaza appeals of family unification rulings in which the Court upheld denials of residency status to spouses living in Arab countries. These did not affect Israeli citizens; hence the state's belligerent occupation arguments respecting the ongoing conflict between Israel and the Arab countries could be made more convincingly than in *Adalah*. The aggrieved person in the latter case was a citizen of Israel, not someone living on disputed land; therefore more plausibility attached to the idea that "[p]ermission granted to a nonresident to reside in the Territories is an act of grace and not a right."[80] Nevertheless, Kretzmer questions why in issues concerning Arabs in the territories humanitarian considerations have been, with the Court's apparent blessing, systematically subordinated to the claim of military necessity.

Part of the explanation for the disparity between the Court's "regular" jurisprudence and its disposition of cases from the territories relates to "the political dimensions of Israel's self-identity and the Zionist narrative of its conflict with the Palestinians."[81] This narrative is only the most recent chapter in an extended saga of survival that finds judges

78. Ibid., xiii. Lahav depicts this important jurist as someone whose utopian aspirations came to be tempered by the catastrophic strand in Zionist ideology. Eventually he embraced "[a] constitutional principle that put the Jewish state above and beyond all other values [to] serve as yet another weapon in the defense of 'never again' " (ibid., 190).

79. Kretzmer, *Occupation of Justice*, 191.

80. Ibid., 110.

81. Ibid., 195.

occasionally invoking the Holocaust as the backdrop for a refusal to interfere with the government's security measures.[82] It is a narrative ingrained in the Israeli collective mindset and very much a part of the ongoing process of constitutional settlement. Much as the concept of militant democracy *(streitbare Demokratie)* has "achieved authoritative status in German constitutional law,"[83] a similar idea—the state rejecting neutrality in confronting its mortal enemies—has acquired constitutional standing in Israel where, to be sure, it does not find the explicit sanction that is present in the German document.[84] Understandably, the Court has given greater license to the doctrine in cases where citizens of the state do not pay the costs of its invocation. But, as we see in *Adalah,* Arab citizens of Israel may also be required to bear the burdens of this historically determined policy.[85] In the next section I examine the jurisprudential

82. When asked what makes Israel a Jewish state, Justice Barak replied, "You can abolish the Law of Return and still be a Jewish State. . . . It's language—Hebrew, it's the Jewish holidays, it's the Jewish history, it's the Holocaust. There are many things that make it a Jewish State and not necessarily the Law of Return." In other words, it's the Jewish story of survival (consider, for example, the meaning of most of the Jewish holidays) that is essential to the Jewishness of the state. Author's interview with Justice Aharon Barak, April 27, 2007. Of course, the Law of Return is an artifact of that story. And according to Justice Cheshin, "It is only a matter of time before the right of return will be raised before the Court." Correspondence with Justice Mishael Cheshin and the author, May 19, 2007. If and when that happens, an interesting question is whether the Court would view that law as necessary to Israeli identity, and if so, not repealable in the manner of an unconstitutional constitutional amendment.

83. Donald P. Kommers, *The Constitutional Jurisprudence of the Federal Republic of Germany* (Durham, NC: Duke University Press, 1997), 34.

84. Several provisions of the German Basic Law make enjoyment of fundamental rights contingent upon accepting the legitimacy of the constitutional order. Article 21, for example, declares parties opposed to the "free democratic order" to be unconstitutional. Justice Barak has been a strong supporter of the concept: "[M]y opinion is that democracy may and must defend itself from those who seek to destroy it. Democracy cannot remain neutral toward two parties that seek to eradicate it. This is the militant democracy that has been written about in Germany. This is the defensive democracy that was discussed in Israel." Barak, *Judge in a Democracy,* 30. Of course the question in *Adalah* was how militant may the state (and the Court) be to defend the security of the Jewish people?

85. As Justice Cheshin wrote: "[A]s long as the security services find it difficult to distinguish between those who aid our enemies and those who do not aid our enemies, the right of the few to have a family life in Israel should yield to the rights of all the residents of Israel to life and security." *Adalah,* at 119.

alternatives that either enhance or diminish the possibility of this happening—and what it means for Israeli constitutional identity.

Identity and Jurisprudence

As the old adage goes, where you stand depends on where you sit. Reflecting on the ruling on family reunification, *Adalah*'s founder and general director was struck more by the similarities in the two main opinions than their differences. As he saw it, "[T]he legal decision between the justices remained within the Zionist framework."[86] What these justices chose not to talk about—demography—much as what they opted to emphasize—security—convinced him that "there [was] no serious debate between them concerning the 'essence' of the definition of the state. . . ."[87] Their disagreements, he concluded, related to pragmatic considerations rather than to issues of principle.

In Hassan Jabareen's account of the case brought by his organization, the "deep-rooted consensus" on the subject of Israeli identity was that "Jewish dominance should be preserved in the State of Israel."[88] Indeed, the justices might have agreed, at least on a general level, with this impression, as the director's judgment that the Court's decision was rendered within a Zionist framework of reference was one with which they doubtless would sympathize.[89] But their assent would very likely be incomplete, for as someone who viewed the issue of Israeli identity from a point external to that frame of reference, Jabareen failed to note or appreciate the further definitional distinctions that were present within the larger canvas of identity upon which the case had been adjudicated.

These distinctions were implicit in the alternative judicial methodologies deployed by Barak and Cheshin. While the immediate significance of the split decision was most apparent in the details of the immigration policy upheld by the Court, any assessment of the ultimate import of the

86. Jabareen, Adalah's Newsletter.

87. Ibid.

88. Ibid.

89. Justice Cheshin said, "As to the Israeli identity, that was not the issue, and I am not sure that there is a great difference between Barak and I." Correspondence with Justice Mishael Cheshin and the author, May 19, 2007.

decision would require further reflection on the connections between constitutional jurisprudence and constitutional identity. Critical to this exercise is the manner in which the balance between the dual aspirations of Israeli *national* identity devolves into a discernible *constitutional* identity; how, that is, the ambiguities of "the values of the State of Israel as a Jewish and Democratic state" acquire clearer constitutive meaning. In *Adalah,* the Basic Law on Human Dignity and Liberty was the instrument through which the opposing sides expected the essentials of national identity to translate into specific constitutional shape and texture. This law had affirmed a necessary principle of constitutionalism; in Justice Barak's formulation, "Human dignity is . . . the freedom of the individual to shape an individual identity."[90] But how much freedom should a judge have in interpreting human dignity in order to shape a constitutional identity? Barak's perception of the 1992 law as a necessary component of constitutional governance was evident also in the very different interpretive strategy of Justice Cheshin. What remained, however, was the adaptation of the dignity principle to the Israeli context, thereby elucidating the character of this specific constitution and the method by which it would come to be known.

The Nucleus and the Periphery

As we have seen, both Justices Barak and Cheshin accepted that the family is an institution protected under the dignity provision of the 1992 Basic Law, and they also agreed in principle that under that law's limitations clause the state's interest in security could override this protection. While Jabareen saw their disagreement in *Adalah* over the character of the means used to enforce this interest as insignificant in the context of the justices' broader concurrence on fundamentals, the most important disparity between Barak and Cheshin did not concern the pragmatics of balancing rights and security, but the methodology for determining the scope of constitutionally protected rights. Moreover, as Barak pointed out, this divergence is "not a mere technical or methodological matter . . . [but one] with deep implications for human

90. Barak, *Judge in a Democracy,* 86.

rights in Israel."[91] As such, it also has deep implications for constitutional identity in Israel.

To see how, we need first to consider the limitations clause in the Basic Law, which reads: "There shall be no violation of rights under this Basic Law except by a law befitting the values of the State of Israel [as a Jewish and democratic state], enacted for a proper purpose, and to an extent no greater than is required."[92] The principal model for this language was the Canadian Charter of Rights and Freedoms, which "guarantees the rights and freedoms set out in it subject only to such *reasonable limits* prescribed by law as can be *demonstrably justified* in a *free and democratic society*."[93] As in the Canadian example, judges in Israel proceed through a sequence of stages to determine whether a law purported to be in violation of a constitutionally guaranteed right is in fact invalid for that reason. As outlined by Justice Barak:

> The *first* stage examines whether the law—in our case the Citizenship and Entry into Israel Law—violates a human right enshrined in the Basic Law. If the answer is no, the constitutional scrutiny ends. . . . If the answer is yes, the legal analysis passes on to the next stage. In the *second* stage, we examine the question whether the violation of the right satisfies the requirements of the limitations clause. Indeed, not every violation of a human right is an unlawful violation. Sometimes a law violates a constitutional human right, but the constitutionality of the law is upheld, since the violation satisfies the requirements of the limitations clause.[94]

As first elaborated in the landmark Canadian case, R. v. Oakes, these stages require that both the rights guaranteed by the document, and the reasonable limits on these rights, be interpreted in light of the document's larger purposes. "The underlying values and principles of a free and democratic society [in Israel: Jewish and democratic] are the genesis

91. *Adalah,* at 107.

92. Basic Law: Human Dignity and Liberty.

93. Canadian Charter of Rights and Freedoms, Section 1.

94. Ibid., at 33.

of the rights and freedoms guaranteed by the Charter [in Israel: the Basic Law on Human Dignity and Liberty] and the ultimate standard against which a limit on a right or freedom must be shown, despite its effect, to be reasonable and demonstrably justified."[95]

In accordance with this procedure, Justice Barak found that the right of the Arab-Israeli spouses to realize their family life in Israel had been violated, as had their right to equality. But the purpose behind the contested law—reducing the risks of terror—was deemed a proper one and thus satisfied the requirement of the limitations clause. Given that twenty-six recorded cases had been cited where spouses admitted for family unification reasons had committed acts of terrorism, the legislation and its blanket prohibition against entry of foreign spouses into Israel was a rational way of pursuing a legitimate social objective. In the end, however, the Court's Barak-led minority felt the law should be held unconstitutional, since the blanket prohibition (as opposed to a system of individual checks), while rational (and no doubt effective in minimizing the risk), was not proportionate in the balance it struck between the benefit it achieved and the damage to the human rights caused by it. Weighing the values and interests in play against the principles of the Israeli legal system, could lead to only one result—the law cannot stand. "Democracy does not act in this way."[96]

Had the Cheshin opinion only differed with the minority on the question of balancing and proportionality, Jabareen's take on the case would be more compelling, which is to say *Adalah* would be a less interesting prism through which to examine the problem of constitutional identity. But the main difference between them lies elsewhere, specifically at the

95. R. v. Oakes, 1 S.C.R. 103 (1990), 136. Justice Barak used similar language in *Adalah:* "Both the human rights and the limitations clause should be interpreted in accordance with the basic principles and basic purposes of the Basic Law. . . . Indeed, human rights and the possibility of violating them derive from the same source." *Adalah,* at 68. For a good analysis of the Canadian limitations clause jurisprudence, see David Beatty, *Constitutional Law in Theory and Practice* (Toronto: University of Toronto Press, 1995). For a thoughtful comparison of how this jurisprudence replicates the legal framework of the police power in American constitutional experience, see Lorraine E. Weinrib, "The Postwar Paradigm and American Exceptionalism," in Sujit Choudhry, ed., *The Migration of Constitutional Ideas* (Cambridge: Cambridge University Press, 2006).

96. *Adalah,* at 98.

initial point when the Court had to determine if in fact there was a constitutional right to realize a family life in Israel with a foreign spouse and child. Absent such a finding, there would be no need to satisfy the conditions of the limitations clause, since there could then be no violation of a constitutional right. To be sure, Cheshin eventually concluded that had resort to the limitations clause been necessary its conditions would have been met; but that question was rendered academic once the justice determined that the scope of the family right guaranteed under the Basic Law's dignity provision did not include reunification with a non-Israeli family member.

He thus disagreed with Barak that such a right "lies at the very nucleus of the right to family dignity."[97] The latter's position was that to exclude the marginal or peripheral cases from the sphere of constitutional protection would defeat the rights-friendly constitutional purpose underlying the commitment to human dignity. The nucleus of human dignity applies equally, he argued, to families where both spouses are Israeli and to those where only one is a citizen of the state. "Our role as judges at this stage of our national life, is to recognize in full the scope of human rights, while giving full strength to the power of the limitations clause to allow a violation of those rights, when necessary, without restricting their scope."[98]

Against this judge-centered view of the derivation of constitutional rights, Cheshin insisted on a greater role for the legislature. Recognition of a constitutional right means excluding the legislature from any interference with the right, as if to say to the lawmaking branch, "take care and keep away."[99] It also means that the protected right embodies universal values; hence, as we noted earlier, Cheshin's depiction of the core family right as rooted in the precepts of natural law. But when the scope of the right is expanded, and constitutional protection is extended to derivative rights at the periphery of their strength, the authority of the Knesset is unduly restricted, and "human dignity [will have] replace[d]

97. Ibid., at 106.
98. Ibid., at 108.
99. Ibid., at 146.

the dignity of statute."[100] The legislative body, according to this view, must have authority over those rights whose normative status do not rise to the level of other rights within the nucleus of generic constitutionalism. Lacking this special connection to "universal basic values," the constitutional arrangements that embody these rights "may be cancelled or changed when times change and the needs of the state change."[101] Such reasoning leads to a conclusion opposite from that of Justice Barak: "The court does not have the power to give a normative status of a basic right—a right that enjoys the normative protection of a Basic Law—to specific rights which by their very nature do not have a normative status of a 'constitution,' unless the constitutive authority in the state included them expressly in the constitution of the state."[102]

This contrast on the respective roles of the legislature and judiciary implicates a familiar point made prominent by Ronald Dworkin, but one about which more can be said in connection with constitutional identity. For Dworkin, courts are the institutional locus for elaborating and affirming principles, which are the propositions that describe rights. Legislatures

100. Ibid., at 147. Quoting from an opinion by Justice Yitzhak Zamir in Local Government Centre v. Knesset.

101. Ibid., at 147. Justice Cheshin cited the U.S. Eighteenth Amendment on prohibition and that Constitution's Second Amendment on the right to bear arms as examples of constitutional arrangements that did not reflect universal values and which therefore could be—as was done in the Twenty-first Amendment—excised whenever historical circumstances suggested the advisability of doing so. This view implies some sympathy with the concept of the unconstitutional constitutional amendment discussed in Chapter 3. Indeed, one Israeli Court observer has suggested that while Justices Cheshin and Barak disagreed about many things, one point on which they agreed was that the Court is authorized to nullify even basic laws that contradict the fundamental principles of the regime. Shahar Ilan, "The High Court's Doomsday Weapon," *Haaretz,* May 15, 2006. Ilan quotes the justices' opinions from the case reviewing the so-called Tal Law, which exempted Yeshiva students from military service. Cheshin: "None of the branches is authorized to 'abolish' the state as a Jewish and democratic state." Barak: "[T]here is room for the idea that a law or Basic Law, that denies Israel's character as a Jewish or democratic state is unconstitutional." Cheshin said of Ilan's account, "I think he is correct." Correspondence with Justice Mishael Cheshin and the author, May 19, 2007. As for Barak, he maintains that after the constitution-making process has been completed, the Indian model of judicial review over the substance of amendments would be appropriate for Israel. Author's interview with Justice Aharon Barak, April 27, 2007.

102. *Adalah,* at 148.

have a different decisional focus involving the determination of policies, which are the propositions that describe collective goals.[103] Courts have the responsibility of ensuring that specific constitutional guarantees (which may involve quite general language) are interpreted to institutionalize the moral rights that define a just society. Or, as Justice Barak framed it in his opinion: "The legislature determines the measures that are to be taken in order to realize social objectives. That is its role. The judiciary examines whether these measures violate the human right excessively. That is its role. One power does not enter the sphere of the other power."[104]

This division of labor embodies certain assumptions about relative institutional priorities. Because rights carry the weight of enduring moral principles, they can only be trumped by policies for which a compelling case of great urgency can be made. In the Israeli constitutional scheme the Court makes this calculation at the second interpretive stage in connection with the limitations clause. Thus, if "[w]e . . . define the weight of a right . . . as its power to withstand such competition,"[105] then judicially expanding the scope of a right by adding mass to its nucleus, renders it a more formidable competitor at this second stage. The effect is to enhance the authority of the Court at the expense of the lawmaking body, which can also be viewed as the jurisprudential path through which, in Hirschl's formulation, the "judicialization of politics has expanded to include the transfer to the judicial arena of foundational nation-building challenges. . . ."[106] Moreover, [p]erhaps nowhere has this trend been as clear as in Israel. . . ."[107]

103. Ronald Dworkin, *Taking Rights Seriously* (Cambridge, MA: Harvard University Press, 1977), 90. Principles of justice vindicate individual rights when, as inevitably happens, they compete with public policies seeking to advance some goal of the community as a whole. Policies are conceptualized as utilitarian goals that, unconstrained by principle, render as vulnerable rights that emerge from moral considerations, rather than from calculations of aggregate good.

104. *Adalah,* at 86.

105. Dworkin, *Taking Rights Seriously,* 92.

106. Ran Hirschl, *Towards Juristocracy* (Cambridge, MA: Harvard University Press, 2004), 169.

107. Ibid., 173. Most of Hirschl's illustrative examples involve the religious/secular disharmony in Israeli society, but his point is equally applicable to the conflict between Arabs

The broader significance of this expansion comes more clearly into focus if viewed as an example of E. E. Schattschneider's classic political science teaching: "[I]n political conflict every change in scope changes the equation."[108] What gives weight to the rights that courts are obliged to take most seriously is their transcendent quality, their embodiment of principles of justice that reflect universal truths and not just the preferences of the local environment within which they are propagated and constitutionalized. "Universal ideas in the culture, ideas concerning equality, consistency, equal protection of the laws, justice, liberty, *freedom of movement,* freedom of speech and association, and civil rights tend to socialize conflict."[109] How does one determine, in the absence of any express textual provision, whether a specific application of these ideas should be incorporated in a constitutionally protected right? For example, assuming widespread agreement that freedom of movement is a necessary element of constitutional order and entitlement, is family reunification across national borders something that should be guaranteed as within the scope of this right?

In *Adalah* the question was asked differently, as the Court focused on human dignity and its generally acknowledged derivative right to a family life. But in both instances, determining the scope of the family right or establishing the reach of the freedom of movement, assessing international experience to evaluate the claim of universality attaching to a purported right has obvious appeal as part of the decision-making process. Thus, in identifying the family as a basic unit of human society, Justice Cheshin noted, "It is not surprising . . . that the right to a family life has been recognized in the international community as a basic

---

and Jews. He wisely points out too, however, that when the judiciary assumes this role in trying to sort out the terms of foundational politics, they often incur a popular backlash that can threaten their institutional authority. In this regard he cites the *Qa'aden* case discussed in Chapter 4, as well as the famous *Shah Bano* case from India, in which the Court's rather heavy-handed effort to intervene in the foundational politics of Hindu/Muslim relations precipitated a political reaction that had profound convulsive repercussions in subsequent Indian political development.

108. E. E. Schattschneider, *The Semisovereign People: A Realist's View of Democracy in America* (Hinsdale, IL: Dryden Press, 1975), 4.

109. Ibid., 7 (emphasis added).

right."[110] In whatever shape and direction Israeli constitutional identity was to evolve, clearly for Cheshin it would have to include this universal right as a salient feature of its makeup. Such is also the case for Justice Barak, but, in his conceptualization of the problem constitutional identity entailed a more capacious scope for rights, with the result that a larger fraction in the identity equation reflected commitments associated with universalistic aspirations in contrast to those concerned with Israeli exceptionalism.

Indeed, in Barak's view an important goal of the constitutional project is the development of a constitutional identity in which the enjoyment of rights is generally consistent with standards commonly recognized within the international environment, and such a goal requires resisting more insular and particularistic definitions.[111] Reflective of this commitment is his extensive reliance on the conventions of international law; for example, the European Convention on Human Rights and Fundamental Freedoms and its granting "of a broad right to the reunification of families for all citizens of the European Union, whether the foreign spouse is a citizen of a member state in the Union or not."[112] Support for the right may also be found in the jurisprudence of many nations, and Barak quoted at length from various foreign decisions to buttress his conclusion that it was "not merely a basic right in common law, but a constitutional right enshrined in the right to human dignity."[113] As we saw in Chapter 4, expanding the scope of the right in question—in this instance the right to a family—correlates positively with an expansion in the scope of constitutional sources available to the judicial decision-making process.

Changing the scope changes the equation, but unlike the categorical rejection of such sources frequently voiced in the United States, Justice Cheshin's heightened solicitude for the indigenous roots of identity argues only for a more modest and cautious use of foreign materials.[114] "I am

110. *Adalah,* at 153.

111. Author's interview with Justice Aharon Barak, April 27, 2007.

112. *Adalah,* at 51.

113. Ibid., at 54.

114. In fairness, Justice Barak does not argue for an uncritical use of foreign jurisprudence. Justice Cheshin's reference to an earlier opinion of his colleague makes this clear:

not antagonistic to looking into what is going on in other states . . . but the intimacy between a constitution and the people of the state should put us on guard."[115] This guardedness is mainly about respecting the narrative of survival so critical to Israeli self-understanding. "Is there any other country that is being asked to allow into its territory the establishment of a family unit in which one of its members is an enemy alien? . . . The status and way of life of [other] countries, and especially the security position in them, are so different from the status of Israel, from the way of life in it and from the security position that prevails in it that an analogy from the legal systems practiced in them—legal systems that reflect what is happening in those countries—is out of place."[116]

Justice Cheshin's critique of the form of external guidance that leads to an assimilative, emulative result is the logical extension of his position on the nucleus and the periphery. What it means, in effect, to be "out of place" is evident in the internal guidance he drew from Justice Barak's predecessor as chief justice, Meir Shamgar, whose opinion in the *Mizrahi* case Cheshin found instructive as he weighed the costs and benefits of judicial engagement with foreign law. "Every constitution," Shamgar had contended, "reflects in the protections of rights that are granted therein the social order of priorities that is unique to it and the outlooks

---

"[E]ach country has its own problems. Even if the basic considerations are similar, the balance between them reflects the uniqueness of every society and what characterizes its legal arrangements . . ." (ibid., at 173).

115. Correspondence with Justice Mishael Cheshin and the author, May 19, 2007. "Although in general it is proper for us to take a look at foreign legal systems, to learn and receive inspiration, we should always remember that normative arrangements that were created and exist against a background of a reality that prevails in those countries and that exists within legal systems that give expression to that reality, and therefore we should not follow blindly . . . normative arrangements that are practiced in those places." *Adalah,* at 173.

116. Ibid., at 175. Cheshin, it should be noted, was not reluctant to borrow extensively from foreign courts to support the position that the particular circumstances of a country should determine the scope of a right. As one example, this reference to an 1892 American case—Ekiu v. United States—was used to present a different view on the obligations of international law. "It is an accepted maxim of international law that every sovereign nation has the power, as inherent in sovereignty, and essential to self-preservation, to forbid the entrance of foreigners within its dominions, or to admit them only in such cases as it may seem fit to prescribe" (ibid., at 157).

that have been adopted in its society."[117] A country's immigration policy will reflect these priorities, which in turn will have been set by a collective political decision in which the specific needs of the place dictate the arrangements suitable for that polity at any given moment. Placed in the context of the Basic Law's limitations clause jurisprudence, the question this raises invites a response that is critical to the construction of constitutional identity. At what stage should the social ordering of priorities assume constitutive significance? Should it occur as part of the inquiry into the substance and scope of a constitutional entitlement, or should it become a factor only at the point when the Court is ready explicitly to confront the balancing procedure mandated by the terms of the Basic Law?

Sooner or Later?

"At the basis of the difference of opinion lies the question whether the Israeli spouse has a super-legislative constitutional right to realize his family life in Israel with his foreign spouse and their joint child."[118] Behind this difference are two paths to the recognition or nonrecognition of such a right. The first (approach A) requires a judge to decide whether there is a moral justification for family reunification that is a necessary extension of the right to human dignity. Whatever the answer, the determination—falling, perhaps, under the rubric of "taking rights seriously"—should be unaffected by contingent circumstances. If, say, the occasion for engaging this deliberative exercise is the state's adoption of an immigration policy, considerations related to the public interest aspects of a particular course of action do not belong in the calculus through which the right is affirmed or not affirmed. For example: "The armed conflict between Israel and the Palestinians in the territories does not change the scope of the human rights belonging to Israeli citizens."[119] In this sequencing the public interest is to be factored in only *if* the right has been upheld, and then only within the framework of examining the conditions of the limitations clause.

117. Ibid., at 174.
118. Ibid., at 103.
119. Ibid., at 109.

The second (approach B) requires taking the public interest into account at the initial stage of constitutional scrutiny in conjunction with the obligation to designate the scope of the family right. By implication this contrasting ordering of assignments also means increasing the scope of the lawmaking power. Thus it is the legislature's responsibility to advance interests and values that must be placed in proper balance with the rights vying for constitutional protection before the Court. These interests and values are in no sense subordinate to the rights under consideration; indeed, the "prerogative of the state has a constitutional status."[120] Commensurate with this status, the public interest "should not be required to bow its head and enter the constitutional debate within the framework of the limitations clause. Its place is on the first page of the constitution, when the values and the basic rights of the individual are being shaped."[121]

In thinking about these two approaches one should look beyond the narrow doctrinal issues incorporated in the differences between them and view these methodological options as an invitation to reflect on the role of the Court in the development of Israeli constitutional identity. Accepting the invitation will draw attention to four propositions:

1. The state has a "strong and decisive interest . . . in protecting the identity of society in Israel."[122]
2. "[T]he place of the public interest within the framework of determining the scope of the human right . . . is likely to reduce the right itself."[123]
3. "A constitution is created, first and foremost, for the people of the land and to regulate life for the residents and citizens of the land *inter se.* The United States constitution is for the people of the United States, the German constitution is for Germans and the Basic Law in Israel is for Israelis and for regulating relations between them and the state and among them *inter se.*"[124]

120. Ibid., at 165.
121. Ibid.
122. Ibid.
123. Ibid., at 107.
124. Ibid., at 166.

4. Israel's constitutional identity embodies a commitment to Jewish and democratic values.

With regard to proposition (1), both (A) and (B) would agree that the state's identity interest is strong, but diverge on its significance as a direct source of constitutive meaning. The insistence by (B) on ensuring that the state's interest appear on "the first page of the constitution" in effect proclaims that the tensions in the preface to the constitution—i.e., the Proclamation of Independence—are to be addressed within the process of conferring meaning to the nation's basic law. If that page is, as (A) might have it, to be reserved for an enumeration of rights unencumbered by the constraints of security considerations (short and long term), then the collective strand in the nation's prescriptive constitution will have given way to, or been absorbed into, the prefatory document's more cosmopolitan commitment. Approach (B), therefore, accepts proposition (2)—at least with regard to the scope of the right—as a necessary consequence of embracing the reality of proposition (3) and clarifying the meaning of proposition (4).

With the exception of proposition (4), the sequencing question—what we might call "the page one problem"—should appear in similar propositional form wherever decisions about a limitations clause are in play. In an early South African case, for example, Justice Kriegler of the Constitutional Court wrote, "The South African Constitution is primarily and emphatically an egalitarian constitution. The supreme laws of comparable constitutional states may underscore other principles and rights. . . . Equality is our Constitution's focus and organizing principle. The . . . role of the right to equality must . . . be understood in order to analyze properly whether a violation of [a] right has occurred."[125] Should the state seek to pursue its interest in advancing the egalitarian identity articulated in this observation, thus clarifying the meaning of the "open and democratic society" mentioned in the limitations clause of Section 36, would there not be, rightly or wrongly, a strong incentive to inscribe this understanding earlier rather than later in the elaboration of constitutional rights pertaining to property?

125. President of the Republic of South Africa v. Hugo, 1997 (4) SA 1 (CC).

The Canadian Supreme Court has regularly confronted the problem in the wake of its landmark *Oakes* ruling. As an illustration, consider the famous 1990 case, Regina v. Keegstra, in which the Court upheld a criminal statute that prohibited the willful promotion of hatred against identifiable groups. Section 2(b) of the Charter guarantees the "freedom of thought, belief, opinion and expression. . . ." If, as in American First Amendment jurisprudence, hate speech, however loathsome, were held to fall within the contours of constitutionally protected expression, then the statute would be seen as violating the Charter provision and upheld only under the stage two application of the limitations clause. But the Court's majority limited the scope of the expression right in much the same way as Justice Cheshin limited the reach of the family right in *Adalah*. "[S]ections 15 and 27 [of the Charter] represent a strong commitment to the values of equality and multiculturalism, and hence underline the great importance of Parliament's objective in prohibiting hate propaganda. . . ."[126] The state, in other words, to borrow from Justice Cheshin's language, had a "strong and decisive interest . . . in protecting the identity of society in [Canada]."

But what does this say about Canadian *constitutional* identity? Chief Justice Dickson explained that in the limitations clause of Section 1 "are brought together the fundamental values and aspirations of Canadian society."[127] That clause "operates to accentuate a uniquely Canadian vision of a free and democratic society."[128] The substance of that vision does not appear in the general language of the limitations clause, emerging only from the interactive dynamic of Parliament's pursuit of the public interest with values incorporated within the Canadian constitutional tradition. This dialogical process specifies and clarifies the principles that make up a "free and democratic society," in the end affirming them as "page one" principles of Canadian constitutionalism.[129]

126. Regina v. Keegstra, 3 S.C.R. 687, (1990), 755.

127. Ibid., at 735–736.

128. Ibid., at 743.

129. The opinions in *Keegstra* included extensive discussions of American free speech jurisprudence. For a thoughtful analysis of the relationship in Canadian jurisprudence between dialogical institutional interaction and judicial engagement with foreign legal materials see Sarah Harding, "Comparative Reasoning and Judicial Review," 28 *Yale Journal*

If this process resembles approach (B) in Israel, it may also provide some insight into the underlying rationale for approach (A)'s more court-centered orientation. A judge confronting the "majestic generalities"[130] of a "Jewish and democratic" society might very well feel less sanguine than his or her counterpart in Canada about the possibilities of achieving a coherent constitutional vision out of creative institutional interaction. The tensions in the commitment to a "free and democratic" society simply do not approximate the magnitude of the disharmonic reality subsumed in the Israeli constitutional dualism. The judicial responsibility in a post-Constitutional Revolution world is, according to Justice Barak, to interpret the Constitution "with the intention of achieving unity and constitutional harmony."[131] How is this to be done? "The content of the phrase 'Jewish state' will be determined by the level of abstraction which shall be given it. In my opinion, one should give this phrase meaning on a high level of abstraction, which will unite all members of society and find the common ground among them. The level of abstraction should be so high, until it becomes identical to the democratic nature of the state."[132]

Ratcheting up the level of abstraction is a familiar interpretive tool to expand the scope of constitutional rights. In the United States, too, the outcomes of family rights cases have sometimes hinged upon the particular plane of generality upon which the Court has settled, in order, according to Justice Brennan, to "defin[e] the scope of the liberty

---

of International Law 409 (2003). She sees *Keegstra* as "a robust example of the eagerness of the Supreme Court of Canada to engage in a cross-border judicial dialogue while still paying close attention to local circumstances" (ibid., at 426).

130. Aharon Barak, "The Constitutionalization of the Israeli Legal System as a Result of the Basic Laws and its Effect on Procedural and Substantive Criminal Law," 31 *Israel Law Review* 3, 5 (1997).

131. Ibid.

132. Aharon Barak, "The Constitutional Revolution: Protected Human Rights," 1 *Mishpat Umimshal* 9, 30 (1992–1993). As Justice Barak explained, "All those notions of Judaism—that God created man in his image, which is the basis of equality, that all men are created equal . . . are also those of democracy. . . ." When both are defined at "a high level of abstraction, then there . . . is a good chance there will be fitness [between them]." Author's interview with Justice Barak, April 27, 2007.

protected by the Due Process Clause."[133] Yet, in his execution of this technique, Barak's objectives have transcended the straightforward, if important, goal of widening the constitutional domain of rights protection. They include increasing the power of the Court relative to that of the legislature and, in connection thereto, reducing—if not eliminating—the tensions in the constitutional legacy of the nation's founding principles. A priority of the Court must therefore be the emergence of a unity of purpose that can be brought to bear on the project of advancing a constitutional future that resembles the progress of other liberal democracies.

But a unity of purpose is not the strong suit of approach (B). That orientation is decidedly more invested in a collaborative constitutional process in which the constitution's first page will come to reflect, in significant part, the concerns of context, contingency, and the public interest that nonjudicial institutions are well positioned to advance and articulate. In Israel these concerns are likely to find expression in the legislative branch and reflect security issues in both their short- and long-term incarnations. The latter incorporates the commitment to the Jewishness of the state in a form that may not be so amenable to harmonious integration into the universal aspirations of its coordinate democratic commitment. The result is a somewhat complex and untidy representation of constitutional identity that reflects the complicated reality of its sources as well as the fact that, as Sujit Choudhry and Robert Howse have noted with respect to Canada, "interpretive responsibility for particular constitutional norms is both shared and divided."[134]

In contrast, approach (A) is more compatible with an "enforcement model," a designation adopted to describe the strongly juricentric focus of the American Court that "rests on the presumption that limitations in

133. Michael H. v. Gerald D., 491 U.S. 110, (1989), 121. In response to Justice Brennan's preference for a high level of generality so as to widen the protection owed to non-traditional family relationships, Justice Scalia wrote: "Though the dissent has no basis for the level of generality it would select, we do: We refer to the most specific level at which a relevant tradition protecting, or denying protection to, the asserted right can be identified . . ." (ibid., at 127).

134. Sujit Choudhry and Robert Howse, "Constitutional Theory and the Quebec Secession Reference," 13 *Canadian Journal of Law and Jurisprudence* 143, 160 (2000).

sources and a well-defined legal hierarchy are essential to the coherence of constitutional interpretation."[135] In the context of limitations clause jurisprudence, the coherence of constitutional norms will likely be enhanced as the level of judicial involvement in defining the substance and scope of protected rights at the initial pre-limitation stage of constitutional engagement rises. The closer this approximates a unilateral role for the Court in determining priorities in the allocation of constitutional values in individual cases, the greater will be the unity of purpose in what can officially be portrayed as the Israeli constitutional identity. For Justice Barak, proposition (2)—inserting the public interest within the framework of determining the scope of the human right will reduce the right itself—is also a prediction about the diminished prospects for securing the substance of an identity consistent with the universalist aspirations of liberal democracy.

Conclusion

"[I]t is important to underscore the limited scope of judicial inquiry into immigration legislation. This Court has repeatedly emphasized that 'over no conceivable subject is the legislative power . . . more complete than it is over' the admission of aliens."[136] The reference was to the American Supreme Court, which in this instance upheld a section of the Immigration and Nationality Act of 1952 that had failed to extend to the illegitimate child of a natural father the right to immigrate to the United States to live with his or her citizen father. The law had only permitted illegitimate offspring to enter the country to secure reunification with their American mother. The Court ruled it was within Congress's power to deny a visa to an alien on the basis of that person's illegitimacy over the objection that the law unconstitutionally discriminated against male citizens.

The dissenters argued that Congress could not distinguish among citizens in this way even if as a general rule "Americans have no constitutional

135. Harding, "Comparative Reasoning," 451.

136. Fiallo v. Bell, 430 U.S. 787, 792 (1977).

right to compel the admission of their families."[137] That the discrimination occurred in an immigration context was not enough, they contended, to insulate it from the highest level of judicial scrutiny. In his *Adalah* opinion, Justice Barak cited the U.S. case as evidence that 'the right to family reunification is protected within the framework of the constitutional protection given to the right to family life."[138] But, this framework also included the majority's lower level of judicial scrutiny, which, much like the majority in Israel, left the justices unpersuaded by the claim that the scope of the fundamental due process family right should be expanded to cover the admission of alien kin to accommodate family reunification.

In fact, the Court seemed barely interested in the state's reason for pursuing a discriminatory policy. "Congress obviously has determined that preferential status is not warranted for illegitimate children, perhaps because of a perceived absence in most cases of close family ties as well as a concern with the serious problems of proof that usually lurk in paternity determinations. In any event, it is not the judicial role in cases of this sort to probe and test the justifications for the legislative decision."[139] A judicial deference so pronounced that the Court declaimed an institutional disregard for minimal probing of the reasons behind a controversial state policy, makes sense—if it does at all—only if the policy in question is perceived as not implicating core constitutional commitments.

The family reunification law in Israel *did* implicate such commitments, and it was not only the minority justices who recognized the connection. To be sure, the dissenters, led by Justice Barak, considered the law to be an unwarranted violation of human dignity and therefore transgressive of the nation's liberal democratic constitutional aspirations. But the majority justices, especially Justice Cheshin, also had an appreciation of the law's constitutive significance. Their main difference with the other side was in the emphasis they attached to the immigration law's bearing on the evolving understanding of the Constitution's meaning. As a statute whose enforcement had an undeniable discriminatory im-

137. Ibid., at 807.
138. *Adalah,* at 53.
139. *Fiallo,* at 798.

pact, it required serious scrutiny from the Court. Yet the very factors that led to the enactment of procedures with questionable legal consequences also required the Court's consideration as relevant input into the particular identity of Israel's constitutional arrangement.

The deference extended the legislature was, therefore, not a sign of the triviality of the issues at stake; on the contrary, to a significant degree it reflected a judgment that they were of critical constitutive importance. The circumspectness of the Court's various references to the "image of society" and the "identity of society" in connection with the state's interest in adopting the Citizenship and Entry into Israel Act, should not detract from the fact that the pursuit of these things was construed as vital to the achievement of a constitutional settlement. Justice Cheshin's opinion embodied the idea that, as Ruth Gavison's has said, "[t]he state and the laws are . . . ways of facilitating life and promoting goals many of which are not civic."[140] The main concern of these goals is the support and encouragement of a nation-state for Jewish self-determination. Achieving it is central to the state's framing of the public interest, which, as we have seen in the discussion of Cheshin's judicial methodology, is to be inserted directly into the constitutional equation rather than factored in subsequently as a nonconstitutional counterweight to judicially sanctioned rights in the balancing deliberations of the limitations clause.

Judicial restraint (which, in his long career, has not always been Justice Cheshin's orientation) may thus be valued for allowing the disharmonic strands in the Israeli constitutional tradition to play out within an ongoing dynamic of institutional interaction. The implicit presumption is that a less juricentric focus will have the effect of evening the playing field in the competition between universalistic and particularistic commitments, with the latter emerging as the major beneficiary of an approach that elevates the profile of the legislative branch in the cauldron of constitutional politics. But, restraint and deference may also be distrusted as providing inadequate safeguards for individual rights, whose largeness in scope is often taken to be the hallmark of a highly developed constitutional polity. As seen from this more skeptical perspective, the

140. Ruth Gavison, "Law, Adjudication, Human Rights, and Society," 40 *Israel Law Review* 13, 30 (2007).

object is not to deny or discount the prominence of the deeply rooted tensions of Israeli constitutionalism, but to achieve their principled reconciliation such that the higher aspirations of liberal democracy correspond with the major precepts of Jewish nationhood. When this reconciliation is accomplished, for example, with judges reasoning abstractly to extend the scope of the family right so that it comports with the best moral thinking within both traditions, interests generated by the political process can be permitted to influence, and perhaps determine, judicial outcomes. These outcomes, however, will not materially affect the substance of constitutional identity.

The issue of family reunification in Israel is bound up in the uncertainties of constitutional identity. In Chapter 3 I noted Alasdair MacIntyre's depiction of personal identity as a phenomenon making sense only in connection with a larger narrative within which it is embedded. The same, I suggested, pertains to the identity of a constitution, and, moreover, what MacIntyre understood as critical to the vitality of traditions—the "continuities of conflict" embodied within them—was also fundamental to the development of constitutional identity. With the family as the specific focus of attention, the *Adalah* case reveals how the abiding disharmonies of the Israeli historical narrative get refracted in different ways through the prism of the legal process to offer alternative visions of a constitutional future.

In concentrating my attention on a specific decision, I want to suggest in concluding this chapter that, as singular as are the fascinating details of the *Adalah* case, the nub of the underlying jurisprudential issue is recognizable in many of the constitutional controversies that have preoccupied the Israeli Supreme Court in its sixty-year history. The dialectic between universal and particular commitments may be seen, for example in the early landmark case, "Kol Ha'am" Co. Ltd. v. Minister of Interior,[141] where the American-born jurist, Shimon Agranat, borrowed freely from the free speech jurisprudence of his native country and then adapted it to his adopted land where deference to security considerations meant that even in "a freedom-loving State"[142]—which, like the

141. "Kol Ha'am" Co. Ltd. v. Minister of Interior, 7 P. D. 871 (1953).
142. Ibid., at 884.

United States, Israel was aspiring to be—the demands of the local environment would ultimately limit the reach of general principles.

More recently, it is observable in the Court's consideration of the legalities surrounding the construction of a security barrier separating the occupied territories from Israel proper. Here the issue was similar to the concerns later raised in the *Adalah* case, as the government's actions were ostensibly predicated on the growing threat posed by terrorists crossing over from the West Bank to carry out murderous bombings in Israeli civilian locations. Unlike in *Adalah,* the Court's application of the proportionality test did not lead it to support the security claim, although the judgment—the first of several—suggested how that might be accomplished. In an opinion by Justice Barak (concurred in by Justice Cheshin), the Court ruled that the "relationship between the injury to the local inhabitants and the security benefit from the construction of the Separation Fence along the route, as determined by the military commander, is not proportionate. The route disrupts the delicate balance between the obligation of the military commander to preserve security and his obligation to provide for the needs of the local inhabitants."[143] As in *Adalah,* the Court's balancing exercise required engagement with complex questions of international law, leading to an interpretation more sensitive to the local security needs than a contemporaneous advisory judgment on the case handed down by the International Court of Justice. And tellingly, much like the subsequent family unification ruling's rejection of the alleged demographic motivations behind the government's actions, the Court concluded that the setting of the barrier had not been prompted by political considerations, a similarity that might be viewed as significant in assessing the substance of Israeli constitutional identity.

143. Beit Sourik Village Council v. The Government of Israel, Isr SC 58 (2005), par. 60. Rhetorically, Justice Barak's opinion emphasized the universalist strand in the nation's dual set of obligations. "This is the destiny of a democracy—she does not see all means as acceptable, and the ways of her enemies are not always open before her. A democracy must sometimes fight with one arm tied behind her back. Even so, a democracy has the upper hand. The rule of law and individual liberties constitute an important aspect of her security stance. At the end of the day, they strengthen her spirit and this strength allows her to overcome her difficulties" (ibid., par. 86).

Numerous additional examples could be assembled from Israel to illustrate the jurisprudence of the disharmonic constitution. They would bear the imprint of the unique array of continuous conflicts that define Israeli constitutional development. But from a wider comparative perspective this development represents an instance of the more general phenomenon described in Chapter 3, the understanding of which enables one to apprehend the essentials of a nation's constitutional identity. For the student of constitutionalism, the ethnographic approach featured in this chapter is the methodological projection of that phenomenon's salient ideas. Thus to see how disharmony and prescription move the process of identity formation one needs to examine the constitutive aspirations of a polity through an immersion that facilitates both intimacy and detachment—the first to appreciate the things that are held most dear, and the second to describe what happens when these things engage each other through intense and often painful legal and political contestation.

CHAPTER 7

Conclusion

> It is still the constitution adopted two hundred years ago, just as a person who lives in an eighteenth-century house lives in a house built two hundred years ago. His house has been repaired, added to, and changed many times since. But it is still the same house and so is the constitution.
>
> —Joseph Raz

> Whatever withdraws us from the power of our senses; whatever makes the past, the distant, or the future predominate over the present, advances us in the dignity of thinking beings.
>
> —Samuel Johnson

Return Visits

Central to this book's inquiry into constitutional identity has been a concern with continuity and change in the constitution. Consider in this connection the challenge to constitutionalist thinking implicit in the oft-raised question: why should we submit to governance by the "dead hand of the past"? In those polities—the United States is the most obvious example—where a constitutional text has been around for a very long time, the reasons for acceding to entrenched commitments made by framers of a decidedly different time and place are not immediately evident. On the other hand, arguments for the irrelevance of these commitments seem also not quite convincing and are likely to be persuasive mainly to those who claim to see no connection between the choices made by the constitution's framers and the identity of the constitutional regime under which they currently live. Founding choices are themselves a blending of continuity and change; what emerges as the earliest manifestation of constitutional identity is a preview of subsequent incarnations, as the balance between new and old is transformed over time.

Imagining a polity in which the live hand of the present was the animating and sole directive source for its constitutive choices is to imagine a polity without a constitutional identity. More to the point, its identity would be contingently changeable, which is tantamount to not having an identity at all. As it is not "the formal legal existence of the constitution but . . . the constitution as it exists in the practices and traditions of the country" with which we are concerned, there is, the legal philosopher Joseph Raz notes, "a presumption in favor of continuity" in societies where constitutional life and legitimacy are taken seriously.[1] Such continuity—recall Burke's account—"disclose[s] [itself] only in a long space of time." For Burke's friend Samuel Johnson, it serves to distinguish human identity from that of nonthinking beings. One need only add that as a uniquely human activity, constitutional practice, conceived as a continuum connecting a distant past with an imagined future, might be thought of in much the same way.

Consistent with this presumption of continuity is an equally strong belief in the necessity for constitutional change and adaptation, a belief provided ample empirical support in research on the endurance of constitutions.[2] Thus, one of the major keys to constitutional longevity is flexibility. "Given the existence of exogenous shocks that change the costs and benefits to the parties to a constitutional bargain, constitutions require mechanisms for adjustment over time."[3] These "mechanisms"

1. Joseph Raz, "On the Authority and Interpretation of Constitutions: Some Preliminaries," in Larry Alexander, ed., *Constitutionalism: Philosophical Foundations* (Cambridge: Cambridge University Press, 1998), 175. This continuity, necessary too in many philosophical treatments of personal identity, makes possible the coherence and fit that integrity—as in an integrated constitution (and personality)—facilitates. Integrity is also prominently featured in non-jurisprudential literatures on identity—mainly the psychological and philosophical—where, by providing meanings accessible to the psyche, it plays a role not dissimilar to its functioning in constitutional identity.

2. See Zachary Elkins, Tom Ginsburg, and James Melton, *The Endurance of National Constitutions* (Cambridge: Cambridge University Press, 2010).

3. Ibid., 81.

are both formal and informal, with much of the latter occurring through exercises in constitutional interpretation by courts and other institutions. Specific changes that result from such exercises are sometimes substantial and may cause one to wonder if the changed constitution is in fact the same constitution it once was.

Raz's house analogy is intended to caution against confusing change with loss of identity, which in general is very good advice. Much as an old person differs in substantial ways from the person of his or her youth, old renovated houses and old frequently altered constitutions are different in salient respects from their earlier incarnations but arguably alike in terms of the properties that establish the sameness of identity.[4] But let us suppose that someone who grew up in a house presided over by loving parents—call them Ozzie and Harriet—returns many years later to catch a glimpse of his childhood address and discovers that it now functions as the law offices of Oswald and Hairston. Would he not be justified in concluding—sadly perhaps—that it was no longer the same house it once was, such that associating the perceived change with a loss of identity would, in fact, clarify more than confuse?

Yet, however clarifying, applying this reasoning to constitutions could also obfuscate matters if it encouraged us to think of identity purely in dichotomous terms rather than as something connected to a continuum. Thus, the language of "loss" and "gain" describes dramatic instances of identity transformation, but framing the issue in this way fails to capture the idea of identity as an evolving phenomenon in which change is compatible with continuity rather than opposed to it. Unlike structures such as houses, constitutions, I have argued, are in decisive

4. The house analogy is a variant of the identity conundrum first introduced by Plutarch in his depiction of the Ship of Theseus. "The ship wherein Theseus and the youth of Athens returned had thirty oars, and was preserved by the Athenians down even to the time of Demetrius Phalereus, for they took away the old planks as they decayed, putting in new and stronger timber in their place, insomuch that this ship became a standing example among the philosophers, for the logical question of things that grow; one side holding that the ship remained the same, and the other contending that it was not the same." Plutarch, *The Lives of the Noble Grecians and Romans,* trans. John Dryden (New York: Modern Library), 14. Indeed, the example continues to be a focal point of debate among philosophers to this day. See, for example, Brian Smart, "How to Reidentify the Ship of Theseus," 32 *Analysis* 145 (1972); and Francis W. Dauer, "How Not to Reidentify the Parthenon," 33 *Analysis* 63 (1972).

ways characterized by disharmony, a condition that generates a dialogical process that may result in changes in identity that, however significant, only rarely culminate in a wholesale transformation of the constitution. The identity of constitutions is therefore also distinguishable from the way this idea is understood in other domains: mathematics, for example. Thus in mathematical terms, an identity is an element of a set that, when combined with another in a binary operation, leaves the second unchanged.[5] But as we have seen, identity in the constitutional arena, elusive a concept as it is, can best be appreciated within a dialogical or transactional "operation" in which all elements, including identity itself, are at least potentially modifiable through their engagement with one another.

Such modifications involve a dynamic of prescriptive and disharmonic elements. The latter has both internal and external aspects to it, the first referring to tensions within a constitutional tradition, the latter to the confrontation between constitutional aspirations and the social/political setting in which they are situated. What Alasdair MacIntyre said of a "tradition of enquiry," that "it is more than a coherent movement of thought," aptly conforms to the disharmonies within the constitutional domain; thus: "those engaging in that movement become aware of it and of its direction and in self-aware fashion attempt to engage in its debates and to carry its enquiries further."[6] But the incoherences are not contained solely within the tradition (or set of constitutional arrangements) itself; occasionally they reveal their incongruities when established practices confront changing social realities that were never justifiable in the full light of the rules and principles meant to govern them.[7]

5. For the operation of addition, zero is the only identity, since $0 + 1 = 1$, $0 + 2 = 2$, . . . $0 + x = x$ for every number x. Thus combining 0 with any other number by the binary operation of addition leaves that other number unchanged. Similarly, for the binary operation of multiplication, 1 is the only identity, since $1 * 0 = 0$, $1 * 1 = 1$, $1 * 2 = 2$, . . . $1 * x = x$ for every number x. So combining 1 with any other number by the binary operation of multiplication leaves that other number unchanged.

6. Alasdair MacIntyre, *Whose Justice? Which Rationality?* (Notre Dame: Notre Dame Press, 1988), 327.

7. See, for example, Robert C. Post, "The Supreme Court, 2002 Term – Foreword: Fashioning the Legal Constitution: Culture, Courts, and Law," 117 *Harvard Law Review* 1 (2003), 10. "[C]onstitutional law will be as dynamic and contested as the cultural values and beliefs that inevitably form part of the substance of constitutional law."

To the Amendment Question

To put an actual face on these concluding observations, I want first to return to Turkey, where, as was mentioned at the outset of this book, the country's highest court had rendered a decision in 2008 invalidating two constitutional amendments that had been adopted with the support of 80 percent of the Grand National Assembly. This extraordinary move by the Constitutional Court resembles the actions taken by several other national tribunals—most notably the Indian Supreme Court—that are discussed in Chapter 2. But as noted in that chapter, the ambitious quality of the judiciary's rejection of a constitutional amendment on substantive constitutional grounds has not been matched by a deeply theorized account of the act's significance for the identity of the constitutions in question. Chapter 3, focusing on prescription and disharmony, was an effort partly to address this insufficiency through an elaboration of a conceptual framework that might elucidate the meaning of constitutional identity and demonstrate its usefulness to comparative constitutional theory. Revisiting the unconstitutional constitution conundrum through the Turkish case will serve to highlight what has been learned. In the next section I revisit the family, which, as we have seen, is an institution of enormous constitutive significance.

The Turkish amendments in question were inspired by concerns about religious liberty that, in the language acceded to by the national legislature, had been draped in an article of clothing. Since the time of Atatürk and his attack on the fez and other items of traditional Muslim attire, garments had become an important symbolic focus for the effort to re-constitute Turkish national identity; indeed, as was well understood by everyone involved in the amendments controversy, the religious liberty issue itself had a constitutive significance that transcended the debate over theologically prescribed head coverings.[8]

8. As has been vividly detailed by Bernard Lewis, Atatürk launched his assault on the fez in an August 1925 speech, in which he and his compatriots wore Panama hats for the occasion. In his speech he made clear how his sartorial concerns implicated a larger purpose: "[T]he aim of the revolutions we have been and are now accomplishing is to bring the people of the Turkish Republic into a state of society entirely modern and completely civilized in spirit and form. This is the central pillar of our Revolution, and it is necessary

Whether or not the underlying purpose of the amendments was, as described by the AK Party leader, to "change the soul of the Turkish Constitution," at a minimum it represented the next logical step in an ongoing political contest over the right of women in Turkey to wear headscarves in institutions of higher learning. For those who opposed the official ban on this religiously freighted apparel choice, the more conventional avenues to achieving their goal had been exhausted, as had been made very clear as early as 1989 in a judgment by the Constitutional Court annulling headscarf-friendly legislation.[9] Nevertheless, societal developments subsequent to that decision (including the enhancement in wealth and status of religious Turks) had markedly improved the political environment for a relaxation of the more demanding of secular requirements, with polls showing overwhelming support for allowing university students to wear the headscarf.[10] As a Turkish constitutional lawyer put it, "The rules [banning scarves, etc.] served a purpose when Turkey was forging a national identity out of the remains of the Ottoman Empire. But now Turkey has outgrown them."[11]

Outgrowing the rules implied a need to amend the principle of laicity (requiring in the Turkish experience a public space free from expressions of religious identity), which its advocates insisted was not tantamount to rejecting the Constitution's commitment to secularism. The debate in Turkey has not for the most part been between opposing forces over the question of whether the country should be committed to secular principles of governance; rather, it has centered on the true meaning of secularism, the proponents of the amendment seeking a more "passive"

---

utterly to defeat those mentalities incapable of accepting this truth." Bernard Lewis, *The Emergence of Modern Turkey*, 3rd ed. (Oxford: Oxford University Press, 2002), 410.

9. The 1989 decision received international legitimacy when the European Court of Human Rights upheld its ruling in 2005 in Leyla Sahin v. Turkey, The European Court of Human Rights, Grand Chamber, 2005, App. No. 44774/98.

10. Only 22 percent of Turks support the headscarf ban, which stands in stark contrast with a similar ban in France, where 72 percent of the population there are supportive. Ahmet T. Kuru, *Secularism and State Policies Toward Religion: The United States, France, and Turkey* (Cambridge: Cambridge University Press, 2009), 193.

11. Quoted in the *New York Times*, July 20, 1997.

secularism that would allow for a greater public visibility for religion.[12] Thus the AK Party has emphatically denied the appeal of Islamism, preferring instead to be identified with a commitment to "conservative democracy," complete with its own list of inspirational Western figures, including Edmund Burke and Michael Oakeshott.[13]

But for the defenders of the divergent Kemalist understanding, the two amendments that explicitly provided for the headscarf right clearly contradicted the very foundations of the secular state. The touchstone for the assertive secularists was Article 24: "No one shall be allowed to exploit . . . religion . . . for the purpose of maintaining personal or political interest, or for even partially basing the social, economic, political, or legal fundamental order of the state on religious tenets." These secular foundations, they maintained, were "irrevocable" under the Constitution, which meant that any effort to amend them would have to be deemed illegitimate. To that end, Article 4 states: "The provisions of Article 1 of the Constitution establishing the form of the state as a Republic, the provisions in Article 2 on the characteristics of the Republic ['a democratic, secular and social state governed by the rule of law'], and the provision of Article 3 [the state as 'an indivisible entity'] shall not be amended, nor shall their amendment be proposed." Translation: the essentials of Turkish constitutional identity are unalterable.

With a decisive nine–two vote the Constitutional Court concluded that the amendments did indeed undermine secularism, "the basic principle of the Republic," and therefore they were in express violation of the mandate of Article 2.[14] But, in doing so, the Court's bold decision raised

12. For the terms "passive" and "assertive" secularism, I draw from the work of Ahmet T. Kuru, who has very ably distinguished the meaning of these alternatives in *Secularism and State Policies Toward Religion*. Kuru analogizes the differences between these two perspectives to the competition in the United States between separationists and accommodationists, the latter more agreeable to an overtly supportive role for government in its relations with religion (ibid., 172).

13. Ibid., 178.

14. The Court's decision led many to believe that its outcome foreshadowed the much-anticipated ruling on the possible banning of the Justice and Development Party (AK Party), which at the time of the headscarf litigation was already before the Court. It came, therefore, as something of a surprise when on July 30, 2008, the Court narrowly rejected the closing option. In doing so, however, it issued a "serious warning" to the Party not to

as many questions about constitutional fundamentals as it answered, particularly with respect to the significance of its own actions. Under Article 148, which establishes the functions and powers of the Constitutional Court, the Court may examine constitutional amendments "only with regard to their form." This limited jurisdiction stands in contrast with its review power over ordinary legislation, where it is authorized to evaluate laws "in respect of both form and substance." Therefore, in striking down the amendments on substantive grounds, the Court exposed itself to the criticism that it was itself transgressing the Constitution.[15] Indeed, the amendment episode contributed a new expression to the Turkish political vocabulary: judiciary *coup d'état*.[16] And so, after its ruling people were urged to express their opposition to "the judiciary's breach of constitutional order and popular sovereignty [by] pressuring their representatives to leave aside political differences and prioritize constitutional change as the most urgent issue facing Turkey today."[17] To be sure, political affiliation can account for the most intense reactions to the decision, as in the ominous declaration, "This is the end of democracy as we know it and the emergence of juristocracy in its place."[18] But partisan hyperbole to the contrary notwithstanding, the subverting of a constitutional change supported by 441 of the country's 550 parliamentarians presents an inescapable challenge to theorists of constitutional democracy.

---

continue steering the nation in an Islamic direction. The outcome probably avoided a constitutional crisis; what remained unclear was the effect of the decision, in connection with the headscarf ruling, on the evolving Turkish constitutional identity.

15. That it did so must have taken some observers by surprise, as this statement written prior to the ruling suggests. "An attempt by the Turkish Constitutional Court to review the constitutionality of amendments made in Article 10 and 42 of the Constitution, which the Turkish Grand National Assembly passed, in terms of content such as laicity, would therefore amount to a blatant violation of the Constitution. We see no possibility that the Constitutional Court would dare to take this route." Mustafa Sentop, "The Headscarf Ban: A Quest for Solutions," *Seta Policy Brief,* March 2008, No. 8, 6. The author's sympathies for the ruling party may have colored his opinion, but given the aggressiveness of the Court's move it is unlikely that he was alone in his prediction.

16. Kuru, *State Policies Toward Religion,* 186.

17. Saban Kardas, "The Turkish Constitutional Court and Civil Liberties: Question of Ideology and Accountability," *Seta Policy Brief,* June 2008, No. 16, 6.

18. Ibid., 2.

However tendentiously put, the antidemocratic critique hardly seems far-fetched in light of the extraordinary display of judicial activism inherent in any judicial invalidation of a duly enacted constitutional amendment. Surely, it provokes one to consider the ironic possibility that in its determination to defend the secular identity of the state the Court had run afoul of its republican identity, yet there is an additional identity-related concern to consider. The indictment of the Court for abusing its authority was only partially based on procedural objections; it also had a substantive dimension: "[t]he judiciary's insistence on a static identity," and its imposition of "an archaic ideology through judicial activism."[19] In short, the accusation against the Court included the contention that it had become an impediment in the way of achieving a necessary convergence between constitutional law and the changing realities of Turkish society.[20] The rejoinder to the charge that the amendments represented a frontal assault on the Constitution's very identity was that identity must be viewed as an evolving phenomenon, the meaning and vitality of which could only be preserved if its content reflected significant shifts in societal mores and behavior.[21]

It is beyond the scope of these concluding observations to attempt anything like a comprehensive assessment of the issues raised by this case, but several points of general significance for the concept of constitutional identity are worth noting.

(1) Invocation of the irrevocability provisions of Article 4 to protect the essentials of the Turkish Constitution rests on the assumption that "the characteristics of the Republic"—i.e., secularism—have a discernible meaning and coherence that will enable political actors (the Constitutional Court?) to defend them when they are under assault, even if the

19. Ibid., 4.

20. Procedure and substance are of course inseparable. Thus "the judiciary's breach of constitutional order and popular sovereignty" prevented the system from "prioritiz[ing] constitutional change as the most urgent issue facing Turkey today," ibid.

21. These shifts are reflected in electoral politics. During the last three decades the AK Party and other center-right parties have won about 70 percent of the votes in elections in that time frame. Yet, as Ahmet T. Kuru points out, assertive secularist dominance in the military and judiciary has severely limited the impact of this electoral success. Kuru, *State Policies Toward Religion,* 183.

assault materializes through the precise form specified in the document. Let us assume that such characteristics establish the basics of the constitutional identity of the Turkish Republic. Let us also assume that we have, based on an extensive documentary record of Kemal Atatürk's radical transformation of state/religion relations in that country, a fairly clear sense of the core meaning of secularism as it had been understood by the framers of the post-Ottoman Constitution and its later incarnations. And, let us further assume that this meaning is closely tied to the Western orientation of the regime's revolutionary founders and their fervently held goal of Turkish modernization, including the belief that traditional Islam was an impediment to the achievement of that goal.

Can we then know with certainty what is and is not irrevocable when speaking of Turkish constitutional identity? Consistent with the stance taken in this book, I would suggest that an affirmative response ought to be received skeptically. The reason for such uncertainty is not unique to the Turkish case, nor does it require adherence to a theory of constitutional indeterminacy, instead it lies in the dynamic quality of identity and the dialogical process by which it is formed and develops. Turkey's secularism, for example, was not a simple product of the imagination, but was and remains embedded in a deep cultural matrix from which counterpressures to the dominant ideology exert a continuing, if irregular, force seeking a more favorable standing for religious identity, specifically for the nation's overwhelmingly Muslim majority (99 percent of the population). As noted by Bernard Lewis, "Westernization has posed grave problems of identity for a people who, after all, came from Asia, professed Islam, and belonged by old tradition to the Middle Eastern Islamic world where, for many centuries, they had been unchallenged leaders."[22] The removal of Islam from the Constitution in 1928 may

22. Lewis, *Emergence of Modern Turkey,* xi. In line with this observation, Serif Mardin concludes, "The Turkish Revolution was . . . primarily a revolution of values in which the revolutionaries still showed the influence of their Ottoman-Islamic background." Serif Mardin, *Religion, Society, and Modernity in Turkey* (Syracuse, NY: Syracuse University Press, 2006), 203. Or as a Turkish scholar has observed about that nation's problem of identity, "[T]he danger with the Republic is that while it tries to eliminate primordialism, it opens itself to being possibly kidnapped by a monological retribalization. In other words, as it shrinks the dialogical space between the public persona and self-identity and it leaves

rightly be taken to have signaled the triumph of legal secularism, but then to understand that subtraction as having excluded a religious presence from the domain of constitutional identity would be highly questionable. Rather, the pervasiveness of Islamic traditions in Turkish society strongly suggests that the content and parameters of the Constitution's secular mandate possess a mutability that varies with the relative strength of these traditions and their more worldly competitors. An Islamic presence relegated to the sidelines by a largely unchallenged judiciary and military will push the boundaries of secularism in the direction of a stronger commitment to religious liberty as its political and economic condition improves. But, any additional push fueled by theocratic ambitions will doubtless be successfully resisted as an unambiguous threat to constitutional identity.

Consequently, one way of interpreting the political struggles in Turkey today is to see them as an integral part of the give and take of identity politics: as a central element of the interactive process intrinsic to a constitutional work in progress. "Turkey is an unfinished symphony. We have been looking for a constitution for the last 150 years."[23] As the actors in this process work to shape a public consensus supportive of their positions on constitutional change and continuity, they seek to turn the discordant notes of Turkey's complex constitutionalism into a harmonious composition that, while serving their political interests, can be presented as the fulfillment of the common good. The headscarf problem is a focal point for these efforts, with both sides to the controversy drawing heavily on different parts of the nation's conflicted tradition to advance their vision of a secular republic true to the authentic voice of the Turkish people.

(2) Unlike symphonies performed for concert, there is no one composer of a constitution to whom the responsibility lies to create a work

---

itself most vulnerable to the distortions of both, when under real or imagined duress." From "Affiliation to Affinity: Citizenship in the Transition from Empire to the Nation-State," in Seyal Benhabib, Ian Shapiro, and Danilo Petranovic, *Identities, Affiliations, and Allegiances* (Cambridge: Cambridge University Press, 2007), 41.

23. Quoting Zuthtu Arslan in Brendan Sweeney, "Turkey's Search for a Workable Constitution," www.humanrights.dk/News/Turkey<#213>s+Search+for+workable=Consti tution.

that, if successful, may dazzle us with its compelling unity and harmonious compositional integrity. For all its distinctive features, the Turkish constitutional arrangement has, in the fashion of its genre, multiple creators with sometimes competing agendas, who may find themselves pressing their cases from different institutional vantage points. As the developments in Turkey illustrate, a constitution is a large piece of a nation's constitutional identity, but it is not coterminous with it. In most cases it lays down key markers of that identity that are then adapted to changing political and social realities in ways that modify, clarify, or reinforce it through the dialogical engagement of various public and private sources of influence and power.

The debate over the legitimacy of a given constitutional amendment reflects this dynamic. In the headscarf case, the Court said that a basic principle—X (secularism)—is unamendable, and that an amendment—Y—was invalid because it contradicted X; thus, its proponents were, in effect, committing an act of constitutional identity theft. The Assembly, on the other hand, while also accepting X as unamendable, viewed Y as consistent with X as well as to its commitment to basic principle Z (republicanism) and its corollary obligation to interpret X in accordance with the sovereign popular will. From its alternative perspective, the Court, by virtue of its aggressive judicial activism, was itself a perpetrator of constitutional identity theft through its improper flouting of Z. Moreover, any claim by the Court that the only valid identity-fixing meaning of X was its *own* rendering of the specific authorial intent behind X, was undermined by the embarrassing detail of X's having been included in 1982 as part of an undemocratically produced document: the only genuine voice of the constituent power was actually located in the legislative branch through its assertion of the amendment power. Therefore, not only did the Court's own unaccountability undercut its assertion of monopolistic authority over constitutive foundational questions, but its critics could argue that the document over which it claimed such authority was, by virtue of its authoritarian adoption, similarly suspect.[24]

24. This a point well made by Andrew Arato. He notes that the Court's act of striking down an amendment follows the example of the Indian Supreme Court, which, as we see in Chapter 2, has been the leading implementer of this practice. The difference? "[T]he In-

(3) The ruling by the Court did not end the legislative/judicial struggle over identity, as was made clear by the Court's subsequent decision not to use its specific power under Articles 68 and 69 to ban the country's governing party for doing things like generating unconstitutional amendments allegedly challenging the secular foundations of the state.[25] Thus, the episodic and untidy process of constitutional definition, with its thrusting and counterthrusting in and out of courtrooms, will proceed in tandem with the increasingly evident disharmony between rules and behavior with no obvious or definitive end in sight.[26] A pivotal idea of this book has been that disharmony, whether manifest in the incongruities lodged within a constitution, or, as in the Turkey case, in the gap between inscribed commitments and external realities, is the main impulse behind the shaping of constitutional identity. But to understand how it works requires serious engagement with sources from within the traditions of a polity that

---

dian Constitution was democratically made, and there the Court could arguably defend the work of the democratic *pouvoir constituant,* against mere governmental organs, including the qualified parliamentary majority. In Turkey the [1982] Constitution was an authoritarian product, and it may seem paradoxical to defend its unchangeable provisions against democratically elected parliaments." Anthony Arato, "The Turkish Constitutional Crisis and the Road Beyond," *American: A Magazine of Ideas,* June 30, 2008.

25. The report in the *New York Times* described the ruling as "hav[ing] something for everyone." *New York Times,* July 31, 2008, A6. Another way of putting it is that the outcome made it very clear that each side in this struggle over first principles came away from the confrontation with ample resources to continue pursuing their respective visions of constitutional identity.

26. As Ahmet T. Kuru notes, "The synchronization or disharmony between religiosity and dominant ideology also has certain implications on the relationship between secularism, liberalism, and democracy." Kuru, *State Policies Toward Religion,* 244. There are a number of thorny theoretical issues here, but one way to begin thinking about them is through the application of Ronald Dworkin's famous concept/conceptions distinction. Thus one might think of a constitutional provision, such as the guarantee of secularism, as laying down a general philosophical principle with which any subsequent formal constitutional change must conform. But an amendment that differs from the specific conception of the principle prevailing at the time of the original provision may still be legitimate if it is responsive to latter-day conditions while retaining the core of the original philosophical commitment. The key question then becomes Which institution, the court or the legislature, is in the best position to engage in the follow-up conceptualizing exercise? See Ronald Dworkin, *Taking Rights Seriously* (Cambridge, MA: Harvard University Press, 1977), 134–136.

extend much farther back in time than the occasions that trigger the impulse.[27]

This engagement might benefit from some of the insights in the American political development literature. As Karen Orren and Stephen Skowronek have argued, "[T]he institutions of a polity are not created or recreated all at once, in accordance with a single ordering principle; they are created instead at different times, in the light of different experiences, and often to quite contrary purposes."[28] Their emphasis on multiple orders and the conflict and reciprocal interactions that define the developmental process is appropriate too as we reflect on the evolution of constitutional identity in Turkey and elsewhere. Both passive and assertive secularism rest upon, and are traceable to, different historical moments from the constitutional pasts of Ottoman and post-Ottoman Turkey, and the contradictions that have endured throughout these periods provide the animating impulse and dynamism for the progressive realization of Turkish constitutional identity. What Orren and Skowronek say of the American Constitution has wider comparative application: "[T]he Constitution stands midway between prescriptive and positive law and in that sense is a perfect example of multiple orders. The framers clearly intended to throw over the past in important respects, but they also sought a relative permanence against the future; thus, on one hand, the difficulty of amending the Constitution and, on the other hand, the fact that the Constitution can be amended at all."[29]

27. What Rogers Smith has offered to students of American politics may have adaptive potential to the study of comparative constitutionalism: "[A] multiple traditions approach leads us to expect that the major political parties and actors will offer varying civic conceptions blending liberal, republican, and ascriptive elements in different combinations, and that important conflicts will occur over all these contrasting elements." Rogers Smith, *Civic Ideals* (New Haven, CT: Yale University Press, 1997), 8.

28. Karen Orren and Stephen Skowronek, *The Search for American Political Development* (Cambridge: Cambridge University Press, 2004), 112. Within this literature the term "intercurrence" has taken hold, meaning that a multiplicity of orders produces a political dynamic in which the resulting conflict moves the developmental process along.

29. Ibid., 180. Consider in this context Anne Norton's insightful comments: "Because it invites its own amendment even as it enjoins allegiance, it invites us to reflect upon change as the guarantor of constancy, and upon the relation of change and constancy in the definition of identity. Because it acknowledges the people as author of a text we know to have authored us, it invites us to recognize the dialectical nature of constitution." Anne Norton,

Finally, constitutionally significant disharmony also extends beyond the nation's borders. At the time of the Turkish Republic's proclamation, there was great uncertainty regarding the retention of the Caliphate, which had been a fixture for centuries in the governance of the Islamic world. Atatürk wasted little time in abolishing it, but before doing so, "The question of the Caliphate aroused interest far beyond the borders of Turkey, and brought anxious inquiries, especially from India, about the intentions of the republican regime."[30] Similar anxieties are present in the contemporary scene, with Turkey's admission into the European Union dependent in large part upon its ability to persuade the existing members of that body of nations that its internal constitutional policies were compatible with the professed values of the EEC.[31] The two sides in the headscarf controversy, for example, were acutely mindful of these distant sensibilities, and their interpretations of the basic principles of secularism and republicanism were developed to appeal to both foreign and domestic audiences. Indeed, from the American Declaration of Independence's gesture to "a decent Respect to the Opinions of Mankind," to the Israeli Declaration's embrace of a set of principles that would gain "them title to rank with the peoples who founded the United Nations," to the framers of the South African Constitution who provided explicit instructions for aligning their law with the standards of the international community, the process of shaping a constitutional identity has entailed dialogical engagement in several dimensions, including the transnational.

"Transubstantiation: The Dialectic of Constitutional Authority," 55 *University of Chicago Law Review* (1988), 472.

30. Lewis, *Emergence of Modern Turkey,* 262.

31. For example, the reaction to the Court's decision not to close the AK Party emphasized this aspect. "[The Court] took the domestic and international context into account. Fierce opposition within the country to the case in general, outright reprimand from the European Union and belated yet consistent probing from Washington all played their part in determining the outcome." Soli Ozel, "The Court Blinks," *G/M/F News,* August 5, 2008, 2.

To the Family

Engagement with the international community, both in achieving conformity (or not) with extra-national norms and charters, and in determining the permeability of constitutional borders, can be an important factor in the evolution of a nation's constitutional identity. Often, as we saw in the attention to the family in Chapter 5, this externally directed engagement is an extension of the more general effort in which, according to Anne Norton, "the material world questions the constitutive text."[32] Such was the case in Ireland, where, as ex-President Mary Robinson (and later United Nations High Commissioner for Human Rights) pointed out, the nation's constitutional identity required continual adaptation to changing material circumstances; therefore, to the extent that the family figured prominently in filling out the substance of Irish constitutional identity, the latter's meaning would be greatly effected by how emerging disharmonies between the constitution of text/tradition and the "constitution of the people"[33] came ultimately to be resolved.

Revisiting the family will facilitate recapitulation of my principal arguments, but instead of returning to the national venues of Chapters 5 and 6, consider another example taken from a very different place: South Korea, where, as in many other nations, the Constitutional Court has come to play a major discursive role in defining and elaborating the fundamentals of constitutional identity.[34] In the Korean context this often means determining the place of Confucianism in that country's political and social life; not surprisingly, the institution of the family is a critical locus for these constitutive determinations.[35]

32. Norton, "Transubstantiation," 470.

33. Ibid., 469.

34. For an excellent treatment of how the Korean Constitutional Court came to play a major role in Korean politics and social life, see Tom Ginsburg, *Judicial Review in New Democracies: Constitutional Courts in Asian Cases* (Cambridge: Cambridge University Press, 2003), 206–246.

35. My focus on Confucianism's place in Korean constitutional identity is not intended to obscure the fact that a complete assessment of this subject would have to concentrate as well on such critical determining factors as the rivalry between North and South, the development of a market economy, and the dramatic political transition from colonial domination.

While the Korean Constitution makes no explicit mention of Confucianism, "Confucian culture provides the tools with which Koreans interpret and give order to the world around them."[36] The Constitution also makes scant reference to the family, and to the extent that it does it says only that marriage and family life must be "sustained on the basis of individual dignity and equality of the sexes."[37] It is widely understood, however, that the family is the basis of individual identity in Korea, and that to one degree or another Confucianism remains a highly salient presence in the configuration and behavior of that institution.[38] That it does is unsurprising, as it is in South Korea perhaps more than anywhere else that Confucian traditions have penetrated deeply into the social relations of the population. Indeed, the absence of any specific reference to Confucianism in the Constitution may be less significant than at first it seems; the opening line of the Preamble speaks of pride in "traditions dating from time immemorial."[39] One of these traditions is Confucianism.

Yet the Preamble also emphasizes the Constitution's "mission of democratic reform," language consistent with Article 36's egalitarian and libertarian commitment to the family, and thus potentially in conflict with the

36. Chaihark Hahm, "Law, Culture, and the Politics of Confucianism," 16 *Columbia Journal of Asian Law* 2003, 257. This view runs in the family. Chaihark Hahm's late father, the noted diplomat and legal scholar, Hahm Pyong-choon, wrote of Confucianism that it "still remains the moral foundation of the nation." Hahm Pyong-choon, *Korean Jurisprudence, Politics, and Culture* (Seoul: Yonsei University Press, 1986), 161. The elder Hahm wrote prior to the adoption of the current and most democratic constitution. It is interesting that this event—and the dramatic changes in Korean society occurring since—does not appear to have led the son, also a distinguished constitutional scholar, to have concluded differently with regard to the importance of Confucian culture.

37. Article 36. In addition, "The State shall endeavor to protect mothers."

38. See, for example, Hahm Chaibong, "Family Versus the Individual: The Politics of Marriage Laws in Korea," in Daniel A. Bell and Hahm Chaibong, eds., *Confucianism for the Modern World* (Cambridge: Cambridge University Press, 2007), 336.

39. As Jibong Lim has noted, "By starting with a reference to tradition and history, the Korean Constitution emphasizes that the political community has not been formed accidentally or even by choice, but is based on a cultural community formed by shared history and tradition." Jibong Lim, "The Korean Constitutional Court, Judicial Activism, and Social Change," in Tom Ginsburg, ed., *Legal Reform in Korea* (London: RoutledgeCurzon, 2004), 22.

Confucian tradition's hierarchical and communitarian norms. So if, as it has been described, the Korean family is not only the foundation of one's identity, "but also the repository of all the values and mores deemed essential for human flourishing,"[40] the balance that is struck between a prescriptive constitution, part of which contains values in tension with the constitutional text and, increasingly, in Norton's terms, with the constitution of the people, will determine to a great degree the substance of Korean constitutional identity.

The prescriptive constitution did not disappear with the commencement of the Sixth Republic under the current Constitution, even if in the minds of some critics in Korea "Confucianism is a dead tradition that has been (justifiably) relegated to the dustbin of history."[41] It did confront the realities of newly codified democratic aspirations and a rapidly modernizing society, that, in the instance of the family, ensured (as we have seen in the Irish case) some movement between the polarities of acquiescence and militancy as far as the Constitution's relations with that institution and the extant social order are concerned. In terms of the conceptual framework detailed in Chapter 5, the acquiescent model was surely dominant during the period of constitutional rule in Korea when the old tradition occupied a more commanding position within the society. "[T]he line between the family and the state never became [for neo-Confucians] so distinct as to make the two realms incompatible. If anything, a great deal of emphasis was placed on ensuring perfect compatibility and harmony between them."[42] But at least since 1945, and certainly after the 1988 constitutional transformation, the traditional, Confucian-based family has been under assault. As a result, a prescriptive constitution comprising a vital Confucian component has increasingly confronted the challenges of constitutional disharmony.

If it were correct that the Confucian component of Korean constitutional culture has become a "dead tradition," its demise, at least in the sense delineated by Alasdair MacIntyre in Chapter 3, might be deemed

40. Ibid., 335.

41. Daniel A. Bell and Hahm Chaibong, "Introduction: The Contemporary Relevance of Confucianism," in Bell, *Confucianism*, 3. This, to be clear, is not the view of the authors, who see Confucian thought as a still vital presence in Korea.

42. Chaibong, "Family Versus the Individual," 356.

attributable to the failure of a monolithic tradition to renew itself over time. For some scholars reports of the tradition's death are decidedly premature, since "Confucianism [has] constantly renewed itself by coming to terms with the dominant philosophical orientations of the time. . . ."[43] Such an understanding is consistent with the view taken in this book; namely, that constitutional identity develops dialogically and usually incrementally and involves interpretive and political activity that follows from the inevitable disharmonies present in the constitutional condition. Chaihark Hahm points out that the Korean Constitutional Court has become a forum "for contesting certain long-standing practices whose normative meanings are supported by Confucian concepts, rhetoric, and symbols."[44] From this arena of contestation one can discern the outlines of an evolving Korean constitutional identity, as "the newer language of rule of law and individual rights becomes intermingled with the older language informed with Confucian signs and symbols."[45] But before it crystallizes into something less ephemeral than an outline, it must engage with other decision-making arenas, most importantly the lawmaking branch, where the imprimatur of legislative endorsement can be attached to, or withheld from, newly interpreted and revised legal conceptualizations.

The Constitutional Court's landmark decision in a uniquely Korean case concerning the family is illustrative of this dynamic. In 1997 the Court considered the constitutionality of a section of the Civil Code (Article 809) that prohibited marriages of persons with the same family name and geographical origin (or "ancestral seat").[46] In Korea, the notion of an ancestral seat *(dongseong bongwon)* has long been important in establishing a person's legal identity, but the prohibition against marriage of two individuals sharing the same surname (e.g., Kim) and ancestral

43. Bell, "Contemporary Relevance of Confucianism," 26. Similarly, Chaihark Hahm writes, "To obsess about arriving at 'the essence' of Confucianism is to ignore the fact that, as a living tradition, Confucianism has always undergone revisions and transformations." Chaihark Hahm, "Constitutionalism, Confucian Civic Virtue, and Ritual Propriety," in Bell, *Confucianism,* 48.

44. Hahm, "Politics of Confucianism," 280.

45. Ibid., 301. Here, as in the Turkish case, Orren and Skowronek's multiple-orders approach might profitably be employed to comprehend these developments.

46. "A marriage may not be allowed between blood relatives, if both surname and its origin are common to the parties."

seat (e.g., Kimhae) also meant that many people were not able to marry in accordance with their wishes.[47] However restrictive such a centuries-old policy might seem to be as a curtailment of individual liberty, it could also be viewed as "the most concrete mechanism by which family identities were maintained, thereby insuring the integrity of the family as a sociopolitical institution."[48] Indeed, in Confucian tradition the achievement of a well-ordered society had long been thought to hinge on the existence of this marriage prohibition, so contesting its validity had potentially significant implications for ascertaining the place of Confucianism in contemporary Korean life.[49]

The Court's decision was a "modified" judgment (or Decision of Disagreement with the Constitution) that the provision of the Civil Code was "incompatible with the Constitution."[50] While seven of the nine Justices thought the section unconstitutional, only five of them held that it should be voided immediately, one less than the constitutional requirement that there be a concurrence of six justices to invalidate a law (Article 113). "Marriage between close relatives should be regulated by civil codes other than Code 809 while the actual extent of the prohibition should be left to social ethics and morality to decide"[51]; thus the ruling was accompanied by instructions to the National Assembly to revise or repeal the provision in light of the judgment of the Court. Failure to act by the end of 1998 would render the law null and void. But until then, all courts and government agencies were instructed not to apply it.

The justices offered competing perspectives on a range of issues, including differing accounts of the indigenous character of the marriage

47. For example, Chaihark Hahm notes that the number of Kims from a place called Kimhae is nearly four million. Inasmuch as South Korea has a population of just over forty-seven million people, "this is not an insignificant restriction on one's choice of marriage partners." Hahm, "Politics of Confucianism," 288. The same problem presented itself to members of the two other large Korean clans, the Milyang Parks and the Jeonju Lees.

48. Chaibong, "Family Versus the Individual," 336.

49. Projecting its significance can also lead to some hyperbole: "The outlawing of the prohibition against interclan marriage will signify the end of one civilization and the beginning of another. What we are witnessing . . . is a 'clash of civilizations'" (ibid., 358).

50. *Same-Surname-Same-Origin Marriage Ban* case (95 Hun-Ka6 on Article 809 (1) of the Civil Act) (1997).

51. Quoted in Chaibong, "Family Versus the Individual," 337.

ban (was it in fact a Chinese import?), and alternative readings of how the dramatic socioeconomic transformations in Korea might have affected the institution of marriage. These disagreements were incorporated within a larger interpretive division over Korean constitutional identity, with the majority emphasizing the specific individualist and egalitarian language of the constitutional text, and the dissenters favoring a more traditional cultural reading consistent with the document's less definitive injunction in Article 9 that "The State shall strive to sustain and develop cultural heritages and to enhance national culture."[52] According to the majority, "The law against marriages between members of the same agnatic lineage descendants violates the dignity of human beings and the right to the pursuit of happiness as guaranteed by the Constitution as well as the right to free marriages and equality."[53] Moreover, "The majority of the public's concept of marriage has changed from one of 'a union between families' to one of 'a union between persons,' reflecting the respect for a person's free will."[54]

The minority's position was consistent with the neo-Confucian embrace of the marriage prohibition as essential to ensuring the survival of a family system whose "sense of identity [was] based on continuity through successive generations. . . ."[55] Extrapolating from the identity of the family to the identity of the broader polity of which that institution has by wide acknowledgment been central, a judicial holding that in effect ended the continuity of cultural practices as constitutive as those involved in the surname/ancestral seat case, would likely have major consequences for Korean constitutional identity. The dilemma was this: clearly the hierarchical, authoritarian, patriarchal nature of the traditional family structure had become increasingly anachronistic in the rapidly changing social order of late twentieth-century South Korea; on the other hand, that family system had its virtues, not the least of which was its role in "fostering a sense of intimacy and caring

52. There is wide agreement among Korean constitutional scholars that the idea of the *Kulturstaat* (derived from German constitutional theory) is an important element of Korean constitutional jurisprudence.

53. As quoted in en.wikipedia.org/wiki/Article_809_of_the_Korean Civil Code.

54. Ibid.

55. Chaibong, "Family Versus the Individual," 356.

that most 'civil societies' tend to lack."[56] Should the Confucian conception of the family be "given a rearticulation that is appropriate for the modern world,"[57] the interactive dynamics of the prescriptive and disharmonic features of the constitutional order would, as described in previous chapters, determine the scope and meaning of the resulting changes.

Indeed, the political follow-up to the Court's decision makes sense precisely in these terms. In November 1998 the Ministry of Justice presented to the National Assembly a reform bill that included the repeal of Article 809. Confucian groups were, of course, intensely opposed to the repeal, and the National Assembly's Sub-committee on Law excised the article from the larger bill. A year later, the Subcommittee stated: "In view of the national sentiment which places a great deal of importance on bloodline the abolition of the law prohibiting marriages between people with the same surnames and ancestral seats is premature."[58] Consistent with this sentiment, an amendment was passed maintaining the prohibition in the face of the other two branches' insistence that the old law had ceased to be operative. The resulting confusion persisted until after the April 2004 elections when the Ministry of Justice reintroduced its Family Law Reform Bill, which the National Assembly passed in March 2005. Included in it was an altered version of Article 809 that maintained the prohibition in a form that had diminished its restrictive impact on the subject population.

According to one insightful account, this episode "highlight[s] the law's entanglement in the process of cultural negotiation and adaptation."[59] It suggests that constitutional adjudication can serve as a critical venue for determining the significance of the Confucian tradition for contemporary Korean identity. This assessment seems eminently reasonable as long as we broaden the venue for ultimate determination of the identity question. What the Court was able to accomplish in deciding the sur-

56. Ibid., 358.

57. Ibid.

58. As quoted in en.wikipedia.org/wiki/Article_809_of_the_Korean Civil Code.

59. Hahm, "Politics of Confucianism," 300.

name/ancestral seat case was to attach a constitutional imprimatur to a radically more individualistic model of the family than had previously been sanctioned by high institutional authority. To be sure, its success in doing so did not require extraordinary flights of imagination, as the nation's constitution—the formal text that is—was easily able to accommodate the greater freedoms associated with the modern nuclear family as we have seen. But, as I have argued in these pages, constitutional identity involves more than just the official charter of a nation; it incorporates the prescriptive constitution as well, which includes long-standing commitments and sanctioned practices that may be at odds with the language of the document currently in force. That text's silence with respect to the Confucian tradition, much like the Turkish Constitution's muteness about Islam, had not denuded Korean constitutional identity of a Confucian presence, even as the demands of modernity challenged assumptions at the very core of its structure of social relations. Even so, as MacIntyre argued, "Incoherences in the established system of beliefs may become evident. Confrontation by new situations, engendering new questions, may reveal within established practices and beliefs a lack of resources for offering or for justifying answers to those new questions."[60]

To become a vital part of an evolving Korean constitutional identity, Confucianism's prescriptive power, which incorporates a presumption in favor of the continuity of settled practices, must also be open to a debate about its mutability. Thus, we see the "renegotiation of Confucianism's cultural meaning"[61] taking place within a constitutionally structured arrangement that deploys disharmony as a valued asset in a necessary process of renegotiation and recalibration. The dialogical interactions among political institutions that connect in different ways to the older tradition is forging a constitutional identity that incorporates the Confucian component of the Korean inheritance as an important cultural strand whose considerable intellectual resources enable it to engage divergent moral sensibilities and become transformed in the

60. MacIntyre, *Whose Justice?* 355.

61. Hahm, "Politics of Confucianism," 301.

process.[62] The National Assembly ensures that there will be an effective voice for maintaining traditional values in family relations, but in confronting the dominant commitment in the constitutional text as voiced through the Constitutional Court, those values are being subordinated, if not totally rejected. Whether this will result in a modified Confucian tradition or an unmodified tradition with a greatly diminished impact on Korean society is for others to say. But as we have seen before, the development of a constitutional self will embody the specific components of an identity that evolves as these elements play off against each other within the circumscribed parameters of the national historical narrative.

The Disharmonic Constitution

Why conclude this study with two examples—Turkey and South Korea—that have not been featured previously? Moreover, unlike these cases, the countries receiving most of my attention—India, Israel, Ireland, and the United States—are sufficiently alike in their histories to constitute a logi-

62. Interestingly, that older tradition did not see disharmony as a virtue; indeed, as Hahm Pyong-choon pointed out, "[T]he traditional culture of Korea . . . took the extreme position of refusing to admit the inevitability, let alone the indispensability, of conflict in human life. . . . Unlike some of the better known strains in the Occidental philosophy which have concluded that human progress derives its motive force from the 'dialectical tension' inherent in a conflict, the Korean [Confucian] culture looked upon conflict as an instance of human failure." Pyong-choon, *Korean Jurisprudence,* 243. One way of making sense of this seeming paradox may be found in an argument put forward by the constitutional theorist Will Harris, which states that "Any distinct constitution will have specific traits matched to itself, as negative *attributes,* which, when assembled, set up a comprehensively negative alternative constitution." Will Harris, "Constitution of Failure: The Architectonics of a Well-Founded Constitutional Order," in Stephen Macedo and Jeffrey Tulis, eds., *The Limits of Constitutional Democracy* (Princeton: Princeton University Press, forthcoming 2010). The claim is that in founding a constitutional order, framers incorporate both positive and negative constitutions within their creation, as exemplified by the Americans, who, Harris contends, did so by establishing a constitution of "chaos and furor" as well as one of "self-sustaining unity and order." Harris, "Constitution of failure." The result, I would argue, is a disharmonic dynamic that provides the energy for the development of constitutional identity, as has been the case in South Korea and elsewhere.

cal cohort for a sustained inquiry into questions concerning identity. All of these nations were at one time under the dominion of British imperial rule, and in all instances their postindependence constitutional identities have been substantially affected by colonial policies bearing directly upon the relations of major population groups within their respective polities.

Nevertheless, this family of nations has seen its individual members develop in very different directions. Their common source of origin may explain certain features peculiar to all of them; for example, the absence of a specially designed court to adjudicate constitutional issues, the presence of a jurisprudence rooted in the common law. On the other hand, the differences are often striking. Israel lacks a formal comprehensive constitutional document; India adopted the longest one in the world. The United States has a constitution that is extremely difficult to amend; Ireland and India provide relatively easy paths to formal constitutional change. And as we have seen with respect to the institutions of civil society—notably the family—there is great variability among these nations with regard to how protective their constitutional orientations are toward existing structures of private power.

Indeed, with respect to two issues that have figured prominently in this study—(1) judicial authority to declare a constitutional amendment unconstitutional, and (2) the constitutional status of the family vis-à-vis the state—the accounts from Turkey and South Korea each arguably bears a stronger resemblance to one or another of the earlier considered countries than we find in the similarities between nations within the featured cohort itself. Thus, the Turkish Constitutional Court's invalidation of the headscarf amendment was comparable in its boldness and audacity to the Indian Supreme Court's overturning of several amendments for transgressing its basic structure doctrine on constitutional inviolability. And, the changes in family structure authorized by the Korean Constitutional Court mirror developments in Ireland that were responsive to a notion of the family conceived in terms of the needs of its individual members, rather than as a unit configured according to traditional gendered and religious (or in the case of Korea, quasi-religious) roles. In both cases a more interventionist and less acquiescent interpretive framework provided legitimation for changes not only for the institution of the family, but potentially also for the larger evolution in constitutional identity of which it was a part.[63]

What this suggests is that the dynamics of constitutional identity are less the result of any specific set of background cultural or historical factors than the expression of a developmental process endemic to the phenomenon of constitutionalism. With important differences in political, cultural, and institutional arrangements there will obviously be great variation across countries in the specific ways in which the process unfolds, but comparative inquiry would do well to pursue the question of constitutional identity in light of a conceptual framework reflective of the constitutional condition more generally.[64] To this end I offer four summary observations that may help in the further exploration of our subject:

(1) The text is a start.

To establish the identity of a constitution, it obviously makes sense to scrutinize carefully the text itself. This provides us with a documentary transcript of how a particular group of framers provided for the governance of their polity, and it often includes their aspirations for its subsequent development. These aspirations may coexist harmoniously within the four corners of the document, or their articulation may reveal, ex-

63. By "mirror" I do not mean to minimize the differences in these two cases. Catholicism in Ireland is explicitly referenced in the Irish Constitution in a way that Confucianism is not in the Korean counterpart. It has also been a more dominant presence in Irish life, with a once-powerful ecclesiastical order possessing sanctions of no small consequence for the Irish people. But the constitutional politics in both countries are comparable as one tracks the legal changes that are occurring as a result of shifting sensibilities in the population on key issues of constitutive significance. The Court majority in the Korean case used language that one might expect to find in a contemporary Irish case: "The traditional culture we should really sustain and develop . . . is the traditional ethics and a sense of morality that fit into the social and economic environment of this epoch and has universal validity in this society." Quoted in Lim, "Korean Constitutional Court," 35.

64. As Beau Breslin points out, "[T]he question of *how* a regime alters its collective identity through the process of constitutional transformation depends on the specifics of a polity's particular historical narrative: no two transformations are exactly alike." Beau Breslin, *From Words to Worlds: Exploring Constitutional Functionality* (Baltimore: The Johns Hopkins University Press, 2009), 30. My point, however, is that transcending the variability in historical narratives is a dynamic that is common to all constitutional polities.

plicitly or implicitly, a certain dissonance that will need to be addressed through the constitutional politics that commences with the adoption of the document. Still, a perfectly harmonious constitution is an illusion, as will be evident once we agree that the object of our interest is only partly incorporated in any given written charter.

Thus, as Hanna Pitkin suggests, "[H]ow we are able to constitute ourselves is profoundly tied to how we are already constituted by our own distinctive history."[65] We need not adopt the specific Burkean formulation of the prescriptive constitution, "whose sole authority is, that it has existed time out of mind," to understand that submission to the authority of constitutional rule is bound up in the narrative of a people's prior experiences, that the constitution is "less something we *have* than something we *are*."[66] But who we are is also entwined in the conflicts of the past, which do not dissipate with the inception of a new constitutional experiment, even one that culminates in a seemingly coherent document. There will be common historical reference points; for example, in our principal cases an extended resistance to a colonial empire that established a political ethos as the backdrop to, and perhaps the backbone of, the new constitutional transition. Invariably, however, these shared memories will be recalled from different places on the political spectrum—in India, by Muslims, Hindu nationalists, and reform-minded Hindus; in the United States, by abolitionists and slaveholders; in Israel, by Zionists of varied persuasions; in Ireland, by conservative ecclesiastically oriented Catholics and affiliates more imbued with the social gospel—and these too will become part of the broader constitutional tradition that will shape and drive the dynamics of constitutional identity. Only by distinguishing the constitutional text from the constitutional order will this process become clear to us.

(2) Bounded fluidity.

The future of constitutional identity is inscribed in its past. Recall the first part of the Indian jurist's injunction: "[*T*]*he Constitution is a precious heritage;* therefore you cannot destroy its identity." For others, of

65. Hanna Fenichal Pitkin, "The Idea of a Constitution," 37 *Journal of Legal Education* (1987), 169.

66. Ibid., 167.

course, the Constitution need not be viewed in this way at all. To them it is the Constitution's *deplorable* heritage that stands out, in which case its identity perhaps *should* be destroyed and reconstituted. Or, as is likely the case for most people, the Constitution's heritage is, in the cold light of political and social transformation, a mixed blessing, leaving open the question of how and whether its identity might be changed.

As to the prescriptive component of identity, there is great diversity among constitutions regarding the degree of continuity that prevails over time. Formal constitutions display varying measures of defiance and compliance toward the legacies bequeathed to the founding generation. While a defiant or confrontational constitution—for example, South Africa's—may proclaim its transformational document as a "birth certificate of a nation," its emerging identity cannot fully escape the past, including some of those aspects that persist as searing memories in the recollections of its new citizens. Even when a nation experiences a great rupture in its constitutional development, "Some core of shared belief, constitutive of allegiance to the tradition, has to survive every rupture."[67] And so, along with the fresh commitment to a regime of universalist aspirations, consistent with Alasdair MacIntyre's reflection on intellectual traditions, the Constitution includes communitarian obligations that, while arguably designed with the best of intentions, carry with them the burdens of a complicated and troubled past.

Much of the mutability of constitutional identity is traceable to the disharmony within the constitution, but the strands that constitute the tension in this disharmony also set limits on the nature of the change engendered. Consider in this regard Eamon de Valera, the principal author of the Irish Constitution, who was at once the embodiment of a democratic vision for his country, but also, as Bill Kissane notes, the "symbol of the intensely conservative society he presided over for so long."[68] The democratic ethos of the 1922 Constitution was retained and

67. MacIntyre, *Whose Justice?* 356. H. Jefferson Powell's discussion of MacIntyre pertains to this point: "[I]f constitutionalism is a MacIntyrean tradition, it should be possible to find at any given time one or more . . . identities that embody the constitutional tradition's commitments and display its virtues." H. Jefferson Powell, *The Moral Tradition of American Constitutionalism* (Durham: Duke University Press, 1993), 37.

68. Bill Kissane, "Eamon de Valera and the Survival of Democracy in Inter-War Ireland," 42 *Journal of Contemporary History* (2007), 211.

expanded in the 1937 incarnation and conjoined with a religious commitment that, while absent in the text of the earlier document, had long been at the core of the nation's prescriptive constitution. Just as the 1922 Constitution had not entrenched a constitutional identity within its text, neither had the 1937 version; but it did establish the broad parameters within which that identity would evolve. Moreover, both the democratic and Catholic traditions were themselves fractured traditions, which, much like the analogous developments in India and elsewhere, provided additional impetus for the dialogical engagements that propelled Irish constitutional identity. As problematic as the idea of an immutable or static identity is, so too is the belief that the modifications of it are unconstrained by the traditions that carried it to its transformative moment.

(3) The disharmonic invitation.

Whether by design or by accident the dissonance in a polity's formal constitution functions as a provocation to change. Much of what derives from the discord will have an interpretive aspect to it—"[i]nterpretation . . . lives in dialectical tension"[69]—although we would be remiss if this led us to a narrow focus on the activity of courts. The judiciary is of course a principal actor in the shaping of constitutional identity, but it is rarely a unilateral actor. As Keith Whittington explains, "The constitutional choices made with the drafting and ratification of the text only partially covers the field. . . . A great deal has to be worked out in subsequent practice, most familiarly through judicial interpretation of the Constitution but routinely and importantly through political action that construes, implements, and extends the constitutional text."[70] Viewed from a comparative perspective, Lincoln's response to the Supreme Court's decision in the *Dred Scott* case, in which he summoned nonrobed political actors to rectify the errors of the Court by addressing the

69. Raz, "Interpretation of Constitutions," 180. "Constitutional interpretation is central to constitutional adjudication because courts are faced with conflicting moral considerations, some militating for continuity, and therefore for giving affect to the constitution as it is at that moment, and some pointing to the need to develop and improve it" (ibid., 183).

70. Keith E. Whittington, *Political Foundations of Judicial Supremacy: The Presidency, the Supreme Court, and Constitutional Leadership in U.S. History* (Princeton, NJ: Princeton University Press, 2007), 291.

most constitutive of all issues facing the nation, seems less remarkable than it sometimes does in the United States. Although the political incentives for passing the buck on a regime's "meta-narrative" from the more transparently political institutions to the courts has been well documented,[71] a pattern of interactive institutional involvement in such questions is nevertheless ubiquitous. As exemplified by the experiences in Israel and Turkey, the contesting strands in a nation's constitutional tradition will find their alternative visions embodied in competing power centers, leading to activity that may serve to clarify the uncertainties surrounding constitutional identity or expand its meaning in a particular direction.

The disharmonic invitation may, as we have seen, extend beyond the nation's borders. This occurs as a stage in the adjudicative process, in which one side of a divided constitutional legacy seeks to benefit from an expansion in the scope of conflict by having its cause adopted by an extraterritorial body with authority to intervene in a domestic dispute, as famously happened in Ireland. For the larger question of identity this should not, however, be viewed as a simple transference of decision making to an external source of authority, so much as it is a step in a multipronged constitutional give-and-take stimulated by the imperfections naturally revealed in disharmony. "[T]hese imperfections" are at once "the source of our troubles [and] . . . the source of our greatness."[72] They may exist as contradictions embodied in a constitutional text or as the inevitable disjunction between the actual and the ideal provided for in a constitutional document. As I argue in Chapter 4, constitutional borrowing, the seeking of guidance from foreign sources, offers appealing prospects for overcoming imperfection, but there is, at least in the United States, fierce opposition to the practice. Often expressed as a

71. See Ran Hirschl, "The Judicialization of Mega-Politics and the Rise of Political Courts," 11 *Annual Review of Political Science* (2008).

72. Norton, "Transubstantiation," 469. In this regard, I basically agree with Sarah Harding: "Dialogue, diversity, and even ambiguity are not indications or harbingers of a weakening system but rather the foundation of a distinctive and stable legal identity." Sarah Harding, "Comparative Reasoning and Judicial review," 28 *The Yale Journal of International Law* 410 (2003), 464. The stability of the legal identity should not, however, be confused with its immutability, a condition never to be presumed.

warning about the loss of identity, this fear is not entirely misplaced, although it is not so much a loss of identity that is at stake as much as it is the direction in which constitutional identity might evolve through engagement with foreign law. Like all invitations, however, this one can be declined, and we should be as interested in the nonacceptances as we are with the acceptances. In both cases they will illuminate the jurisprudence of the local court, and through it, the constitutional identity of the larger constitutional order.

(4) The balance of internal and external disharmonies.

The disharmony internal to a constitutional text will ordinarily not be as prominent as it is, for example, in Israel. Indeed, in many polities it will be deftly obscured in the mists of compromise language authored by determined constitution makers. But for the comparative constitutional theorist, Israel's evolving formal constitution only renders more transparent than elsewhere a process that is unusual in that nation mainly for the quality of its translucence. The same dynamic, however, is in place—if in less bold relief—wherever competing commitments or aspirations internal to a constitution engage each other while concurrently being deployed in a dialectical relationship with energized forces in the larger social order. This is, in fact, likely to be the case wherever we look, with the development of constitutional identity varying to the extent that internal and external disharmonies are weighted differently as we travel from country to country.

If constitutions are distinguishable according to the degree to which their internal disharmonies are deeply inscribed, so too are they diversely situated commensurate with their relationship to the surrounding social order. For example, the constitutional texts in polities such as India, South Africa, and Turkey display an aggressive stance toward entrenched societal structures, whose existence became suspect under the provisions and ethos of the document adopted in those polities. To be sure, in each of these places status quo interests were not left bereft of constitutionally sanctioned recourse to defend their interests, but the balance between internal and external disharmonies was weighted more heavily toward the latter, such that the earliest constitutional identity in the three countries possessed a fairly unambiguous confrontational character. As the course of constitutional politics unfolded, the dissonance within the document (a reflection of divisions within the society) served to mitigate or restrain the movement toward an unalloyed realization of the identity embodied in the dominant official ethos of constitutional militancy.

Finally, consider the American Constitution. On its face, the 1787 document can scarcely be called confrontational with respect to the institution of slavery; indeed, there is language that is clearly complacent toward its existence. But even that language—requiring, for example, the end of the slave trade in twenty years—indicates a level of internal disharmony that is at least consistent with the many contentious debates surrounding that issue during the framing of the Constitution. However, once the constitutional order is widened to include a philosophical tradition that incorporates the nation's founding document, American constitutional identity assumes an aspirational dimension incompatible with the holding of human beings as property. This was the view held by Abraham Lincoln and eventually Frederick Douglass, both of whom in effect emphasized the profound discordance between constitution and social order.

One need not adopt their aspirational perspective—and many progressives in their time as well as prominent scholars in ours have not—to recognize the dynamic through which an antidiscrimination principle became a fundamental component of American constitutional identity. In contrast with India and Turkey, over the years the American document (if not always its interpretation) took on a more aggressive stance toward entrenched interests, at least those implicated in the most egregious of the society's inequalities. The Civil War and the amendments that followed in its wake either radically reconstituted the American polity or enabled it in time to make due on its inaugural promise. While I favor the second account, the dialogical interaction of internal and external constitutional disharmonies is discernible regardless of one's interpretive preference. Thus, codification by the post-war amendments of the principle of equal treatment was a signal moment in the development of American constitutional identity, marking the official ascendance of the universalist strand in the nation's conflicted constitutional tradition. But the system's highly fragmented distribution of political power guaranteed that the other more particularistic strand in that tradition would not lack for institutional muscle as its advocates fought to undermine the constitutive significance of the changes wrought through the amendment process. The constitutional identity of the text may have changed, but the constitutional identity of the American people (citizens and public officials) was only beginning its transformation. Ultimately, stability in the identity of the constitutional order depended on convergence of the two.

In considering the much chronicled struggle that followed, a protracted contest involving multiple interventions by political actors distributed across institutions and between levels of government, all responding differently to pressures emanating from a constantly shifting social landscape, there is good reason to portray the process as a uniquely American story.[73] A century after the Constitution's altering, the gap between the ideal and the actual was greatly narrowed, as the "unending dialectic of becoming and overcoming"[74] produced rough alignment between text and behavior. The "promise of disharmony"[75] was, indeed, the aptly turned phrase of Samuel Huntington to describe the exceptional character of American politics. That the characterization works as well for how we think about constitutional identity is, however, unrelated to the question of exceptionalism; rather, it speaks to the presence of a constitutional dynamic of more general comparative applicability. Thus, the uniqueness of the American story—or for that matter the uniqueness of the Indian, Irish, and Israeli stories—should be understood as a variation on a common theme. In this sense, constitutions are a lot like music: their disharmonies are intrinsic to their nature, conditioned by local circumstance and tradition, and necessary for the realization of the enterprise.

73. See, for example, Michael Klarman, *Unfinished Business: Racial Equality in American History* (Oxford: Oxford University Press, 2007).

74. Norton, "Transubstantiation," 463.

75. Samuel Huntington, *American Politics: The Promise of Disharmony* (Cambridge, MA: Harvard University Press, 1981).

Index

Abortion, 188; information amendment, 46, 48, 49, 265; Ireland and, 191, 195–201, 259–266; rape victims and, 191n161; militant constitutions and identity, 259–266

Abortion Information case, 199

Ackerman, Bruce, 15–16, 17, 17n40, 32, 44n23, 81n119, 95n29

Acquiescent constitutionalism, 11, 23, 25, 153; militant constitutions, 226–252. *See also* India; Ireland

Adalah v. Minister of Interior, 278

Adalah v. Municipality of Tel Aviv, 166n92

African Americans, 223n27. *See also* Slavery

After Virtue (MacIntyre), 91

Agnes, Flavia, 250

Agranat, Shimon, 295n67

AK Party. *See* Justice and Development Party

Alford, William, 141, 142

Amar, Akhil Reed, 39n13

Ambedkar, B. D., 148, 170, 213, 220, 249

Amendments, 17n40; unconstitutional constitutions and, 34–83; dismemberment, 50; nullifying, 59–60, 59n63; problematic, 70; question of, 327–337

Amendments, India: twenty-fourth, 54; thirty-ninth, 56–57; forty-second, 57, 241n81; thirty-eighth, 57

Amendments, Ireland: process, 41–49; eighth, 45, 196–198, 254n118; fourteenth, 45–46, 69–70, 196–197; seventeenth, 70

Amendments, Sri Lanka, thirteenth, 58–69, 62, 70, 186

Amendments, U.S.: eighteenth, 36, 306n101; nineteenth, 36; thirteenth, 36, 36n5, 61, 71n87; twenty-first, 42, 42n19, 306n101; fourteenth, 60n65, 61, 64n73, 71n87, 165, 268

Amish, 236n70

Amrit Kaur, Raj Kumari, 243

Analogies: table, 5–7, 77; house, 325n4

Appiah, Kwame Anthony, 91–92, 92n19, 93n22, 122, 123

Arabs, 28; Israel's immigration policy and, 26, 161n77, 271, 273, 277, 283, 288–289, 292, 295, 301, 311, 317–318; Jewish state and, 160, 163, 164n86, 166, 166n93; equality for Jews and, 164n86; constituents and family, 222; Palestine, 272–275; dignity, family and paths of law, 275–277

Arato, Andrew, 334n24

Aristotle, 8n15, 13, 24, 124, 145, 159, 295n67; state's identity, 7–8, 10; family as subordinate institution, 215n4

Articles: V, 36, 60, 72; 76, 45; 41, 47, 48; 79, paragraph 3, 59n63

Ashoka (Mauryan king), 128

Aspirational content: identity, 103, 104–107; continuity in consciousness, 104; radical transformation, 107

Atatürk, Mustafa Kemal, 1, 8n15, 12, 327, 327n8, 332, 337

Attorney General v. Reid, 183n139

Attorney General v. X, 264

Austin, Granville, 54n49, 169, 207n200, 246
Ayodhya incident, 173, 177, 179, 179n133
Azad, Nandini, 250n106

Bagehot, Walter, 89, 89n9, 266n142
Baird, Robert D., 221
Bantustan system, 91n14
Barak, Aharon, 150; constitutional borders and Israel, 152n44, 155–156, 160, 162, 166; enlightened opinions, 153n48; constitutional borders and Ireland, 188, 195n170; juridical objection, 208; family, state, and identity, 271, 278, 279, 280, 290n53; on human dignity, 283n29; on Jewish statehood of Israel, 300n82; on human rights and valid law, 302–303; on Judaism and democracy, 315n132
Barden, Garrett, 105n65
Barresi, John, 108n72
Basic Law on Human Dignity and Freedom, 151–152, 278, 281, 284n33, 291, 300n84, 302
Baxi, Upendra, 109–110
Beatty, David, 176n127
Beit Sourik Village Council v. The Government of Israel, 321n143
Bentham, Jeremy, 261n130
Bétaille, André, 5, 87nn4, 244n90
Bhagwati, P. N., 71
Bharatiya Janata Party (BJP), 157n64
Bhargava, Rajeev, 129
"Birth certificate of a nation," 117, 121, 350
Black, Hugo, 53, 72
Border, constitutional: introduction, 136–144; permeability, 136–212; disharmonic gap, 144–150; Israel, 150–168; India, 168–171; recipient court, 172–179; donor court, 180–187; Ireland, 187–202; imperfection and permeability, 202–205; cultural objection, 206–208; juridical objection, 208–212
Bork, Robert, 137, 150, 165, 169, 200n179, 204, 208
Bowers v. Hardwick, 138, 139, 189n152
Brazil, constitution, 58, 58n61
Brennan, William J., 315, 316
Breslin, Beau, 348n64
Brown, Nathan, 222
Brown v. Board of Education, 161, 164n86, 165, 167, 208
Brubaker, Rogers, 5n9
Buddhists, 58–69, 62n68, 185, 188
Burg, Avraham, 288n45
Burke, Edmund, 19, 28, 34, 40, 48, 70, 73, 74, 76, 78, 80, 82, 127, 130, 136, 324, 329; prescription, 75, 77, 96–97, 99, 100; views on India, 76n109; on Hastings's impeachment, 88, 88n8; constitutions as embodiments of national history, 95; criticism of British imperialism, 95n30, 96, 97–98; reform and innovation, 98; identity, 100n47; East India Bill, 170n103
Burt, Robert, 230

Cachalia, Firoz, 119n112
Cahill, Edward, 29n60, 255
Calhoun, John C., 72
Canada, 314
Canadian Charter of Rights and Freedom, 303
Canavan, Francis P., 77
Caste system, 220–221, 221n20
Catholic Church, 31, 90; Catholicism, 24, 29, 29n60, 182, 193n168; Irish national identity, 254–255, 255n117; rejection of Irish confessional state, 256n119
Chakra, 81
Chandrachud, Y. V., 56, 58
Change, constitutional, 15–17, 59n64; disharmony as precondition for, 5, 6, 87–89, 87nn4; legitimacy question and unconstitutional constitution, 34–40; India, 49–58; Harris on, 54n50; problematic amendments, 70
Chapman, Gerald, 78n116
Charrad, Mounira M., 222n23
Chatterji, Bankim Chandra, 136
Cheshin, Mishael: Israel, 165–166, 166n92, 167, 167n94, 301n89; family, state and identity, 271, 278, 279, 280, 285, 290n52, 308
Children, 163, 241; families and, 193, 237n73, 238, 240, 271, 288; rights, 250,

258n125; colonialism and, 287; preferential status and illegitimate, 318
Choudhry, Sujit, 21, 122, 158n65, 316
Christianity, 17, 21, 62n68
Chubb, Basil, 30n62, 31
Cicero, 242
Citizenship: equality, 129, 160, 292, 293n64; family and Israeli law, 276; identity and, 289–301
Citizenship and Entry into Israel Law, 276, 276n11, 319
Civil Rights Act of 1964, 269
Civil Rights Cases, 268
Civil War, American, 36, 354
Coleman v. Miller, 72
Colonialism, 287
Commerce Clause jurisprudence, 42n19
Comparative analysis, 15, 72n95, 169
Comparative case selection, 144n23
Confucianism, 94, 338, 338n35, 339–341, 348n63
Conrad, Dietrich, 45n24, 58n62
Constituent power, 34, 38, 44, 48, 55, 57, 59
Constitutional identity, dynamics, 355; text and, 348–349; bounded fluidity, 349–351; disharmonic invitation, 351–353; balance of internal/external disharmonies and, 353–354
Constitutional principles (CPs): South Africa, 119, 120n116; Namibia, 119n110
Constitution Restoration Act (CRA), 20–21
Constitutions: suicide and changing, 8; militant, 22–23; unconstitutional, 34–83; reforming and re-forming, 71; prescriptive, 96; historically tied to framing and revision, 106; differences, 347
Constitutions, unconstitutional: change, legitimacy question and, 34–40; conundrum, 34–83; India, heritage and, 37, 49–58; sovereignty claims, 38n10, 39; Ireland, process, substance and, 41–49; repeal of prohibition and connection to, 42, 42n19; Sri Lanka, thirteenth amendment and, 58–69, 70, 186; continuity and, 69–79; conclusion, 79–83
Continuity, 97–98, 97n37; idea, 69–79; aspirational content, 104; Raz on, 324n1
Cooper v. Aaron, 165, 197
Corwin Amendment, 36, 36n5, 61, 71n87
Coughlan, Anthony, 266n142
Cultural objection, 206–208

Daly, Cathal, 255
Dannemann, Gerhard, 144n23
Davis v. Beason, 235n67
de Gaulle, Charles, 59n64
Dellinger, Walter, 39
Democracy: dualist, 16; EU and sustainable constitutional, 114; Barak on Judaism and, 315n132
Derrett, J. Duncan M., 250, 251n109
de Valera, Eamon, 29n60, 45, 255, 257, 259n127, 350
Dhavan, Rajeev, 159n69
Dialogical articulation: identity and, 103, 107–112; history's connection to present and, 111; India and, 111
Dickson, Brian, 314
Directive Principles of State Policy, 216n7, 251; India, 50, 54, 147, 147n32, 148n35; Ireland, 147–148, 188
Disharmony: critical to development of constitutional identity, 4–5; precondition for change, 5, 6, 87–89, 87nn4; identity and prescription, 103, 128, 322, 327; gap and constitutional borders, 144–150; family, state and identity, 271–275; Turkey and South Korea's constitutions, 346–355; constitutional identity and bounded, 351–353; constitutional identity and balance of internal/external, 353–354
Dismemberment, 50
Donor court, constitutional borders and, 180–187
Dormant power, 42n19
Douglas, William, 227, 269
Douglass, Frederick, 106, 133
Downs v. City of Birmingham, 72n95
Dred Scott decision, 105, 110, 351
D'Souza, Jerome (Rev.), 238–241
Dualist democracy, 16
Dual state, 124n125
Due Process Clause, 316

Dworkin, Ronald, 4, 69, 109–110; recipient court, 174, 174n121; identity and jurisprudence, 306, 307n103; concept/conceptions distinction, 335n26

East India Bill, 74, 75, 170n103
Egypt, 29n58
Einstein, Albert, 35
Eisgruber, Christopher, 72, 100
Eliot, T. S., 19
Elshtain, Jean Bethke, 215
Ely, John Hart, 4
Enabling Act of 1933, 45, 45n24
England, 28, 144
English Constitution, The (Bagehot), 89
Entrenchment, 6, 6n12, 55
Epstein, Richard, 4
Equality, 178; social and economic, 55, 86n3, 149; norm, 87n5; human, 105, 127, 156–157, 168, 315n132; citizenship, 129, 160, 292, 293n64; rule of, 163; Arabs and Jews, 164, 164n86; militant constitutionalism and, 218–226; gender, 225, 259, 339; women's, 250n106
Erikson, Erik, 9, 10; on identity, 125n129
European Convention on Human Rights and Fundamental Freedoms, 309
European Court of Human Rights, 136, 199, 208, 259n128
European Union (EU): constitution, 11, 116; sustainable constitutional democracy, 114; Lisbon Treaty and, 116n103
Expressivism, 12

Family: rights, 26, 47; unification, 26; children and, 193, 237n73, 238, 240, 271, 288; constitutions referencing, 215n2; subordinate institution, 215n4; principles of justice applied to, 218–219, 219n12; caste system and, 220–221; Arab constituents and, 222; Saudi Arabia's constitution and, 222n23; French constitution and, 224n28; state and identity, 271–322; reunification and immigration, 274; dignity and paths of law, 275–281; citizenship and entry into Israeli law, 276; Palestinian obstacles to reunification, 276n11; French reunification policy, 277n12; conclusions, 338–346; as basis of individual identity in South Korea, 338n35, 339–346; integrity, 342
Federalist, The, 97, 145
Ferguson, Niall, 28
Fez, attack on, 327, 327n8
Finn, John, 16
Firat, Dengir, 1
Fitzgibbon, 42, 50
Flag Burning Amendment, 45–46, 49, 69–79
Fluidity, constitutional identity and, 349–351
Foundationalism, 16
Fox, Charles James, 74
Framers, 126; American, 146; Irish, 146; Indian, 169
Framing process, 122n117
France, 224n28; constitution, 6, 6n11, 224n28; family reunification policy, 277n12
French Conseil Constitutionnel, 6n11
French Revolution, 59, 59n64, 98
Fuller, Lon, 18, 74

Galanter, Marc, 25n52, 247n98, 251, 251n109
Gallie, W. B., 12n26
Galston, William, 228, 229
Gandhi, Indira, 70, 75, 88, 129, 149n38; amendment problem, 52, 53–54, 56, 57; election of 1971, 54; twenty-fourth amendment and, 54; power quest, 54n49, 56–58; electoral fraud and emergency regime, 56–57; thirty-ninth amendment, 56–57; thirty-eighth amendment, 57
Gandhi, Sanjay, 244n90
Gans, Chaim, 292–293
Gavison, Ruth, 112, 112n87, 155–156, 319
Gay marriage, 86n3, 215n2
Gay rights, 20
Gaza Strip, 25, 299
Geertz, Clifford, 141
Gender equality, 225, 259, 339

Generic/local balancing: identity, 103, 112–117; inner morality of law, 113–114
George III (king), 40
Germany: constitutional identity, 18; amendment process, 44, 58–60; basic law, 300n84
Ghai, Yash, 149
Ginsburg, Ruth Bader, 205
Glendon, Mary Ann, 200n179, 201
Glenn, H. Patrick, 92n21, 128n134, 171n108
Gödel, Kurt, 34, 35, 49, 83
Golak Nath v. State of Punjab, 52, 54
Goldsworthy, Jeffrey, 102n57
Graber, Mark, 104
Granholm v. Heald, 42n19
Greenfield, Liah, 224n28
Grimm, Dieter, 114, 115
Griswold v. Connecticut, 227, 254n114
Guaranty Clause (Art. IV, sec. 4), 73; U.S. Constitution's, 6

Habermas, Jürgen, 115, 116
Hahm, Chaihark, 339n36, 341, 341n43
Hahm, Pyong-choon, 339n36, 346
Hamas, 287, 287n41. *See also* Palestine
Hamilton, Liam 46
Hand, Learned, 82
Harari Resolution, 281n23
Harding, Sarah, 352n72
Harlan, John Marshall II, 99, 226, 237n73, 268–269
Harris, William, 54n50, 69n85, 346n62; on positive/negative constitutions or disharmony, 87n6; constitutional identity, 108n73
Hartz, Louis, 223, 223n27
Hastings, Warren, 40, 74, 76, 88, 88n8
Headscarf ban, 328, 328n10, 333, 337, 347
Hindu Code laws of 1950s, 249, 250n105, 252
Hindu Marriage Act, 249n104, 251n108
Hindus, 28, 29, 111, 128n134, 179, 183, 185, 245n92; Sri Lankan, 62n68; India, 63; rights, 129n136
Hindutva Cases, 174, 174n122, 177, 186, 208
Hirschl, Ran, 8n15, 14, 26, 29n58, 166n92, 216n5
History: constitutional future and ties to, 94n28; constitutions as embodiments of national, 95; dialogical articulation and connection to present, 111; plurality of societies and cultures, 111n84
Hogan, Gerard, 253
Holmes, Oliver Wendell, 56, 57
Holocaust, 300
Homosexuals: gay rights, 20; gay marriage, 86n3, 215n2; sodomy statute, 136–137; criminalization, 259n128
Honduras: unamendable presidential term limits, 79–80, 79n117; Zelaya and military coup, 79–80
House analogy, 325n4
Howse, Robert, 316
Hume, David, 93, 95, 287
Humphreys, Richard, 195n170, 261
Huntington, Samuel, 87n4, 156, 355

Identity, 3; disharmony critical to development of constitutional, 4–5, 15, 103–117; table analogy and certifying constitutional, 5–7; Aristotle on state's, 7–8, 10; scheme of composition, 8; constitutional changes and continuous, 8–9, 9n18, 48; national and constitutional, 10; collective, 12; Sinhalese Buddhist national, 58–69; DNA, 102, 102n55; aspirational content and, 103, 104–107; prescription and disharmony, 103, 128, 322, 327; unity and fundaments of, 103–117; dialogical articulation and, 107–112; generic and local balancing, 112–117; Soviet Union's constitutional, 117; constitutions acquiring specific, 118; Catholic Church and national, 254–255, 255n117; militant constitutions and abortion, 259–266; family and state, 271–322; dignity, family and paths of law, 275–281; different citizens and, 289–301; state and jurisprudence, 301–311; house analogy and, 325n4; zero, 326n5; Turkey and re-constituting national, 327–337; dynamics of constitutional, 347–355; stability of legal, 352n72
"I Have a Dream" (King), 145

Immigration: Israel's policy, 26, 161n77, 271, 273, 277, 283, 288–289, 292, 295, 301, 311, 317–318; family reunification and, 274; Jewish, 274; law, 284n32
Immigration and Nationality Act of 1952, 317
Imperfection, 202–205
Imperialism, 95n30, 96–98, 144
Incorporation, unconscious acts, 107n69
India, 14, 17, 19, 23–24, 25, 27, 28, 29, 32, 33; religion's imprint, 30, 51–52, 68n81; constitution, 37, 49–58, 87n4, 125–132, 181n136, 216; supreme court, 37, 50–54, 55n51, 56n54, 60, 65n74, 68n83, 73, 81, 119–120, 125, 142–143; unconstitutional constitution and heritage, 37, 49–58; amendment and dismemberment, 50; directive principles of state policy and, 50, 54, 147, 147n32, 148n35; social reconstruction and, 50; constitutional limits, 51; essentials of religion test, 51, 51n39; twenty-fourth amendment, 54; natural rights/law, 54–56; thirty-ninth amendment, 56–57; forty-second amendment, 57, 241n81; thirty-eighth amendment, 57; Hindus, 63; Sri Lanka's political model compared to, 64n71; Burke's view, 76n109; chakra, 81; dialogic interaction, 111; preliminary applications and unity, 125–132; secularism, 126–128, 126nn132, 133; England, imperial governance and, 144; comparative case selection, 144n23; judicial empowerment, 149n38; uniform civil code debate, 157n64; universalism, particularism and constitutional borders, 168–171; framers, 169; recipient court, 172–179; donor court, 180–187; caste system, 220–221, 221n20; polygamy in, 245
Indo-Sri Lanka accord of 1987, 62
Inheritance, 19, 101, 249, 265; principle, 77, 96, 128; conflicted, 95; constraints, 98; laws, 243; Korean, 345
Integrity, 69, 125n130, 324n1, 334, 342
Iran, 158, 215n1; ruling clerics, 158n65
Iraq, 28
Ireland, 9, 11, 17, 23–24, 25, 27, 28, 29, 33, 66; constitution, 12, 31, 41–49, 192n164, 252; *lex posterior*, 41; Public Safety Act, 41; unconstitutional constitution, process and substance, 41–49; eighth amendment, 45, 196–198, 254n118; fourteenth amendment, 45–46, 69–70, 196–197; supreme court, 51, 143–144, 199; Lisbon Treaty rejection, 116n103; England and imperial governance, 144; comparative case selection, 144n23; framers, 146; directive principles of state policy, 147–148, 188; adaptation, culture, prudence and constitutional borders, 187–202; abortion in, 191, 195–201; constitutional identity, 252–258; constitutional polarities and, 252–259; Catholic Church's rejection of confessional state, 256n119; abortion and identity, 259–266
Irish Free Constitution of 1922, 41
Islam, 222, 222n23, 329, 332, 333, 337, 345; traditional political philosophy, 158n65; conversion, 182–183, 184
Israel, 14, 25, 26, 27, 29, 29n58, 31, 32n68, 33, 109, 353; supreme court, 25, 25n52, 26, 150; immigration policy, 26, 161n77, 271, 273, 277, 283, 288–289, 292, 295, 301, 311, 317–318; religion's imprint, 30; as Jewish and democratic state, 103; identity conflict, politics and, 112; England and imperial governance, 144; comparative case selection, 144n23; external sources, identity and constitutional borders, 150–168; Basic Law on Human Dignity and Freedom, 151–152; judicial activism and, 154n54; Katzir Cooperative Society, 160; Jewish state, 160–161, 163–164, 164n86, 272–275; personal laws, 247n98; proclamation of the establishment of the state of, 273n3; family reunification policy, 275; basic law and, 276–277, 281n23
Israeli Law of Return, 273–274; eligibility disputes, 273n2

Jabareen, Hassan, 301
Jackson, Vicki, 142n22
Jains, 185

James, Christine, 254n114
Janatha Vimukthi Peramuna (JVP), 62
Japan, 94
Japanese Americans, internment, 297, 297n75
Jayawardene, J. R., 62
Jefferson, Thomas, 50
Jenks, Edward, 242n82
Jesuits, 29n60
Jethmalani, Ram, 131n142
Jewish Agency, 160, 161n77
Jewish National Fund, 161n77
Jewish state, 164n86, 166, 166n93; equality for Arabs and, 164n86; Palestine and, 272–275; Barak on, 300n82. *See also* Israel
Johnson, James, 111n84
Johnson, Samuel, 323, 324
John XXIII (pope), 254
Joppke, Christian, 274n4, 284n32
Judges. *See specific judges*
Judicial activism, 154n54
Judicial empowerment, 149n38
Juridical objection, 208–212
Jurists. *See specific jurists*
Justice and Development Party (AK Party), 2, 328–329

Kahn, Paul, 102n56
Karachi Resolution of 1931, 130
Katz, Elai, 72n95
Katz, Stanley N., 5n10
Katzir Cooperative Society, 160
Kennedy, Anthony, 84–85, 97, 136–137, 139n16
Kennedy, Finola, 256, 258n125
Kennedy, Hugh, 41–42, 42n19
Kenny, Michael, 13
Kersch, Ken, 138, 205
Kesavananda Bharati v. State of Kerala, 53, 53n48, 54, 55n51, 57, 58, 67, 71, 73, 73n98, 74, 81, 120
Khanna, Hans Raj, 71, 74n101, 77
Kimmerling, Baruch, 9n19, 32n68, 98n39
King, Martin Luther, Jr., 16, 106, 145
King v. Perumal, 183
Kissane, Bill, 350
Klug, Heinz, 113
"Kol Ha'am" Co. Ltd. v. Minister of Interior, 320
Korematsu v. United States, 297n75
Kretzmer, David, 292n60, 296n70, 299
Kriegler, Johann, 91, 313
Krishnan, Jayanth, 25n52, 247n98
Kumari, Raj, 243
Kuru, Ahmet T., 329n12, 331n21, 335n26

Lahav, Pnina, 298
Landau, Moshe, 152
Lasch, Christopher, 218
Laski, Harold, 74n100
Lawrence v. Texas, 20, 137, 139, 171, 208, 210
Laws, 60; morality of, 18; personal, 25n52; *lex posterior*, 41; India and natural rights, 54–56; natural rights and, 54–56; generic/local balancing and inner morality, 113–114; Israel and, 151–152, 247n98, 273–274, 273n2, 276–277, 281n23; militant constitutions, unity of society and fundamental, 213–218; inheritance, 243; Hindu code, 249, 250n105, 252; dignity, family and paths of, 275–281; basic, 276–277; immigration, 284n32; Germany and basic, 300n84; human rights and valid, 302–303
"Letter Concerning Toleration, A" (Locke), 159
Levinson, Sanford, 12n26, 44n23
Levy, Jonah, 224n28
Lewis, Bernard, 327n8, 332
Liberation Tigers of Tamil Eelam (LTTE), 62
Lim, Jibong, 339n39
Limits: constitutional, 51, 59; implied, 58; presidential term, 79–80, 79n117
Lincoln, Abraham, 16, 36n5, 49, 105, 105n63, 105n65, 145
Lisbon Treaty, 116n103
Local/generic balancing, 103, 112–117
Locke, John, 93, 95, 108n72, 159
Loughlin, Martin, 34

Luther v. Borden, 72
Lutz, Donald S., 5n10, 24

Maastricht Treaty on European Union, 6n11, 262
MacArthur, Douglas (general), 94
Macedo, Steven, 228n45
MacIntyre, Alasdair, 4n7, 19; compelling unity, 90, 98, 107, 128; identity and, 92–93; tradition, 101, 108n70, 111, 326; unity of narrative quest and, 115; continuities of conflict and, 129; militant and acquiescent constitutionalism, 245, 268; family, state and identity, 320
Madison, James, 39, 39n13, 97, 124, 134
Magna Carta, 74–75
Maier, Charles S., 298
Maitland, F. W., 84
Mansfield, Harvey, 231
Marbury v. Madison, 54
Mardin, Serif, 332n22
Marks, Jonathan, 134n147
Marriage, 284n31; gay, 86n3, 215n2; foundation for civilized society, 248; Hindu Marriage Act, 249n104, 251n108; bill of 1954, 250; citizenship and entry into Israel law, 276; disallowable, 341n46. *See also* Polygamy
Martin, Raymond, 108n72
Mate, Manoj, 171n109
Mazie, Steven V., 164n86, 166n93
McCrudden, Christopher, 182
McGee v. Attorney General, 190, 208, 260, 265
Mehta, Uday, 76n109, 98
Meierhenrich, Jens, 124n125
Meiji Revolution, 94
Meta-narrative questions, 26
Michael H. v. Gerald D., 139n16, 316n133
Michelman, Frank, 9n18, 110
Militant constitutionalism, 22–23; fundamental law and unity of society, 213–218; born equal or not, 218–226; acquiescent constitutionalism and, 226–252; within constitutional polarities, 252–259; abortion and identity, 259–266; U.S. and, 266–270
Mill, John Stuart, 76n109, 92, 218, 243, 258
Miller, Samuel F., 64n73
Minerva Mills, Ltd. v. Union of India, 51n40, 57, 67, 71
Minow, Martha, 227, 230, 231
Misgav, Haim, 289n50
Mitra, Subrata, 126n132
Montesquieu, 175, 211n206
Moore, Wayne D., 64n73
Moore v. East Cleveland, 231
Morality of law, 18, 113–114
More, Thomas, 279, 295n67
Mormons, 232–234, 232n58, 233n59
Morrill anti-bigamy act, 232
Mostov, Julie, 101
Moynihan, Daniel Patrick, 213
Murphy, Walter, 4n8, 10, 11n23, 17, 71, 106, 264n139; importance of history to constitutional futures, 94n28
Muslims, 25n52, 28, 32, 178, 183, 185, 222n23, 247n98; Sri Lankan, 62n68; attack on traditional attire, 327

Namibia, 119n110
Nandy, Ashis, 180n134
Naor, Miriam, 297n75
Nationality and Entry into Israel Law, 25
National Religious Party, 162
Natural rights/law, 54–56, 60
Nazis, 34, 45
Negation, conscious acts, 107n69
Nehru, Jawaharlal, 52n42, 68, 128, 129, 149n38, 242, 249
Nehru Constitutional Draft of 1928, 130
Normative state, 124n125
Norris v. Attorney General, I. R., 189n152, 199
Norton, Anne, 14, 296–297
Nullification, amendments and, 59–60, 59n63
Nyerere, Julius K., 134

Oakeshott, Michael, 329
O'Connell, Daniel, 259n127
O'Higgins, Thomas, 189n152
Okin, Susan Moller, 218, 277, 278

Orren, Karen, 236, 238, 247, 336
Osiatynski, Wiktor, 153, 154

Pakistan, 54
Palestine, 28, 117; Israel's immigration policy, 26, 161n77, 271, 273, 277, 283, 288–289, 292, 295, 301, 311, 317–318; family, state and identity, 271–322; Arabs, 272–275; Jewish state and, 272–275; family reunification obstacles, 276n11, 294; prisoner exchange, 287, 287n41
Particularism, 168–171
Particularities, 158n65, 169, 176; prescription and, 75; moral, 101; national legal, 158n65
Permeability: constitutional border and, 136–212; imperfection and, 202–205
Perry, Michael, 11, 96
Personal laws, 25n52
Peru, 37
Pierce v. Society of Sisters, 232
Pitkin, Hanna, 4n8, 349
Planned Parenthood v. Casey, 264
Plato, 7, 127
Plutarch, 325n4
Poland, 9, 90, 91n14
Polarities, 226, 340; authenticity-existentialism, 129; militant constitutionalism within, 252–259
Political Liberalism (Rawls), 172
Politics of Aristotle, The (Aristotle), 7–8, 8n15, 145
Polygamy, 182–183, 233, 235, 243–244, 245, 251n108
Positive secularism, 178
Posner, Richard, 206, 208
Post, Robert C., 13, 268
Powell, Lewis, 231
Power: constituent, 34, 38, 44, 48, 55, 57, 59; dormant, 42n19; Gandhi's emergency quest, 54n49, 56–58; devolution, 58–69; in hands of people, 66; judicial, 149n38
Prasad, Rajendra, 249
Preliminary applications: South Africa, 117–125; India, 125–132
Prerogative state, 124n125
Prescription, 96, 99, 127; Burke on, 75, 77, 96–97, 99, 100; identity, disharmony and, 103, 128, 322, 327
Presumption, 100
Preuss, Ulrich K., 49n35
Prisoner exchange, 287, 287n41
Privacy of Communications Case, 59n63
Proccacia, Ayala, 297n75
Proclamation of the Establishment of the State of Israel, 273n3, 274n4
Prohibition: eighteenth amendment and, 36, 306n101; twenty-first amendment and repeal, 36n101, 42, 42n19
Protectionism, constitutional, 140
Public Safety Act, 41
Publius, 145, 146, 202
Putnam, Robert, 193n168

Qa'adan v. The Israel Land Administration et al., 160, 162–163, 164, 165, 167, 208

R. v. Oakes, 302, 304n95
Radicalism, 50, 107
Rapacznski, Andrzej, 207n200
Rape, 191n161
Rawls, John: recipient court, 172, 173n117, 175n125; family as basic societal structure, 218, 219n12; militant and acquiescent constitutionalism, 225–226, 234, 237; family, state and identity, 277
Raz, Joseph, 3, 323, 324, 324n1
Recipient court: Western concepts in judicial opinions and, 172; constitutional borders and, 172–179
Reconstruction, India and, 50
Regina v. Keegstra, 314, 314n129
Reid, Thomas, 71, 93, 95, 265
Reincorporation, 107n69
Religion, 21, 30; state, 17; imprint, 30, 51–52, 68n81; India and essentials of, 51, 51n39; conversion, 182–183, 184. *See also specific religions*
Republican revival, 110
Revolution, 17n40, 112n87; judiciary's status and, 152n44; Iranian constitutional, 158n65; constitutional, 279n16

Reynolds v. United States, 232, 233n60
Richards, David A. J., 211n206
Rights: gay, 20; family, 26, 47; natural, 54–56, 60; Hindus, 129n136; children's, 250, 258n125; valid law and human, 302–303
Ritter, Gretchen, 229, 230
Robinson, Mary, 258, 338
Rodrigues, Valerian, 250n105
Roe v. Wade, 194n169, 254n114, 260
Roosevelt, Franklin D., 216
Rosen, Jeffrey, 38, 46, 49
Rosenblum, Nancy, 233
Rosenfeld, Michel, 18, 107n69
Rousseau, Jean-Jacques, 8n16, 134n147
Rubenfeld, Jed, 7n13, 115n101, 116, 130–131
Rubenstein, Amnon, 274n5
Rubin, Eva, 230
Rudolph, Lloyd, 95
Rudolph, Susanne, 95
Ryan case. *See* State (Ryan) v. Lennon

S. R. Bommai v. Union of India, 65n74, 125n130, 177
Sachs, Albie, 86n3, 120, 205
Sager, Lawrence, 82
Saint Patrick, 255
Sajo, Andras, 10n22
Sarla Mudgal v. Union of India, 183–184, 248
Saudi Arabia, 222n23
Saunders, Cheryl, 207
Scalia, Antonin, 20; unconstitutional constitution, 85; permeability of constitutional borders, 137, 138, 139, 139n16, 141, 154, 155, 195n170, 200n180, 204n187, 205, 208, 209n203; family, state and identity, 316n133
Schattschneider, E. E.: permeability of constitutional borders, 204, 205, 208, 210; militant and acquiescent constitutionalism, 229, 248; family, state and identity, 308
Schauer, Frederick, 58, 107n69, 108n72, 140, 200
Schmitt, Carl, 44–45, 44n23, 48–49, 57; on constitutional limits, 59; on popular sovereignty and constitutional change, 59n64
Secularism, 126–128, 126nn132, 133; Turkey's, 6; misguided, 131n142; positive, 178; critique of Western, 180n134
Self, constitutional: unity and, 89–103; moral particularities, 101; moving from personal to political, 104
Sen, Sarbani, 81, 81n119
Shalit, Gilad, 287, 287n41
Shamgar, Meir, 163, 310
Sharvananda, Suppiah, 64–65
Shi'ites, 28
Shourie, Arun, 129n136
Sick textiles case. *See* Minerva Mills, Ltd. v. Union of India
Sikhs, 185
Sikri, 56n54
Singh, Jaspal, 249n104
Singh, Kuldip, 184–185, 186
Sinhalese: Buddhists, 58–69, 62n68, 185, 188; Tamils' ethnic struggle with, 62–63, 67; political/religious imprint, 68n81
Skowronek, Stephen, 336
Slaughter-House Cases, The, 64n73, 268
Slavery, 36, 72, 223n27, 354; constitutional aspirations, 104, 105, 105n63
Smith, Adam, 42n19
Smith, Anthony D., 100n48, 130n138
Smith, Rogers, 105n63, 223, 336n27
Sodomy, 136–137
South Africa, 86; supreme court, 86n3, 91; constitution, 91, 113, 113n93, 117–125, 270n147; "birth certificate of nation" and, 117, 121, 350; preliminary applications and unity, 117–125; constitutional principles, 119, 120n116; certification process, 119n112, 123; principles, 123, 123n122; as dual state, 124n125
South Korea, 27, 338; family as basis of individual identity, 338n35, 339–346; constitution, 339n39; inheritance, 345; disharmonic constitution, 346–355; attitudes toward conflict, 346n62

Southwest Case, 59n63
Sovereignty claims: as means to amend constitutions, 38n10, 39; French Revolution's, 59n64
Soviet Union, 10, 97n37; constitution, 97n37; constitutional identity, 117
Spain, constitution, 72n95
Special Marriage Bill of 1954, 250
Sri Lanka, 17, 181; unconstitutional constitution, thirteenth amendment and, 58–69, 70, 186; supreme court, 61, 62n68; devolution, 62, 63n70; religious groups/government ministries, 62, 62n68; Sinhalese/Tamil ethnic struggle, 62; Hindus, 62n68; India's political model compared to, 64n71; referendum's required, 64n72
Ssemogerere et al. v. Attorney General, 37n6
Stamka v. Minister of Interior, 285n36
Stanlis, Peter James, 96n45
State (Ryan) v. Lennon, 41, 44, 46, 49, 50, 188n150
States: ethnic nation, 271–275, 272n1; introduction, 271–275; family and identity, 271–322; dignity, family and paths of law, 275–281; on not doing something special, 281–289; different citizens, 289–301; identity and jurisprudence, 301–311; sooner or later, 311–317; conclusion, 317–322
Stevens, John Paul, 42n19, 84
Stone-Sweet, Alec, 109
Subjection of Women, The (Mill), 218, 243
Suicide, 8, 191n161, 264
Sumner, Charles, 72
Sunnis, 28
Sunstein, Cass, 163, 163n84
Supreme Courts: U.S., 20, 33, 42n19, 53, 64n73, 84–86, 136, 165; Israel, 25, 25n52, 26, 150; India, 37, 50–54, 55n51, 56n54, 60, 65n74, 68n83, 73, 81, 119–120, 125, 142–143; Peru, 37; Ireland, 51, 143–144, 199; Sri Lanka, 61, 62n68; Honduras, 79–80; South Africa, 86n3, 91; Canada, 314
Swayne, Noah H., 64n73
Table analogy, 5–7, 77
Tamils, 62–63, 67, 68
Taney, Roger, 105, 105n65
Taylor, Charles, 92, 93n22, 107, 108n70, 123, 130
Teitel, Ruti, 169
Text, constitutional identity and, 348–349
Thapar, Romila, 111n84
Theseus, 325n4
Thiemann, Ronald, 174
Thirteenth amendment: unconstitutional constitution and Sri Lanka's, 58–69, 62, 70, 186; decentralization-agreement roots, 62
Thomas, Clarence, 42n19, 208
Thomas, George, 133
Tocqueville, Alexis de, 24, 31, 157, 193n168, 219, 220, 223, 224, 229, 270; women's happiness and, 225
"Tract on Popery" (Burke), 48
Tradition, 101, 108n70, 111, 326; living and dying, 96n42, 99; disharmonic constitutional, 105
Transformation, 50, 107
Tribe, Laurence, 3, 4, 4n7, 96n34, 246n95
Tulis, Jeffrey, 17n40
Turkey, 11, 19, 27, 29n58; secularism, 6; Kemalist constitutions, 10; constitution, 12–13, 14, 22, 331–332; re-constituting national identity, 327–337; headscarf ban, 328, 328n10, 333, 337, 347; disharmonic constitution, 346–355
Tushnet, Mark, 12

Uniform civil code debate, 157n64
United Mizrachi Bank v. Migdal Cooperative Village, 279
United States: constitution, 3, 6, 12, 15–16, 21, 29n60, 34, 42, 96–97, 115, 354–355; supreme court, 20, 33, 42n19, 53, 64n73, 84–86, 136, 165; eighteenth amendment, 36, 306n101; nineteenth amendment, 36; thirteenth amendment, 36, 36n5, 61, 71n87; twenty-first amendment, 42, 42n19, 306n101; fourteenth amendment, 60n65, 61, 64n73, 71n87, 165, 268;

United States (*continued*)
England and imperial governance, 144; framers, 146; militant constitutionalism, 266–270; constitution: preamble, 106
Unity: introduction, 84–89; quest for compelling, 84–135; constitutional self, 89–103; fundaments of identity, 103–117; aspirational content, 104–107; dialogical articulation, 107–112; generic and local balancing, 112–117; preliminary applications, 117; South Africa, 117–125; India, 125–132; conclusion, 132–135
Universalist interpretation, 158n65
Utopia, 295n67
Uyanganda, Jayadeva, 64n71

Vatican II, 254, 255, 259
Verma, J. S., 174, 174n122

Waldron, Jeremy, 281
Walker, Neil, 34
Walsh, Brian, 192, 192n164, 194n169, 197–198, 208, 265
Walzer, Michael, 159, 159n68, 274n6
Wanasundera, R. S., 66–67
War: American Civil, 36, 354; metaphor, 242n82
Weber, Max, 246n95
Weiler, J. H. H., 11, 12, 20n47, 114n96
West Bank, 25, 299, 321
We the People (Ackerman), 44n23
Whittington, Keith, 351
Whyte, Gerry, 253
Wiley, Norbert, 92n19
Wilson, James, 39n13
Wineries, 42n19
Wisconsin v. Yoder, 232, 236n70
Women, 234; happiness, 225; equality, 250n106; state's protection of home life, 256; headscarf ban, 328, 328n10, 333, 337, 347
Wood, Gordon, 39n15

Yakobson, Alexander, 274n5

Zelaya, Manuel, 79–80
Zero identity, 326n5
Zionists, 349

Harvard University Press is a member of Green Press Initiative (greenpressinitiative.org), a nonprofit organization working to help publishers and printers increase their use of recycled paper and decrease their use of fiber derived from endangered forests. This book was printed on recycled paper containing 30% post-consumer waste and processed chlorine free.